Constable London

Ex Libris. Book plate of a
Lewis Carroll collector. 'Life,
what is it but a dream?' Acrostic poem
from Through the Looking-Glass

Lewis Carroll by
Oscar Gustave Rejlander

*'It isn't manners for us to
begin, you know,' said the Rose.
Screenprint by Peter Blake*

6

First published 1954
by Constable & Company Ltd
10 Orange Street, London
WC2H 7EG

Copyright © 1954 by Derek
Hudson

New illustrated edition 1976

ISBN 0 09 460590 4

Filmset and printed by
BAS Printers Limited,
Wallop, Hampshire

Also by Derek Hudson

A Poet in Parliament
(Life of W. M. Praed)

Thomas Barnes of 'The Times'

British Journalists and Newspapers

*Norman O'Neill: A Life of
Music*

Charles Keene

*Martin Tupper: His Rise and
Fall*

James Pryde

*The Royal Society of Arts,
1754–1954*
(In collaboration)

Sir Joshua Reynolds

Arthur Rackham

*The Forgotten King and other
essays*

Writing between the Lines
(Autobiography)

Holland House in Kensington

Kensington Palace

Munby: Man of Two Worlds

For Love of Painting
(Life of Sir Gerald Kelly)

'It isn't manners for us to
begin, you know,' said the Rose.
Screenprint by Peter Blake

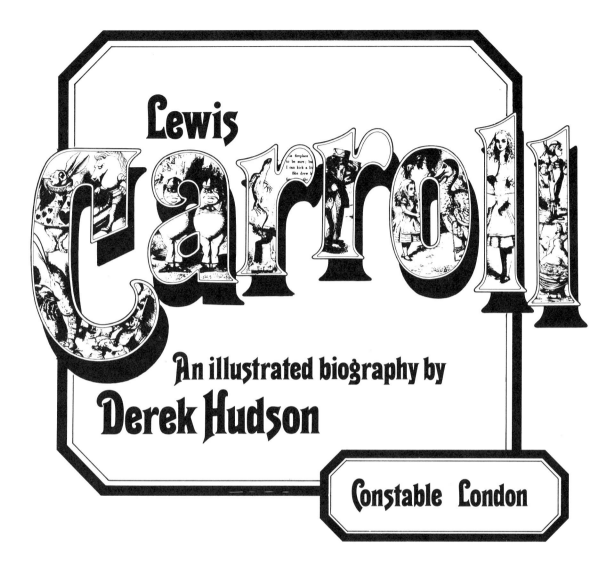

Lewis Carroll

An illustrated biography by

Derek Hudson

Constable London

6

First published 1954
by Constable & Company Ltd
10 Orange Street, London
WC2H 7EG

Copyright © 1954 by Derek
Hudson

New illustrated edition 1976

ISBN 0 09 460590 4

Filmset and printed by
BAS Printers Limited,
Wallop, Hampshire

Also by Derek Hudson

A Poet in Parliament
(Life of W. M. Praed)

Thomas Barnes of 'The Times'

British Journalists and Newspapers

*Norman O'Neill: A Life of
Music*

Charles Keene

*Martin Tupper: His Rise and
Fall*

James Pryde

*The Royal Society of Arts,
1754–1954*
(In collaboration)

Sir Joshua Reynolds

Arthur Rackham

*The Forgotten King and other
essays*

Writing between the Lines
(Autobiography)

Holland House in Kensington

Kensington Palace

Munby: Man of Two Worlds

For Love of Painting
(Life of Sir Gerald Kelly)

'The have-been is eternal, as well as the will-be. We are not only elderly men, but young men, boys, children'
Thackeray

To my daughter

Katherine ('Dilly')

with much love

Contents

Preface to the Second Edition **13**
Author's Note to the First Edition (1954) **16**

1 The End and the Beginning **19**
2 Daresbury Days **34**
3 Croft Rectory **42**
4 The Undergraduate Years **61**
5 A Victorian Don **74**
6 Photographer and Clergyman **91**
7 Alice **112**
8 Moscow and Guildford **131**
9 Through the Looking-Glass **148**
10 Love and Lewis Carroll **159**
11 Towards the Snark **174**
12 Lewis Carroll as a poet **184**
13 As Man to Man **194**
14 Sugar and Spice **207**
15 Sylvie and Bruno **222**
16 'Death is over Now' **235**

Appendices

a Last Memories of Lewis Carroll
By Viscount Simon, Mrs A. T. Waterhouse,
Miss H. L. Rowell and Mrs Arthur Davies **248**
b Introduction to 'The Guildford Gazette
Extraordinary' by Lewis Carroll **256**
Notes and References **258**
A Select Bibliography **265**
Index **267**

Colour frontispiece, reproduced by courtesy of Peter Blake and Waddington Galleries

Lewis Carroll's grave at Guildford photographed by Jeremy Marks **18**

Lewis Carroll cot. Photograph reproduced by courtesy of The Hospital for Sick Children, Great Ormond Street, London **22**

Plaque on the gate-post of The Chestnuts photographed by Colin G. Futcher **28**

Biscuit tin reproduced by courtesy of the Guildford Muniment Room and photographed by Colin G. Futcher **28**

Illustrations from *The Illustrators of Alice*, edited by Graham Ovenden, Academy Editions, London, 1972 **29-31, 33**

'An unusually large saucepan . . .'. Illustration reproduced by courtesy of William Heinemann Ltd **32**

Jig-saw reproduced by courtesy of the Guildford Muniment Room and photographed by Colin G. Futcher **39**

The earliest photograph of Dodgson reproduced by courtesy of *The Daily Telegraph* **46**

Henrietta, Dodgson's youngest sister, Guildford Muniment Room **46**

Dodgson's aunts, the Misses Lutwidge reproduced by courtesy of the Gernsheim Collection, University of Texas **60**

Christ Church Hall reproduced by courtesy of The Governing Body of Christ Church, Oxford **77**

Dodgson at twenty-five reproduced by courtesy of the Dodgson family **78**

Landseer's 'Titania and Bottom' reproduced by courtesy of the Melbourne National Museum, Australia **85**

Mrs Liddell and Dean Liddell reproduced by courtesy of the Mansell Collection **88**

John Ruskin reproduced by courtesy of the Mansell Collection **91**

William Makepeace Thackeray reproduced by courtesy of the Mansell Collection **93**

Agnes Grace Weld and Alfred, Lord Tennyson reproduced by courtesy of the Gernsheim Collection **94**

Irene MacDonald, George Macdonald and Lily reproduced by courtesy of the Gernsheim Collection **100**

Professor Jowett by Hay Cameron **107**

Alice Liddell reproduced by courtesy of the Gernsheim Collection **108**

Alice Liddell reproduced by courtesy of the New York Public Library Picture Collection **110**

Alice Jane Donkin reproduced by courtesy of the Gernsheim Collection **111**

Folly Bridge reproduced by courtesy of the Central Library, Oxfordshire County Council 113

Rhoda Liddell and Liddell sisters reproduced by courtesy of the Mansell Collection 116

Sir John Tenniel reproduced by courtesy of the Mansell Collection 117

Rossetti family reproduced by courtesy of the Gernsheim Collection 135

John Ruskin and Holman Hunt, John Ruskin and Rossetti reproduced by courtesy of the Mansell Collection 136

Charlotte M. Yonge, Gernsheim Collection 138

The Chestnuts photographed by Colin G. Futcher 143

Sitting Room at Christ Church, photograph in Guildford Muniment Room 144

Tiles from the De Morgan Potteries reproduced by courtesy of the Governing Body of Christ Church, Oxford 146

Alice's Shop, St Aldates, Oxford, the Guildford Muniment Room 148

'I only hope the boat won't tipple over' reproduced by courtesy of Granada Publishing Ltd 150-151

'The Sisters' reproduced by courtesy of Mrs B. A. F. Hervey-Bathurst 162

Ellen Terry photographed by Jeremy Marks at the Watts Gallery, Guildford 163

Ellen Terry reproduced by courtesy of the Gernsheim Collection 164

Coates reproduced by courtesy of the Gernsheim Collection 213

Photographs of Dodgson in his forties and fifties, Guildford Muniment Room 242

Alice in Wonderland Memorial, Central Park, New York. Photograph by courtesy of the Guildford Muniment Room 247

Since this biography was first published in 1954, interest in Lewis Carroll has greatly increased. There are now active Lewis Carroll societies both in England and America. I do not, of course, state this as cause and effect!

While I was writing the book, my principal object was to put in order and reassert the facts of Lewis Carroll's life, which I felt were being obscured and even distorted by a growing accretion of psycho-analytical and Freudian theory. I had discovered the intriguing possibilities of this theorising earlier than most people, because a great friend of mine Tony Goldschmidt (later Goldsmith) contributed an article 'Alice in Wonderland Psycho-analyzed' to the *New Oxford Outlook* in 1933, when we were both Oxford undergraduates.

Tony's short paper is the earliest in date of the 'Freudian Interpretations' assembled in *Aspects of Alice*, edited by Robert Phillips (Gollancz, 1972). The piece is enigmatic but magisterial, as befits a pioneer. In four pages Tony conveyed the Freudian sexual significance of falling down 'what seemed to be a very deep well'; of a tiny golden key; of the little door with the curtain; and of much else. He presented his case in the quiet throw-away manner which I so well remember, and he did not go on fussing about it – an example neglected by his successors. Whether his deductions were all technically sound, I don't know, but they seemed quite startling at the time.

Tony Goldsmith was a brilliant and delightful young man who was killed in action in Tunisia in 1941, leaving devoted admirers from Sir Terence Rattigan to Spike Milligan. Though the article proved perspicacious, and prophetic of much to come, Tony's tongue was halfway into his cheek; he was very willing to laugh at his discovery, which is more than can be said of those who followed him.

Here perhaps lies the clue to my own attitude towards the psycho-analysing of *Alice*; I had encountered it in circumstances where it was impossible to take it too seriously. Not unnaturally, I preferred as a biographer to emphasise that Lewis Carroll had sent Alice down the rabbit-hole for the immediate pleasure of three small Victorians rather than for the future benefit of a generation of Freudians.

This did not mean that I believed the Rev C. L. Dodgson's numerous little-girl friendships, though based on a genuine love of children, could be described as entirely 'normal'. Nor would I describe as 'normal' the similar predilections of another Victorian clergyman, the diarist Francis Kilvert. They were too obsessive for that.

Indeed in Dodgson's case I found most illuminating the evidence of a phrenologist and a graphologist who had studied his head and hand – whereas Freudian interpretations of *Alice in Wonderland* struck me as likely to hinder a biographer more than they helped. When Lewis Carroll gaily improvised the opening chapters of *Alice*, sitting in the boat with Canon Duckworth and the Liddell girls in July, 1862, *he* did not know, poor fellow, that falling down a well would be called a symbol of coitus, or that a little door with a curtain in front of it might be interpreted as a female child and her clothes. If Canon Duckworth had been able to enlighten him, he would have collapsed in horror into the bottom of the boat, and we should have had no *Alice in Wonderland*. (Altogether, Freud can hardly have provided much encouragement for those stories about tunnels and secret passages which so many children have enjoyed.)

There is danger in giving retrospective sanction in a responsible biography to all this theorising. First and foremost, Freud must not be allowed to cast his analytical blight on spontaneous high spirits. But there is another risk: psycho-analysis may not only be seriously misleading as to a man's character, but also about the historical facts of his life.

Two years after Tony Goldsmith's Oxford paper, a much more elaborate psychological essay by William Empson was published (1935). Empson referred to the theory that Alice's pool of tears represented the amniotic fluid, the whole passage being supposedly associated with evolution and the birth trauma. Yet in plain fact the pool of tears was an allusion to a river expedition that Lewis Carroll and the Liddell sisters had made to Nuneham on a very wet day a fortnight earlier.

Fortunately, Freudian theorising, at least in its literary application, has become much less fashionable than it was when this book first appeared. I have felt no temptation to change my original policy and discuss Freudian interpretations of episodes in the first half of *Alice in Wonderland* (this being the favourite hunting-ground for Lewis Carroll's 'subconscious'). I have allowed the original text to stand generally unaltered; but I have brought it up to date here and there, corrected errors of fact, and introduced additions and improvements, for many of which I am indebted to the generous promptings of Philip Jaques, Denis Crutch and Morton Cohen.

Freudian theorising was only attractive because it was supposed to 'explain' the remarkable and lasting qualities of *Alice in Wonderland* by reference to sexual symbolism and bachelor frustrations. In practice, Freud has not been helpful even to the latter part of that book – let alone to *Through the Looking-Glass* as a whole, or (I believe) to *The Hunting of the Snark*, or to Dodgson's many delightful nonsense letters to children. The psycho-analytical critics have not really got around to all this later creativity. They are content to allow that it was not so much 'inspired' as 'hammered out' intellectually – disregarding the fact that many consider *Through the Looking-Glass* to be a better book than its predecessor. The psycho-analysts have not even tackled, so far as I know, the first verse of 'Jabberwocky' which bears the early date 1855.

I believe, as I said in an essay published in 1958 (*Lewis Carroll*, Longmans for the British Council), that 'it is misguided to apply this method to a work of imaginative literature, and that, so far from heightening appreciation, the clinical dissection of an author's mind may tend to belittle his creation and impair enjoyment.' Remarkably mature at twelve and thirteen, Lewis Carroll never entirely outgrew his childhood. Remaining 'fixated' to his early years, his intimation of Wonderland was recorded on his mind, to be developed like a photograph when he was past thirty. As a life-long stammerer, he was always happiest with children; his love of children, focusing on Alice Liddell, inspired the *Alice* books. But it was his unusual training as logician and mathematician that gave Carroll's writing the inimitable quality which has held readers of all ages for a century.

I have thought it best to retain the Author's Note to the first edition, which gives a fairly full list of those who helped me produce the book of 1954. In the meantime several of those mentioned have died or have left the positions they then held. But to find what has happened to each would be a great work of research, with little point to it; I prefer to leave them all gratefully preserved in a sort of literary aspic – generous collaborators in the original venture.

Some losses, however, are much in my mind. The death of Menella Dodgson, who had charge of her uncle's literary estate for many years, and was so unfailingly courteous and obliging to all who approached her, including myself, must certainly be regretfully recorded. Everyone interested in Lewis Carroll should remember her with great respect.

In the past twenty years, several collectors of this author have died. One whom I knew personally and found most helpful was Alfred C. Berol, an American business man who collected both Lewis Carroll and Arthur Rackham. His Carroll collection is now at New York University. Others now gone are my friends Michael Sadleir and Ralph Arnold of the firm of Constable; they took a special scholarly interest in this book; I remember their distinguished partnership in Orange Street with lasting appreciation, and it would have pleased them both to see how Ben Glazebrook has given new life to the old house. Caryl Hargreaves, son of the original Alice, and Christopher Hassall, an old friend of my Oxford days, have also died since the book appeared.

Mr Edward Charlesworth is no longer Rector of Croft; Miss Enid Dance has been replaced by Miss G. M. A. Beck as the attentive curator of Guildford Muniment Room, which now houses most of the Dodgson Family Collection. Mrs Irene Jaques and her two sisters are now the only surviving nieces of Lewis Carroll, and Mrs Jaques' son Philip is the efficient custodian of his memory. I am more grateful than I can say to Mr Jaques for his advice and encouragement for this second edition.

Mrs Margaret Davies, who contributes memories of Lewis Carroll's last years in Appendix A, died in 1971 at the age of 87. I remember her as a strong wise person, a great rider of the bicycle in Battersea. Her relics of Lewis Carroll are now in possession of her son Rear-Admiral A. Davies, of 25 The Cloisters, Windsor Castle.

I thank Messrs Macmillan for correcting my earlier figures for the printings of *Alice in Wonderland*; and once again I thank my old friend Colin Futcher for travelling to Guildford and taking, with the blessing of Mr Jaques and Miss Beck, some splendid new photographs of 'The Chestnuts' and of items in Guildford Muniment Room. Further thanks are due to the British Council and Messrs Longman for allowing me to adapt the select bibliography which appeared in the second edition (1966) of my essay on Lewis Carroll in the 'Writers and their Work' series. This should help to shore up my documentation of what has become an extremely complicated subject.

Derek Hudson

Hindhead,
March, 1976

Author's Note to the First Edition

'Until the publication of Dodgson's Diary takes place, there is no real call for a new Life of Lewis Carroll', wrote Falconer Madan, at the outset of his *Handbook of the Literature of the Rev C. L. Dodgson*.

This, then, is the first biography to appear since the Diaries were published in January of this year, under the editorship of Mr Roger Lancelyn Green, and I am greatly indebted to Miss Menella Dodgson for permission to see the full text before its publication, and to her and Messrs Cassell for allowing me to quote from it. Mr Green's ready help has also been invaluable.

My debt to Miss Dodgson is far more than this, however, for she has generously placed at my disposal much unpublished material in possession of the family and has most kindly co-operated with me throughout in my attempt to produce the definitive biography of her uncle which we both, I think, felt was needed. At the same time, I must make it clear that I alone am responsible for the opinions which I have expressed.

I have been fortunate in being allowed to make use of a great many hitherto unpublished letters, including some of the most interesting and revealing that Lewis Carroll wrote. In fact, more than three-quarters of the letters I have used are new to print. I am especially indebted to Messrs Macmillan for allowing me to quote from the many letters (more than four hundred) which Dodgson wrote to his publishers, and which have never before been employed in a biography. I have also received invaluable and most courteous help from many American collectors, including the libraries of Harvard, Yale and Princeton, the Huntington Library, San Marino, and Mr Alfred C. Berol, Mr Warren Weaver, Mrs Elizabeth Hartz and Dr Lall G. Montgomery.

It was a stroke of luck that Professor Duncan Black should have discovered a mass of documents at Christ Church, Oxford, in 1952, concerning Dodgson's period as Curator of the Common Room, and I am much obliged to him and to the Christ Church authorities for allowing me to use them; as well as individually to Mr W. G. Hiscock, Dr T. B. Heaton, Mr R. H. Dundas and Mr Geoffrey Bill – all of Christ Church – for their willing co-operation and encouragement in various ways. Letters written by Dodgson to Michael Ernest Sadler, when he was Steward of Christ Church, and kindly lent to me by Mr Michael Sadleir, have also helped to throw light on his college life.

I am most grateful to Viscount Simon, Mrs A. T. Waterhouse, Miss H. L. Rowell and Mrs Arthur Davies for the last memories of Lewis Carroll which appear in Appendix A; and to Miss Rowell and Mrs Davies for allowing me to publish letters.

The Rector of Croft, near Darlington, the Rev G. Edward Charlesworth, has placed me in his debt by kindly showing me the Rectory, where Lewis Carroll spent so much of his youth, and the interesting finds that he has recently made there; I owe thanks, also, to Miss Florence Pimm for her hospitality at 'The Chestnuts', Guildford.

I have been particularly indebted to Dr M. J. Mannheim for the great trouble he has taken over the analysis of specimens of Dodgson's handwriting at different times of his life; his conclusions have been exceedingly interesting and helpful. I should make it clear, in this connection, that Dr Mannheim approached the study of the handwriting with no knowledge of Dodgson's life except that he was an author and an Oxford don.

The illustrations and handwriting reproductions are included by kind permission of Miss Menella Dodgson, Harvard College Library, Mr Michael

Sadleir, Mr Helmut Gernsheim and the University of Texas, Wing Commander Caryl Hargreaves, Mrs Audrey Skimming, Mrs Irene Jaques, Miss Florence Pimm and Mr George Buday, author of *The Story of the Christmas Card*, published by Odhams Press. Mr Colin G. Futcher has taken many of the excellent photographs.

I must thank Miss Marghanita Laski (Mrs John Howard) for trying out 'The Game of Logic' with her children, Wing Commander Caryl Hargreaves for much wise advice and assistance, and the following for helping me in various ways: Mrs Audrey Skimming, Mrs Irene Jaques, Mrs Hester Thackeray Fuller, Mrs Frances Stockwell, Dr F. L. Pleadwell, Professor Lionel Stevenson, Mr J. M. Thompson, Mrs Alice Collet, Mr R. E. Thompson, Miss F. Mary Tyrwhitt, Miss Hilda D. King, Miss Enid Dance (Curator of Guildford Museum), Mr Amos Chalcraft, Professor C. A. Coulson, F.R.S., the President of Corpus Christi College, Oxford, Mr T. A. Meade Faulkner, Mr Charles Dougan, Canon H. E. Hone, Miss J. Whillis, Mr F. R. G. Duckworth, Mr Cecil G. Keith, Mr Christopher Hassall, the Borough Librarian of Eastbourne, Mr Peter Alexander, Mr W. Todd Furniss, the late Aleyn Lyell Reade, Mr Jeffrey Dell, Messrs. Harper and Brothers (as publishers of *Harper's Magazine*) and Messrs John Murray (as publishers of the *Cornhill Magazine*). I owe grateful thanks to Mr Michael Sadleir and Mr Ralph Arnold of Constable for their encouragement and advice. There have also been many others to whom I should apologise for not giving individual mention.

The fact that I have largely relied on new material does not mean, of course, that I am not indebted to biographies of Lewis Carroll and other books already published. I have acknowledged my particular indebtedness in the Notes and References at the end of the book.

Finally, after recording so much fruitful support, I feel I should mention one venture that did not come off, but in which I am nevertheless grateful to have had the help of Mr Herbert Elliott and Mr George Savage of Eastbourne. Mr Elliott owns a Victorian oil-painting of a little girl reading *Punch*, which has on the back of it an inscription to the effect that it was painted by Lewis Carroll. It is not a very good picture, but if it had been genuine I should have liked to reproduce it as Dodgson's only known attempt in oils. The signature, however, seems best interpreted as 'E.D.', and, according to Lewis Carroll's diary, a young friend, Edith Denman, presented him with an oil-painting of a village child in November, 1881. Therefore the explanation must be, I think, that Dodgson gave away Miss Denman's picture to an Eastbourne friend. I cannot exactly blame him for this, and if we may not hail Dodgson as an artist in oils, it is perhaps as well that the attribution should have been investigated, even though it was found to be mistaken.

Derek Hudson

Haslemere,
February, 1954

THY WILL BE DONE

WHERE I AM. THERE SHALL
ALSO MY SERVANT BE.

REV. CHARLES LUTWIDGE DODGSON,
(LEWIS CARROLL.)
FELL ASLEEP JAN. 14. 1898.
AGED 65 YEARS.

"HIS SERVANTS SHALL SERVE HIM."

Lewis Carroll's grave in the
Cemetery, Guildford

One

The eighteen large pages of *The Times* of January 15th, 1898, opened with an opulent crackle. Readers seeking the page marked 'Latest Intelligence' turned from the aftermath of the Dreyfus case, the Sicilian *fêtes*, the bad news from Prague, to a long right-hand column headed 'Obituary'. The name at the head of it will have been to most of them, in some degree, familiar. 'We regret to announce the death of the Rev Charles Lutwidge Dodgson, better known as "Lewis Carroll", the delightful author of *Alice in Wonderland*, and other books of an exquisitely whimsical humour. He died yesterday at The Chestnuts, Guildford, the residence of his sisters, in his 66th year. . . .'

It had been in the sixties, the obituary recalled, that '*The Adventures of Alice in Wonderland* burst upon an astonished world', and the chronicle continued:

'Few would have imagined that the quiet, reserved mathematician, a bachelor, who all his life was remarkable for his shyness and dislike of publicity, possessed the qualities necessary to produce a work which has stood the test of more than 30 years, and still captivates young and old alike by its quaint and original genius. . . . It is curious to note how frequently *Alice in Wonderland* is quoted in reference to public affairs, as well as to the ordinary matters of everyday life. Hardly a week passes without the employment of its whimsicalities to point a moral or adorn a tale. . . . In many a home and many a schoolroom there will be genuine sorrow to-day when it is announced that the author of *Alice in Wonderland* and *Through the Looking-Glass* has passed away.'

Those who took in other papers found the same news and the same measure of appreciation. '"Alice" and "The Snark" must remain with us for all time', said the *Daily Mail*. 'He richly deserved the epithet of the unique', said the *Daily Telegraph*. 'The voices he raised in that Kingdom of Nowhere will not die so long as the language of Shakespeare continues to be spoken.' And there was a final paragraph:

'In truth, Lewis Carroll was moulded of the porcelain clay of human kind. His salient characteristic consisted in a curious combination of poet, mathematician, and man of the world, such as has probably never been seen before. The man "Lewis Carroll" has passed away from among us, but his works are destined to endure.'

Best served were the readers of the *Daily News*, who were given an obituary of over a column and a long leading article asserting that 'Mr Dodgson was a man of genius . . . the two "Alices" have never been superseded. It is possible that they never will be'. The obituary, written from intimate knowledge, was able to show the photographer as well as the writer: 'The smell of the collodion he used to pour on to the negative, while his small "subjects" watched him open-mouthed the while, lingers in the memory of many whose childish days he helped to brighten.'

Yet, even on the morning after Lewis Carroll's death, there was a hint that not all recollections of him were going to be unclouded. The *Daily Chronicle* printed a long and critical article 'By One Who Knew Him' (and who apparently did not like him). The writer recognised his importance as a children's author, but sounded some discordant notes – he 'could be almost insolent' – and concluded that 'he was a humorist oppressed by a sense of gravity'. As a memory this was bitter-sweet.

His oldest friend, the Rev T. Vere Bayne (Plate p. 176), like Dodgson a Student of Christ Church, allowed no emotion of any kind to appear in the sparse entry of his singularly uncommunicative diary: 'Chas. L. Dodgson died yesterday of Pneumonia foll^g on Influenza. I come up to Ch. Ch. Wilfred Dodgson comes to see me.'[1] (A few days later he was noting that Wilfred Dodgson was 'appalled at the mass of papers, etc., in his brother's rooms'; and many things were then destroyed that would eventually have become valuable.)

Although Dean Paget, Professor William Sanday and other Oxford men spoke and wrote feelingly about Dodgson at this time, it was probably the young who felt his loss most keenly, and who loved him the most; a girl like Ethel Rowell, for instance, who on a morning in her third year at Holloway College 'saw in *The Times* that Mr Dodgson had died':

'To me the printed words seemed to bear no sense, the fact stated seemed impossible. He had always been so vividly alive to me, and I had never imagined life without him; for days I went on asserting to myself that he *couldn't* be dead, asserting it doggedly but hopelessly against those also strangely insistent paragraphs in the newspapers.

I heard no details of his last illness or of the way of his death, and perhaps the lack of news increased my feeling that it had all happened absolutely irrationally, and simply could not be accepted. It gave me a feeling of forlornness such as I had never known. No one around me was aware of my plight. And there was nothing I could do as an expression of my sorrow – or so it seemed, till finally I hit upon an odd and childish device: I made a large badge out of some black ribbon I had by me, and I fastened this black badge to my petticoat in front just under my shirt blouse. I felt I could not wear the badge outside; people would ask what it was and after all he was no relation; yet I knew I must in some manner "wear black" for Mr Dodgson.'[2]

Close in spirit to Ethel Rowell's gesture was the poem which appeared in *Punch* on January 29th, 1898, with its final verse:

> Farewell! But near our hearts we have you yet,
>   Holding our heritage with loving hand,
> Who may not follow where your feet are set
>   Upon the ways of Wonderland.

Two

In the meantime Lewis Carroll's brothers Wilfred and Edwin, in pursuance of their duties as executors, had examined 'the last Will and Testament of me Charles Lutwidge Dodgson, Student of Christ Church, Oxford', which had been signed on November 4th, 1871, and by which he did 'give devise and bequeath all the real and personal estate of which I shall be possessed or entitled to at the time of my decease to be divided into equal shares one share to go to each of my brothers and sisters who shall be then living and if any one of them be then deceased but have married one share to be divided equally among the children if any be then living of such brother and sister'. The document was typical of him, and of the strong family affection that was a feature of his life. For many years his books had brought him a considerable income, but he had been generous with his money and had no large fortune to leave – to be exact, £4,596 7s. 7d.[3]

The executors also had before them a paper written by their brother on June 4th, 1873, shortly after the death and funeral of his favourite uncle Skeffington Lutwidge. It was headed 'Directions regarding my Funeral, etc.' and ran as follows:

'I request of those who arrange for my Funeral that no Pall may be employed, and that no hat-bands or scarfs may be worn at the Funeral or given to any one. Also that it may be a walking funeral, unless the distance or other cause should make that arrangement inconvenient. Also that the Coffin may be quite plain and simple, and that there be not an inner coffin, unless that be necessary for some reason other than custom.

And generally I request that all the details be simple and inexpensive, avoiding all things which are merely done for show, and retaining only what is, in the judgement of those who arrange my Funeral, requisite for its decent and reverent performance. But this clause is not to override any preceding clause, or any subsequent clause.

I further request that no plumes may be carried, either on the hearse, or on the horses, if there be horses. Also that the Coffin be not black, nor covered with cloth.

Also that there be no expensive monument. I should prefer a small plain head-stone, but will leave this detail to their judgement.'[4]

The instructions were scrupulously followed. Only flowers lay on the plain coffin, which was carried from 'The Chestnuts' to the near-by parish church of St Mary's, where Dr Paget, the Dean of Christ Church, and Canon Grant, the Guildford Rector, conducted the service. Thence it was taken, again on a hand-bier, to the cemetery. The mourners walked – up a very steep hill. There were not many of them: members of the family, some old friends from Oxford and Guildford, and G. L. Craik, who had so often battled with Lewis Carroll's exacting correspondence at Macmillan's. Dr Paget read the committal sentences, and the choir sang 'Peace, perfect peace'. The wreaths were placed on the grave; many were from child-friends; one came from 'Alice' (Mrs Hargreaves).

Having been so careful about the plumes and the horses, the executors may have felt entitled, perhaps, to use their own judgement about the 'small plain head-stone'. It may well have seemed to them that their own respect – and, indeed, England's affection – required slightly more elaborate expression. And so, in due course, a monument consisting of three steps surmounted by a marble cross rose over the grave. On the lowest step were inscribed the texts 'His Servants Shall Serve Him' and 'Father in thy Gracious Keeping leave We now thy Servant Sleeping'; on the next step 'Revd. Charles Lutwidge Dodgson (Lewis Carroll) Fell Asleep Jan. 14. 1898, aged 65 Years'; on the top step 'Where I am, There Shall also my Servant be'; and on the cross itself 'Thy Will be Done'.

The visitor, turning away from the quiet sanctuary on the hillside, looks down over the old town of Guildford, through whose narrow streets Lewis Carroll had so often walked – looks down, too, to the busy world of men in which he dreamed his dreams.

Three

In his 'Easter Greeting to Every Child who Loves "Alice"', Lewis Carroll said: 'If I have written anything to add to those stores of innocent and healthy amusement that are laid up in books for the children I love so well, it is surely something I may hope to look back upon without shame and sorrow (as how much of life must then be recalled!) when *my* turn comes to walk through the valley of shadows.' One of his child-friends now made the most appropriate suggestion for a memorial to him. Audrey Fuller, aged fourteen, wrote a letter that was published by the *St James's Gazette*: 'I have been wondering if all the children who knew and loved him, and the children who only knew him by his books, could not all join together and do some lasting good in remembrance of him. Perhaps we might collect enough money to have a cot in the Children's Hospital, and call it the *Alice in Wonderland* cot.'

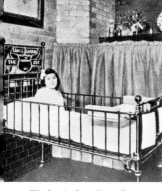

The Lewis Carroll cot, Great Ormond Street Hospital for Sick Children

The *St James's Gazette* took up the idea and opened a subscription list; money came in steadily, much of it in small sums from children; and in October, 1898, the subscribers were able to present to the Great Ormond Street Hospital the £1,000 which was required to 'endow the cot for ever'. Audrey's mother, Mrs Herbert Fuller – who in earlier days, as Minnie Drury, had herself been one of Lewis Carroll's child-friends – acted as honorary secretary of the fund, and prepared for her daughter a large scrapbook full of press cuttings and letters which she received concerning the appeal. This scrapbook conveys better than any other single source what English people felt about Lewis Carroll in the year of his death.[5]

From the black-bordered note with which 'The Brothers and Sisters of Lewis Carroll' enclosed their loyal contribution, we turn to a letter in a graceful and dignified hand signed 'Alice Pleasance Hargreaves'. 'The great thing,' wrote 'Alice' herself, 'will be to make the memorial a real success which I do not doubt.' Later comes a letter from Canon Robinson Duckworth, who was able to speak of the genesis of *Alice in Wonderland* with an authority second only to that of Mrs Hargreaves:

'I have pleasure in sending £2 2s. od. towards the Lewis Carroll Memorial. During my Oxford Tutorial days I was intimate with Mr Dodgson, and I was "stroke" of the "pair" of which he was "bow" in the famous voyage from Oxford to Godstow, when *Alice in Wonderland* was created. The quaint story floated over my shoulders to the pretty trio of sisters, daughters of Dean Liddell, on that beautiful summer afternoon in the Long Vacation which is described in the introductory verses to the story. I am the "duck" which figures in it, and it was by my urgent persuasion that Mr Dodgson gave it to the world.'

Canon Duckworth was not the only person who claimed to have persuaded Dodgson to publish *Alice in Wonderland*, but he wrote with understandable pride and pleasure in his memories. So, too, did another old friend of Lewis Carroll's, who had not made the historic trip to Godstow but who triumphantly joined the voyage at a later stage. In asking to be excused from writing a letter for publication, Sir John Tenniel showed a modesty and sensitivity reminiscent of Dodgson himself:

'. . . I need hardly assure you that the movement itself has my warmest sympathy, in every way; I am proud to have my name on the Committee, and would gladly and most willingly – so far as I am able – do anything in my power towards the success of the undertaking: at the same time, I habitually shrink from "*publicity*", and must, therefore, beg to be excused from taking any sort of conspicuous action in that direction; – indeed – and seeing my very intimate association with poor Mr Dodgson for so many years – even to within a few months of his death – I could hardly do so without incurring the risk of a possible charge of "*advertising*" *myself* (which I loathe!) in the reflected light of "Alice's" world-wide popularity, over the grave – so to speak – of my poor dead friend.'

Several members of the Royal Family were among the contributors. Princess Alice was particularly enthusiastic and allowed her name to appear as a supporter. There were letters from many members of the nobility and leaders of the Church, and one from Sir Michael Hicks-Beach, the Chancellor of the Exchequer, who was a Christ Church contemporary of Dodgson's.

But it is naturally to the response from the literary world that one turns with the greatest interest – to George Meredith's remark that 'Nothing better in the form of a Memorial could have been chosen'; to George MacDonald's good wishes and willingness to 'let you use my name'; to J. K. Jerome's 'I enclose you a guinea. It ought to be more'; to Lady Ritchie's reminder that 'Mr Dodgson was always so kind a friend to *old* children as well as young ones'; to S. R. Crockett's announcement that, along with his own contribution, came half a crown from a little girl, which 'represents five weeks' pocket-money so that is a good deal for her'; to the notes from W. M. Rossetti, Anthony Hope-Hawkins, Alice Meynell (who wrote a special article for the *St James's Gazette*); to the lament from R. D. Blackmore: 'It would have been a pleasure, and a pride, to me to subscribe for your good purpose, if I had anything to subscribe with. But through the utter loss of crop last year, and other adverse circs, I am now obliged to confine myself to what I cannot help, which is manifold.'

The letter which said most, and in a short space said it supremely well, came in the spidery handwriting of Sir Walter Besant:

'. . . It is now thirty years since I first made the acquaintance of Alice and I should not like to count the number of copies of that incomparable work which I have given to little girls of my acquaintance since that time. It is the only child's book, perhaps, which can be read with equal pleasure by old and young. I should frequently read it still, but for the fact that I know it by heart. It is also the only child's book of nonsense which is never childish though it always appeals to a child; where there is no writing down to the understanding of a child, though it can always be understood by a child. It is, in a word, a book of that extremely rare kind which will belong to all the generations to come until the language becomes obsolete.

I cannot doubt that your cot will be more than provided. If there is any doubt upon the subject you have only to ask us all to double our subscriptions.'

Artists proved generous contributors – among them Holman Hunt, Alma-Tadema, Herkomer, and Walter Crane, who wrote: 'From the time when his delightful *Alice in Wonderland* first appeared I have always been a great admirer of his delightful invention, whimsical fun and fancy, and childlike sympathy with children.' Many bishops and clergymen supported the fund. Equally strong was the response from the stage. Sir Henry Irving wrote from the Lyceum, Kate Terry Lewis from the Globe, and Madge Kendal (on tour) from the North Western Hotel, Liverpool. 'Any work associated with the name of Lewis Carroll must command widespread interest and sympathy,' said Irving, 'more especially anything which is concerned with the care and happiness of children.' Most touching of all were the efforts made by the children themselves. 'My pupils', wrote a Cambridge head-mistress, 'always make a point of saving during Lent and this year we unanimously determined to give our offerings to the "Lewis Carroll cot".' . . . 'We thought we should like to help,' wrote twelve girls at Bath High School. . . . 'Money collected at a small concert given by the pupils of Derwent House School, Carshalton', was enclosed in another letter. And so it went on.

Of course not all the correspondence was constructive. There was a lady in the Fulham Road who had never heard of the book called 'Alice' and requested to be informed where she could obtain a copy. And Gladstone's daughter, Mrs Mary Drew, who herself had 'boundless reverence and love and gratitude' for Lewis Carroll, reported a lack of sympathy in a higher quarter:

'I am sorry to say that I entirely failed when the old Alices came out first in interesting Mr Gladstone in them. It did not appeal to his particular sense of humour, therefore I do not think it is worth while trying to interest him in the Memorial, in spite of Mr Dodgson's distinctions in other things.'

Curious, too, in another way, was the letter from Frederick Hollyer, the portrait-photographer, who had 'had the pleasure of knowing Mr Dodgson for many years' but had been 'quite unaware he was the author of *Alice in Wonderland* until a few days ago'.

Four

We have been able to sense some of the emotions that were stirred, in the early months of 1898, by the death of Lewis Carroll. Outstanding among them was the feeling that a most unusual man had departed, a man who might be termed a genius, a man who had achieved something unique that would never be surpassed in its own line. There was already an agreement of opinion on that point, from the newspapers, from men of letters, artists, actors, above all from children and those who understood children. At the same time we can sense that an impenetrable barrier shut off certain intellectual minds (though a minority) from an enjoyment of his gift – Mr Gladstone, for instance, had not been 'interested'; and we are made aware of a widespread feeling that there was about him a mystery even more complex and individual than that which commonly surrounds the man of genius. Moreover, despite the general deep affection he had inspired, there are already hints of asperities and angularities, of baffling turns of character that had disappointed some of those who revered and loved him for the happiness he had given to the world.

More than seventy-five years have passed since January 14th, 1898. They have seen the gradual growth of an imposing *corpus* of Lewis Carroll literature which has testified to ever-increasing interest on both sides of the Atlantic. Yet two of the most valuable contributions to an understanding of C. L. Dodgson appeared in the year of his death. The Rev T. B. Strong, subsequently Bishop of Oxford, writing from intimate knowledge, contributed to the *Cornhill* of March, 1898, a cool and lucid analysis of the man and his works that has not been displaced as criticism, though it has been very charmingly supplemented by Walter de la Mare's long and delightful essay published in 1932. He wrote of him as one who had 'paroxysms' of work when he was 'apt to forget his meals, and toil on for the best part of the night', admitted that 'to a large extent, especially in his later years', he lived as a recluse, but added that 'those who knew him ceased to find it puzzling' that he had produced the 'Alice' books: 'There was always the same mind displayed in his talk'.

It was hardly to be expected that Bishop Strong's attitude of friendly but not uncritical detachment should have been adopted in the 'official' life of Lewis Carroll by his nephew S. Dodgson Collingwood, which also was published in 1898. Considering the rapidity with which Collingwood must have worked in order to get together this substantial volume of four hundred pages in a matter of months, the result – apart from the index – was surprisingly successful: his book remains an indispensable source. As early as December 3rd, 1898, T. Vere Bayne was able to write in his diary: 'Dodgson's Nephew, Stuart D. Collingwood, gives to C. R. [i.e. Christ Church Common Room] a copy of his Uncle's life and letters'. But it was naturally limited in its scope by the circumstances of its composition. The deep affection and gratitude which his brothers and sisters felt for Lewis Carroll understandably precluded any critical approach. The biography – full of interesting information – stands as a pious Victorian memorial to a life which, many years later, has to be viewed in different perspective. If his nephew does at one point admit that 'Mr Dodgson was no easy man to work with', that is as far as he is prepared to go – peculiarities are not denied; but there is no admission here of what many would now consider proved, that his uncle was one of the great Victorian eccentrics.

Anyone who attended the sale of Lewis Carroll's property at the Holywell Music Room, Oxford, on May 10 and May 11th, 1898, must, however, have suspected the presence of a highly individual and engaging eccentricity, especially as he ran his eye down the section of the catalogue headed 'Personal Effects'.[6] Watches, clocks, opera glasses and telescopes were much in evidence here. An aneroid, a microscope, a 'pair of combination "Field, Marine and Theatre" glasses in case' and a 'pocket sun dial' lead gracefully into this moving sequence:

'Set of chessmen in case, backgammon and draughts.
Artist's model of a hand and foot.
Human skull and skeleton of a hand and foot.
Two artist's lay figures and sundries.
Two rules, ivory angle rule, 2 paper knives, 2 small inlaid boxes, box of mathematical instruments and a box of geometrical solids.
Two Whiteley exercisers, bundle of walking sticks and umbrellas, and pair of boot trees.
Two pairs of dumb bells, 2 small clothes brushes, silk tidy, etc.
Photo album, containing coloured photos, and a musical album.'

After many more photograph albums and loose photographs, we come to such items as '6 travelling inkpots', 'Dr Moffatt's Ammoniaphone (for voice cultivation)', the '"Trytograph" printing press', the 'Nyctograph in case' (this was Dodgson's invention for taking notes in the dark), a 'Japanese tea-pot in basket' and two boxes of homoeopathic medicines. If this was not the inventory of a Victorian White Knight, it was something very like it.

The auction upset many people, among them Professor York Powell, a Christ Church colleague, who wrote a poem that is published in the second volume of his biography by Oliver Elton:

> Poor playthings of the man that's gone,
> Surely we would not have them thrown,
> Like wreckage on a barren strand,
> The prey of every greedy hand.
>
> Fast ride the Dead! Perhaps 'tis well!
> He shall not know, what none would tell,
> That gambling salesmen bargain'd o'er
> The books he read, the clothes he wore,
>
> The desk he stood at day by day
> In patient toil or earnest play,
> The pictures that he loved to see,
> Faint echoes of his Fantasy.
>
> He shall not know. And yet, and yet,
> One would not quite so soon forget
> The dead man's whims, or let Gain riot
> Among the toys he loved in quiet:
>
> Better by far the Northman's pyre,
> That burnt in one sky-soaring fire
> The man with all he held most dear.
> 'He that hath ears, now let him hear'.

Five

Lewis Carroll's genius did not lack appreciation among his contemporaries, and they were glad to read, as a supplement to his biography, S. D. Colling-wood's *The Lewis Carroll Picture Book*, published in 1899, and also Saki's parody *The Westminster Alice* of 1902 – but, on the whole, in the early years of the new century, interest in him slackened considerably. As Falconer Madan put it, 'he came to be regarded as, after all, only a Victorian, whose significance began and ended with that age'.[7]

Towards the end of the 1914–18 war this attitude began to change. It may well be that the horrors of war turned men's hearts and minds back to the remembered innocence of childhood, to 'the happy summer days'. Probably there were many who re-read 'Alice' in the trenches, and others beside Osborne in *Journey's End* who may have answered Trotter's 'Why, that's a kid's book!' with 'Yes', and his further question 'You aren't *reading* it?' with another 'Yes'.

For whatever reason, it came to be generally understood at about this time – or perhaps one should say, it was rediscovered – that Lewis Carroll was something much more than a temporary Victorian phenomenon, that in the 'Alice' books he had captured the essence of the wonder of childhood with such loving insight that he must belong not only to his own century but to all the centuries to come. A significant increase in the prices paid at auction for his manuscripts and first editions was noticeable in 1917, continued progressively throughout the nineteen-twenties, and reached a sensational climax in 1928 when Dr A. S. W. Rosenbach, the well-known rare-book dealer, paid £15,400 at Sothebys for the manuscript of the original version of *Alice's Adventures in Wonderland*, and resold it in the same year for nearly double that sum to Eldridge R. Johnson of New York.

Lewis Carroll's reputation was kept alive by American enthusiasts at a time when he was ignored in England. Prominent among those individuals responsible was Morris L. Parrish of Philadelphia, who was one of the first Americans to form a big Carroll collection and who published two bibliographies of it for private distribution.

The values reflected in the sale of Lewis Carroll items during the boom period immediately before and after his centenary (1932) were, like those of all sought-after literary rarities, greatly exaggerated. In 1948 Dr Luther Evans, the Librarian of Congress, presented the 'Alice' manuscript to the British Museum on behalf of a group of American admirers of Great Britain's part in the war. This delightful gesture was made possible by the generosity of Eldridge R. Johnson and by subscriptions from American sympathisers to the amount of £12,500. There is irony in the contrast between this figure, reduced though it was from the peak payment of 1928, and the total receipts of the Lewis Carroll sale of 1898, when his whole library, including two first editions, association copies, original drawings, proof engravings, photographs, etc., as well as all his furniture and effects, realised only £729 2s. 6d. It is understandable that the Dodgson family should feel sad at this thought, and in retrospect they may well agree with York Powell and Sir Charles Oman, who wrote in his autobiography that these things 'ought never to have come under the hammer'.

Cash values, however, though interesting, are a most inadequate and unromantic index to an author's fame. The years which centred round the centenary of Lewis Carroll's birth in 1932 saw the publication of several works which provided indispensable material for a proper understanding of the man. First came that remarkable compilation, a sort of Bible for Carrollians, the *Handbook of the Literature of the Rev. C. L. Dodgson (Lewis Carroll)*, by S. H. Williams and Falconer Madan (1931), which was revised by Roger Lancelyn Green and re-issued as *The Lewis Carroll Handbook* in 1962. It was followed in 1932 by the publication of two of his early manuscript magazines, *The Rectory Umbrella* and *Mischmasch*, by Walter de la Mare's essay, a biography from Langford Reed, and an edition of the *Collected Verse*; and in 1933 by *A Selection from the Letters of Lewis Carroll to his Child-friends*. In 1939 the Nonesuch Press published *The Complete Works of Lewis Carroll*, which, though far from complete, had the advantage of presenting in convenient form many lesser works that would otherwise be difficult of access. In 1954 came *The Diaries of Lewis Carroll*, edited by Roger Lancelyn Green. The years since 1932 also saw the appearance, on both sides of the Atlantic, of a number of other biographical studies, of which Helmut Gernsheim's *Lewis Carroll: Photographer* deserves special praise. In 1952 Henri Parisot contributed to the series 'Poètes d'Aujourd'hui' the most ambitious account of Lewis

Carroll that had so far appeared in France. In subsequent years French interest has increased, and has culminated in Jean Gattégno's *Lewis Carroll: une vie* (1974).

The centenary of 1932 not only inspired a most interesting exhibition of Carrolliana, held at Messrs Bumpus's premises in Oxford Street (where more than ten thousand people saw it), but also provided the occasion for the publication of an illustrated book *The Lewis Carroll Centenary in London 1932* which contains, besides the complete catalogue of the exhibition, a certain amount of unpublished material. Steps were also taken at this time to initiate a more substantial memorial in the form of an entire Children's Ward at St Mary's Hospital, Paddington, and this project was launched by a letter in *The Times* in March, 1932, signed by Ramsay MacDonald, Stanley Baldwin, J. M. Barrie, Alice Pleasance Hargreaves, A. P. Herbert, E. V. Lucas, Frederick Macmillan, Walter de la Mare, A. A. Milne, the Bishop of Oxford, P. Wilson Steer and J. C. Squire. Many famous actors and actresses took part in a special Lewis Carroll *matinée* at the St James's Theatre in July, 1932. The success of the appeal was largely due to the enthusiasm of Dodgson's nephew, Professor B. J. Collingwood – Professor of Physiology at St Mary's Medical School and himself a figure beloved by all who knew the hospital* – and to the generosity of Guy Harben, chairman of the memorial committee, who made up the difference between the £3,000 subscribed by the public and the £10,000 needed for the ward.

Left: Plaque on the gate-post of The Chestnuts, Guildford, designed by Graily Hewitt
Right: Lewis Carroll biscuit tin – one of the commercial manifestations of Lewis Carroll's popularity (1892).

The Lewis Carroll Ward at St Mary's was opened in November, 1937, and visited in that month by Queen Elizabeth. Decorations and furniture were designed by Sir Edwin Cooper, R.A., and from the twenty-six cots children can see majolica panels of *Alice in Wonderland* characters by F. V. Blundstone. These same characters look down, now, from a stained-glass window

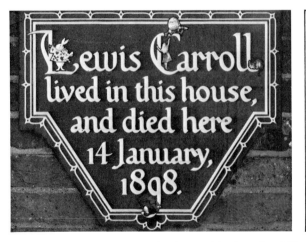

in the parish church of Daresbury, where Lewis Carroll was born. They also greet visitors from an ornamental plaque designed by Graily Hewitt at the gate of 'The Chestnuts', Guildford, where he died (Plate p. 143).

For since the death of Lewis Carroll his characters have consolidated their

*Among Dodgson's instructions to his executors was the following, dated June 11th, 1891: 'Now that my nephew, Bertram Collingwood, is studying for the medical profession, I should like him to have what he likes of the books on the subjects of Anatomy, Physiology, Pathology, and Kindred Subjects' (Harvard College Library). He put them to good use.

hold on the imaginations of men, women and children throughout the world, to a degree unattained by the characters of any other author with the exception of Shakespeare, Dickens, and, perhaps, Sir Arthur Conan Doyle. Even their creator was able to send 'The Lewis Carroll Biscuit Tin' (Plate p. 28) as a present to his friends, but his imagination might have boggled at the extent to which the White Rabbit, the March Hare, and the rest, have since been employed by cartoonists, parodists, advertisers, and designers in every medium from cigarette-cards to tea-services. English editions of 'Alice' have been innumerable. Like Sherlock Holmes, she has long ago captured America, and, apart from the Bible and one or two other works, there are probably more partial or complete translations of *Alice's Adventures in Wonderland* than of any other book that has ever been written.* A little black Alice even talks Swahili.

The dramatic adaptations of 'Alice', by Kate Freiligrath-Kroeker and by Savile Clark, which Lewis Carroll knew, have been followed by many others since his death, perhaps the best of these being Clemence Dane's, presented at the Scala Theatre, London, in 1943, with charming music by Richard Addinsell. Other composers who have written for 'Alice' include Walter Slaughter (Savile Clark's collaborator), Norman O'Neill (who wrote an 'Alice' ballet), Sir Walford Davies (Humpty Dumpty Cantata), H. Fraser-Simson, who set the songs, and Deems Taylor (composer of a *Through the Looking-Glass* suite). The B.B.C. has broadcast Max Saunders's brilliant musical version of *The Hunting of the Snark* – a work which combines a gay irresponsibility with passages of becoming seriousness and gravity; and *Through the Looking-Glass*, whose episodes have often been staged as part of *Alice in Wonderland*, has been successfully dramatised and televised on its own.

What employment has been derived from Lewis Carroll, then, by artists of

The illustrators of Lewis Carroll's characters: 1 Lewis Carroll. 2 Sir John Tenniel. 3 Arthur Rackham

all kinds! – especially by the illustrators, from Tenniel to Mabel Lucie Attwell, and from Arthur Rackham to Marie Laurencin. The cinema has attempted more than once to capture the spirit of 'Alice'. High praise has been given to a little-known version made at Denham by Dallas Bower and Lou Bunin. Unfortunately, Walt Disney's interpretation, of which much was hoped,

*Warren Weaver's *Alice in Many Tongues* (1964) is the best authority on these. He assembled a personal collection of about 160 copies of *Alice in Wonderland* in 42 languages. It is now at the University of Texas.

proved a sad disappointment. The 'book of the film' spoke of his 'meticulous handling of the characters' and claimed that 'the true spirit of the humorous classic' was 'faithfully preserved'. Alas, it was impudent bluff. The film turned out to be a vulgar and noisy travesty, made all the more disappointing by the few artistic passages in which Disney showed what he might have made of the subject if he had been in better mood.

Six

What manner of man was it who achieved all this, where so many have failed? The question remains real and insistent. Lewis Carroll is remembered in remote corners of the world where most of his donnish contemporaries have never been heard of. From a contemplation of the powerful outer eddies of his fame, the onlooker turns back to the centre of the mysterious pool, where Dodgson's little stone, thrown diffidently a century ago, made such an unexpected splash. And at the heart of the disturbance, clearer now than he was, is still the Rev C. L. Dodgson of Christ Church, with his name painted in white letters over his door, withdrawn, reserved, sending out now and then his shy half-smile, toiling at his 'mass of papers', fussing, helping those in need, reproaching himself before God for his shortcomings, but always looking forward eagerly to the next work that he had set himself to do.

In recent years writers have hunted Lewis Carroll's secret as persistently as any Snark:

> They sought it with thimbles, they sought it with care;
> They pursued it with forks and hope . . .

Some of the forks drawn from the *batterie de cuisine* of Dr Freud have been sharp. One or two writers have shown a surprisingly hostile and superior attitude – a tendency to 'rub salt', as it were, into the wounds that modern psychological diagnosis has thrown open.

The fantasy of Lewis Carroll has, in its turn, inspired some far-fetched fantasy from his biographers. It may be advisable to re-establish some facts; often prosaic and angular, they will at least have the period interest of the Victorian furniture in Dodgson's study, the 'massive mahogany dining-table', the 'settee in crimson rep'.

Accepting the repressions that can now be recognised, accepting the help of scientific analysis, there is still room for sympathy and understanding. If there was weakness in C. L. Dodgson, there was also great strength, the strength of Christian belief. He deserves to be approached not with prurient curiosity but with gratitude for his genius, with affection for all the pleasure he has given to the world, with respect, too, for the way in which he fought against his difficulties and managed to live what was, on the whole, a happy and certainly a useful life. No one can belittle the force of words that have, more than once, been heard by the present writer from those who knew him as children – 'he was so kind.'

Opposite: *The illustrators of Lewis Carroll's characters (continued): 4 A. E. Jackson. 5 Gwynedd Hudson. 6 and 7 Charles Robinson.* *8 Mervyn Peake. 9 Philip Gough. 10 A. L. Bowley. 11 Arthur Rackham. 12 Robert Hogfeldt. 13 Millicent Sowerby.* Right: *14 Mabel Lucie Attwell*

14

'*An unusually large saucepan
flew by it, and very nearly carried
it off*'. *Arthur Rackham's
colour illustration for* Alice's
Adventures in Wonderland

33

Middle: *Charles Robinson.*
Above: *Willy Pogany.* Below:
Willy Pogany

The illustrators of Lewis Carroll's
characters (continued): Above
A. E. Jackson. Below *J. Morton
Sale*

Right: *Willy Pogany*

Daresbury Days

Archdeacon and Mrs Dodgson, the parents of Lewis Carroll. From the silhouettes in the possession of the Dodgson family

One

Visitors to the race-course at Haydock Park must occasionally have pondered the names of some of the races on the card – the Lewis Carroll Hurdle Race, for instance, the Wonderland Steeplechase, or the White Rabbit Steeplechase. They are neighbourly tributes to Lewis Carroll, who, as Charles Lutwidge Dodgson, began his own hurdle race at the parsonage of Daresbury, Cheshire, on January 27th, 1832, in an England torn with political unrest. It may be appropriate that the great reformer of English humour should have made his appearance in the year of the great Reform Bill. But there was certainly no Radical tendency in the political horoscope of that 'little Conservative' who was then 'born into the world alive'.

The third child and the eldest son of the eleven children of the Rev Charles Dodgson by his marriage to his first-cousin Frances Jane Lutwidge, he was descended from two ancient and distinguished North-country families, and inherited from the Dodgsons especially a tradition of service to the Church and from the Lutwidges a tradition of service to the State.[8] His great-great-grandfather, the Rev Christopher Dodgson, held a Yorkshire living early in the eighteenth century, and Christopher's son Charles (who died in 1796) rose to become Bishop of Ossory and Ferns, and later Bishop of Elphin – romantically improbable titles that may well have fed his great-grandson's poetic imagination.

The Bishop's daughter, Elizabeth Anne, by marrying Charles Lutwidge of Holmrook, Cumberland, initiated the connection of the Dodgsons with a family that had many ramifications in Cumberland, Lancashire and Cheshire. Lewis Carroll's great-grandfather, Thomas Lutwidge (1660–1745), and married Lucy, daughter of Sir Charles Hoghton and of Mary Skeffington, who in her turn was the daughter of the second Viscount Massareene in the peerage of Ireland. Sir Charles Hoghton traced his descent by Adam de Hoghton from Matilda, illegitimate daughter of William the Conqueror. And it was at the table of Sir Richard Hoghton, the first Baronet, that King James I is supposed to have solemnly 'knighted' the loin of beef – a legendary incident that may have inspired the famous introduction in *Alice Through the Looking-Glass*: 'Alice – Mutton: Mutton – Alice'.

Bishop Dodgson had, beside his daughter, three sons, of whom two died young. The surviving son, again Charles, became a captain in the 4th Dragoon Guards, and was married to Lucy Hume (whose sister Mary married the Rev E. Smedley, uncle of Frank Smedley, the novelist). Captain Dodgson, killed by a rebel in Ireland in 1803,* left two sons – Charles, the father of Lewis Carroll, and Hassard, who eventually became a Master of the Court of Common Pleas.

It will be seen even from this brief summary that Lewis Carroll possessed an unusually large number of verifiable ancestors and relatives. His Uncle Hassard further complicated the genealogical tree by marrying a cousin Caroline Hume and begetting ten children. With all his vast family of cousins, aunts and uncles, Lewis Carroll kept up an acquaintance that varied in intimacy; he acquired a strong affection for his brothers and sisters, and (as

---

*The text of a letter dated January 27th, 1804, from John Longfield to Major Lutwidge of the 1st Royal Lancashire Infantry, kindly communicated to me by Mrs Irene Jaques, shows that Lewis Carroll's grandfather died gallantly while attempting with Longfield the arrest of some rebels in a house at Philipstown, but does not corroborate the account of the incident given by Collingwood (*Life and Letters of Lewis Carroll* (1898), p. 6) in all its details.

time wore on) for a batch of nephews and nieces.

Two

The family background explains much in Lewis Carroll's character – his sense of religion and tradition, of loyalty and service; a certain pride in social standing; an innate conservatism that struggled with his own originality of mind. It is necessary now to detach from the rich confusion of this parade of gifted relatives, the substantial figure of his father Charles Dodgson, who was born at Hamilton, Lanarkshire, in 1800.

A photograph of the father of Lewis Carroll, which appears in Collingwood's Life of his son, shows a solid and rather gloomy-looking divine, though one whose obvious authority and piety admit the lurking possibility of a sense of humour. We are assured that he had 'the rare power of telling anecdotes effectively', although Collingwood adds that 'his reverence for sacred things was so great that he was never known to relate a story which included a jest upon words from the Bible' (the same might be said, word for word, of Lewis Carroll as he developed).

In fact, there is no doubt that Lewis Carroll's father had a remarkably vivid, profuse and indeed ruthless sense of fantastic fun. He demonstrates it generously in an unpublished letter, written to his son Charles at the age of eight, which is among the Dodgson Family Papers:

'. . . I will not forget your commission. As soon as I get to Leeds I shall scream out in the middle of the street, *Ironmongers – Iron*-mongers – Six hundred men will rush out of their shops in a moment – fly, fly, in all directions – ring the bells, call the constables – set the town on fire. I *will* have a file & a screwdriver, & a ring, & if they are not brought directly, in forty seconds I will leave nothing but one small cat alive in the whole town of Leeds, & I shall only leave that, because I am afraid I shall not have time to kill it.

Then what a bawling & a tearing of hair there will be! Pigs & babies, camels & butterflies, rolling in the gutter together – old women rushing up the chimneys & cows after them – ducks hiding themselves in coffee cups, & fat geese trying to squeeze themselves into pencil cases – at last the Mayor of Leeds will be found in a soup plate covered up with custard & stuck full of almonds to make him look like a sponge cake that he may escape the dreadful destruction of the Town. . . .'

And so he goes on, until he concludes:

'At last they bring the things which I ordered & then I spare the Town & send off in fifty waggons & under the protection of 10,000 soldiers, a file & a screwdriver and a ring as a present to Charles Lutwidge Dodgson from his affec^{nte} Papa.'

Surely no boy of eight could ever have received more direct encouragement to devote himself to the writing of nonsense than this? The Rev Charles Dodgson was heavy-handed; his son refined the process to a sensitive art. But the element of ruthlessness in this letter reappears in the work of Lewis Carroll, and the Mayor of Leeds in the soup plate anticipates the White Queen in her tureen.

The father would not now be remembered if it were not for his son, but he had in abundant measure the qualities necessary to the success of a nineteenth-century clergyman, and they brought him in due course to the Archdeaconry of Richmond and to a Canonry at Ripon Cathedral. He was a distinguished classical scholar who took a 'double first' at Christ Church, Oxford, published a translation of Tertullian and a number of books on theological and religious subjects, and, besides all this, had a special interest in mathematical studies. His generosity to the poor was proverbial in his parishes. There is much here that is immediately recognisable in the character of his famous son – though more, perhaps, that belongs to the formal presentation of C. L. Dodgson, the Oxford don, than to the artist who wrote as Lewis Carroll.

Dr M. J. Mannheim, whose graphological analysis has been of great value in the preparation of this book, deduces from Canon Dodgson's handwriting that he had 'great perseverance and much dignity and poise, and behind it all considerable irritability usually controlled behind a benign façade'. He sees him as somewhat narrow in his emotional range, 'austere, puritanical and fond of power', unlikely to make allowances for shortcomings or disobedience. His more human side would be likely to show itself, Dr Mannheim feels, 'with people in trouble or children whom he would protect, provided that his authority was not challenged'.

These are, of course, only conjectures, and may err in their critical assessment of a man with some humour and full of 'good works'. But it is beyond dispute that Lewis Carroll modelled his outward character largely on his authoritarian father. This would make it all the more likely that, as a grown man, he would turn back again and again to his memories of the love of an affectionate mother, who died on the day before his nineteenth birthday. It seems clear that students of heredity must look to his mother for much of the gentleness, the graceful simplicity, and perhaps, too, the whimsical poetry,

The Parsonage, Daresbury

without which the 'Alice' books could never have been written. In his 'Easter Greeting', written long afterwards, he remembered 'a Mother's gentle hand that undraws your curtains and a Mother's sweet voice that summons you to rise'. Collingwood quotes an estimate of Mrs Dodgson as

'one of the sweetest and gentlest women that ever lived, whom to know was to love. The earnestness of her simple faith and love shone forth in all she did and said; she seemed to live always in the conscious presence of God. It has been said by her children that they never in all their lives remember to have heard an impatient or harsh word from her lips.'[9]

This picture might appear almost too idealised to be quite convincing. But a perusal of some of Mrs Dodgson's letters – written in a sensitive, swiftly running hand – show that she was essentially a practical angel, who lived effectively on this earth: a very busy person who often wrote 'in a tearing hurry' or 'at a gallop', and whose family, husband, house, garden and servants filled her life.

The childhood years of Lewis Carroll were so important to him, so pregnant with meaning for his future creative work, that it is a pity that we do not know more about his Daresbury days. The parsonage (demolished after a fire in the eighteen-eighties) was situated a mile and a half from the village on a glebe farm, and seems from a photograph to have been a plain, homely build-ing of very moderate size. The Lewis Carroll Society of Daresbury has marked its site with a bronze plaque. Daresbury is now on the outskirts of the busy and overgrown town of Warrington, but was then so secluded, as Collingwood says, that 'even the passing of a cart was a matter of great interest to the children'. 'Charlie' (as he was called) had not many friends outside his own family; one of them was Vere Bayne (Plate p. 176), son of the headmaster of Warrington Grammar School, with whom he later renewed acquaintance at Christ Church. He played in the fields, climbed trees and scrambled in and out of the old marl-pits; he was interested in the little animals more than in the larger, and made friends with toads, snails and even earthworms. Probably he got into the shrubberies and gardens of Daresbury Hall, which would have made a natural playground. We know, too, that one family holiday was spent at Beaumaris on the Isle of Anglesey, and Mr R. L. Green legitimately supposes that he may have explored the ruined castle, with its long, dark passages and deep garde-robe pits with their openings at every level[10] – an experience that might well have emerged from his subconscious mind when he came, years later, to describe Alice's adventures underground.

The first of his letters that has survived was written, apparently, to his nurse, while he was away from home. How old he was at the time is a matter of guess-work, but clearly he had been helped in the writing and had his hand guided. The note is addressed on the back, in the hand of the guider, 'For dear kind Bun, from little Charly.' Here is the letter, which has not been published before:[11]

My dear Bun,

I love you very much, & tend you a kitt from little Charlie with the horn of hair. I'd like to give you a kitt, but I tan't, betause I'm at Marke. What a long letter I've written. I'm twite tired.

> My dear Burn,
>   I love you very much
> & send you a kitt from little
> Charlie with the horn of hair
> I'd like to give you a kill, but I
> can't, because I'm at Marke. What
> a long letter I've written. I'm twite
> tired.

The writing cannot, of course, be accepted as a fully authentic autograph – still less the language, foisted on to him by some well-meaning grown-up. Perhaps, however, he originated some of the expressions. It is interesting to note that the baby-talk, fortunately absent from the 'Alice' books, reappeared with deplorable effect in *Sylvie and Bruno*.

Three

In 'Faces in the Fire', written in 1860, Lewis Carroll looked back affectionately to his childhood at Daresbury parsonage –

> 'An island-farm, mid seas of corn
> Swayed by the wandering breath of morn –
> The happy spot where I was born.'

To his father, the compact parsonage in the corn-fields was not quite the paradise that it was to 'little Charlie with the horn of hair'. He had many anxieties. The living to which he had been presented by Christ Church in 1827 was what is known as a 'perpetual curacy', a 'chapelry' under the 'mother-church' of Runcorn (the church containing the memorial window to Lewis Carroll is not the same as that in which his father preached, for it was entirely rebuilt, except for the tower, in 1870). Charles Dodgson's stipend can only have been small, and from the time of his arrival at Daresbury children were born to him at regular intervals of eighteen months or two years. His whole family of seven girls and four boys made its appearance at Daresbury, with the exception of the last child.*

*The following is a list of Archdeacon Dodgson's children, kindly supplied to me by Miss Menella Dodgson with the dates of their births and deaths and particulars of their marriages where they occurred. Genius, as so often, was relatively short-lived. All the children except Lewis Carroll lived to be over seventy, and three to be over eighty: Frances Jane (1828–1903), Elizabeth Lucy (1830–1916), Charles Lutwidge (Lewis Carroll) (1832–1898), Caroline Hume (1833–1904), Mary Charlotte (married C. E. S. Collingwood) (1835–1911), Skeffington Hume (married I. M. Cooper) (1836–1919), Wilfred Longley (married A. J. Donkin) (1838–1914), Louisa Fletcher (1840–1930), Margaret Anne Ashley (1841–1915), Henrietta Harington (1843–1922), Edwin Heron (1846–1918).

Charles Dodgson supplemented his income by taking pupils and did not neglect to urge on the authorities of Christ Church the need to increase his stipend. A letter of his to the Rev Dr Bull of Christ Church, written on January 23rd, 1832, a few days before the birth of Lewis Carroll, shows that the College were then trying to secure payment of a potato tithe, which Dodgson estimated would be worth 'nearly £200 a year' to him if it could be obtained. 'I wish all possible success to your laudable undertaking,' he wrote; 'the Revenues of the Perpetual Curacy of Daresbury certainly *admit* of improvement.' He mentioned that he had spent nearly £30 in manuring part of the land of the small farm attached to the curacy: 'I have preferred this course to that of letting the Farm at a lower Rent, and as my successor therefore may possibly derive a great share of the advantage, the Chapter may perhaps be disposed to take the matter into their consideration.'

He ends his letter despondently, no doubt with the thought in his mind that there would be another mouth to feed in a few days' time:

'I am very glad to hear a good account of my old Friends – for myself I am going on as well as a man can be supposed to do, without prospects, living upon a precarious Income and subject to constant drawback on his domestic comforts. I already begin to experience the anxieties incidental to my situation, having at this moment two Vacancies for Pupils unfilled.'[12]

During the sixteen years that he spent at Daresbury, Charles Dodgson established a Sunday school, organised lectures, did much for the poor, and saw a steady increase in the numbers of his congregation – all this we know from a grateful address given by his churchwarden when he left the parish.[13] Collingwood tells us that Lewis Carroll as a boy at Daresbury also had charitable ideas: 'he used to peel rushes with the idea that the pith would afterwards "be given to the poor", though what possible use they could put it to he never attempted to explain'. One of the toys Lewis Carroll played with in the Daresbury nursery was a jig-saw of 'The Life of Christ' (Plate below) which has

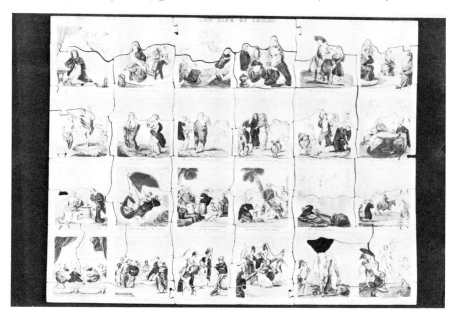

Jig-saw: 'The life of Christ' in twenty-four pictures, used by Dodgson as a child. Forty-nine pieces (one missing) in a wooden box inscribed 'Children, Parsonage, Daresbury.'

survived at Guildford (with one piece missing!). His father gave special attention to the needs of the bargemen who worked on a canal that ran through his parish, and thanks to the generosity of a large landowner in the district, Lord Francis Egerton, was able to turn one of the barges into a chapel for them. Altogether, there is no doubt that Charles Dodgson won the esteem of the parishioners of Daresbury, and when, in 1843 – shortly after his appointment as chaplain to the Bishop of Ripon – the desirable Crown living of Croft in Yorkshire fell vacant, Lord Francis Egerton wrote a warm letter of recommendation to the Prime Minister, Sir Robert Peel, on his behalf:

Worsley. Jany. 7, 1843.

My Dear Sir Robert,

I understand that the Bishop of Ripon is bringing under your consideration the claims of the Revd C. Dodgson, one of his chaplains, for preferment to a living at present vacant in his Diocese. Mr Dodgson has held for 16 years a small living in Cheshire in which I have some property. I am able from this circumstance to bear testimony to the zeal & efficiency with which he has discharged his office since I became acquainted with the district in question, & the care which he has extended to a very generally neglected but not ungrateful class, that of the canal navigators. To his qualities & attainments you will have received better testimony than mine, but I have a recollection of him at Ch. Ch. as a double first class man, & I know from opportunities of personal observation in this county that he has not belied the promise of distinction in his profession which his college success held out.

Believe me,
My dear Sir Robert,
Very faithfully yours
F. EGERTON.

The Rt Ho^{bl} Sir Robt Peel.[14]

The anxiety with which the Rev Charles Dodgson must have awaited Peel's decision can readily be imagined. He was now the father of ten children, and the Croft living was a good one, which would give him a net income of nearly £900 a year. It would be understandable if he had not discouraged some active lobbying on his behalf. Peel, in fact, complained to the Bishop of Ripon that he wished he had not received so many letters in his favour, 'necessarily involving me in a very extensive correspondence and not influencing my decision'.[15]

The grounds for that decision were adequately set out in the following letter, which one hopes that Charles Dodgson opened and read with something less than his usual poise:

Whitehall. Jan. 12, 1843.

Sir

There is no part of my public Duty which is more gratifying to me, than the appropriation of such Church Patronage as may be at my disposal, to the Reward and Encouragement of active professional Exertions by men of unblemished private Character and great intellectual attainment. In conformity with this principle, and exclusively upon the ground of your professional services and claims, I have resolved to appoint you to the Living of Croft in the N. Riding of Yorkshire.

I am unwilling that you should receive the first intimation of this from any other quarter than from myself – and therefore have not mentioned my intentions to any other Party.

I make the offer to you upon the full understanding, in the case of a Living of so much value, that you will be enabled to reside upon the Living and to discharge the Parochial Duties in Person.

I have, &c., &c.,

ROBERT PEEL.

You are quite at liberty in the receipt of this to mention to any one, with whom you may wish to communicate, my intentions in respect to the Living of Croft.

The Revd Charles Dodgson.[16]

In his reply the new Rector of Croft rose to the importance of the occasion. As he wrote, he turned over the most important page in his life, and one of great significance to his eldest son.

Daresbury – Warrington.
Jany. 14, 1843.

SIR

I regret that my absence from home yesterday has caused the delay of a Post in my reply to your letter of the 12th Instant.

I find it utterly impossible to describe the feelings of pleasure & gratitude, with which I have received a communication so highly important to me, and so much enhanced in its value by the peculiarly kind terms in which it is conveyed. It would be intrusive in me to trouble you by detailing the many circumstances connected both with my domestic happiness, and with the performance of my official duties in the Diocese of Ripon, which render the appointment so especially desirable and advantageous to me: but I should be doing culpable injustice to my own feelings, did I fail to express how deeply sensible I am of the high distinction conferred by the notice with which you have honoured me.

I beg to assure you that I shall be anxious to commence my residence at Croft with as little delay as circumstances will admit of: and I earnestly trust that I may be enabled so to devote myself to the duties of my Care, as, in some measure at least, to justify your choice, & repay your kindness.

I have the honour to remain, Sir, with unfeigned respect,

Your most obedient humble Servant,

CHARLES DODGSON.

The Right Hon: Sir Robert Peel, Bart,
&c., &c., &c.[17]

Croft Rectory

One

Those who go northwards by train from King's Cross are not often distracted from their newspapers by striking natural scenery until they have passed through York. Indeed one of the first interesting views that they can see is about three miles south of Darlington, where they may catch a momentary glimpse, to the left of the line, of a long, handsome bridge over the Tees, and, beyond it, a little church surrounded by trees and a cluster of houses. The train rushes out of Yorkshire into Durham, leaving a fleeting impression of something typically English, reassuringly peaceful and permanent. This 'something' (though the traveller may not know it) is the village of Croft.

One day in 1953 the bookstall at Darlington station displayed a thriller, with a lurid cover, by an American author Fredric Brown; its title – *Night of the Jabberwock*. Mr Brown showed a considerable knowledge of Lewis Carroll and had filled his story – not otherwise a very good one – with references to the Master and quotations from his works. 'When Fredric Brown joins forces with Lewis Carroll,' said the blurb, 'a heady brew is almost certain to result. . . .' Agreed; yet there was something satisfying about finding Lewis Carroll represented, however oddly, on Darlington station in 1953 – on the platform that he must have trodden so often, in the years between 1843 and 1868, at the end of a homeward journey from Rugby, London, or Oxford.

A watercolour (signed C. W. H., 1851) of Croft Rectory.

Three miles away, just inside the Yorkshire boundary, the Georgian rectory of Croft stands to the outward view very much as it must have appeared to the Dodgson family when they saw it in 1843, soon after that magical letter from Sir Robert Peel had altered the scope and tenor of their lives. 'The house is a good old-fashioned Rectory, with no *beauty* outside or inside', wrote the Rev Charles Dodgson when he first visited it.[18] To us, who are sated with later horrors, this seems an error of taste. Croft Rectory is undeniably pleasing.

The house is close to the church and surrounded by a large rambling garden, of the kind very attractive for children to play in, full of trees and shrubs.

On the front lawn are the withered remains of the acacia tree under which an ancient inhabitant could still, in 1932, remember Lewis Carroll sitting or lying full-length on the grass, writing.[19] The old yew-tree, known as the 'umbrella-tree', which stands by the lawn to the left of the house, has been found as convenient for climbing by subsequent Rectory children as ever it was by the young Dodgsons. At the back, the large walled kitchen-garden – its long paths intersecting at the centre – was obviously an ideal place for the 'railway game', devised by young Charles for his brothers and sisters with a train made out of a wheelbarrow, a barrel and a small truck, and 'stations' arranged at intervals along the paths.

Some of Lewis Carroll's rules for the railway can now be seen in Harvard College Library:[20]

'Station master must mind his station, and supply refreshments: he can put anyone who behaves badly to prison, while a train goes round the garden: he must ring for the passengers to take their seats, then count 20 slowly, then ring again for the train to start. . . . Passengers may not go on the line on any pretence: parents responsible for their children: may not get in or out of the train when moving: the money is divided equally among all except drivers: the parents take their childrens': any one without money works at one of the stations.'

This is all characteristically methodical and didactic, foreshadowing the man. Perhaps the most Carrollian touch comes in the rule which stipulates: 'All passengers when upset are requested to lie still until picked up – as it is requisite that at least 3 trains should go over them, to entitle them to the attention of the doctor and assistants.'

A plan of the Rectory as it was when the Dodgsons arrived in 1843 shows that this elaborate establishment must have required a number of servants.[21] Besides a large dining-room and drawing-room, a library and a 'small library', a big kitchen, a nursery and numerous bedrooms and dressing-rooms, the plan records such period amenities as a 'House Keeper's Room', 'Butler's Pantry', 'Servants' Hall', 'Bacon House', a room marked 'Pastry', a 'Needle-work Room', two maids' bedrooms and a 'Men Servants' Room.' Outside were the 'Laundry', 'Brew House', 'Wash House', stable, etc.

When Lewis Carroll made a little drawing of the Rectory for his family magazine *The Rectory Umbrella*, he doubled the number of windows in the building and added an imaginary third storey, as if to emphasise its monumental proportions – a great change from Daresbury. The drawing illustrated this verse, part of a parody of Macaulay:

> Fair stands the ancient Rectory,
> The Rectory of Croft,
> The sun shines bright upon it,
> The breezes whisper soft.
> From all the house and garden
> Its inhabitants come forth,
> And muster in the road without,
> And pace in twos and threes about,
> The children of the North.

Two

The inhabitants of Croft Rectory now 'come forth' by way of a different front-door from that known by Lewis Carroll. Formerly, the door was at the side of the house; it is now in the centre of the main front, and has been constructed out of one of the dining-room windows. Inside, the house has been re-modelled to provide three flats, of which that on the ground-floor is occupied by the Rector.

During the alterations to the house, in October, 1950, the then Rector, the Rev G. Edward Charlesworth, made some discoveries which are of absorbing interest in considering the recreations of the 'children of the North', and in particular the development of Lewis Carroll, the leader in all their games. Family tradition had already spoken of a loose board in the nursery floor which had been used to give access to a hiding-place; and it was underneath the floor of the old Dodgson nursery on the second storey that the finds were made. Mr Charlesworth brought out a highly miscellaneous collection of treasures: a hair-slide, a lid from a doll's tea-set and some other pieces of china, an attractive child's embroidered handkerchief, three pieces of clay pipe, a small penknife, a scrap of paper in Mrs Dodgson's handwriting, a fragment of parchment (which Mr Charlesworth rather reluctantly guessed to come from Archdeacon Dodgson's induction paper), the shell of a lobster, a crochet instrument, a letter from a child's alphabet – and, last but not least, these significant objects, a small thimble, a child's white glove in excellent condition, and a child's left-hand shoe.

Any lover of 'Alice' must view these three childish relics with considerable emotion. We know from 'The Hunting of the Snark' – 'they sought it with thimbles, they sought it with care' – that thimbles exerted an abiding fascination for Lewis Carroll; but it is, of course, the Dodo's presentation to Alice that forms the *locus classicus* of thimble literature. 'What else have you got in your pocket?' the Dodo asked Alice:

Alice and the Dodo, from Alice's Adventures in Wonderland

'Only a thimble,' says Alice sadly.

'Hand it over here,' said the Dodo.

Then they all crowded round her once more, while the Dodo solemnly presented the thimble saying 'We beg your acceptance of this elegant thimble'; and, when it had finished this short speech they all cheered.

If the thimble suggests the Dodo, the little white glove recalls the White Rabbit, and how he dropped his pair of white gloves, and how Alice discovered – when she became very small – that she could put one of them on. And then there is the left-hand shoe: to find a quotation for that we must turn to the White Knight's song in *Through the Looking-Glass*, or rather to the poem 'Upon the Lonely Moor', which formed the basis of the song, but which was written as early as 1856 and already contained the lines:

> And now if e'er by chance I put
>   My fingers into glue
> Or madly squeeze a right-hand foot
>   Into a left-hand shoe. . . .

It is at least an interesting conjecture – and, in the case of one so 'fixated' to his childhood as Lewis Carroll, it is plausible – that the thimble, the glove, and the shoe, hidden beneath the floorboards of the nursery at Croft, lingered in his subconscious mind, to find their way into literature after the lapse of years. Young Charles had, of course, outgrown the nursery by the time he came to Croft at the age of eleven, though he occupied a bedroom not far away from it, on the same floor; but that he was the leading spirit in these surreptitious proceedings can scarcely be doubted, from our knowledge of his character. Mr Charlesworth made some further discoveries that go far towards proving it. He found – in the same place as the other things – three small pieces of wood, roughly sawn by the workmen and each bearing a few words written in pencil. Two of these inscriptions have the same date and both refer to the new floor which the Rev Charles Dodgson ordered to be laid in the nursery when he came to the Rectory – presumably with the idea of getting some more sleep for himself and his wife, whose bedroom was exactly below. One of the inscriptions is hard to read, but the other is perfectly clear: 'This floor was laid by Mr Martin and Mr Sutton June 19th 1843.'

The White Rabbit, from Alice's Adventures in Wonderland, *and Alice and the White Knight, from* Through the Looking-glass

Juvenile handwriting changes so frequently that it is difficult to pronounce upon it with absolute certainty, but there seems to be little doubt that this is in Lewis Carroll's hand. The words on the third block of wood are undoubtedly written by him and comparable to a specimen of his hand at the age of about fifteen. Oracular and mysterious, this inscription – at first sight puzzling – becomes, on reflection (and in the light of our knowledge of the later Lewis Carroll) strangely satisfying. These are the words:

> And we'll wander through
> the wide world
> and chase the buffalo.

Miss Winifred Mansbridge has suggested that they are a misquotation from the song 'The Buffalo' of the early eighteenth century: 'We'll wander through the wild woods and we'll chase the buffalo.' Lewis Carroll certainly kept up an interest in buffaloes. The Mad Gardener in *Sylvie and Bruno* sings:

> He thought he saw a Buffalo
> Upon the chimney-piece . . .

– 'a strange wild song'. And the White Knight's song, which gave us in its early version the 'left-hand shoe', gives us also, in its final form:

> . . . Who snorted like a buffalo –
> That summer evening long ago,
> A-sitting on a gate.

But the literary associations of the lines – odd lines, surely, for any ordinary boy to scribble on a piece of wood and hide under the floor – are less moving than their spiritual undertones. They sound very much, in Lewis Carroll's case, like a *cri de coeur*, evidence, perhaps, of an early longing to escape into some sort of Wonderland.

Three

As a boy Lewis Carroll devoted himself wholeheartedly to the entertainment of his brothers and sisters; and because the sisters were in the majority he naturally acquired from an early age those special skills in amusing little girls which he practised so willingly for the rest of his life. The minute box of carpenter's tools (Plate p. 46), measuring 2 inches by $1\frac{1}{2}$ inches and inscribed on the lid 'Tool box E.L.D. from C.L.D.', which he made for his sister Elizabeth at Croft, shows that he was remarkably deft with his fingers.[22] He was a successful conjurer, and, according to Collingwood, he made, with the assistance of the village carpenter and members of his family, a troupe of marionettes and a theatre for them to perform in – thus early establishing his life-long passion for the stage.

Miniature tool box (2 × 1½ ins)
made by Dodgson for his sisters.

The earliest photograph of
Dodgson, with a younger sister
and their nurse

Henrietta, Dodgson's youngest
sister

Canon Dodgson tolerated home-theatricals, but he disapproved so strongly of the commercial theatre that his son Charles, who later became a frequent theatregoer, must eventually have found it advisable, on his visits to his father, to turn the conversation into other channels. For the moment, however, he was allowed to manipulate his marionettes and to write plays for them, two of the most popular being *The Tragedy of King John* and *La Guida di Bragia*, a 'ballad opera' devised as a skit on Bradshaw's Railway Guide, which contains a reference to 'wandering through the wide world' and shows humour and promise.[23] As a young man of twenty-three he was still organising such performances. On April 11th, 1855, he complained in his diary of the lack of suitable plays for puppet theatres: 'All existing plays for such objects seem to me to have one of two faults – either (1) they are meant for real theatres, and are therefore not fitted for children, or (2) they are overpoweringly dull – no idea of fun in them. The three already written for our theatre have at least the advantage of being tested by experience and found to be popular.'

It may not be out of place to insert here some remarks made many years later by a Christ Church friend of Lewis Carroll:

'My own view has always been that Dodgson was a great dramatic genius, who had found his opening as "Dramatist of Childhood": this was his work in life, and was consciously, or, perhaps more often, subconsciously, present to him in seeking the friendship of children: it was a "dramatic" as well as a "personal" friendship that he sought.'[24]

Lewis Carroll never did, in fact, complete a play for the professional stage, and in later life produced only a very few prologues, etc., for amateurs, although, as we shall see, he once seriously considered writing a play and got so far as sketching an outline for it. There is no doubt, however, that the dialogues which contribute so much to the success of the 'Alice' books are informed with a keen dramatic sense; and he cast his *Euclid and his Modern Rivals* effectively into dramatic shape. It is important therefore to understand that his early enthusiasm for the drama was an essential element in his crowded childhood.

But, soon after his arrival at Croft, he also began to write poems and stories, and to set aside a special little book for humorous sketches, in which he was already taking great pleasure. Throughout his life he continued to draw with remarkable zest and perseverance, never attaining to a professional facility, but showing more than ordinary talent. His drawings were naïve, but enjoyed the advantages of sincerity and simplicity; the best of them are masterpieces of the amateur, and have their own validity as expressions of character. Thus we can trace the progress of his artistic talent from the lively, grotesque, uninhibited drawings of his first youth – which often have a wild brilliance; through the imaginative but still primitive designs for the first draft of *Alice's Adventures in Wonderland*; until it peters out in conventional sketches of little girls at the seaside, painstaking but weak.

At Croft he was soon illustrating the manuscript magazines which he edited, and largely composed, for the amusement of his family (his interest in illustration, persisting throughout his life, helps to explain the usually happy results that he obtained from artist-collaborators in his later books). The first of the family magazines was *Useful and Instructive Poetry*, composed for 'W.L.D.'

and 'L.F.D.', his younger brother and sister, Wilfred (aged seven) and Louisa (aged five). The editor tells us that it was written 'about the year 1845' and 'lasted about half a year'. Many of the verses poke fun at copybook maxims. Thus, 'Rules and Regulations':

Silhouette of Dodgson aged eight

Learn well your grammar,
And never stammer,*
Write well and neatly,
And sing most sweetly,
Be enterprising,
Love early rising,
Go walks of six miles,
Have ready quick smiles,
With lightsome laughter,
Soft flowing after.
Drink tea, not coffee;
Never eat toffy.
Eat bread with butter.
Once more, don't stutter.*
Don't waste your money,
Abstain from honey.
Shut doors behind you,
(Don't slam them, mind you.)
Drink beer, not porter.
Don't enter the water
Till to swim you are able.
Sit close to the table.
Take care of a candle.
Shut a door by the handle,
Don't push with your shoulder
Until you are older.
Lose not a button.
Refuse cold mutton.
Starve your canaries.
Believe in fairies. . . .

The first poem in the magazine, which the editor declares was suggested by a piece in Praed's *Etonian*, takes up the theme of belief in fairies in a manner intimate and personal. It is called 'My Fairy':

I have a fairy by my side
    Which says I must not sleep,
When once in pain I loudly cried
    It said 'You must not weep'.

*These allusions were something more than convenient rhymes. Several of the children stammered, among them Lewis Carroll, who suffered from a hesitation of speech throughout his life. But four of the children did not stammer at all. Wilfred was one of those who escaped the affliction.

If, full of mirth, I smile and grin,
　　It says 'You must not laugh';
When once I wished to drink some gin,
　　It said 'You must not quaff'.

When once a meal I wished to taste
　　It said 'You must not bite',
When to the wars I went in haste
　　It said 'You must not fight'.

'What may I do?' at length I cried,
　　Tired of the painful task.
The fairy quietly replied,
　　And said 'You must not ask'.

　　　Moral: 'You mustn't'.

This tiresome fairy, conjured up by Lewis Carroll at the age of thirteen, seems to have kept in touch with him during most of his life, and to have been particularly assiduous in its attentions after he had passed forty. Was this the fairy who gave him his insomnia and his stoicism, who set such strict bounds to his natural humour, who put him on to a sparse diet, and who ultimately told him 'You must not ask' as the answer to several large questions? There is no end to the almost uncanny anticipations that we find in this remarkable childhood. The same magazine contains 'A Tale of a Tail', with a drawing of a very long dog's tail which seems to anticipate the Mouse's tail in 'Alice', and a poem about someone who insisted on standing on a wall but eventually fell

A page from The Rectory Umbrella

off it – strongly suggestive of Humpty Dumpty. The pages are as full of 'Morals' as the conversation of the Ugly Duchess. There is also a significant emphasis throughout on dreams and visions, and a hint – at thirteen! – of what G. M. Young has called 'the new, unpietistic handling of childhood'. It is not quite enough to say of Lewis Carroll that the child was father of the man. In his case the child and the man were curiously, indeed uniquely, blended.

Useful and Instructive Poetry, roughly bound up into a little volume, remained in the possession of the Dodgson family until 1953. Enough has been quoted to show that, from the literary point of view, it was remarkably precocious (though the illustrations were relatively cruder).[25] It was followed by a series of other manuscript magazines – *The Rectory Magazine*, *The Comet*, *The Rosebud*, *The Star*, *The Will-o'-the-Wisp*, *The Rectory Umbrella* dating from 1849 or 1850, and *Mischmasch* (a scrapbook compiled at Oxford between 1855 and 1862). In some of these Lewis Carroll's share was small. The two last were, however, almost entirely his own work, and they are so amusing that they fully deserved publication at the time of the centenary, under the editorship of Florence Milner of Harvard.

Four

Charles Dodgson began his schooldays at the age of twelve, by going to Richmond Grammar School, ten miles from Croft. But he had already learned a great deal at home from his father. One day, when he was very small, he had approached him with a book of logarithms and asked: 'Please explain.' Although Mr Dodgson told Charles that he was too young for logarithms, he persisted, '*But*, please explain!'

By the time he was twelve Charles had received a thorough grounding in mathematics. The earliest surviving letter to him from his mother – which he treasured so much that he wrote on the back 'No one is to touch this note, for it belongs to C.L.D.' – shows that the Classics were also broached to him. 'It delights me, my darling Charlie,' wrote Mrs Dodgson, 'to hear that you are getting on so well with your Latin, and that you make so few mistakes in your exercises.' His Latin never appealed to him in the same way as that book of logarithms, however. Mr Tate, the Richmond headmaster, told his father in his first report that he had 'passed an excellent examination just now in mathematics, exhibiting at times an illustration of that love of precise argument, which seems to him natural', but that he 'frequently sets at nought the notions of Vergil or Ovid as to syllabic quantity. He is moreover marvellously ingenious in replacing the ordinary inflexions of nouns and verbs, as detailed in our grammars, by more exact analogies, or convenient forms of his own devising'. Yet Mr Tate did not attempt to conceal that he was deeply impressed. 'You may fairly anticipate for him a bright career. . . . You must not entrust your son with a full knowledge of his superiority over other boys. Let him discover this as he proceeds.'[26]

The first surviving letter of Lewis Carroll's that was written entirely in his own hand (now in Harvard College Library) was addressed to his two elder sisters from Richmond School on August 5th, 1844. It shows that he received rather a boisterous welcome, but suggests that he could hold his own: 'The boys play me no tricks now.' He mentions those he likes best, and characteristically notes the presence of 'a little girl who came down to dinner the first day, but not since'. The letter ends with a succinct postscript for his younger brother Skeffington – 'Roar not lest thou be abolished': an early exercise in nonsense-ruthlessness, comparable to his poem in *Useful and Instructive Poetry* with the moral 'Never stew your sister', which must have been written about the same time as Lear's lines (published in 1846):

> There was an Old Man of Peru,
> Who watched his wife making a stew;
> But once by mistake, in a stove she did bake,
> That unfortunate Man of Peru.

Whether this is coincidence or, as is just possible, imitation, cannot be ascertained owing to the vagueness of the dating of *Useful and Instructive Poetry*.

Perhaps the most interesting thing about this early letter from Richmond

A page from Useful and Instructive Poetry

School (the final sheet of which is reproduced on p. 65) is the quality of the handwriting. Dr M. J. Mannheim has studied it, and finds it 'outstanding in maturity, tenderness and sensitivity. The maturity and promise are of a rare order.' But he also notes that 'the demands on himself are very high and there are signs of stress that he feels overburdened. One wonders what happened to bring him forward so prematurely. . . .'

The signs of stress might perhaps be explained by the fact that this was a new boy's letter from his first school; but on the wider questions raised by the letter, Dr Mannheim comments:

'A letter written with such outstanding maturity at the age of 12 is puzzling for two reasons. First, there is the absence of disturbance commonly found at that age. Where one would expect turmoil there is maturity. I am astonished that he appears to have cut out of his development the strange turmoil of adolescence. The second reason for surprise is the incredible attainment of a personality usually accomplished much later. If such precocity is very rare, there is also a negative aspect: important influences can no longer affect him.'

Charles stayed at Richmond only a year and a half, but he looked back on his time there with pleasure and spoke of Mr Tate as his 'kind old schoolmaster'. He composed some Latin verses – not very good ones – and wrote a story for the school magazine. His inscription inside one of his school books, *The Tutor's Assistant* (reproduced opposite), was intended to strike fear into the heart of any potential thief who might wish to steal the property of 'Carolum Ludrigum Dodsonum', but tailed away characteristically into some fanciful and elegant doodling. When the time came for Charles's departure, Mr Tate was still impressed: 'Be assured that I shall always feel a peculiar interest in the gentle, intelligent, and well-conducted boy who is now leaving us.'[27]

Five

He went to Rugby at the beginning of 1846, and did not enjoy his stay at the School House there in the least. A few years after he had left, he set down his considered opinion of the place in his diary:

'During my stay I made I suppose some progress in learning of various kinds, but none of it was done *con amore*, and I spent an incalculable time in writing out impositions – this last I consider one of the chief faults of Rugby School. I made some friends there, the most intimate being Henry Leigh Bennett . . . but I cannot say that I look back upon my life at a Public School with any sensations of pleasure, or that any earthly considerations would induce me to go through my three years again.'[28]

He compared Rugby unfavourably to Radley, which he visited in 1857. Radley appealed to him as 'a very well arranged establishment':

'I was particularly struck by the healthy happy look of the boys and their gentlemanly appearance. The dormitory is the most unique feature of the whole: in two large rooms, by a very trifling expense in wood-work, every boy has a snug little bedroom secured to himself, where he is free from interruption and annoyance. This to little boys must be a very great addition to their happiness, as being a kind of counterbalance to any bullying they may suffer during the day. From my own experience of school life at Rugby I can say that if I could have been secure from annoyance at night, the hardships of the daily life would have been comparative trifles to bear.' (Diary, March 18th, 1857.)

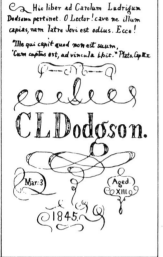

Inscription in a school book

Signature in a school book, with comment in another hand

Read together, these entries leave no doubt that Charles Dodgson was miserable at his public school, and they do not encourage a biographer to investigate his Rugby years at all closely. It is obvious that he suffered from bullying – indeed this is suggested by an inscription in one of his school books, bearing a date in his first year, where his signature C. L. Dodgson is followed by the direct comment 'is a muff' in another hand. He had no appreciation of games and said that at Rugby he only played cricket once. Put on to bowl, he delivered one ball, and was then taken off, 'the captain remarking that the ball, if it had gone far enough, would have been a wide.'[29]

The stock tragedy of the studious, talented, sensitive boy who is no good at games has been so often enacted at English public schools that there is no point in recapitulating its subtleties here. If you have a delicate plant nurtured in a Rectory garden, not the most encouraging treatment is to sit on it. The young Lewis Carroll made the best of a difficult situation. He worked exceedingly hard; brought home many prizes for mathematics, classics, history, composition and divinity; may eventually have achieved the grudging tolerance that is reserved at a public school for the successful 'swot'; and probably won with his humour a few friends among the less lumpish of his companions. His mother wrote proudly about his many school successes to other members of the family. The following is part of a letter to her sister, Lucy Lutwidge, dated simply June 25th but attributable to 1847:

'. . . dearest Charlie came home safely yesterday, bringing with him *2* handsome Prize Books! one gained last Christmas, *Arnold's Modern History* – the other *Thierry's Norman Conquest* just *now* gained for having been the best in Composition (Latin & English Verse & Prose) in his Form during the Half – he is also 2nd in Marks – 53 boys in his Form – they have marks for *everything* they do in their daily work & at the end of the Half they are added up – he is to go into a higher Form when he returns to School – dearest Charlie is *thinner* than he was but looks well & is in the *highest* spirits, *delighted* with his success at School – he is going to write to you himself – he sends you his love & *humblest* apologies & says he *will* write very soon. . . .'[30]

Naturally Charlie would not have allowed his unhappiness to appear in the dutiful letters that he wrote home; those that have survived are all quite cheerful in tone. There is a very long and interesting letter in the Huntington Library, San Marino (published in full by Mrs F. B. Lennon and Mr R. L. Green), which describes a visit to the Roman camp at Brinklow, discusses *David Copperfield* and Macaulay with great intelligence, and displays a keen curiosity regarding all the details of home life in his absence. A shorter letter which is reproduced below – and can be dated tentatively to 1847 – has not, apparently, been published before, apart from a few sentences in Mrs Lennon's book. Written to his elder sister, it may be taken as typical of his Rugby letters:

School House
Oct: 9.

DEAREST ELIZABETH,

Thank you for your letter: in reply to your question I *do* get a prize, value one guinea. I have chosen for it Butler's Analogy in 2 vols. which exactly comes up to the value, one vol: Analogy, the other Sermons. As to the other prize prize [*sic*] I am not yet decided: Papa has taken no notice of the book I had set my fancy on getting, Whiston's Josephus, in 2 vols, 24*s*. Will you ask him what he thinks of it? Clarendon's Rebellion is in double columns, and Hallam's looks very dry – Whiston wd. require a Bohn to make up the value, I was thinking of Wheatly on the Common Prayer.

I have *not* got any warm gloves yet but I must do so soon. Now I think of it, I shd. like 10*s*. of my own money to be sent: I can settle about the gloves afterwards. I must not forget to send my hearty thanks to Papa and Mamma for their kind present. I cannot in the least decide what to get, and should be glad of some advice on *this* head.

Thanks for your explanation of a *drawn* bonnet. I suppose *shot* silk or satin is to be explained on the same principles: I hope you never wear it. I am glad to hear of the 6 rabbits. For the new name after some consideration I recommend Parellelopipedon.* It is a nice easy one to remember and the rabbit will soon learn it.

The report is certainly a delightful one: *I* cannot account for it; I hope there is no mistake. As to the difference between Walker and myself (Papa seems satisfied about Harrison) it must be remembered that he is in the 6th and has hitherto been considered the best mathematician in the school. Indeed no one but me got anything *out* of the 6th (I hope you understand this last sentence). As to the tutor marks, we did not go the 1st week and the Prize examinations have prevented the 4th. The Lower Mathematical Prizeman, Fisher, unfortunately broke his arm yesterday by falling down: it had been broken before, or I do not think so slight a thing could have done it.

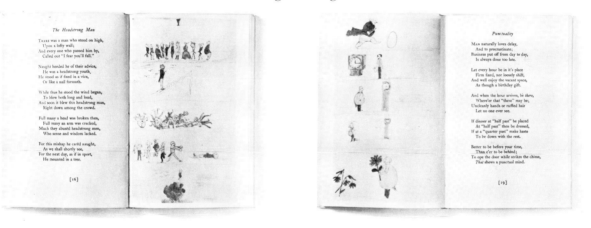

Is w.l. and l.f's 'Useful and Instructive Poetry' finished binding yet? I enclose for Papa *the* Geometrical problem worked out by Mr Mayor. It is

*This word, which he has misspelled, not surprisingly, is the Greek form of 'parallelepiped', 'a regular solid bounded by six parallelograms, the opposite pairs of which are parallel'. It appears to have fascinated Lewis Carroll throughout his life, for he makes the narrator in *Phantasmagoria* (1869) take leave of the friendly little ghost that has been haunting him with

> Old Brick, or rather, let me say,
> Old Parallelepiped!

and goes on to reflect that

> . . . after such a splendid word
> I felt that it would be absurd
> To try it any farther.

one of the most beautifully neat ones I ever saw. Pray ask him to take *great* care of it. There are some books I shd. like to have leave to get: these are – Butler's Ancient Atlas [*crossed out*] (On 2nd thoughts not yet). Liddell & Scott's Larger Greek-English Lexicon. Mr Paice quite despises the little one and says it is only fit for my younger brothers. It is hardly any use in Demosthenes. Cicero's Epistles, this we do in school. If he consents will you ask him to send the leave on a piece of paper by itself. With best love to all I remain –

Your most affte brother

C.L.D.[31]

This is a letter that implies a vast amount of conscientious application and sets the pattern for a most hard-working life. Charles was clearly taxing his strength and did not avoid some illness. During a serious attack of whooping-cough his mother wrote to Lucy Lutwidge: 'I cannot of course *help* feeling anxious & fidgetty about him', but he got over it so well that he was soon busily entertaining his brothers and sisters again in the Rectory garden. 'At the *Railroad* games, which the darlings *all delight* in, he *tries* & *proves* his strength in the most persevering way.'

Towards the end of his Rugby days he suffered from mumps. He had already been slightly deaf in the right ear, and this illness seems to have made the deafness worse. Mrs Dodgson told her sister that her husband had informed Dr A. C. Tait (the headmaster of Rugby) about 'Charlie's former deafness & its source (Infantile fever) & requesting him to take the best medical opinion within his reach & to report it immediately to us . . .'. Several years later, that opinion was still being sought. 'Called on Mr Toynbee, the aurist', wrote Charles in his diary of June 18th, 1856. The deafness was not cured but did not spread to the other ear.[32]

Six

It must have been a great relief for Charles finally to make his escape from Rugby to the more congenial atmosphere of Croft. This he achieved at the end of 1849, after nearer four than the three years of his later estimate. Dr Tait wrote most cordially about him in a letter to Archdeacon Dodgson:

'. . . I must not allow your son to leave school without expressing to you the very high opinion I entertain of him. . . . His mathematical knowledge is great for his age. . . . His examination for the Divinity prize was one of the most creditable exhibitions I have ever seen. During the whole time of his being in my house, his conduct has been excellent . . .'.[33]

For the next year, 1850, Charles worked steadily at home, preparing for Oxford. Probably he gave up part of his time, however, to *The Rectory Umbrella*, which is an engaging mixture of prose, verse and drawings (Cassell, 1932)

Frontispiece to The Rectory Umbrella *by Dodgson*

deserving study as something of a junior classic. A frontispiece shows a very jolly old poet reclining beneath a capacious umbrella marked Tales – Poetry – Fun – Riddles – Jokes. To him appear seven graceful maidens designated respectively as Mirth, Content, Cheerfulness, Good Humour, Taste, Liveliness and Knowledge. They bear their tributes to him in little baskets; while in the air above a number of ill-disposed imps, manifesting every symptom of impotent rage, throw down upon the umbrella craggy lumps of rock labelled Woe, Crossness, Alloverishness, Ennui, Spite and Gloom.

After this optimistic prelude, we find the body of the magazine conceived throughout in a spirit of intelligent parody. A medieval mystery 'The Walking-Stick of Destiny' unrolls itself in eight chapters; there is a series of humorous 'Zoological Papers', including one of prophetic import on 'The Lory'; and there are several delightful skits on pictures 'in the Vernon Gallery', with agreeable caricatures of the work of Reynolds (a young hippopotamus as

For the steed is very strong,
And backward moves its stubborn feet,
And backward ever doth retreat,
And drags its guides along.

And now the knight hath mounted,
Before the admiring band,
Hath got the stirrups on his feet,
The bridle in his hand.
Yet, oh! beware, sir horseman!
And tempt thy fate no more,
For such a steed as thou hast got,
Was never rid before!

But thy steed will hear no master,
Thy steed will bear no stick,
And woe to those that beat her,
And woe to those that kick!
For though her rider smite her,
As hard as he can hit,
And strive to turn her from the yard,
She stands in silence, pulling hard
Against the pulling bit.

And now two roads to choose from
Are in that rider's sight:
In front, the road to Dalton,
And New Croft upon the right.
'I can't get by!' he bellows,
'I really am not able!
Though I pull my shoulder out of joint,
I cannot get him past this point
For it leads unto his stable!'

Round turned he, as not deigning
Their words to understand,
But he slipped the stirrups from his feet
The bridle from his hand
And grasped the mane full lightly,
And vaulted from his seat,
And gained the road in triumph,
And stood upon his feet.

Drawings and extracts for 'Lays of Sorrow No 2' in The Rectory Umbrella, *drawn about 1850 by Dodgson*

'The Age of Innocence'), Herring, Collins, Wilkie, Callcott, Landseer and Etty. It was all Charles's own work, as he made clear at the end in 'The Poet's Farewell':

> But in thee – let future ages
>   Mark the fact which I record,
> No one helped me in thy pages,
>   Even with a single word!

The Rectory Umbrella was a very clear foretaste of what was to come. One must in fairness add that it is hard to imagine that the author, and especially the illustrator, had not seen Edward Lear's *A Book of Nonsense*, published in 1846. Lewis Carroll's illustration for the lines in 'Lays of Sorrow: No. 2':

> They gave him bread and butter,
>   That was of public right,
> As much as four strong rabbits,
>   Could munch from morn to night

There was an old man of Calcutta,
Who perpetually ate bread and butter;
Till a great bit of muffin, on which he was stuffing,
Choked that horrid old man of Calcutta.

is distinctly reminiscent of Lear's drawing of the Old Man of Calcutta, 'who perpetually ate bread and butter'. And, by the way, was not the Duchess's 'uncomfortably sharp chin', which rested on Alice's shoulder, a recollection of Lear's Young Lady whose chin 'resembled the point of a pin'? But on the subject of his nearest rival in nonsense, Carroll maintained complete silence; neither did Lear ever put on record his estimate of the author of 'Alice'.

Wilfred Dodgson (1838–1914), Lewis Carroll's brother, photographed by him

Seven

Those must have been pleasant days – in that last year at Croft, with his charming mother and his brothers and sisters, before he went up to Christ Church – days full of hard work but with leisure for lying under the acacia-tree on the front lawn, strolling through the kitchen garden and looking up at the many tall chimneys of the old house, wandering into the greenhouse to peer at the famous cactus, the night-blowing Cereus. The Rectory, tangibly marked by the initials C. L. D. on a back window-pane, is still redolent of memories of that strange, exciting childhood and early manhood. And with the Rectory there must always have been linked in his mind the little church of St Peter, over the road, where Charles gazed at the fantastic Milbank pew and listened to his father's services – 'My dear father was what is called a "High Church-man", and I naturally adopted those views, but have always felt repelled by the yet higher development called "Ritualism".'[34] Perhaps a walk over the bridge or along the bank of the Tees brought him sometimes into the churchyard to sit on one of the flat tomb-stones – a peaceful place, not threatening.

We shall see that towards the end of his life Lewis Carroll talked about happiness, and expressed his own belief that it was usually discovered in retrospect; one did not so much appreciate that one was happy at the time, but realised later that one had been happy. Perhaps he came to feel like this about his own early days, and especially about the year 1850 at Croft. For Charles Dodgson's golden age, roughly broken by the Rugby years and renewed for this further brief spell, was now coming finally – and in one important respect, unexpectedly – to a close.

Having matriculated at Christ Church on May 23rd, 1850, he went into residence as a Commoner on January 24th, 1851. But he could hardly have unpacked his belongings before he had to hurry home again, numbed by the shock of the sudden death of his adored mother. Soon he was standing with a little group in the churchyard – in the shadow of the church on the north side – looking into the grave that was to be covered by a stone 'Sacred to the Memory of Frances Jane the Beloved Wife of the Revd Charles Dodgson, Rector of this Parish, who died January 26th, 1851. Aged 47'.

The exact cause of his mother's death is nowhere stated. One can only assume that she was worn out by the strain of child-bearing, and of managing the large rectory and its servants and her family of eleven children. That she had no regrets for her life at Croft, no doubts of present happiness, is abundantly clear from a letter written to Archdeacon Dodgson by his aunt Mary Smedley on February 13th, 1851:

'. . . What a crowning blessing to all your comforts is the recollection of the happy *happy* life of our sainted Fanny. I do not think I ever heard of anyone so highly favoured – as daughter – wife & mother – & few surely have ever passed into glory knowing so little of earthly stain or sorrow. The last walk we took together she spoke to me of her rare and exceeding happiness – She told me that she was very happy at Daresbury but that while you took pupils there was always a drawback & she used to be continually picturing such a life as she led at Croft as the perfection of earthly happiness – & she said that sometimes when remembering this it was almost startling to find how exactly her wishes had been fulfilled & that for seven (I think) years she had been living precisely the life that she had most delighted to dwell upon in fancy, – & then she spoke most touchingly & beautifully of the responsibility incurred by a lot of so much happiness – & that it really at times was "alarming" to look round her & feel that she had not a wish unfulfilled – I could have said "nor a duty also" but I felt that she was above my praise . . .'.[35]

What the readers of *Alice in Wonderland* owe to Mrs Dodgson for providing her son with his happy childhood, for offsetting the austere (though affectionate) domination of his father, and for giving him the loving sympathy which helped him to become a writer, has not hitherto been fully recognised and cannot even now be properly estimated. Something vital went out of his life when she died. He would surely have given much to have received at Oxford more of those letters to 'dearest Charlie', which he had treasured from the first, and whose frequent underlinings were echoed in his own later letters and in the many italicised words in his books (a sign of weakness in formal writing, perhaps, but in letters a proof of sincerity and feeling).

If there was one lesson above others that he brought away from Croft, it was that he could never in future, so long as he lived, be without the companionship of children. They had already become a necessity of his existence. His abiding reverence for his mother is shown by a note written, nineteen years after her death, to his sister Mary Collingwood, congratulating her on the birth of a son (who lived to become his biographer):

Jan. 13, 1870.

My Dearest Mary,

I must write one line to *yourself*, if only to say – God bless you & the little one now entrusted to you – & may you be to him what our own dear mother was to *her* eldest son. I can hardly utter for your boy a better wish than that.

Your loving brother,

C. L. Dodgson.[36]

Dodgson's seven sisters photographed by himself

Dodgson's aunts, The Misses Lutwidge, taken by him

One

The life of an undergraduate must go on – even though his mother lies dead, and he has to write to a sister to look for the 'silk neck handkerchiefs' that he has left at home. ('The only things of the kind I possess here are the handkerchief I now have on, and a black satin tie for the evening.') This letter of March 6th, 1851, to his sister Mary shows Charles Lutwidge Dodgson, as he signs himself, turning resolutely from his private grief to lose himself in the discipline of work. He is distressed that he has been late for morning Chapel:

'For some days now I have been in the habit of – I will not say getting up, but of being called at $\frac{1}{4}$ past 6, & generally managing to be down soon after 7. In the present instance I had been up the night before till about $\frac{1}{2}$ past 12, & consequently when I was called I fell asleep again, & was thunderstruck to find on waking that it was 10 min: past 8. I have had no imposition, nor heard anything about it. It is rather vexatious to have happened so soon, as I had intended never to be late.'

He tries to think of something that might cheer up the sorrowing household at Croft, and remembers an incident that had occurred that day:

'This afternoon I was sitting in my room when I heard a sudden shrieking of dogs, as if fighting: I rushed to the window, but the fight, if any, was over, having lasted for about the space of 3 seconds, and every thing & every body was flying from the scene of combat: six dogs went headlong down the steps, which lead into the quad, yelling at the very top of their voices: six sticks came flying after them, & after that came their six masters, all running their hardest, and all in different directions. For a little time none of the dogs knew which way to go, so they went darting about, tumbling over each other, screaming, & getting hit by the sticks, & their masters did the same only they screamed in a different manner: at last 3 dogs got away & ran straight home, screaming as they went, 2 others were hunted up & down the quad by their masters, I suppose with the intention of beating them, but were never sufficiently caught for that purpose, & the sixth went home with its master, but even *it* screamed all the way. Never was such desperate vengeance taken for so small an offence: I should think *all* the dogs will rue the day: the two combatants will never wish to fight again, nor the others to be aiders or abettors.'[37]

This little sketch of a dog-fight makes a doubly appropriate introduction to Charles's prolonged Oxford career. It is interesting, first, for the light it throws on its author. It reveals him as a keen observer of detail; the words are carefully chosen, as by a discriminating writer; and the incident is of a kind that Lewis Carroll was later often to imagine and describe with the same wild gusto. The number of dogs and masters is so exactly recorded, with their precise movements, that the whole passage seems about to develop at any moment into one of those complicated mathematical problems in which C. L. Dodgson took such keen delight.

But the dog-fight serves another purpose, by making us realise something of the remote and still almost medieval character of the university to which Charles Dodgson now belonged. Dogs are no longer a feature of life at

Left: *One of the earliest photo-*
graphs of Dodgson as a young
man, taken before he was twenty.

Right: *At twenty-three.* Below:
A year later, probably taken by
Reginald Southey

Christ Church, but at this time, while Gaisford was still the Dean, his Verger (Keys) was regularly to be seen standing at the entrance to the choir of the Cathedral, holding a stout whip, with which to discourage dogs from following their masters into the interior. He was kept busy; the dogs of Christ Church seem on the whole to have been roughly handled. Keys also administered a beer-store in a cupboard below the pew on the north side of the choir. As H. L. Thompson says, 'Dog-whip and beer were both summarily ejected by Dean Liddell, to the old verger's great annoyance.'[38]

Young Dodgson came up to an Oxford that was still almost entirely confined within the remains of its walls. In 1851 the railway had only recently reached Oxford, and it was only on this side of the city that there had been any serious and discordant development. Elsewhere the untouched meadows hemmed in the ancient streets and buildings, still mellow and unspoiled in their grey and yellow stone. The red brick of North Oxford scarcely threatened; the view from Headington Hill was much as Turner had painted it. In the words of Sir Charles Mallet's history of the University: 'Cowley marsh was a rush-grown common. No houses broke the quiet of the Iffley road.'

If the Oxford of those days gave a young man – for perhaps the last time – a sense of the grave beauty of the medieval university, it was not without practical disadvantages. Undergraduates at Christ Church were treated like overgrown schoolboys, and were even subject to such punishments as impositions. In an obituary article about his old friend, one of Dodgson's contemporaries, who matriculated with him and renewed their acquaintance as Commoners, has shown that dining in Hall was a primitive business. Collingwood seems to have seen this article by 'G. J. C.-B.'* and to have used it as material for a paragraph in his biography, but it is worth quoting at greater length:

'Members of "The House", whose memories can carry them back to the period, will call to mind the batches of half-a-dozen undergraduates who dined together at the different tables in the hall, and the disgraceful way the dinner at that time was served. The hour then was five. Though the spoons and forks were silver – some of them very old, the gift of former members of The House – the plates and dishes were pewter. The joint was pushed from one to another, each man hacking off his own portion, and rising from the table without waiting for one another, without even waiting for the ancient Latin grace, said by one of the junior students in response to the invitation of the senior scout (a stout man with a squeaky voice) always in the same drawling tone, "Gra-ace, Gen-tlemen, plea-ease." For the reform of all this sumptuary slovenliness, and other customs "more honoured in the breach than in the observance", we are indebted to the late Dean (Liddell). . . .'

In Dodgson's "mess" were young Philip Pusey, whose crippled frame enshrined a pure soul and a cultivated intellect; the late Rev G. Woodhouse; the present rector of St John's, Edinburgh, and others equally unknown to fame. The features, however, of one of our number are immortalised in "The Hatter", who figures in the "Mad Tea-Party" in *Alice in Wonderland*. Among our

*The Rev G. J. Cowley-Brown, Rector of St John's, Edinburgh. G. J. Brown matriculated at Christ Church in 1850, and apparently later added Cowley- to his name. His article appeared in *The Scottish Guardian* of January 28th, 1898.

Sir John Tenniel's illustration of
The Hatter *in* Alice's
Adventures in Wonderland

contemporaries, bachelor or undergraduate, were the late Lord Lothian, a man of the very highest promise; the late Lord Carnarvon, and his successor in the vice-royalty of Ireland, Lord Cowper; Lord Harrowby, the late Duke of Newcastle, the present Bishop of Gibraltar, Lord Justice Vaughan Williams, Sir Henry Longley, Canon Jelf, Mr Talbot, one of the present members for the University; the present Chancellor of the Exchequer, Sir Michael Hicks-Beach; Mr Oswald, afterwards curate of St John's, Edinburgh; Malcolm of Poltalloch, and many others more or less known to fame. We all, however, I may safely say, sat in the same hall and some of us even at the same table with Dodgson without discovering (perhaps from our own want of it) the wit, the peculiar humour, that was in him. We looked upon him as a rising mathematician, nothing more. He seldom spoke, and the slight impediment in his speech was not conducive to conversation. . . .'

The Doormouse and The Hatter

But this shy and silent young man was acutely sensitive. He was grateful for a friendly word. Forty-six years afterwards he wrote to the widow of Woodhouse, his early companion in Hall: 'Of all the friends I made at Ch. Ch., your husband was the very *first* who spoke to me – across the dinner-table in Hall. . . . I remember, as if it were only yesterday, the kindly smile with which he spoke.'[39]

Two

We see, then, that – though the humour lurked inside him and sprang out more often in his characteristic half-smile as he increased in confidence – Charles Dodgson's early days at Christ Church were marked by a strong sense of serious purpose. From his Rectory upbringing, and from his father's example, one might have expected this to be so. His sense of fun saved him from priggishness, however, and he was certainly not 'soft'; he had already begun his habit of taking long walks and soon started to go for expeditions on the river. The robust world of Tom Brown and Verdant Green was remote from him, but his letters show that he took an intelligent interest in the sporting activities of his fellow undergraduates even though he did not participate in them.

Illustration by Henry Holiday

With very little money to spend, and with the disability of a stammer to handicap his enjoyment of society, it was not surprising that Charles kept himself largely to himself, making many acquaintances but comparatively few friends. He held to a moderate course in religion, which was always the driving force of his life. The evangelicalism that had been fashionable at Oxford twenty years earlier, when Gladstone and Tupper were at Christ Church, had been superseded for most of the intervening period by the Tractarian Movement, which now in its turn was giving way to a liberal spirit of reform encouraged by the appointment of the first University Commission in 1850. Dodgson always retained an admiration for Newman, and when, in 1876, he was shown a letter which the Cardinal had written to a friend about *The Hunting of the Snark*, he copied it out meticulously for the benefit of his sister-in-law, making no comment on Newman's suggestion that the style of the dedicatory poem was 'so entirely of the School of Keble, that I think it could not have been written, had the Christian Year never made its appearance.'[40] That Dodgson was, indeed, like so many clergymen of the period, profoundly influenced by Keble, Newman and Manning cannot be doubted. It is equally certain that neither he nor his father were ever in danger of going over to Rome. In fact, as he grew older, Charles Dodgson turned more and more towards simplicity in the services of the church and showed an ever-widening tolerance towards all Christian sects. In *Sylvie and Bruno Concluded* he made the Earl say: 'How slight the barriers seem to be that part Christian from Christian, when one has to deal with the great facts of Life and the reality of Death!'

Few letters survive from his undergraduate years. One that is quoted by Collingwood shows him to have been an appreciative visitor to the Great Exhibition of 1851. He also paid visits to London to stay with his Uncle Skeffington, a barrister and Commissioner in Lunacy, for whom he had a great affection, and whose truly Victorian enthusiasm for gadgets and inventions he particularly appreciated. In a letter to his sister Elizabeth of June 24th, 1852, now in Harvard College Library, he noted that his uncle was:

'Looking very well, and if anything, *rather* stouter than when I last saw him. He has as usual got a great number of new oddities, including a lathe, telescope stand, crest stamp (see the top of this note-sheet), a beautiful little pocket instrument for measuring distances on a map, refrigerator, &c., &c. We had an observation of the moon and Jupiter last night, & afterwards live animalculae in his large microscope: this is a most interesting sight, as the creatures are most conveniently transparent, & you see all kinds of organs jumping about like a complicated piece of machinery, & even the circulation of the blood. Everything goes on at railway speed, so I suppose they must be some of those insects that only live a day or two, & try to make the most of it.'

He proceeds to give a lively account of the Encaenia ceremony in the Sheldonian Theatre. A sheet of his letter, describing the intense effort that was required to get inside the building, is reproduced below, alongside the conclusion of his letter written from Richmond School eight years earlier. This enables us to compare the quality of the two handwritings and to note the remarkable change that has occurred in his script during the interval.

It will be recalled that Dr M. J. Mannheim found the letter of 1844, 'outstanding in maturity, tenderness and sensitivity'. Having studied the letter of 1852, Dr Mannheim writes:

Left: *Page of a letter by Dodgson from Richmond School on 5 August, 1844, showing the remarkable maturity of his handwriting at the age of twelve.* Right: *Page of a letter written by Dodgson to his sister Elizabeth on 24 July, 1852, showing his handwriting at the age of twenty*

'While he was still impressionable and open to stimulation at the age of twelve, the letter written at the age of twenty shows clearly that he is now rigidly set in his ways. The later script is in the true sense not more but less "juvenile" than the previous one: with decreased sensitivity and openness to events and people, he is now decidedly introverted, i.e. prompted from "within". There is also much more egotism in the second script than in the first. The past-fixation of impulses is strong. In the second script there is the façade of social adjustment, behind that façade is a *very* rebellious mind.

The quality of the second script is still high; there is some beauty in certain of his letters. Both scripts give clear indications of unusual artistic or literary ability. The second shows a love for a systematic approach and for intellectual matters that do not involve one emotionally.'

It seems clear that something fundamentally disturbing – over and above the normal claims of puberty and adolescence – must have occurred to upset Charles Dodgson's development between twelve and twenty. There need be no mystery about what it was; having advanced so precociously at home, he had passed, shy and stammering, through a chastening experience at his public school, and then had suddenly lost a mother whom he greatly loved. This left a wound which healed very slowly, and never healed completely. Two years after her death he was still, one may think, seriously affected by the tragedy. In a poem called 'Solitude', already influenced by 'The School of Keble', he wrote of meditating in 'the stillness of the wood', and continued:

> Here may the silent tears I weep
>   Lull the vexed spirit into rest,
> As infants sob themselves to sleep
>   Upon a mother's breast.
>
> But when the bitter hour is gone,
>   And the keen throbbing pangs are still,
> Oh, sweetest then to couch alone
>   Upon some silent hill!
>
> To live in joys that once have been,
>   To put the cold world out of sight,
> And deck life's drear and barren scene
>   With hues of rainbow-light.
>
> For what to man the gift of breath,
>   If sorrow be his lot below;
> If all the day that ends in death
>   Be dark with clouds of woe?
>
> Shall the poor transport of an hour
>   Repay long years of sore distress –
> The fragrance of a lonely flower
>   Make glad the wilderness?
>
> Ye golden hours of Life's young spring,
>   Of innocence, of love and truth!
> Bright, beyond all imagining,
>   Thou fairy-dream of youth!

> I'd give all wealth that years have piled,
>> The slow result of Life's decay,
> To be once more a little child
>> For one bright summer-day.

This nostalgic poem is unusual for a young man to write at twenty-one, and it is a little disturbing to read, even though we realise that the mood in which it was composed might have changed in a matter of hours or days to one of exuberant fun. The 'past-fixation' of its author, already so strong, was to deepen with the years. And yet the character of Lewis Carroll was so rich in its complexity and originality, that there were always many positive qualities to offset his recurrent melancholy. Some of these appear to have been discovered by Edward Hamilton, an Edinburgh phrenologist who 'felt his bumps' in 1852, and whose report will be read with particular interest, as it has not been published before:

'This Gentleman has eight very prominent traits in his Character, namely, a strong love of children; a strong love of friends; much emulousness *and* amiability; much Circumspection; Lofty generous sentiments; much good taste for order & dress & elegance; Excellent analogical reason; & deep penetrating causality to trace the relation between cause & effect.

All these mentioned Organs of *the faculties* in your large Brain counteract each other & constitute your mental nature to be considerably *harmonious*; *and* the great activity & volatile action of your mind is caused by the mixed sanguine nervous temperament – however you wd. do well to cultivate Nos. 3, 13 & 22 in the Chart to give fixity of purpose, patience in application, & *close* attention to simple facts, details, Names, Numbers, Dates, &c. Your memory is good for great things. You could compose well by practice & you have good taste & judgment to criticise, discriminate & *select*. In fact, there is more by far of refinement than any tendency to coarseness or insipidity. As medical man you cd. excel. Do not stress the brain too much at time [*sic*] because it is not firmly knit yet.

Upon the whole a good Head.'[41]

The phrenologist, though in general somewhat optimistic, had made several palpable hits. He had gone first to the 'strong love of children', had emphasised 'refinement', and had been shrewd in his appraisal of Dodgson as a potential 'medical man' – an estimate fully justified by the many medical books and pamphlets in his library.* We cannot now identify 'Nos. 3, 13 & 22 in the Chart' which he was asked to cultivate, but, if he did apply himself in that direction, he did so to good purpose. The patience and attention to detail that he acquired were remarkable.

Three
The fact that we now study Lewis Carroll's handwriting and phrenology with curious interest is our tribute to what he eventually made of his life. Perceiving something of his difficulties, we can appreciate his courage in

*After mocking at homoeopathy in *The Rectory Umbrella*, Dodgson lived to appreciate its advantages.

facing them. For him the going was always hard.

His strenuous exertions as an undergraduate were rewarded by a Boulter Scholarship in November 1851 and by a Second in Classical Moderations and a First in Mathematics at the end of 1852. 'You shall have the announcement of the last piece of good fortune this wonderful term has had in store for me', he wrote to his sister Elizabeth on December 9th, 1852, 'that is, *a 1st class in Mathematics*. Whether I shall add to this any honours at collections I cannot at present say, but I should think it very unlikely, as I have only to-day to get up the work in, (The Acts of the Apostles, 2 Greek Plays, & the Satires of Horace) & I feel myself almost totally unable to read at all: I am beginning to suffer from the reaction of reading for Moderations'. Later in the same letter, he adds: 'I am getting quite tired of being congratulated on various subjects: there seems to be no end of it. If I had shot the Dean, I could hardly have had more said about it.'*42

This success in Moderations was followed on Christmas Eve, 1852, by nomination to a Studentship of Christ Church (which in other colleges would have been called a Fellowship). He owed his nomination to his father's old friend, Dr E. B. Pusey. The preferences of college loyalty, and even of mutual high Anglican sympathies, must have been present to the mind of Pusey, but he emphasised that there was no element of favouritism in his choice. 'I cannot desire stronger evidence than his own words', wrote Archdeacon Dodgson to his son, 'of the fact that you have *won*, and well won, this honour for *yourself*, and that it is bestowed as a matter of *justice* to *you*, and not of *kindness* to me.'43

The honour had indeed been fully earned by hard work. In some respects, however, Charles Dodgson was fortunate in his hour. His Studentship was among the last to be granted under the ancient system of college privilege, by which the Dean and Canons of Christ Church nominated to Studentships in turn. The removal of restrictions in Fellowships was one of the principal recommendations of the University Commissioners who completed their report in April, 1852. Where comparisons are possible, it is obvious that the advantages of this reform were incontestable. As Sir Charles Mallet points out: 'Balliol, with nearly all its Fellowships and Scholarships thrown open, had won twenty-two First Classes between 1841 and 1850. Christ Church, more than twice the size, with its Fellowships and Scholarships in the patronage of the Dean and Canons, had not won in the same period more than thirteen.'

Dodgson would probably have obtained his Studentship even if he had had to compete for it in open examination, according to the changes instituted in 1858. But such a hypothetical question cannot be satisfactorily debated. He was now a Student of Christ Church for life, so long as he remained unmarried and proceeded to Holy Orders. To one with his preference – and probably his inner need – for system and security, the situation thus early established must have profoundly influenced all his thoughts and plans. We shall see that he duly fulfilled the conditions and that he remained a Student until his death.

There is very little available information about Dodgson's life in the year 1853, but a letter to his cousin Frank, the son of his uncle Hassard Dodgson, who was two years younger than himself, and was about to come up to Christ

*Collingwood in his biography makes it appear that these last two sentences were written in 1854, and this mistake has been repeated by other writers.

Church from Westminster, shows him conforming, at least outwardly, to
the conventional undergraduate existence:

Ch: Ch:
May 4th, 1853.

Dear Frank,

I listened to the names of the successful Westminster candidates with much
the same feelings that I did to the Mathematical class list when I was expecting
a 1st, and I cannot tell you how delighted I am at your success and how heartily
I congratulate you on it. For my own sake, I was very glad to hear of your
being among the Oxford names, but I will not congratulate on that, as I think
you said you would prefer Cambridge of the two. I suppose it will not be long
now before you come up to matriculate: pray let me know how soon you are
coming, & whether Uncle Hassard will come with you or not.

Sidney Joyce was with me when I heard it: he was very much pleased, but
seemed a good deal vexed at Gilbert's going to Cambridge instead of Oxford.

We have been fortunate enough to get a classical 1st (Brown) in the Great-
go schools: another man (Lord Lothian) who was expected to be a double
1st, took his name off, as it was said, because he was afraid of missing his
1st, & wanted to make sure next time.

I am afraid you will hardly get here in time to see any of our boat-races, as
Saturday week will be the last night of them: we have not made a bump yet,
but have very fair hopes of doing so before they are over.

With repeated congratulations on your success,

I remain,
Your very affte Cousin,
Charles L. Dodgson[*44]

Four

The next scholastic hurdle was the 'Greats' examination in the Classical School,
which took place in the Easter term of 1854. Although he worked thirteen
hours a day for three weeks beforehand, Dodgson was only placed in the
Third Class, philosophy and history being uncongenial subjects to him. But
he could now devote himself to his main object, the Final Mathematical
School, and for two months of the Long Vacation of 1854 he worked at Whitby
with a reading-party under Professor Bartholomew Price. In a letter to his
sister Mary, written on August 23rd, he talks of 'getting on very swimmingly'
with Professor Price at Integral Calculus. The letter shows that the reading-
party found time for recreation – also that Charles Dodgson at twenty-two
was not a namby-pamby:

'I have just been out to buy some note-paper, & am returned breathless &
exhausted: there is a strong wind blowing off shore, & threatening to carry
Whitby & contents into the sea. There is sand & sharp shingle flying in the
air, that acts on the face like the sharp cut of a whip, & here & there the painful
sight of an old lady being whirled round a corner in a paroxysm of dust &
despair. On the whole it is more pleasant in than out, so I sit down to give you
a more detailed account of our trip to Goathland. It was nominally to see a
cascade, yclept "Mallyan's Spout", tho' by a mis-reading of the guide we asked

*Frank Dodgson later emigrated to Australia, which his 'very affte Cousin' thought a
'mad idea'.

our way of every one we met to "Mary Ann's Spout": you may imagine the ludicrous effect it must have had. Before leaving the station at Goathland we examined the machinery used for drawing the trains up the incline, which is about a mile long, & the steepest I should think in England. There is a very strongly-made piece of machinery, the spokes of the flywheel being about 12 feet long, to wind up the rope, which is about 2 inches thick & consists entirely of wire. At every few yards along the line there is a little wheel erected, à la grindstone, in the middle of the rails, for the rope to run on. We tried to conceive what the result wld. be if the rope broke when the train had nearly reached the top, but imagination failed: the subject was too stupendous. The road down to the cascade consisted of mud & water, with a preponderance of the latter, so I was rash enough to set the example of returning up the side of the cliff, instead of by the road. Only one of the men followed at first, & he did so, thinking the ascent would be easy: a little earth, he says, came crumbling down upon him, but he thought I was throwing it down in fun. However when my cap came flying down upon him, & at the same moment he received a clod of earth in each eye, he began to think more seriously of it. At that precise moment both my feet had lost hold at once, & if the root I was hanging to had broken, I must have come down, & probably carried him with me. I had now reached a point where retreat was hopeless, & the only thing to do was to go on: the ascent took about $\frac{1}{4}$ of an hour: every here & there came a little platform where one could rest & consider the next thing to be done. Just at the top it was hardest of all; it was only to be done by crawling up through the mud, holding by 2 roots, without whose help it would have been impossible. My companion took about 5 minutes longer, & subsequently 4 other men reached the top, all covered with mud. Mr Price & the remaining man more wisely went back as they came. We joined him again at the station, & boasted as much as possible of our feat, to prevent ridicule at our appearance. The Spout itself is a "poor little feeble, fluttering thing", scarcely worth so much trouble to see. However we had had a very pleasant expedition, & such a scramble as I have rarely engaged in.'[45]

Dodgson's Whitby amusements were not all so violent. Already this year he had written two poems – neither of which has been preserved – for a short-lived publication, *Hall's Oxonian Advertiser*. And now, over the unexplained initials 'B. B.', he contributed a poem, 'The Lady of the Ladle', and a story, 'Wilhelm von Schmitz', to the *Whitby Gazette*. These are his first published works to have survived. Both contain allusions of local Whitby interest. Neither is remarkable in itself – the story is rather long-winded – but each shows considerable talent and promise (all the more easily recognisable, perhaps, in retrospect).

But this Whitby visit of 1854 has been endowed with portents and promises of a much more exciting kind. In 1898, at the time of the appeal for the Lewis Carroll cot at Great Ormond Street Hospital, Dr Thomas Fowler, then President of Corpus Christi College, Oxford, sent a subscription to the *St James's Gazette* and with it a few lines of reminiscence which were published in the issue of March 11th, 1898. This is what Dr Fowler said:

'Dodgson and I were both pupils of Professor Bartholomew Price (now Master of Pembroke) in a mathematical Reading Party at Whitby in the summer of 1854. It was there that "Alice" was incubated. Dodgson used to sit on a rock on the beach, telling stories to a circle of eager young listeners of both sexes. These stories were afterwards developed and consolidated into their present form.'

Dr Fowler's recollection has caused considerable surprise, for, if we accept it, the 'official' version of the origins of 'Alice', attested both by Lewis Carroll and by Alice Liddell (Mrs Hargreaves) – namely, that it was first told on a river-picnic at Oxford on July 4th, 1862 – must be modified. Several writers have speculated as to what portions of *Alice in Wonderland* might be attributed to the story-telling at Whitby. Walter de la Mare* thought of 'The Walrus and the Carpenter'; A. L. Taylor has ingeniously conjectured that Dodgson

---

The Walrus and the Carpenter

THE sun was shining on the sea,
　Shining with all his might:
He did his very best to make
　The billows smooth and bright—
And this was odd, because it was
　The middle of the night.

The moon was shining sulkily,
　Because she thought the sun
Had got no business to be there
　After the day was done—
" It's very rude of him," she said,
　" To come and spoil the fun ! "

The sea was wet as wet could be,
　The sands were dry as dry.
You could not see a cloud, because
　No cloud was in the sky:
No birds were flying overhead—
　There were no birds to fly.

The Walrus and the Carpenter
　Were walking close at hand;
They wept like anything to see
　Such quantities of sand:
" If this were only cleared away,"
　They said, " it *would* be grand ! "

" If seven maids with seven mops
　Swept it for half a year,
Do you suppose," the Walrus said,
　" That they could get it clear ? "
" I doubt it," said the Carpenter,
　And shed a bitter tear.

" O Oysters, come and walk with us ! "
　The Walrus did beseech.
" A pleasant walk, a pleasant talk,
　Along the briny beach:
We cannot do with more than four,
　To give a hand to each."

The eldest Oyster looked at him,
　But never a word he said:
The eldest Oyster winked his eye,
　And shook his heavy head—
Meaning to say he did not choose
　To leave the oyster-bed.

But four young Oysters hurried up,
　All eager for the treat:
Their coats were brushed, their faces washed,
　Their shoes were clean and neat—
And this was odd, because, you know,
　They hadn't any feet.

Four other Oysters followed them,
　And yet another four;
And thick and fast they came at last,
　And more, and more, and more—
All hopping through the frothy waves,
　And scrambling to the shore.

The Walrus and the Carpenter
　Walked on a mile or so,
And then they rested on a rock
　Conveniently low:
And all the little Oysters stood
　And waited in a row.

" The time has come," the Walrus said,
　" To talk of many things:
Of shoes—and ships—and sealing-wax—
　Of cabbages—and kings—
And why the sea is boiling hot—
　And whether pigs have wings."

" But wait a bit," the Oysters cried,
　" Before we have our chat;
For some of us are out of breath,
　And all of us are fat ! "
" No hurry ! " said the Carpenter.
　They thanked him much for that.

" A loaf of bread," the Walrus said,
　" Is what we chiefly need:
Pepper and vinegar besides
　Are very good indeed—
Now if you're ready, Oysters dear,
　We can begin to feed."

" But not on us ! " the Oysters cried,
　Turning a little blue.
" After such kindness, that would be
　A dismal thing to do ! "
" The night is fine," the Walrus said.
　" Do you admire the view ?

" It was so kind of you to come !
　And you are very nice ! "
The Carpenter said nothing but
　" Cut us another slice:
I wish you were not quite so deaf—
　I've had to ask you twice ! "

" It seems a shame," the Walrus said,
　" To play them such a trick,
After we've brought them out so far,
　And made them trot so quick ! "
The Carpenter said nothing but
　" The butter's spread too thick ! "

" I weep for you," the Walrus said:
　" I deeply sympathize."
With sobs and tears he sorted out
　Those of the largest size,
Holding his pocket-handkerchief
　Before his streaming eyes.

" O Oysters," said the Carpenter,
　" You've had a pleasant run !
Shall we be trotting home again ? "
　But answer came there none—
And this was scarcely odd, because
　They'd eaten every one.

---

might have turned to good account a discussion with Professor Price on the Statics and Dynamics of Particles and there and then invented some of Alice's reflections as she fell down the rabbit-hole; R. L. Green remembers that the poem 'She's all my fancy painted him', which formed the basis of the White Rabbit's 'evidence' at the trial of the Knave of Hearts ('They told me

Tweedledee's recitation from Through the Looking-glass

*Walter de la Mare unwittingly created a certain amount of confusion by attributing the Whitby reminiscence to Dean Paget. I have no doubt that de la Mare's source was the same as mine, i.e. the *St James's Gazette*, and I can only conjecture that he misinterpreted the words 'President of C.C.C., Oxford' as 'Dean of Christ Church, Oxford' (Dr Fowler's name not being mentioned). Dean Paget could hardly have had any recollections of the kind, because at the time of the Whitby reading-party he was only three years old, whereas Fowler was an exact contemporary of Dodgson.

you had been to her', etc.), was composed some time in 1854 and might have provided a partial justification for Dr Fowler's statement.[46] And we might add, having just read about the expedition to 'Mary Ann's Spout', that the name of the White Rabbit's housemaid was Mary Ann!

Rear-Admiral Noel Wright contributed a closely argued letter to *The Times Literary Supplement* in 1951 in support of the view that 'The Walrus and the Carpenter' was written at Whitby in 1854. The beach certainly has 'such quantities of sand', and in those days apparently there was a pile of rocks about a mile from the pier which would have been 'conveniently low' for resting. Admiral Wright also made an intriguing comparison between the opening verses of 'The Walrus and the Carpenter' and a passage in J. R. Bellot's *Journal d'un voyage aux mers polaires*, published in 1854. On the other hand, the famous verses did not appear in print at this time, and they are not included in the family magazine *Mischmasch* which contains the verses written between 1853 and 1862 that Dodgson considered worth preserving. Nor are they mentioned in his Diary (although admittedly the volume for 1854 is missing). Moreover, Whitby has a serious rival claimant in Whitburn, near Sunderland, which Dodgson often visited when staying with the Collingwoods or his cousins the Misses Wilcox – and where the original Walrus is proudly identified with a stuffed specimen in Sunderland Museum, and the Carpenter with the numerous ships' carpenters in their distinctive dress who were a feature of the Sunderland streets in Dodgson's day.[47]

On the whole it seems wisest to approach the Whitby theories with caution. It is most interesting to know that Dodgson was already in the habit of telling stories to children with facility, and it is possible that at Whitby he recited

Two illustrations by Dodgson from Mischmasch

STUDIES FROM ENGLISH POETS Nº IV

"She did so; but 'tis doubtful how or whence —" Keats.

'She's all my fancy painted him' – not a very acceptable offering for children, however, outside its classic context in 'Alice'? – and *perhaps* other tales or verses approximating to items in the famous book. He might even have been able to retain some of these miscellaneous fragments in his mind for as long as eight years, for he had a very good memory. But it seems probable that

Dr Fowler, having a recollection of Dodgson entertaining children at Whitby in 1854, jumped to conclusions when he wrote his account more than forty years later and unconsciously enlarged on the facts. His version of the genesis of 'Alice' is not confirmed by any other source.

The main interest of the Whitby visit lies not in any particular conjectures, but in the knowledge that, while he was there, Dodgson was establishing his character as a *raconteur* and as a freelance humorous journalist. Not until eight years later did he give *Alice in Wonderland* its first unfinished form; but from 1854 onwards he was always accumulating material and learning to express himself. Gradually – and with no very ambitious motive – he began to give literary shape (though not always in writing) to some of those whimsical intimations and impressions that had haunted him since childhood, fantasies that belonged (as we now know) to the Wonderland country and to the other side of the Looking-Glass. For the 'Alice' books were in some degree an autobiographical miscellany, woven together with extraordinary skill: an Odyssey of the subconscious.

His Whitby recreations cannot have impeded his studies, for at the end of October he obtained a First Class in the Final Mathematical School, and on December 18th, 1854, he brought his undergraduate years to a close by taking the degree of Bachelor of Arts.

A Victorian Don

One

In the course of 1854 Dodgson began to keep a diary, which henceforth he wrote up at regular intervals in his immaculate hand, and which by the end of his life filled thirteen octavo volumes. It was not in any way a sensational diary; nor was it ever intended to be more than a private record for his own use. Nevertheless, it does contain a proportion of more personal and intimate passages, and it is naturally the most authoritative source of information available on matters of fact.

Unfortunately only nine of the thirteen volumes have survived intact. These have been published under the careful editorship of Roger Lancelyn Green (Cassell, 1954). The complete diary was available to S. D. Collingwood when he wrote his *Life and Letters* in 1898, for he quotes passages from all the missing volumes, but by 1930 four volumes had disappeared – the first (1854), the third (covering the last three months of 1855), and the sixth and seventh (covering the period April, 1858, to May, 1862). Probably their loss was entirely accidental and occurred in the course of various family moves, and redistributions of property, at a time when Lewis Carroll's reputation had not yet risen to the spectacular heights it attained in the nineteen-thirties, and when his diaries were not handled with any particular care.*

It is, then, at the beginning of the year 1855 that we are first enabled to study Charles Dodgson 'in the round', and from the accumulation of small details to piece together a picture of his daily life. The entries for the early days of January, 1855, set a pattern which was to be maintained so long as the diary was written. Basically, Dodgson's problem did not alter and may be thus expressed: How was a man with such wide interests in art and photography, in the theatre, in children, in literature and poetry, in religion, science and medicine ever to find time enough to do all the work that he knew was necessary if he was to make a success of his career in the sphere that he had specially chosen for himself – the sphere of mathematical and logical studies? It was a question that he never managed to answer to his entire satisfaction, and that was to keep him, over many years, labouring well into the small hours (and thus appreciably, one may think, to shorten his life).

'Meant to have begun work to-day, but fell to at illumination instead.' 'Failed again in beginning work. Began on the second volume of Haydon's Life.' 'Got about two hours of Mathematics in the morning, and afterwards did nothing but illumination and sketching.' 'No work done. Got my likeness photographed by Booth. . . .'

These entries of January, 1855 – written in the vacation at Ripon (while his father was fulfilling his duties as Canon Residentiary) – must not be taken to imply that Dodgson failed to concentrate on his academic work when he returned to Christ Church. The reverse is true; he worked hard and well. In February, 1855, he was made Sub-Librarian, and in May was given a Bostock scholarship – thus gaining a helpful addition to his income, from both sources, of £55 a year. 'This very nearly raises my income this year to independence,' he wrote. 'Courage!'

But the internal struggle revealed in those diary entries is important to our understanding of his complex character. Those who met Dodgson casually at this time might have carried away the impression of a handsome, serious youth whose mind was entirely set on his studies. When they looked at the book he was reading – and he often had a book in his hand – they might have

*But see p. 105, *infra*.

been puzzled as to exactly what those studies were. It could, of course, have been a mathematical book or part of his divinity reading for ordination. ('This should take precedence over all other. I must consult my Father on the subject', he resolved in the diary.) But it might equally well have been one of the English poets – Shakespeare, Milton, Byron, Coleridge, Wordsworth, was the order he set them in, and soon he added Tennyson; or something French or Italian – he liked Tasso better than Dante; or the latest popular novel by Dinah Maria Mulock, who had yet to write *John Halifax, Gentleman*. In March, 1855, he was gallantly resolving, in the same breath as it were, to read Scott's novels 'over again' (!) and to 'finish Mill and dip into Dugald Stewart'. A young man might well cry 'Courage!' who set himself such formidable tasks.

The age in which he was living demanded much from a thoughtful and sensitive mind like Charles Dodgson's. 'Of all decades in our history,' Mr G. M. Young has maintained, 'a wise man would choose the eighteen-fifties to be young in.' Yet to relish to the full the dangers of the Crimea and the Mutiny, the clashes of Church and State, the challenge of social and educational reform, needed a tougher mental constitution than was given to Dodgson. It was not that he did not feel the progressive wind, which stirred the sails even of the ancient galleon of Christ Church. So far as print and paper could help him, he was anxious to learn; he was eager to explore the exciting new worlds revealed at the far end of Uncle Skeffington's telescope and microscope. But in great issues, and it was a time for greatness, his need for certainties kept him cautious and conservative. His reaction, in the diary of January 7th, 1856, to Kingsley's *Alton Locke* shows clearly where he stood:

'Finished *Alton Locke*. It tells the tale well of the privations and miseries of the poor, but I wish he would propose some more definite remedy, and especially that he would tell us what he wishes to substitute for the iniquitous "sweating" system in tailoring and other trades.

If the book were but a little more definite, it might stir up many fellow-workers in the same good field of social improvement. Oh that God, in His good providence, may make me hereafter such a worker! But, alas, what are the means? Each has his own nostrum to propound, and in the Babel of voices nothing is done. I would thankfully spend and be spent so long as I were sure of really effecting something by the sacrifice, and not merely lying down under the wheels of some irresistible Juggernaut.

. . . How few seem to care for the only subjects of real interest in life. – What am I, to say so? Am *I* a deep philosopher, or a great genius? I think neither. What talents I have, I desire to devote to His service, and may He purify me, and take away my pride and selfishness. Oh that *I* might hear "Well done, good and faithful servant"!'

The cry still has power to move us, coming from a simple-hearted young man beginning to make his way earnestly in the world, disclaiming genius, yet already conscious of unusual powers that awaited expression. The dynamic qualities of the reformer were missing. With his need for something 'more definite', his need to be 'sure of really effecting something'. Dodgson will never be a leader in that crusade of Kingsley's. One feels that he really understands this, and shows instead a quiet determination to live a modest, Christian, charitable life in his own way.

But it was not all so simple as the copybook resolution in Dodgson's diary might suggest. We have to reckon with the '*very* rebellious mind' which Dr Mannheim discovered in his youthful handwriting. The year 1855 provides a curious example of the way in which that mind was working.

At some unknown date in 1855 (probably towards the end of the year, for there is no mention of it in the surviving portions of his diary) Dodgson wrote a four-line stanza in parody of Anglo-Saxon poetry. He provided some highly scholarly and entertaining explanations of the thoroughly obscure words in this stanza – for 'there are plenty of hard words there', as Humpty Dumpty said – and then copied the whole piece into his current scrapbook, *Mischmasch*, dating it 'Croft, 1855'. To the family who read it at the time, this was nothing more or less than an ephemeral *jeu d'esprit*; to us who read it a century later it comes with the familiarity of an old friend.

STANZA OF ANGLO-SAXON POETRY.

'Twas brillig, and the slithy toves
  Did gyre and gimble in the wabe;
All mimsy were the borogoves,
  And the mome raths outgrabe.

The genesis of 'Jabberwocky', and Tenniel's illustration for the verse in Through the Looking-glass

Collingwood says that the poem 'Jabberwocky', of which this is the beginning, was composed while Dodgson was 'staying with his cousins, the Misses Wilcox, at Whitburn, near Sunderland. To while away an evening the whole party sat down to a game of verse-making, and "Jabberwocky" was his contribution.'[48] It appears probable from this that Dodgson wrote the body of the poem at Whitburn, not the first verse. What is certain is that the famous first stanza was composed in 1855 and remained unknown in his scrapbook for seventeen years – until it was published with the rest of 'Jabberwocky' in *Through the Looking-Glass* in 1872, with only a few small alterations of the spelling.*

The significance of this discovery to any student of Dodgson's life must be

*Roger Lancelyn Green has shown that there is a strong probability that the rest of the poem was influenced by 'The Shepherd of the Giant Mountains', a translation by Menella Smedley from the German of Fouqué (*Times Literary Supplement*, 1 March, 1957).

obvious. Here is the classic stanza of nonsense poetry – a form of poetry which, as Emile Cammaerts has pointed out, if 'not necessarily the highest type of poetry', is in a sense the most poetical, being the most musical – and we find that it is the casual inspiration not of a man of forty but of a youth of twenty-three. Its musical cadences immediately acquire a more romantic glow. The lines have always sounded singularly unforced and melodious – and it is agreeable to be able to assume, as in the light of this knowledge we may, that they were not 'hammered out' like the rest of 'Jabberwocky' but one day dropped unbidden into young Dodgson's mind, perhaps as he reclined in a tin bath at Croft.

Dodgson becomes in a moment more of a poet, less of a professional humorist. 'Twas bryllyg' shows that the artist, who buried beneath the nursery floor-boards his wish to 'wander through the wide world and chase the

buffalo', was still alive within him. By thus embarking on the 'Kubla Khan' of nonsense, he gives assurance that he will one day send Alice on her wanderings 'through caverns measureless to man'.

Christ Church Hall, circa 1863

Two

The quarters which Dodgson occupied at Christ Church have been listed by Williams and Madan and others.[49] He appears to have had four different sets of rooms. As an undergraduate he lived in Peckwater Quad; next he moved to the Chaplain's Quadrangle, pulled down in 1862; for the following six years he was in the Old Library, a building which was removed to give place to the Meadow Buildings; and in November, 1868, he was installed in the spacious apartments on two floors in the north-west corner of Tom Quad which he retained until his death.

The dignified stability of his Christ Church background was to be an exceedingly important factor in Dodgson's life. Something of the kind was necessary to him, and he always remained proudly grateful to 'The House' for providing it. When he was nearly fifty, he had occasion to defend the college against adverse criticism in the *Observer*. 'The truth is', he wrote, 'that Christ Church stands convicted of two unpardonable crimes – being great, and having a name. Such a place must always expect to find itself "a wide mark for scorn and jeers". . . .' And he concluded by saying that if the writer of the article had found 'a set of young men more gentlemanly, more orderly, and more pleasant in every way to deal with, than I have found here, I cannot but think him an exceptionally favoured mortal'.[50]

Dodgson at twenty-five

A photograph of 1857 shows that the orderly young man in the Chaplain's Quadrangle was neat in appearance, and by holding himself very straight in his long black coat and high butterfly collar contrived to suggest that he was rather taller than his moderate height of five feet nine. One is faintly reminded of Dickens's remark that the High Churchman of 1850 was the dandy of 1820 in another form. In later life Dodgson was not always quite so neat, and the white tie which he then affected was inclined to straggle.

For his twenty-third birthday Dodgson received a photograph of his father, to stand on his mantelpiece, no doubt, as a daily admonition. His aunt Lucy Lutwidge, who had kept house for the family since his mother died, sent him a sofa-cover and his sisters a copy of Hook's *Church Dictionary*. He purchased five quires of folio scribbling-paper. The box belonging to the 'Bachelors' table' in Hall was brought to him, so that as 'caterer' he could manage the accounts and order the dinners (someone obviously having noted him as a methodical and obliging person). Periodically he would go along to supervise the library and catalogue the books.

To his rooms there now entered a succession of pupils, beginning with a youth called Burton, 'who seems to take in Algebra very readily'. By April, 1855, he had fourteen of these private pupils to look after, but in the autumn of the same year he began new and more important duties as 'Mathematical Lecturer' of Christ Church, the counterpart of the Tutor of modern days. These were soon to keep him very busy, partly in giving tuition to undergraduates in his rooms, but also with an increasing number of public lectures.

No Englishman could live through 1855 without thinking often of the Crimean War, and Dodgson's diary records both the 'melancholy news' of the repulse of the Allies' attack on the Malakoff in June and the 'glorious intelligence' of the fall of Sebastopol in September. Christ Church was also conspicuous in the newspapers during the year. In June, 1855, Dean Gaisford died – 'our old Dean, respected by all and I believe regretted by many.' Dr H. G. Liddell, the Headmaster of Westminster and collaborator with Dr Robert Scott in the famous Greek lexicon, was appointed to succeed him. 'The selection does not seem to have given much satisfaction in the college', noted Dodgson, but it was later to have various important consequences for himself, and it had one immediately satisfactory result – that in honour of Dr Liddell's appointment he was made a 'Master of the House' (i.e. was given all the privileges of a Master of Arts within the walls of Christ Church). He did not take the ordinary M.A. degree until 1857.

The year 1855 was thus a most important year for him. He showed in his final diary entry that he fully realised its significance:

'I am sitting alone in my bedroom this last night of the old year, waiting for midnight. It has been the most eventful year of my life: I began it a poor bachelor student, with no definite plans or expectations; I end it a master and tutor in Ch. Ch., with an income of more than £300 a year, and the course of mathematical tuition marked out by God's providence for at least some years to come. Great mercies, great failings, time lost, talents misapplied – such has been the past year.'[51]

He may perhaps have felt that he had lost time and misapplied his talent by writing 'Twas bryllyg, and the slythy toves . . .'

Three

Mr R. L. Green has collected together, in his edition of the Diaries, a number of contrasting views on Dodgson's lectures. The general opinion of them was that they were not only dull but that they were most uninspiringly delivered. Dodgson's need to overcome his shyness and his stammer may have largely accounted for this. To the frivolous he was sometimes an object of amusement as a lecturer. Mr Fred Sim of Christ Church used to say that Dodgson once asked him, 'Sim, what are you laughing at?' To which the reply was: 'I'm afraid we were laughing at *you*, Sir!'[52] On the other hand, there is evidence that those who were really interested in the subject found his explanations extremely lucid. He was no doubt much more successful in his *tête-à-tête* 'tutorials' than in his public performances.

Probably Dodgson soon realised that, though he had a natural love of teaching, he had not a natural gift of communicating to an assembled class. Much of the work he felt to be a waste of time. He wrote in his diary of November 26th, 1856, that he was 'weary of lecturing and discouraged. I examined six or eight men to-day who are going in for Little-Go and hardly one is really fit to go in. It is thankless, uphill work, goading unwilling men to learning they have no taste for. . . .' Canon Scott Holland believed that Dodgson ought to have lived in the Middle Ages in the palmy days of Scholasticism, when his peculiar gifts of mind would have enabled him to rout all other schoolmen and to produce subtleties and dialectical terms which would have confounded the whole of Europe. He pictured Dodgson lecturing to eleven thousand students who had flocked to him from Paris, Padua and Bologna, to hear him turn the theories of all the other great men inside out![53] It is a vision that has more relation, of course, to Dodgson's later attempts to propound his theories of logic than to his early efforts as a teacher of mathematics.

As a young man he tried very hard to master the art of teaching. His initial experience was obtained in the boys' Sunday School at Croft on July 8th, 1855, when he noted: 'I liked my first attempt in teaching very much'; and in January, 1856, he eagerly followed this up by accepting a part-time engagement to teach the boys at St Aldates School, Oxford. The first lesson, to a class of eight boys, he found 'much more pleasant than I expected', though he remarked that the contrast between town and country boys was 'very striking': 'here they are sharp, boisterous, and in the highest spirits – the difficulty of teaching being, not to get an answer, but to prevent all answering at once.' Before long these interesting town-bred peculiarities were seen to have their drawbacks, as successive entries in the diary indicate:

'(Feb. 8, 1856.) The school class noisy and inattentive – the novelty of the thing is wearing off, and I find them rather unmanageable.

(Feb. 15.) School class again noisy and troublesome – I have not yet acquired the arts of keeping order.

(Feb. 26.) Class again noisy and inattentive – it is very disheartening and I almost think I had better give up teaching there for the present.

(Feb. 29.) Left word at the school that I shall not be able to come again for the present. I doubt if I shall try again next term: the good done does not seem worth the time and trouble.'

It had obviously been a humiliating experience, which may have contributed materially to Dodgson's distaste for little boys, a distaste which gradually increased as he grew older.

He had much to occupy his mind, however, apart from academic difficulties. Other things beside Euclidean figures and mathematical symbols began to appear on those quires of scribbling-paper. Through his cousin Menella Smedley, herself a poet, Dodgson obtained an introduction to her cousin Frank Smedley, the crippled novelist and author of *Frank Fairlegh*, who proposed to him in July, 1855, that he should write for the *Comic Times*, a new periodical which was about to commence publication under the editorship of Edmund Yates. 'I do not think I have yet written anything worthy of real publication (in which I do not include the *Whitby Gazette* or the *Oxonian Advertiser*),' Dodgson declared in his diary, 'but I do not despair of doing so some day.' He sent Smedley a parody of some lines in Moore's *Lalla Rookh*, beginning 'I never loved a dear gazelle', and had the satisfaction of seeing it appear in the second number, although it had previously been rejected by *Punch*. Three further contributions by him appeared during the short life of the *Comic Times* – the paper succumbed in November, 1855, after sixteen issues – including 'She's all my fancy painted him', written the year before, which may be a parody of some undiscovered original and which was later used in 'Alice' as the White Rabbit's Evidence. He also submitted some humorous drawings, but, on being informed that they were 'not up to the mark', resolved not to send any more.

The disappointed staff of the *Comic Times* formed themselves into a company to produce another humorous paper, again under the editorship of Edmund Yates. This time it was a monthly called *The Train* which made its début in January, 1856. Dodgson thought the opening number 'only average in talent, and an intense imitation of Dickens throughout', but he was soon offering Yates some contributions. The first of several pieces to appear in *The Train* was the poem 'Solitude', quoted in the last chapter, which he had written three years before. He submitted it under the mysterious initials 'B.B.', but this form of signature did not please Yates, who asked him to choose a *nom de plume*.

Dodgson thereupon proposed 'Dares', the first half of his birthplace, Daresbury. Yates thought this 'too much like a newspaper signature', and so he had to try again. On February 11th, 1856, he recorded in his diary:

'Wrote to Mr Yates sending him a choice of names: 1. *Edgar Cuthwellis* (made by transposition out of 'Charles Lutwidge'). 2. *Edgar U. C. Westhill* (ditto). 3. *Louis Carroll* (derived from Lutwidge . . Ludovic . . Louis, and Charles). 4. *Lewis Carroll* (ditto).'

On March 1st he added a note: '*Lewis Carroll* was chosen.' We find therefore that we owe the famous signature, in the last resort, to Edmund Yates, and must be grateful to him for deciding as he did. There would not perhaps have been much to choose between Louis and Lewis, but the other alternatives are clearly unthinkable. 'Edgar Cuthwellis lived in this house. . . .' No, it does not bear contemplation. And Edgar U. C. Westhill could only have written sentimental novels for maidservants.

The poems by Dodgson in *The Train* included a parody of Wordsworth's 'Resolution and Independence', called 'Upon the Lonely Moor', published in October, 1856. This was not one of the contributions signed by Lewis Carroll – in fact it appeared anonymously – but that Lewis Carroll did not disdain it is shown by the fact that he used it as the basis of the White Knight's song in *Through the Looking-Glass*. Indeed in 1893 he told R. Brimley Johnson that 'the character of the White Knight was meant to suit the speaker in the poem'.*

'*I shook him well from side to side, until his face was blue*'

Four

Early in 1855 Dodgson had a bad fall while skating, thus anticipating a similar mishap suffered by another master of light verse, C. S. Calverley, which unfortunately had more serious results. In June, 1855, he went to the Varsity match at Lord's. In March, 1856, he followed the University boat race in a steamer with his cousin Frank and saw Oxford lose by half a length, being inclined to blame 'bad steering' for the result. All this shows that he did not withdraw himself from the sporting activities of his contemporaries, though he found his favourite recreations in books, pictures and the theatre.

Between the years 1855 and 1858, of which we have a complete diary record, he not only read deeply in the work of the great poets of the past, but also missed little that was worth discovering in contemporary prose or verse, enjoying

*Brimley Johnson had asked Dodgson whether the White Knight had been inspired by two highly suggestive passages in Samuel Butler's *Hudibras*. 'I have certainly no consciousness of having borrowed the idea of the inventions of the White Knight from anything in *Hudibras*', replied Dodgson, 'of which poem all that I have read, to the best of my recollection, is contained in the little book of selections herewith enclosed.' The book of selections, about 3 inches by 2 inches, was probably one of the 'Beauties' series published during the first thirty years of the nineteenth century. It did not contain the passages in question. (See *Literature*, March 5th, 1898.)

Patmore's 'The Angel in the House' and appreciating Tennyson's 'Maud' better at a second consideration. *Wuthering Heights* he thought an 'extraordinary book': Heathcliff and Catherine were 'original and most powerfully drawn idealities', but he confessed that 'it is of all novels I ever read the one I should least like to be a character in myself'. (No one, certainly, was likely to cast him as Heathcliff.) Kingsley's *Hypatia*, again, seemed to him 'powerful' but 'outrageous to taste in some parts'. Dodgson was now beginning to build up his library, which ultimately included a most comprehensive collection of the English poets, novelists and philosophers, numerous children's books, thirty-eight volumes of *The Theatre* and more than a hundred volumes of *Notes and Queries*. There were also many books on puzzles and games – Ranjitsinhji's *Jubilee Book of Cricket* coming as rather a surprise – and works on spiritualism and medicine. Dodgson's interest in medicine was first aroused in March, 1856: an Oxford acquaintance had an epileptic fit while he was passing, and Dodgson 'caught him as he fell' and did what he could for him. The next day he ordered *Hints for Emergencies*.

In his twenties Dodgson, with or without his father's approval, began to pay an increasing number of visits to the London theatre. When he saw Charles Kean and Ellen Tree in *Henry VIII* at the Princess's Theatre, Oxford Street, in 1855, he thought it 'the greatest theatrical treat I ever had or ever expect to have'; but Ellen Terry was to give him many equally memorable experiences in later life. By chance, on another visit to the Princess's Theatre in the following year, he happened to see her first professional appearance on the stage, aged eight. It was in 1855, also, that he recorded a visit to Bellini's *Norma* at Covent Garden; and as an after-piece to that opera he watched his first ballet, which did not please him at all. 'The instinctive grace of cottage children dancing is something far more beautiful,' he considered: 'I never wish to see another ballet.' If someone had told him that evening that a ballet, based on a book of his own as yet unwritten, would be danced in the year 1953 in a huge London Festival Hall on a site then covered by warehouses and factories on the Surrey side of the Thames, he would have been understandably incredulous.

'Cheshire-Puss,' she began, 'which way should I go from here?' from Alice's Adventures in Wonderland

Yet intimations of the future 'Alice' and of her dream-world continued to visit him, as he accumulated ideas and impressions. Take this entry, in the diary of February 9th, 1856, with its foreshadowing of the Cheshire Cat's 'We're all mad here':

'Query: when we are dreaming and, as often happens, have a dim consciousness of the fact and try to wake, do we not say and do things which in waking life would be insane? May we not then sometimes define insanity as an inability to distinguish which is the waking and which the sleeping life? We often dream without the least suspicion of unreality: "Sleep hath its own world", and it is often as lifelike as the other.'

It should not be imagined that the thoughtful young don who transcribed such reflections as these could not laugh, or that Lewis Carroll, who gave the wildest amusement to other people, was not himself a 'laughable' person. Some such silly idea may have been implanted in many minds by the sharp and sophisticated distinction drawn by certain writers between the twin identities of C. L. Dodgson and Lewis Carroll. But there was, in fact, nothing of the Jekyll and Hyde about him at all. In every great humorist we search first, and naturally enough, for the man who made us laugh. We have our own ideas of his character – perhaps we imagine him as a little like ourselves in our happiest moments – and we are often puzzled, sometimes disappointed, to find that beneath the iridescent surface the waters run deep and dark. In Dodgson's unusual case the mathematician, the logician, the artist, even the churchman, permeated the humorist, shaping and refining his paradoxes until they formed the inimitable crystal. At the centre was a complex character, made up of too many conflicting elements to bring peace of mind; but we do not help ourselves, or our understanding of Dodgson, by looking for two men instead of one.

If this is true – and if, in later years, he usually showed no more than a half-hidden smile – it is important to know that as a young man Dodgson could on occasion laugh unashamedly and without restraint. He did so, for instance, when a solemn guide lectured him monotonously on a visit to the ruins at Barnard Castle in the Tees valley. 'I was immediately seized with a fit of laughter,' he wrote in his diary of August 30th, 1856, 'which I only just succeeded in stifling, and sat for ten minutes or more looking fixedly out of the window, in a state of agony, and longing for escape. We seized on the opportunity of the first pause he made to fee him and take our departure: the relief of getting into the garden was indescribable – we almost lay down and rolled – I think he must have heard our shouts of laughter, all the more violent for being pent up so long.'

Five

Such hearty laughter was probably not often heard from Dodgson after his childhood days. Fundamentally he was a serious man, and, although he had a considerable capacity for enjoyment, he found a conscientious urge to analyse his emotions. In the diary of September 3rd, 1855, for example, he reflected on his preference for light or popular music:

'There is a peculiar pleasure in listening to what I may call "unsatisfactory" music, which arises, I think, from the fact that we do not feel called on to enjoy it to the utmost: we may take things as they come.

In listening to first-rate music there is a sense of anxiety and labour, labour to enjoy it to the utmost, anxiety not to waste our opportunity: there is, I verily believe, a sensation of pain in the *realisation* of our highest pleasures, knowing that now they must soon be over: we had rather prolong anticipation by postponing them. In truth we are not intended to rest content in any pleasure of earth, however intense: the yearning has been wisely given us, which points to an eternity of happiness, as the only perfect happiness possible – "Thou wilt keep him in *perfect peace*, whose soul is stayed on thee".'

This preoccupation with his reactions is again evidenced by the episode of Dodgson's visit to Bart's in December, 1858. Ever since he had come to the rescue of the youth with the epileptic fit, he had wanted to discover whether he could bear to see an operation. Now he watched an amputation of the leg above the knee, which lasted more than an hour, and was greatly surprised to find he could bear it perfectly well. 'This is an experiment I have long been anxious to make,' he wrote, 'in order to know whether I might rely on myself to be of any use in cases of emergency, and I am very glad to believe that I might. Still, I don't think I should enjoy seeing much of it.'

In fact, if Dodgson had not been safely settled in his academic groove, it appears highly probable that he might have done useful hospital work. 'As medical man you cd. excel', the Edinburgh phrenologist had said. He had a great longing to serve others, and his interest in medicine, combined with his habit of analysing his own emotions, gave him an unusually sympathetic understanding of the feelings of those under stress. That there should be memorials to him in children's hospitals is something far more than a sentimental satisfaction to us; it is a logical sequel to the thought of his lifetime which would have greatly pleased him.

No one can have read even so far as this in the life of Charles Dodgson without appreciating that he was fast becoming one of those busy Victorian polymaths whose strong sense of purpose and responsibility, and whose endless enjoyment in natural and scientific discovery, have made them the wonder of a less robust and versatile age. Mirrored in Dodgson's character are reflections of Tom Hughes, Tupper, Kingsley, Trollope, Henry Cole and many more: men who were artists at heart but whose energy and compassion carried them far into fields of public or patriotic service. One may feel that they, like Dodgson, might have achieved more by attempting less – though one may well be wrong in thinking so. Dodgson holds his unique place in mid-Victorian history because he employed a mathematical mind and a logician's precision to crystallise a poetic genius that might not, of itself, have had the force for survival. But by instinct he was, like other 'little Leonardos' of the period, a graphic and visual artist. Preferring figures to landscape, he continued the habit of drawing them throughout his life, and neglected no opportunity of seeing art exhibitions or visiting the studios of those artists, like Millais, Holman Hunt or Arthur Hughes, whose work he chiefly admired. It is possible that Landseer's 'Titania', which he saw at Ryman's in 1857, may have given him the idea of the White Rabbit in 'Alice'. 'There are some wonderful points in it,' he wrote in his diary, 'the ass's head and the white rabbit especially.'

For a time Dodgson toyed with the idea of turning his talent for drawing to profitable use as a free-lance humorous artist. After the *Comic Times* had returned his sketches in 1855 he seems to have accepted the decision that what he could do was not good enough (though in fact many of his early attempts were little, if at all, inferior to Lear's nonsense drawings). One important event of the following year may be, in part, attributable to this renunciation of professional ambitions as a draughtsman. On March 18th, 1856, he bought his first camera.

Detail of Dodgson's illustration of Alice being ordered home by the Rabbit in Alice's Adventures Under Ground

Six

The new art of photography was just then sweeping England, interest in it having been greatly stimulated, first, by the photographic section of the Great

Landseer's 'Titania and Bottom',
which may have given Dodgson
the idea for the White Rabbit

Exhibition of 1851 and, secondly, by the invention of the collodion or wet-plate process which gave the amateur photographer the opportunity to take his own pictures free from patent restrictions. From 1855 onwards tripod-stands were being unpacked and assembled all over the countryside; cameras were being trained and focused on the soft landscapes and noble architecture that had for so long been the exclusive subjects of oil-painters and water-colourists; while, after the pictures had been taken, earnest amateurs could be seen disappearing with serious expressions into portable tents, there – beneath calico curtains – to grapple with the elaborate mysteries of 'coating, developing, fixing and varnishing.'

Dodgson had observed his enterprising uncle Skeffington Lutwidge taking photographs at Croft in September, 1855, and had naturally been intrigued, although Uncle Skeffington's pictures of the church and the bridge had not come out very successfully. He went with his uncle on a photographic outing to Richmond, Yorkshire, and a week later composed a sketch, 'Photography Extraordinary', which appeared in the *Comic Times*. In January, 1856, he visited the annual exhibition of the Photographic Society in London, which so far increased his interest that he wrote to his uncle from Oxford on January 22nd and asked him to get him a photographic apparatus, 'as I want some other occupation here than mere reading and writing.'[54]

As a matter of fact, Uncle Skeffington did not buy him his camera; instead, Dodgson went up to town with a fellow Student of Christ Church, who was also a keen amateur photographer, Reginald Southey (Plate p. 87), and with his help he bought a camera from T. Ottewill, of Charlotte Street, Caledonian Road. 'The camera with lens, etc., will come to just about £15', he noted in the diary. This did not include the necessary paraphernalia, the chest containing the bottles of chemicals, dishes, glass plates, scales and weights, measures and funnels – and the portable tent.

For the next twenty-five years the handling of this unwieldy apparatus was to be one of its owner's principal cares. The outfit usually remained at Oxford, but in the earlier years Dodgson often took it with him on his travels, which were frequent. Although he could send it in advance by rail, he was obliged to sit in London cabs surrounded by boxes and tripods on the way to the homes of his sitters. The amount of time and trouble involved in packing and unpacking the equipment shows him, once again, to have been a man of infinite patience. But to Dodgson all this was a labour of love, for he had found a pastime that appealed equally to the artist and to the scientist in him. In planning the details of a composition, he was able, at one and the same time, to satisfy both his longing for orderly arrangement and his fastidious aesthetic taste. 'It is my one recreation,' he wrote in his diary of December 31st, 1856, 'and I think it should be done well'.

Just how well it was done we are able to judge by studying the sixty-four plates in Helmut Gernsheim's *Lewis Carroll: Photographer* (1950). Of these about a dozen are photographs of contemporary celebrities, the remainder being family groups or studies of children; there is only one landscape – an exterior view of Tennyson's home, Farringford, and even this has been re-moved from a revised edition of 1969. The selection accurately represents Dodgson's preferences in photography; students of nineteenth-century England owe gratitude to Mr Gernsheim for establishing his pre-eminence in this field, as well as for tracing the whereabouts of his albums, some of the most interesting of which from his own collection are now at the University of Texas.

Having regard to Dodgson's many other activities, Gernsheim concluded that 'his photographic achievements are truly astonishing: he must not only rank as a pioneer of British amateur photography, but I would also un-hesitatingly acclaim him as the most outstanding photographer of children in the nineteenth century. After Julia Margaret Cameron he is probably the most distinguished amateur portraitist of the mid-Victorian era.' And Gernsheim added: 'He was a master of composition, which was one of Mrs Cameron's weak points.'[55]

Dodgson was therefore not destined, after all, to be the visual artist *manqué* that might have been anticipated. The chance that his early manhood coin-cided with the advent of popular photography gave him a remarkable oppor-tunity to express a highly individual talent. He took brilliant advantage of it. With our new understanding of his importance as a photographer, we may well study his drawings with fresh interest.

Seven

The outlines of the young Lewis Carroll begin to emerge from the accumula-tion of diary entries, letters and books. Something is missing, however, that a biographer might have expected to find in a young man's life. There are none but the most formal meetings with young women; there is not a hint – in the

diary or elsewhere – of the most innocent flirtation. It is a far cry from this restrained and unnatural existence to the gallant encounters of even such a studious young poet as Winthrop Praed, who, at Cambridge, thirty years earlier, would not have refused an invitation to a ball even though it was on the night before an examination.

Dodgson's ordeal as a stammerer may provide at least a partial explanation of his attitude. Those who have suffered similarly will testify that during childhood their stammering, such as it was, did not worry them (and hence they have tended to look back to their childhood, as Dodgson did, with a somewhat exaggerated and nostalgic affection). In the unsympathetic atmosphere of a public school, the situation is very different. As the stammerer begins to make his way into adult society the barrier between him and the rest of the world becomes increasingly formidable. He tends to withdraw into himself and to avoid any situation that might provoke embarrassment. It is a curious fact that he is often at his happiest in the company of children. He can talk to them, he finds, quite naturally and freely – probably because they expect less of him and are ready to take him as he comes. These circumstances are fully exemplified in Dodgson's life. His delight in the companionship of children – particularly of little girls – was to sustain and encourage him until his death. It had all begun, of course, when he played with his brothers and sisters and their friends at Daresbury and Croft; but we see the process continuing in the first surviving diary of his early manhood. On August 21st, 1855, at Tynemouth, he met the 'three nice little children' of a Mrs Crawshay, and wrote: 'I took a great fancy to Florence, the eldest, a child of very sweet manners – she has a very striking, though not a pretty face, and may possibly turn out a beautiful brunette.' At about the same time he made the acquaintance at Whitburn of Frederika Liddell, a niece of Dr Liddell, the new Dean of Christ Church – 'one of the most lovely children I ever saw, gentle and innocent looking, not an inanimate doll-beauty'. He sketched her on the seashore, and she soon became 'one of the nicest children I have ever seen, as

Left: *Ivo Bligh, son of Lord Darnley*. Middle top: *Dean Liddell's house*. Middle below: *Three girls, Croft Rectory*, Right: *Reginald Southey*. *All photographs taken by Dodgson*

well as the prettiest: dear, sweet, pretty little Frederika!' But Frederika had a younger sister who also caught his eye: 'The youngest Liddell, Gertrude, is even prettier than my little favourite, Freddie: indeed she has quite the most lovely face I ever saw in a child' (September 21st, 1855).

Collingwood's remark that 'his first child-friend, so far as I know, was Miss Alice Liddell'[56] is therefore misleading. Dodgson had made friends with a number of children before he ever met Alice, including two of her cousins. It is not surprising that, as an artist, he should have been attracted primarily to good-looking children – and the Liddell family, as a whole, seems to have been exceptionally well-favoured. Soon after Dean Liddell had installed himself at Christ Church, Dodgson was on friendly terms with his two eldest children, Harry, aged eight or nine, and Lorina, aged six or seven. The diary of March 6th, 1856, records: 'Made friends with little Harry Liddell (whom I first spoke to down at the boats last week): he is certainly the handsomest boy I ever saw.' It seems that he did not meet the second daughter, Alice, who was nearing her fourth birthday, until April 25th of that year, when he went over to the Deanery with his friend Southey to try to take a photograph of the Cathedral from the garden. 'The three little girls' – the third was Edith, about two years old – 'were in the garden most of the time, and we became excellent friends: we tried to group them in the foreground of the picture, but they were not patient sitters.' Although the photographs of the Cathedral proved failures, and although the diary gives no further details, there must

Mrs Liddell and Dean Liddell

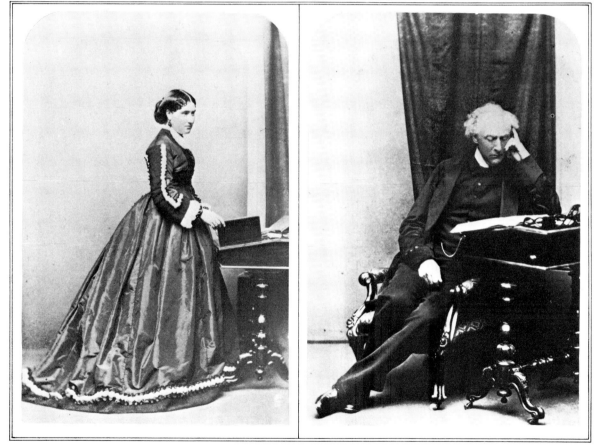

have been some special quality about this first meeting with Alice Liddell that impressed Dodgson, for he added to his diary entry a comment which he reserved for outstanding occasions: 'I mark this day with a white stone'.

Thereafter Dodgson was frequently at the Deanery. In June he photographed the young Liddells, and, with his cousin Frank, took Harry and Ina (as Lorina was generally known) on a successful river excursion. But his early photographic attempts often ended in failure, especially when he tried to take pictures in bad light. He soon discovered that Mrs Liddell, the mother of these desirably 'photogenic' children, was as formidable as she was handsome; and before long she had apparently decided that Dodgson's photography was becoming a nuisance. After twice attempting to take photographs of Harry and Ina in November, Dodgson wrote in his diary (November 14th, 1856):

'I found Mrs Liddell had said they were not to be taken till all can be taken in a group. This may be meant as a hint that I have intruded on the premises long enough: I am quite of the same opinion myself, and, partly for this reason, partly because I cannot afford to waste any more time on portraits at such a bad season of the year, I have resolved not to go again for the present, nor at all without invitation, except just to pack up the things and bring them back.'

It was a passing cloud: a hypersensitive young man's readiness to seize offence. Within a few days he was dining at the Deanery and attending a musical party there. Yet it appears probable that Mrs Liddell did not take particularly kindly to Dodgson, for when he offered to teach Harry Liddell his sums, she 'seemed to think it would take up too much of my time'. (He succeeded eventually in his determination, though the lessons did not last long.)

In 1856 Dr Liddell's health compelled him to winter in Madeira. His wife accompanied him. It is noteworthy that – the very day after they left in December – Dodgson went over to the Deanery and stayed to 'nursery' dinner.

Despite the temperamental difficulties of associating with Mrs Liddell, Dodgson soon established himself as a close friend of her children – he gave 'little Alice' a present for her fifth birthday and he obviously gained the confidence of their governess, Miss Prickett. Even this had its drawbacks in Victorian Oxford, however, for on May 17th, 1857, he commented: 'I find to my great surprise that my notice of them (the children) is construed by some men into attentions to the governess, Miss Prickett.' After a serious discussion with a colleague about this unexpected problem, he decided that, 'though for my own part I should give little importance to the existence of so groundless a rumour, it would be inconsiderate to the governess to give any further occasion for remarks of the sort. For this reason I shall avoid taking any public notice of the children in future, unless any occasion should arise when such an interpretation is impossible'.

Miss Prickett – 'Pricks' to the children – was not, according to Alice's son, Caryl Hargreaves, 'the highly educated governess of the present day'; in due course she became Mrs Foster and died the proprietress of the Mitre Hotel.[57] The idea that Dodgson might have been attracted to her is delightfully absurd. Indeed, the very suggestion shows that Dodgson's contemporaries simply could not contemplate the possibility that a young man in his twenties might have a disinterested love of children for their own sake.

When the Liddells went again to Madeira, in the winter of 1857, their family accompanied them, and Dodgson found that 'it took a long time to get to the end of the adieus of the dear, loving little children'. Did Mrs Liddell stand by with some impatience during this leave-taking? – and was she, in some odd way, a little jealous of this strange young man who could read the hearts of her children? It is a question that will recur.

I should like to know, for curiosity, who that sweet-looking girl was, aged 12, with a red nightcap. I think she had a younger sister, also with a red nightcap. She was speaking to you when I came up to wish you good-night. I fear I must be content with her _name_ only: the social gulf be-tween us is pro-bably too wide for it to be wise to make _friends_. Some of my little _actress_-friends are of a rather lower _status_ than myself. But, below a certain line, it is hardly wise to let a girl have a "gentleman" friend — even one of 62! Always affectionately yours, C.L.D.

Letter, 16 February, 1894, to
Beatrice Hatch, one of the few
girls who remained friends with
Dodgson after her childhood

One

The happy, prosperous eighteen-fifties were good years for the clever son of an archdeacon to be alive in. They saw a revolution in the outlook of the English middle class and an impressive advance in its intellectual and artistic culture. The public schools and the universities were building a new Victorian patriciate which was to dominate English thought until long after the death of the Queen. Thackeray published *Esmond* and *The Newcomes*. Ruskin wrote *Stones of Venice*. Tennyson, the new Laureate, thrilled the nation with 'The Charge of the Light Brigade' and bequeathed 'In Memoriam' and 'Maud' to posterity. George MacDonald published *Phantastes*, and Holman Hunt painted 'The Hireling Shepherd' and 'The Light of the World'.

Before the fifties were out, Charles Dodgson of Christ Church had made the acquaintance of all these remarkable men. He did not meet them on equal terms, as a celebrity, but as a diffident, stammering youth, whose future fame could scarcely have been prophesied. Under the pseudonym of Lewis Carroll, he had so far written nothing important. But, though personally unknown, he was a fellow of a great Oxford college – at a period when Oxford's prestige stood high. In course of time he was bound to be introduced to many famous people: he first met Holman Hunt, for instance, in the Christ Church Senior Common Room on June 13th, 1857. But the local lions were already, so to speak, sitting on his doorstep.

It is rather surprising that he did not encounter Hunt's determined champion, John Ruskin, who was an old member of the House, before October 27th of the

John Ruskin

same year, when he found him eating the Common Room breakfast. Dodgson was able to talk to him then, though not for long enough 'to bring out anything characteristic or striking in him'. He was somewhat disappointed in his appearance – 'a general feebleness of expression, with no commanding air, or any external signs of deep thought, as one would have expected to see in such a man'. But the *rencontre* was memorable enough for the day to be marked in his diary as '*Dies notabilis*'.

The acquaintance with Ruskin never developed very far. Dodgson asked him his opinion of his drawing and was told 'that he had not enough talent to make it worth his while to devote much time to sketching'[58] – a fair enough criticism in its way, though Ruskin was not the man to detect or to encourage the wild brilliance of some of his amateur fantasies. Dodgson later consulted Ruskin again about Henry Holiday's illustrations for *The Hunting of the Snark*. 'He much disheartened me', says the diary entry of November 23rd, 1874, 'by holding out no hopes that Holiday would be able to illustrate a book satisfactorily' – a gloomy prophecy that was not fulfilled, for Holiday, in fact, did the difficult job quite well. On June 3rd, 1875, Dodgson persuaded Ruskin 'with some difficulty' to be photographed and to stay to lunch. Collingwood reproduces the photograph – a hunched-up, uncomfortable-looking Ruskin. Probably the two men were both too sensitive, too touchy, to come to intimate terms. And Ruskin, we are bound to note, was another admirer of little girls and by no means indifferent to Dean Liddell's daughters (he taught Alice drawing).

Apparently Dodgson met Thackeray only once, on May 9th, 1857, six years before the novelist's death. Again, the meeting was at breakfast, traditionally an Oxford social occasion, the host being Thomas Fowler, then Fellow of Lincoln and later President of Corpus Christi College, whose reminiscences of Whitby in 1854 have been quoted in Chapter IV. Thackeray had delivered his lecture on George III the night before and 'seemed delighted with the reception he had met with'. Dodgson was 'much pleased with what I saw of him – his manner is simple and unaffected: he shows no anxiety to shine in conversation though full of fun and anecdote when drawn out'. A cousin of Thackeray's, Francis St John Thackeray, was another Fellow of Lincoln (which explains why the great man stayed there), and later in the year he tried to persuade Thackeray to sit to Dodgson for his photograph. 'He consented to come,' says the diary, 'but had not time then.' The photograph was never taken.

Two

Photography has always been a costly amusement. It is not surprising that Dodgson should have wondered whether he could pay some of his expenses by occasionally selling prints or disposing of a negative and its copyright to a professional firm. In 1857 he did a little business with Ryman's, the picture-dealer's in the High at Oxford, and through them sold a number of copies of a photograph of Quintin Twiss, a Christ Church undergraduate actor, in a sailor's costume. Later he took an excellent photograph of Twiss in the character of 'The Artful Dodger'. To begin with, he photographed everything that came his way, his interest in medicine even inducing him to take a whole series of photographs of skeletons which he also offered to Ryman's.

Though photography was not always or necessarily the actual cause of Dodgson's meetings with the great, the subject probably could not long be kept out of his conversation; not only did it provide an excuse for introduc-

William Makepeace Thackeray,
May 1863

Left: *Agnes Grace Weld as Little
Red Riding Hood, 1852.* Right:
a later photograph. Below:
*Alfred, Lord Tennyson, 28
September, 1857. All by
Dodgson*

tions, but there was often a faint *arrière pensée* – 'if I take a good picture, I *may* be able to sell it'. In these early days it was not Lewis Carroll, the author, whom celebrities were conscious of meeting, but young Mr Dodgson of Christ Church, the ardent amateur photographer. And he could be very persistent in pursuit of a desirable quarry.

The story of his relationship with Tennyson is salutary. Dodgson had long and ardently (though not uncritically) admired the Laureate's verse, dissecting it in his diary, discussing it with his family and friends, and losing no opportunity of reading new or unfamiliar poems. He had even parodied Tennyson's 'The Two Voices' in *The Train*. Being keenly on the watch for a chance of meeting the poet, his hopes were considerably raised in August, 1857, when Mrs Charles Weld, Tennyson's sister-in-law, who was staying in the neighbourhood, came over to Croft Rectory with her daughter Agnes Grace. The child was not a beauty, as Dodgson noted in his diary, but she had rather an intriguing, piquant little face; Palgrave had already addressed a sonnet to her. Dodgson took at least two photographs of Agnes Grace, and one of these, for which he dressed her as 'Little Red Riding-Hood', proved distinctly unusual and attractive. He sent a print of it 'for Tennyson's acceptance' through Mrs Weld, and was pleased to learn that Tennyson pronounced it 'indeed a gem'. (Dodgson exhibited the study at the Photographic Society in London in the following year, and it is reproduced on p. 94.)

During the summer of 1857 Tennyson and his wife stayed at Tent Lodge, Coniston, home of his friend Julia Marshall and the scene of his honeymoon seven years earlier. Whether by accident or design, Dodgson also found himself in the Lake District that September, on the way back from a holiday in Scotland. He reconnoitred Tent Lodge, 'at last made up my mind to take the liberty of calling', and humbly submitted his visiting card with an explanatory note in pencil: 'Artist of "Agnes Grace" and "Little Red Riding-Hood".'

Tennyson was away, but Dodgson was kindly received by Mrs Tennyson and met the two boys, Hallam and Lionel, 'the most beautiful boys of their age I ever saw' (their good looks apparently superseded those of Harry Liddell). He obtained permission to photograph them; and Mrs Tennyson 'even seemed to think it was not hopeless that Tennyson himself might sit, though I said I would not request it, as he must have refused so many that it is unfair to expect it'. Dodgson added: 'Both the children proposed coming with me when I left – how far seemed immaterial to them.' The Pied Piper already exercised a potent spell.

He was back at Coniston a few days later to take the children's pictures, and was shown into the drawing-room:

'After I had waited some little time the door opened, and a strange shaggy-looking man entered: his hair, moustache and beard looked wild and neglected; these very much hid the character of the face. He was dressed in a loosely fitting morning coat, common grey flannel waist-coat and trousers, and a carelessly tied black silk neckerchief. His hair is black: I think the eyes too; they are keen and restless – nose acquiline – forehead high and broad – both face and head are fine and manly. His manner was kind and friendly from the first: there is a dry lurking humour in his style of talking.' (Diary, September 22nd, 1857.)

Thus was Dodgson's ambition fulfilled. He had much conversation with Tennyson that day and received personal explanations of passages in 'Maud' that had puzzled him – Tennyson said 'there had never been a poem so misunderstood by the "ninnies of critics" as "Maud"'. Lewis Carroll's parody of 'The Two Voices' was not, apparently, among the subjects discussed, but Dodgson showed him albums of his photographs and the Laureate 'threw out several hints of his wish to learn photography, but seems to be deterred by a dread of the amount of patience required'. No wonder that this was signalled in the diary as '*Dies mirabilis!*'

About a week later, Dodgson took several photographs of Tennyson and his family – Tennyson coming out very dark and swarthy, like a Velasquez self-portrait. Any lurking commercial motives had surely been swamped by hero-worshipping affection, so that it may seem a little graceless to mention that one of these photographs was published as a *carte-de-visite* by Joseph Cundall of Bond Street in 1861.[59]

Dodgson next saw Tennyson in 1859, at his home, Farringford, in the Isle of Wight. He denied that he had 'followed the Laureate down to his retreat' and declared that he went 'not knowing that he was there, to stay with an old college friend at Freshwater', but it is certainly a coincidence that he should twice have happened to find himself in the poet's neighbourhood, first at Coniston and then at Freshwater! Tennyson was, of course, the celebrity of the age, and he was greatly bothered by sightseers at Farringford, so that it is not surprising that he did not give young Dodgson a very enthusiastic welcome when he appeared in his garden on a May morning while he was mowing the lawn 'in a wideawake and spectacles'. He did not recognise him at first – he was very short-sighted – and Dodgson had the embarrassment of having to introduce himself. But after 'he had finished the bit of mowing he was at', Tennyson became more hospitable, led him into the house, showed him that his photographs of the family 'were hung "on the line"', and reintroduced 'the beautiful little Hallam (his son), who remembered me more readily than his father had done'. Afterwards came invitations to tea on that evening and to dinner the following day, and much friendly talk on both occasions. The proofs of the 'Idylls' were lying about, but Tennyson would not let Dodgson see them. Sir Charles Tennyson in his biography of his grandfather, suggests that this may have been because Tennyson remembered Dodgson's parody of 'The Two Voices'. But probably Tennyson never connected Dodgson with this early effort of Lewis Carroll's, because, after mentioning that he often dreamed long passages of poetry in his sleep, he turned to Dodgson and said: 'You, I suppose, dream photographs?' – which suggests that he thought of him primarily, and from his point of view quite understandably, as a photographer.[60]

Dodgson's admiration of Tennyson continued. The third volume of the Oxonian compilation, *College Rhymes*, which Dodgson edited for a time in the early sixties, was dedicated 'To Alfred Tennyson, Esquire, Poet Laureate . . . by his obedient servant, the Editor', and Dodgson asked the Laureate's permission to prepare, in collaboration with his sisters, an index to 'In Memoriam'. Tennyson consenting, this labour of love, containing about three thousand references in double columns, was issued anonymously by Tennyson's publisher Moxon in 1862. Dodgson occasionally saw Tennyson at Farringford on his holidays, and in 1862 he copied out his verses 'Upon the Lonely Moor' for little Lionel Tennyson's benefit[61] (not, be it noted, for his father's). He took some more photographs at Farringford in 1864, and gave Tennyson a copy of *Alice in Wonderland* in 1865 – and the acquaintance, which could never have become intimate, might have vaguely persisted, or gracefully faded out, as so many youthful admirations of the Laureate must have done, if Dodgson had not been a trifle too insistent and punctilious, and if Tennyson had not been easily irritated.

What actually happened can now be told. In 1870 Dodgson wrote the Laureate the following letter:

> Ch. Ch. Oxford.
> Mar. 3. 1870.
>
> DEAR MR TENNYSON,
>
> It is so long since I have had any communication with your family that you will have almost forgotten my name by this time, I fear. I write on a matter very similar to what I have written about to you on two previous occasions. My deep admiration for your writings (extending itself to your earlier poems as well) must be my excuse for thus troubling you.
>
> There is a certain unpublished poem of yours, called 'The Window' which it seems was printed for private circulation only. However it has been transcribed, and is probably in many hands in the form of M.S. A friend, who had had a M.S. copy given to him, has in his turn presented me with one. I have not even read it yet, & shall do so with much greater pleasure when I know that you do not object to my possessing it. What I plead for is, first, that you will make me comfortable in possessing this copy by giving your consent to my preserving it – secondly, the further permission to *show* it to my friends. I can hardly go so far as ask for leave to give away copies of it to friends, tho' I should esteem such a permission as a great favour.
>
> Some while ago, as you may remember, I had a copy lent me of your 'Lover's Life' – & a young lady, a cousin of mine, took a M.S. copy of it. I wrote to you about it, & in accordance with your wish prevailed on her (very reluctantly, I need hardly say) to destroy the M.S. I am not aware of any other copies of *that* poem in circulation – but *this* seems to me a different case. M.S. copies of the 'Window' are already in circulation, & this fact is unaffected by *my* possessing, or not possessing, a copy for my own enjoyment. Hoping you will kindly say you do not object to my – first reading – & secondly preserving the M.S. that has been given me, & with kind remembrances to Mrs Tennyson & your sons,
>
> I remain,
> Very truly yours
> C. L. DODGSON[62]

'The Window' or 'The Loves of the Wrens' was a song-cycle which Tennyson wrote in 1866 for Sullivan to set to music and which did not please him. Tennyson could not prevent publication of the songs, however, because he had committed himself to Sullivan, and they eventually appeared in December, 1870; if Dodgson had only waited a little longer, he could have read them with a clear conscience. 'The Lover's Tale' – not 'Lover's Life', as Dodgson calls it – was a very early poem, written when Tennyson was eighteen, which it is more understandable that he should have wished to remain private, though eventually, in 1879, he published this also. Dodgson's letter was scrupulously correct and courteous – and, even though this and other requests may have irritated Tennyson, he did not deserve the stinging rebuke that was now administered to him by Mrs Tennyson:

DEAR SIR

It is useless troubling Mr Tennyson with a request which will only revive the annoyance he has already had on the subject & add to it.

No doubt the 'Window' is circulated by means of the same unscrupulous person whose breach of confidence placed 'The Lover's Tale' in your hands.

It would be well that whatever may be done by such people a gentleman should understand that when an author does not give his works to the public he has his own reasons for it.

Yours truly,
EMILY TENNYSON[63]

Dodgson replied to this letter as follows:

Ch. Ch. Oxford,
March 7, 1870.

DEAR MR TENNYSON,

Understanding the letter I received this morning as coming really from yourself, tho' written by Mrs Tennyson, I must trouble you with one or two remarks on it.

First, let me express my sincere sympathy with you in all the annoyance that has been caused you by the unauthorised circulation of your unpublished poems. Whoever it was that thus wantonly betrayed the confidence you had reposed in him, he has, in my opinion, done a most dishonourable thing.

Next, as to your conclusion that Mr Moxon is to blame for this new instance of such circulation – as my silence on this point might be interpreted as assent, let me, in justice to Mr Moxon, assure you that, so far as I know, he has had nothing to do with it.

Lastly, I must in justice to myself call your attention to your concluding sentence. 'It would be well that, whatever may be done by such people, a gentleman should understand that, when an author does not give his works to the public, he has his own reasons for it.' This sentence certainly implies, however unintentionally, a belief that I have done something ungentlemanly. Let me then remind you that in all these matters I have been a purely passive agent, & that in all cases I have consulted your wishes & scrupulously followed them. It is by no act of mine that this poem is now in circulation, & that a copy of it has come into my hands. Under these circumstances I may fairly ask you to point out what I have failed to do that the most chivalrous sense of honour could require.

I hope I have not written harshly. I have not intended to do so. Feeling as I do, that I have done nothing which could deserve so grave a charge, I would fain hope & am quite ready to believe, that you had no intention of implying it. With kind regards to Mrs Tennyson, I remain,

Sincerely yours,
C. L. DODGSON[64]

This was a studiedly moderate answer which deserved a conciliatory response. We do not know the terms of Tennyson's next letter (or letters, for there may have been more than one), but he certainly did not satisfy Dodgson and even seems to have further embittered the proceedings by a grudging and qualified withdrawal. The following communication from Dodgson, written more than three weeks later, concluded the correspondence. It begins abruptly with a passage of dialogue:

'Sir, you are no gentleman.'

'Sir, you do me grievous wrong by such words. Prove them or retract them!'

'I reiterate them. Your conduct has been dishonourable.'

'It is not so. I offer a full history of my conduct. I charge you with groundless libel: what say you to the charge?'

'I once believed even worse of you, but begin to think you may be a gentleman after all.'

'These new imputations are as unfounded as the former. Once more, what say you to the charge of groundless libel?'

'*I absolve you.* Say no more.'

This is followed by the words 'Turn over'. A formal letter appears on the reverse of the sheet:

Mar. 31, 1870.

MY DEAR SIR,

Thus it is, as it seems to me, that you first do a man an injury, and then forgive him – that you first tread on his toes, & then beg him not to cry out!

Nevertheless I accept what you say, as being in substance, what it certainly is not in form, a retraction (though without a shadow of apology or expression of regret) of all dishonourable charges against me, & an admission that you had made them on insufficient grounds.

Sincerely yours

C. L. DODGSON[65]

It had been a foolish business, quite unnecessary and most undignified. Dodgson still managed to think kindly of the Tennysons, however (especially of the children), and after attending a lecture by a Dr Lewin on his cure for stammering, in June, 1872, he wrote to Tennyson to suggest that his son Lionel, who had suffered from the same trouble, might benefit from the treatment. Tennyson's reply was as follows:

June 23/72.

MY DEAR SIR

I am obliged to you for telling me of Dr Lewin, but as Lionel, who is at present with us, does not seem to care to consult him, & as his stammering is much ameliorated & will possibly pass or nearly pass away with advancing life, I scarce think it worth while to send him to Sheffield.

Yours very truly,

A. TENNYSON[66]

Something had been irretrievably lost. After such a display of duelling-

Above: *'It won't come smooth'*,
Irene MacDonald, 1863. Below:
George MacDonald and Lily, 1863

ground punctilio, no friendship could have survived undamaged, and Dodgson did not seriously attempt to take up the threads. The glad cry of '*Dies mirabilis!*' echoes sadly as we read his brief diary entry of October 6th, 1892: 'Death of Alfred Tennyson.'

Three

The story of Dodgson's relations with Tennyson – not an uncommon sequence of youthful enthusiasm and eventual disillusionment – has taken us beyond the events of the eighteen-fifties. But there may be an advantage in this, if it has taught us something of Dodgson's character that we shall anyway have to learn by an accumulation of small instances. Endowed with a most exacting conscience, he set himself the highest standards of personal conduct and was incessantly engaged in a struggle for perfection. Thus from one aspect he might appear fussy, difficult, touchy; from another – the side that was turned most often to women and children – he would be all generosity and kindness. Of his essential goodness there is no doubt; but an artist had been mixed up with a puritan – and Dodgson's goodness was not of the sort that makes for inner tranquillity. A man of lower ideals, less jealous of his own integrity, would never have involved himself in that correspondence with Tennyson, nor driven himself so uncompromisingly into some of the difficulties of his later life.

Basically, Dodgson – a fastidious non-smoker and a very moderate drinker – probably had little except their mutual love of the beautiful in common with Tennyson, who smoked like a chimney and drank port by the pint. On the other hand, George MacDonald, poet, novelist, writer for children and Christian philosopher and teacher, was a man entirely after Dodgson's own heart.

Dodgson's endless but unsuccessful quest for a cure for his stammer, which we have encountered in a later phase at the end of his acquaintance with Tennyson, was the prime cause of his first meeting with MacDonald; for he was introduced to him by Dr James Hunt, the great authority on stammering, when he consulted him at his house at Ore, near Hastings, in 1859. This was the beginning of a friendship that proved rewarding to them both. Each was a Christian teacher with no great wish to be called 'the Rev.',* and with a mystical longing for a poetic fulfilment that was not wholly Christian; Lewis Carroll by way of the little door into the garden, perhaps; MacDonald surely up a magic staircase (for he had a great passion for stairs). The gaiety in both men was mixed with sadness. It is pleasant to know that Dodgson was one of those who could make MacDonald laugh – for he needed his laughter. 'How happily could my father laugh over this loving humorist's impromptu drawings', said his son Greville, 'full of the absurdities, mock-maxims and erratic logic, so dear to the child-heart, young or old!' He could 'laugh till tears ran at his friend's ridicule of smug formalism and copy-book maxims'.[67] This was still the young Dodgson who had written *Useful and Instructive Poetry* with the moral: 'Never stew your sister.' Formalism of a kind became necessary to him; there was always too much nervous tension to nourish smugness.

---

*In thanking a friend for a personally inscribed copy of a book in 1896, Dodgson wrote 'I have erased the words "The Rev.", which do not seem to me to suit the inside of a book.' (Letter to Mr Langbridge, Alfred C. Berol Collection, New York University.)

The children of George MacDonald seem to have been the first of the many who knew him as 'Uncle Dodgson'. When Greville was about four, in 1850, he sat to Alexander Munro, the sculptor, for his fountain of the boy and dolphin in Hyde Park. Dodgson visited the studio and endeavoured to persuade Greville, who wore his hair long, of the advantage of having a marble head of his own which would not have to be painfully brushed and combed. 'Do you hear *that*, Mary?' said the little boy to his sister, 'It needn't be combed!' But Dodgson called the joke off when further reflection suggested to Greville that he wouldn't be able to speak.[68]

Greville MacDonald has recorded that 'one annual treat was Uncle Dodgson taking us to the Polytechnic for the entrancing "dissolving views" of fairytales, or to go down in the diving bell, or watch the mechanical athlete *Léotard*. There was also the Coliseum in Albany Street, with its storms by land and sea on a wonderful stage, and its great panorama of London. And there was Cremer's toy-shop in Regent Street – not to mention bath-buns and gingerbeer – all associated in my memory with the adorable writer of "Alice".' Here is evidence enough that Dodgson could make himself pleasant to little boys when he wanted to, which latterly was not often – but his earliest surviving letters to children outside his own family were sent to a little girl, Greville's sister Mary.

These are highly entertaining letters and contain some of his most amusing nonsense. The first letter (May 23rd, 1864) opens with a splendid piece of bogus science:

'It's been so frightfully hot here that I've been almost too weak to hold a pen, and even if I had been able, there was no ink – it had all evaporated into a cloud of black steam, and in that state it has been floating about the room, inking the walls and ceiling till they're hardly fit to be seen: today it is cooler, and a little has come back into the ink-bottle in the form of black snow – there will soon be enough for me to write . . .'

He went on to explain that the hot weather had made him so sad and sulky that he had thrown a book at the head of a visitor, the Bishop of Oxford, 'which I am afraid hurt him a good deal'.* And then, thinking perhaps that he had gone too far, and that Mary MacDonald might report this act of violence to her father, he added:

'Mem: this isn't quite true – so you needn't believe it – Don't be in such a hurry to believe next time – I'll tell you why – If you set to work to believe everything, you will tire out the muscles of your mind, and then you'll be so weak you won't be able to believe the simplest true things. Only last week a friend of mine set to work to believe Jack-the-giant-killer. He managed to do it, but he was so exhausted by it that when I told him it was raining (which was true) he *couldn't* believe it, but rushed out into the street without his hat or umbrella. . . .'

*The Bishop of Oxford, who ordained Dodgson, was Samuel Wilberforce ('Soapy Sam'), and quite a lot of people would have been glad to throw a book at his head. It would be rash to infer a piece of wishful thinking on Dodgson's part, however, for he had often agreed with Wilberforce in the past, though he did not share his views on the dangers of theatregoing for the clergy nor support his stand in the controversy on Church Ritual.

There is a parable here for students of *Finnegan's Wake* or the later works of Picasso. In another letter of the same year, after apologising to Mary for not having written earlier, Dodgson went on to say:

'Do not suppose I didn't *write*, hundreds of times: the difficulty has been with the *directing* – I directed the letters so violently at first, that they went far beyond their mark – some of them were picked up at the other end of Russia. Last week I made a very near shot, and actually succeeded in putting "Earl's Terrace, Kensington", only I overdid the number, and put 12000, instead of 12. If you enquire for the letter at No. 12000, I daresay they'll give it you. After that, I fell into a feeble state of health, and directed the letters so gently that one of them only reached the other side of the room . . .'.[69]

By this time Dodgson had already completed, though he had not published, *Alice's Adventures in Wonderland*, and in these letters, which it is important to remember were called forth by a child, he was writing inspired nonsense in no way inferior to that in 'Alice'. Indeed, as with the 'Alice' books, the style and thought in these and other passages of his letters to children cannot be fully appreciated except by adults. This does not mean, of course, that the fun in 'Alice' and the letters could not be whole-heartedly enjoyed by the children for whom it was primarily intended – they enjoyed it enormously at the time and their successors will go on enjoying it into a distant future. But it does suggest that the secret of the great children's classics – and how few they are! – lies in the acceptance of no strongly marked frontier between childish and adult thought and language. A limpid prose that can hold the attention of grown-ups is that most likely to retain the affection of children, as Kenneth Grahame and Beatrix Potter understood, though the mixture must be infinitely subtle and delicate.

Dodgson poured into his letters to children a great quantity of delightful nonsense that might, if he had been a different man, have gone into another children's classic. Just occasionally we can trace a link between one of these letters and a passage in his published works. The letter to Mary MacDonald on 'believing', for example, has reminded Mr R. L. Green that the White Queen in *Through the Looking-Glass* sometimes 'believed as many as six impossible things before breakfast'. But to read Lewis Carroll's 'Letters to his Child-friends' is to be impressed by his unselfishness and to realise that here, as in the 'Alice' books, his immediate aim was to afford pleasure to children. He gave the best of his talent to that end, without ulterior motive. If this fact had been properly taken to heart, we might have been spared some of the more sophisticated interpretations of his fantasies which have been published.

Four

'An unimaginative person', said Ruskin, 'can neither be reverent nor kind.' It is a perceptive remark, and may properly be applied to C. L. Dodgson, in whom there was much kindness, not always revealed on surface acquaintance, and deep inherent reverence. This being the case, it was natural that he should have been greatly exercised in his mind when the time came for him to decide whether he should take Holy Orders, a necessary step if he was to continue in his Christ Church Studentship, which he had no wish to abandon.

Many years later (September 10th, 1885) he wrote an important letter to his cousin and godson William Wilcox, who was then himself contemplating the priesthood, which will be read with interest:

'. . . I will tell you a few facts about myself, which may be useful to you. When I was about 19, the Studentships at Ch. Ch. were in the gift of the Dean & Chapter – each Canon having a turn: & Dr Pusey, having a turn, sent for me, & told me he would like to nominate me, but had made a rule to nominate *only* those who were going to take Holy Orders. I told him that was my intention, & he nominated me. That was a sort of "condition", no doubt: but I am quite sure, if I had told him, when the time came to be ordained, that I had changed my mind, he would not have considered it as in any way a breach of contract.

When I reached the age for taking Deacon's Orders, I found myself established as the Mathematical Lecturer, & with no sort of inclination to give it up & take parochial work: & I had grave doubts whether it would not be my duty *not* to take Orders. I took advice on this point (Bp Wilberforce was one that I applied to), & came to the conclusion that, so far from educational work (even Mathematics) being unfit occupation for a clergyman, it was distinctly a *good* thing that many of our educators should be men in Holy Orders.

And a further doubt occurred – I could not feel sure that I should ever wish to take *Priest's* Orders – And I asked Dr Liddon whether he thought I shd be justified in taking Deacon's Orders as a sort of experiment, which would enable me to try how the occupation of a clergyman suited me, & *then* decide whether I would take full Orders. He said "most certainly" – & that a Deacon is in a totally different position from a Priest: & much more free to regard himself as *practically* a layman. So I took Deacon's Orders in that spirit. And now, for several reasons, I have given up all idea of taking full Orders, & regard myself (tho' occasionally doing small clerical acts, such as helping at the Holy Communion) as practically a layman.'[70]

This was Dodgson's view of his commitments as he looked back, when he was past fifty, on his career as a clergyman. In summarising the story, he did not touch on many considerations that had been important to him at the time.

It was, no doubt, the general intention in his family, from very early days, that he should marry and settle down as a parish priest in one of the Christ Church livings, as his father had done. Canon Dodgson diligently proposed to him a system of personal saving and insurance which had this in prospect, but Dodgson eventually came to the decision 'that it will be best not to effect any insurance at present, but simply to save as much as I reasonably can from year to year. If at any future period I contemplate marriage (of which I see no present likelihood), it will be quite time enough to begin paying the premium then.' (Diary, July 31st, 1857.)

That he was still a bachelor when the time came for him to take a decision about his ordination must obviously have been an influencing factor, for the idea of relinquishing an agreeable existence at Christ Church to settle down as a solitary country curate or parson cannot have had many attractions. Moreover, there were other important considerations. Dodgson was already an ardent theatregoer; yet Bishop Wilberforce – to whose pronouncements as Bishop of Oxford Dodgson was obliged to give ear – had expressed the opinion that the 'resolution to attend theatres or operas was an absolute disqualification for Holy Orders', so far as the parochial clergy was concerned.[71] And, perhaps most conclusive of all, there was the disability of his stammer.

In view of all these obstacles, it is not surprising that Dodgson should have abandoned any half-formed idea of attempting parochial work. That he felt himself generally unfitted for the day-to-day encounters of a parish can be gathered from a remark which he made in his diary after an argument with his brother Wilfred on college duties and the need for submission to discipline (in which Dodgson apparently believed more strongly than Wilfred): 'This also suggests to me grave doubts as to the work of the ministry which I am looking forward to – if I find it so hard to prove a plain duty to one individual, and that one unpractised in argument, how can I ever be ready to face the countless sophisms and ingenious arguments against religion which a clergyman must meet with!' (Diary, February 2nd, 1857.)

We should certainly know more about Dodgson's emotional reactions as he approached ordination if the volumes of his diary covering the period April, 1858, to May, 1862, were not missing for he was much in the habit of committing his 'pious ejaculations' to paper – a common practice at the time. The end of each year saw him making touching confession of his shortcomings and registering his determination to do better in future with God's help. Thus, as 1857 became 1858, we find him compiling a list of things that could conveniently be learned by heart during his railway journeys, and continuing: 'What do I propose as the work of the New Year?

(1) Reading for Ordination at the end of the year – and settling the subject finally and definitely in my mind.

(2) Making myself a competent Mathematical Lecturer for Christ Church.

(3) Constant improvements of habits of activity, punctuality, etc.

On all which and other good works I pray God's blessing in the first hour of 1858.'

It has already been suggested* that the most plausible explanation of the disappearance of four of Dodgson's diaries is that they were accidentally lost in the period following his death, after Collingwood had used them for his biography in 1898. One finds it hard to imagine any reason why the two earlier volumes, of 1854 and 1855, should have been deliberately destroyed. In regard to the missing volumes of 1858–62 the possibilities are admittedly different – and it has been surmised that Dodgson's sisters might have 'done away with' this portion of the diary, either because it revealed too openly their brother's religious doubts and difficulties or because it provided evidence of an unhappy love-affair (a question that will be discussed in a later chapter). However, a far better reason for destroying these volumes might be found, to quote R. L. Green, 'in certain other family matters which had no personal connection with Charles Dodgson himself, other than the constant help and sympathy which he was always so ready to extend to any member of his family'.[72] To be a little more precise: two of Dodgson's younger brothers were up at Oxford at about this time and may have caused him a certain amount of anxiety. But the balance of probability still lies with the accidental loss of all four volumes in the course of various family moves.

There is no evidence that Dodgson was disturbed in his faith, or that his

*Supra, p. 74.

hesitations over ordination derived from anything but his own sense of diffidence and unworthiness. In the end he decided to take Deacon's Orders – as he put it, 'as a sort of experiment' – and after studying at Cuddesdon was ordained by the Bishop of Oxford on December 22nd, 1861. The diary shows that, after he had been ordained Deacon, Dean Liddell maintained that he was obliged to take Priest's Orders, but on further reflection the Dean did not press the point.

That he sufficiently conquered his stammer to undertake even a small part in the services of the Church is a great proof of Dodgson's courage. There are records in the Croft baptismal register of his conducting baptisms on August 2nd, 1863, and on September 11th, 1864 – his entry as 'Officiating Minister' on that occasion followed immediately after an entry in his father's hand, a comparison of the two writings suggesting how closely he identified

Page 17.						
BAPTISMS solemnized in the Parish of *Croft* in the County of *York* in the Year 1864						
When Baptized.	Child's Christian Name.	Parents Name.		Abode.	Quality, Trade, or Profession.	By whom the Ceremony was performed.
		Christian.	Surname.			
1864 Augᵗ 14 No. 129.	George	Richard and Margaret	Benson	Dalton	Labourer	C Dodgson Rector
Septᵗ 11ᵗʰ No. 130.	Annie	Joseph and Anna	Gibbon	Croft	Labourer	C. L. Dodgson Officiating Minister

Extract from the Register of Baptisms, Croft, 1864, showing entries by C. L. Dodgson and his father

himself with his father. His diary shows that he first conducted a funeral on October 5th, 1862. He was able to preach occasional sermons, and did so with increasing success in his later years, though he always had to speak slowly. But the stammer – much though he worked at it, by reciting scenes from Shakespeare – remained a constant problem. The diary of Sunday, August 31st, 1862, records that he read the service that afternoon in the church at Putney, where his uncle lived: 'I got through it all with great success, till I came to read out the first verse of the hymn before the sermon, where the two words 'strife, strengthened', coming together were too much for me. . . .' And thirty years later his friend Vere Bayne noted (December 10th, 1891) that 'Dodgson read the Lesson in Mornᵍ Chapel, but got into difficulties towards the end'.[73] It was indeed the curse of his life.

Five

The late eighteenth-fifties saw Dodgson still working steadily at his mathematics and planning his first published book, *A Syllabus of Plane Algebraical Geometry* . . . 'by Charles Lutwidge Dodgson, M.A. Student and Mathematical Lecturer of Christ Church, Oxford', which appeared in 1860. This was a forbidding volume of about 170 pages, bound in black cloth, very dry, the precursor of numerous treatises of the same order. Part I only appeared. In the same year he published a little pamphlet, *Rules for Court Circular*, which was somewhat more characteristically Dodgsonian – being the rules of a new and peculiar card game he had invented – but not particularly attractive either.

These were the first tricklings from the dam, the first tentative drops in the great flood of print which was to be released by Dodgson – either under his own name, or, more rewardingly, under the pseudonym Lewis Carroll – throughout the next forty years. All that he published, famous and forgotten alike, was scrupulously listed by S. H. Williams in the classic 'Handbook' which he prepared in collaboration with Falconer Madan: a work revised for a re-issue by R. L. Green as *The Lewis Carroll Handbook*. No one who glances at that catalogue could deny that Dodgson was one of the busiest men and most industrious authors who ever lived; and we may reflect, further, that with his passion for print and paper Dodgson must have enjoyed himself. Unfortunately, no one who studies this mass of literature closely can fail to discover that it is not only a conglomeration of mathematics, logic, university ephemera, games, puzzles, children's stories and light verse, but also a striking mixture of good, bad and indifferent. It is hardly too fanciful to suppose that Dodgson's pen was bewitched, and that eventually the magic got out of control, though not before it had made its master one of the immortals.

On January 1st, 1861, he assumed a vast methodical labour by beginning his Register of Correspondence, which was to include details of every letter he wrote or received from that date until January 8th, 1898. Apart from forty-five sheets of the year 1861 which were discovered at Christ Church in 1952, none of this Letter Register has survived; but Warren Weaver has shown by careful study of the numbers he inscribed on his correspondence – the last is 98,721 – that from 1861 until about 1870 he registered approximately 460 items a year, from 1872 until about 1881 approximately 2,315 items a year, and from 1881 until his death approximately 3,760 items a year.* Not all the items were letters, though most of them were; sometimes he gave numbers to proof-sheets, pamphlets, etc.[74] The whole elaborate undertaking, which grew progressively more formidable, would have been a life's work in itself for a man of less energy.

The year 1861 also gives us another new picture: of an obstinate Dodgson rising to his feet for the first time in Congregation on November 20th and earnestly opposing any increase in the totally inadequate stipend of £40 a year paid to Benjamin Jowett for his vigorous services as Professor of Greek. Dodgson was a Conservative and Jowett a Liberal whose contribution to *Essays and Reviews* had revived allegations of heresy against him; but Dodgson took his stand on the objection that Jowett's was a Regius Professorship, which implied political influence in university affairs. Once on his feet, he said more than he 'at first meant, and defied them ever to tire out the opposition by

Professor Jowett

*His correspondence as Curator of the Common Room at Christ Church (1882–92) was additional to this, and has more than five thousand items.

perpetually bringing the question on', adding the diary note: '*Mem*: if I ever speak again I will try to say no more than I had resolved before rising.' Two days later, inspired by the same affair, he published his first Oxford 'squib', a mild foretaste of his better-known and ingenious pamphlet *The New Method of Evaluation as applied to π which appeared in 1865*.

Dodgson did not write much of literary interest between 1858 and 1862: his main efforts were the story 'A Photographer's Day Out', a number of serious poems (one of which appeared in *All the Year Round*) and several humorous poems – of which two were notably successful, 'A Sea Dirge', in which he pretended to detest the sea-side which he actually loved, and 'Poeta Fit, non Nascitur'. Most of the verses were printed in *College Rhymes*, a termly publication which flourished at Oxford between 1859 and 1873, and which drew a large proportion of its contributions from members of Christ Church. Dodgson was editor of *College Rhymes* for the Michaelmas Term, 1862, and the Lent Term, 1863. He then resigned for an unknown reason, noting in his diary of March 25th, 1863, that he had written 'to some of the contributors to return them their MSS. and to ask whether they would help any future such magazine under my editorship'. But he never edited any other magazine.

Alice Liddell, photographed by Dodgson, circa 1859

Six

Meanwhile his friendship with Dean Liddell's children continued, the second daughter Alice attracting him more and more as she grew older. In February, 1861, after listing seven mathematical books that he had written or was writing and commenting 'doesn't it look grand?' he told his sister Mary Collingwood:

'My small friends the Liddells are all in the measles just now. I met them yesterday. Alice had been pronounced as commencing, & looked *awfully* melancholy – it was almost impossible to make her smile. I need not say I have given them a copy of *College Rhymes*, they say the Sea-Dirge is "not true" – rather a sweeping condemnation. . . .'[75]

Alice was now eight, a pretty child with an oval face, dark hair and shy fawn-like eyes. Dodgson's happy association with the children was tolerated, but he seems never to have been on really cordial terms either with their mother Mrs Liddell, or their father the Dean, whose determined flourishes with the new broom in college affairs increasingly upset him. It is not probable that he would have been invited to stay *en famille* with the Liddells, yet at the age of eighty Alice was quoted as telling the *Daily Dispatch*: 'I remember with great pride Mr Lewis Carroll's visits to Gogarth Abbey, Llandudno, which my father, Dean Liddell, took for several summers, and our games on the sandhills together.'[76]

This statement of Alice's (which, incidentally, may have been inaccurately reported), coupled with a confident local tradition that some at least of *Alice in Wonderland* was suggested by Dodgson's visits to Llandudno, has helped to create another of those minor mysteries which beset the student of Lewis Carroll. As there is no mention of any such visit in his surviving diaries, one is driven to conclude that Dodgson, if he visited the Liddells at Llandudno at all, did so in the period April, 1858–May, 1862, for which his diaries are missing; he is surely unlikely to have failed to record such a significant occasion. But the 'Gogarth Abbey' to which Alice refers is apparently identical with 'Penmorfa' (now known as the 'Gogarth Hotel'), the house which Dean Liddell built for his family on land purchased in 1861 and which – according to his biographer H. L. Thompson – was excessively slow in building and was not ready for occupation until 1865.[77] It seems, however, that Thompson was mistaken, and that the Liddells first occupied the house in the summer of 1862.

Thus the problem of Lewis Carroll's alleged association with Llandudno bristles with difficulties. A question-mark lingers over the town, persistent as the grin of the Cheshire Cat.

The evidence assembled by Mr R. L. Green, who has gone into the question more thoroughly than anyone else, and published by him in his edition of the Diaries, tends to the conclusion that Lewis Carroll never went to Llandudno at all. In his diary for April, 1863, Dodgson recorded a visit to the Liddells at Charlton Kings, near Cheltenham, which is the only certain visit he paid to them away from Oxford. But we need not be dogmatic. Perhaps he *did* stay at Llandudno with the Liddells – maybe in lodgings on his own, or in some house that they rented before 'Penmorfa' was built. Perhaps the wild rabbits that scurried over the Great Orme's Head *did* turn his thoughts towards rabbit-holes. Perhaps the long stretch of wet sand *did* provide a setting for the

Gryphon and the Mock Turtle. . . . But he had many other opportunities of observing rabbit-holes and sand (he stayed often with his aunts at Hastings, for instance, during this period and was certainly there in 1860). Alas, the local pride of Llandudno is involved; otherwise, the matter has little importance.

Whether or not he amused the Liddell sisters at Llandudno, and probably he never did, we know on Alice's authority that Dodgson had told them 'many, many stories'[78] before, on July 4th, 1862, he and his audience embarked on the Isis for one of the most famous pieces of story-telling in the history of the world.

Alice Liddell, photographed by Dodgson in 1862

Opposite: *Alice Jane Donkin posing for 'The Elopement', taken by Dodgson, Barmby Moor, 9 October, 1862*

Alice

One

Little girls are rarely seen in Oxford colleges. Married dons live outside the precincts – some as far away as North Oxford or Boar's Hill – and they do not encourage visits from their daughters except on special occasions: nor, for that matter, do married undergraduates (a recent phenomenon). Occasionally a crocodile of schoolgirls, shadowed by the grey stone walls, advances deliberately on hall and chapel; or a solitary child jumps doggedly in a rain-puddle until its elders, closing the guide-book, invite it to desist. But, from a combination of awe and apathy, young visitors to Oxford tend to be subdued.

'Youth is full of pleasance, age is full of care'; in an ancient college the voice of a child rings incongruously; elders of learning may resent it, as being, in more ways than one, a disturbing challenge. Rarely indeed do children live in these surroundings at a university – only, as a rule, when the Head of a college is also the head of a growing family in his official residence. Alice Pleasance Liddell and her sisters were privileged little girls.

As time went on, and as they developed into attractive young women, surrounded by several hundred susceptible young men, the privilege brought them a great deal of fun and just a little danger – there was some justification for Mrs Liddell's vigilance. So long as they remained children, few members of Christ Church took an active interest in them. There was always Mr Dodgson, though, who had watched them playing in the Deanery garden from his window in the library when he was sub-librarian, and whose eyes did not cease to brighten whenever he saw them. . . .

Two

Tom Quad at Christ Church is the largest quadrangle in Oxford. If you stood at the gate, gazing across the grass and the pool called 'Mercury', and happened to see three little girls coming out of the Deanery front-door on the far side, they would look very small – almost like specks in the distance. And so must Ina (aged thirteen), Alice (aged ten) and Edith Liddell (who was eight) have appeared to anyone watching them in the early afternoon of July 4th, 1862, as, in their white cotton dresses, big-brimmed hats, white openwork socks and black shoes, they walked under the escort of Miss Prickett along the gravel path – it is now paved with stone – from the Deanery to the Hall archway, and disappeared from view in the direction of Mr Dodgson's rooms in the Old Library.

It was an innocent little party, giving no indication that it was about to play an essential part in work of literary importance. The three children went in to Mr Dodgson's rooms and presently re-emerged, freed from Miss Prickett's restraining hand, in the safe but more exciting company of two clergymen of the Church of England.

Dodgson had had lunch with a friend, F. H. Atkinson, and a Mrs and Miss Peters. After he had taken their photographs and shown them his album, they had departed for the museum. Then he had signalled a festive occasion by assuming a hard white straw-hat instead of a topper and white flannel trousers instead of his usual black; he still retained his black boots. Alice remembered that, as usual, he 'carried himself upright, almost more than upright, as if he had swallowed a poker'.

Robinson Duckworth, then a fellow of Trinity and later Sub-Dean and Canon of Westminster, was an excellent choice for the fifth member of the

One of Tenniel's interpretations of Alice taken from Alice's Adventures in Wonderland

Folly Bridge

expedition. He had been on similar excursions before and the three Liddells knew him quite well. Like Dodgson, he remained a life-long bachelor, but he was fond of children and had a powerful and rich sense of humour, as well as a pleasant singing voice. Others may have enjoyed the 'Alice' books as much as he did; no one has enjoyed them more.

With the men carrying the picnic-baskets, the party made their way through Christ Church Meadows to Folly Bridge, chose their boat and set off – up-stream for a change, because they usually went down-stream. Duckworth rowed stroke, Dodgson bow. At what stage in the afternoon Lewis Carroll began to tell his story of *Alice's Adventures Under Ground* is not exactly known, but Duckworth testified that it 'was actually composed and spoken *over my shoulder* for the benefit of Alice Liddell, who was acting as "cox" of our gig. I remember turning round and saying, "Dodgson, is this an extempore romance of yours?" And he replied, "Yes, I'm inventing as we go along"'.

Twenty-five years later, Lewis Carroll well remembered this day that saw the beginning of 'Alice':

'Full many a year has slipped away, since that "golden afternoon" that gave thee birth, but I can call it up almost as clearly as if it were yesterday – the cloudless blue above, the watery mirror below, the boat drifting idly on its way, the tinkle of the drops that fell from the oars, as they waved so sleepily to and fro, and (the one bright gleam of life in all the slumberous scene) the three eager faces, hungry for news of fairyland, and who would not be said "nay" to: from whose lips "Tell us a story, please," had all the stern immutability of Fate!'

Elsewhere in the same article (in *The Theatre* for April, 1887) Lewis Carroll recalled how, 'in a desperate attempt to strike out some new line of fairy-lore', he had sent his heroine 'straight down a rabbit-hole, to begin with, without the least idea what was to happen afterwards'.

Alice and Duckworth have both declared that the day was fine and confirmed Lewis Carroll's recollection of 'the cloudless blue above'. Canon Duckworth's letter in which he mentioned 'that beautiful summer afternoon' has already been quoted.* Alice later described in the *Cornhill Magazine* (July, 1932) 'that blazing summer afternoon with the heat haze shimmering over the meadows where the party landed to shelter for awhile in the shadow cast by the haycocks near Godstow'.

One would have supposed that such unanimity of testimony must be conclusive of a 'golden afternoon'. But ours is a sceptical age. A correspondence in the *Observer* in 1950 provoked an enquiry at the Meteorological Office, which showed that July 4th, 1862, at Oxford was 'cool and rather wet'. The weather record affirmed, most unpoetically, that in the twenty-four hours from 10 a.m. on July 4th, 0·17 of an inch of rain fell, mostly between 2 p.m. on the 4th and 2 a.m. on the 5th.

It is a little difficult to know what to make of this. The essential fact remains that the weather was good enough for the expedition to be carried through without any immediate adverse comment from Dodgson in his diary. Admittedly, it had been an uncertain summer. Dodgson had intended to take the children on the river the previous day (July 3rd) if it had not rained – and it had also undoubtedly rained, very heavily, a fortnight before when Duckworth and he, accompanied by his sisters Fanny and Elizabeth, had escorted the three Liddells on an expedition to Nuneham. Perhaps the memory of other sunny afternoons on the river misled the three principals of July 4th into assuming that the most famous of all their outings was made under cloudless skies. If they were mistaken, if the sun was weaker and more intermittent than they later imagined, romantics will allow them a degree of poetic licence. For, to adapt a phrase of George Stephenson's, *Alice in Wonderland* – despite the Meteorological Office's wet-blanket – has long been 'bottled sunshine'.

Anyway, the boat and its crew went three miles up the river to Godstow, and, according to Alice, sheltered for a while 'in the shadow cast by the haycocks'. Lewis Carroll's stories that afternoon seemed to her even 'better than usual'. But the time inevitably came to pack up the picnic-baskets, and later the host methodically described the day:

'Duckworth and I made an expedition *up* the river to Godstow with the three Liddells: we had tea on the bank there, and did not reach Christ Church again till quarter past eight, when we took them on to my rooms to see my collection of micro-photographs, and restored them to the Deanery just before nine.'

On the opposite page of the diary, he added on February 10th, 1863: 'On
Supra, p. 22.

which occasion I told them the fairy-tale of *Alice's Adventures Under Ground*, which I undertook to write out for Alice. . . .'

Duckworth remembered 'how, when he had conducted the three children back to the Deanery, Alice said, as she bade us goodnight, "Oh, Mr Dodgson, I wish you would write out Alice's Adventures for me." He said he should try, and he afterwards told me that he sat up nearly the whole night, committing to a MS. book his recollections of the drolleries with which he had enlivened the afternoon.'[79]

Three

The decisive day was over, though for Dodgson the process of creation had by no means ended. Whether or not he actually worked the whole of that night, as Duckworth declared, his diary shows that the idea of committing his entertainment to paper had taken hold of him, for on the way up to London the next day, July 5th, to see the 1862 Exhibition, he wrote out the 'headings' – whatever that may mean – of *Alice's Adventures Under Ground*.

On August 1st he heard the three Liddells sing 'Beautiful Star', the popular song by J. M. Sayles – a significant occasion, because this was the song parodied in 'Alice' under the title 'Turtle Soup', the line 'Star of the evening, beautiful Star' becoming 'Soup of the evening, beautiful soup!' and the elongated vowels 'Beau-ootiful Soo-oop!' poking fun at the conscientious performers in the Deanery as well as at a multitude of professionals outside. A few days later (August 6th) he took the children on another trip to Godstow, this time in the company of A. G. Vernon Harcourt, Senior Student of Christ Church. Dodgson tried to escape his usual rôle by sponsoring a game called 'the Ural Mountains'; when this proved unpopular, he 'had to go on with my interminable fairy-tale of *Alice's Adventures*'.

During the next few weeks he saw little of the Deanery family. Mrs Liddell may have felt that the friendship with her daughters was becoming too close; at all events, she was in one of her frigid moods, and when Dodgson invited her help on October 28th, on behalf of a local artist whom he had engaged to colour some of his photographs of the children, 'she simply evaded the question'. 'I have been out of her good graces ever since Lord Newry's business', commented Dodgson mysteriously.

When he happened to meet Ina, Alice and Edith in the quadrangle on November 13th and stopped to talk to them, he called this 'a rare event of late'. Perhaps Alice then reminded him of his promise about the book, for the same diary entry continues: 'Began writing the fairy-tale for Alice, which I told them July 4th, going to Godstow – I hope to finish it by Christmas.' This presumably refers to the formal manuscript he was preparing; rough notes will already have been in existence.

The whole association with the young Liddells seems to have been governed by the whims of Mrs Liddell, and these in turn were probably influenced by the caution natural to a Victorian mother, by a little mild jealousy, and by doubts whether any grown-up man could have an entirely disinterested love for her children. That Lewis Carroll was an unusual man may be admitted, but the whole story of his life, and the many unclouded memories that he left behind with his child-friends, leaves no question that he did possess, to an exceptional degree, this rare gift of winning and deserving a child's confidence.

In the case of the young Liddells, then, we see periods of close association

Alice

Dodgson's drawing and title pages for Alice's Adventures Under Ground

alternating with long periods of separation. The children's obvious delight in 'Mr Dodgson's' companionship often made them petition their mother to be allowed to see him. Thus in the diary of November 21st, 1862, Dodgson says that he 'was surprised by a message from Mrs Liddell asking whether the children should come over to me, or if I would go to them.' When he arrived at the Deanery, he 'found that Alice and Edith had originated the idea . . . . Mrs Liddell did not appear'.

The year 1863, when Alice was eleven, was the last in which Dodgson saw her with any regularity. He took her to watch the fireworks and illuminations in celebration of the marriage of Edward and Alexandra, and was delighted to notice how much she enjoyed herself. In April he stayed at Cheltenham, visiting the children at their grandparents' house at near-by Charlton Kings. The river expeditions were resumed that summer, but their enjoyment was diminished by the participation of Miss Prickett, whose presence was now required by Mrs. Liddell.

Left: *Rhoda Liddell*. Centre: *The Liddell sisters painted by Sir William Blake Richmond*. Right: *photograph of the Liddell sisters*

Dodgson admitted that Ina, at fourteen, was 'now so tall as to look odd without an escort'. In fact, a painting of the three sisters by W. B. Richmond shows that they had all inherited their mother's dark beauty – a beauty which Richmond thought to be 'of a Spanish type' – and were maturing early. In 1864 Mrs Liddell decided not to let any of the children go out on the river with Lewis Carroll any more ('rather superfluous caution', he thought). He made a new friend in December, 1864 of Ellen Terry, who was nearly seventeen. And in May, 1865, he found thirteen-year-old Alice 'changed a good deal, and hardly for the better – probably going through the usual awkward stage of transition'.

The Alice idyll had run its course. Henceforth her meetings with Lewis Carroll were relatively few and comparatively formal. But, for simply being receptive and trusting and good, she had earned an unusual reward; she had fired the train of genius and left behind her a childhood that would be remembered.

Four   **Alice**

Lewis Carroll finished writing *Alice's Adventures Under Ground* some time before
February 10th, 1863, and soon afterwards sent it to his friend George Mac-
Donald for his opinion. Mrs MacDonald read the manuscript to her assembled
family with such success that the verdict was not in doubt. On May 9th, 1863,
the author noted that they wished him to publish it.

So much is clear from the diary. But Duckworth maintained[80] that Henry
Kingsley saw the manuscript at the Deanery, and that it was Kingsley's
advocacy – to which Duckworth added his own (coupled with a warm
recommendation of John Tenniel as the illustrator) – that induced Dodgson to
decide on publication. Both Kingsley and Duckworth presumably gave advice
at some point, but as it stands, this account is open to doubt; for Dodgson
himself embarked on the slow process of illustrating his original manuscript
for Alice's benefit, and this took him such a long time that he did not get it done
until the autumn of 1864, so that he only sent the manuscript book to Alice

An engraving of Sir John Tenniel

at the Deanery on November 26th, 1864.

By that time – and after much consultation with many people – several things had happened. Dodgson had enlarged the 18,000 words of *Alice's Adventures Under Ground* into the 35,000 words of his famous book; and John Tenniel had read it, had consented to draw and was well advanced on the illustrations.

Two distinct undertakings were therefore in progress, and were overlapping. Mr Dodgson was painstakingly decorating the shorter manuscript as his private present for Alice Liddell – the *'Ur-Alice'*, as the Germans would call it – and John Tenniel, working on the enlarged version, was making the professional illustrations which all the world knows and which will never be bettered. The artist was 'very friendly' from the first, when Dodgson called on him in January, 1864, with an introduction from Tom Taylor. Though increasingly busy with his work for *Punch*, Tenniel was still not averse to undertaking the occasional illustration of books, especially when he could introduce plenty of animals, which he was particularly good at. The French artist J. J. Grandville apparently inspired him in his animal fantasies.

Tenniel had made his name with his drawings for the Rev Thomas James's version of *Æsop's Fables*. These had conditioned his style in such later com-

Illustrations by Tenniel for Aesop's Fables *which gave rise to his choice as the illustrator for* Alice

missions as the illustration of Tupper's *Proverbial Philosophy* and Barham's *Ingoldsby Legends*. By the time he came to 'Alice', a dignified and somewhat archaic formalism was ripe for blending with the lighter touch of the *Punch* artist. It is interesting to notice, on looking back, that the girl who is having a letter read to her in Tupper's chapter 'Of Writing' is almost a prototype of Alice herself; while the solemn trial scene illustrating Tupper's reflections 'Of Estimating Character' is parodied in the comic trial of the Knave of Hearts.

Tom Taylor's recommendation would naturally have predisposed Tenniel in Dodgson's favour, and after reading the text (or parts of it, though one must assume it was virtually complete by now) he anounced his willingness to collaborate in April, 1864. Dodgson promptly got into touch with the Clarendon Press at Oxford – whom he had decided should print the book at his expense – and was able to send Tenniel the first 'slip proofs' (galley-proofs, they would now be called) as early as May 2nd. It was not until the following

year, when many of the drawings were already done, that Dodgson introduced
Tenniel to a photograph of Mary Hilton Badcock, daughter of Canon Badcock
of Ripon, whom he recommended as an excellent model for Alice.[81] But
Tenniel did not like using models. The resemblance to Mary Badcock, not
striking in *Alice in Wonderland*, is only slightly more suggestive in *Through the
Looking-Glass*. Moreover, Professor A. Adrian in his biography of Mark
Lemon (1966) has proposed Kate Lemon as the model of the second Alice.
Anyway, it is probable that these girls provided, at most, only a small part of
Tenniel's inspiration, and that he was largely influenced by his own pre-
conception of an ideal maiden. Whether Lewis Carroll's own drawings affected
him appreciably is doubtful.

The book was really making progress at last. Dodgson gave anxious
thoughts to a suitable title. *Alice's Adventures Under Ground* was pronounced
'too like a lesson book about mines'. He contemplated *Alice's Golden Hour* –
but there was already in existence a book called *Lilian's Golden Hours*. Then

he wondered about *Alice Among the Elves* (or, if need be, among the Goblins). *Alice's hour in Elf-land? Alice's doings in Elf-land* (or in Wonderland)? By a process of elimination he came to *Alice's Adventures in Wonderland*, and on June 10th he announced his preference for this title in a letter to Tom Taylor.[82]

Lewis Carroll was fortunate in being able to persuade a leading firm like Macmillan's to publish 'Alice' on a commission basis. It was a natural choice in every way; Macmillan's were publishers for Oxford University; and Kingsley's *The Water Babies*, in its dark-green binding, had been issued by them as recently as May, 1863. For his own binding, Lewis Carroll preferred red. The following letters in Macmillan's files carry the story of 'Alice' to the end of 1864:

Ch. Ch. Oxford,
Nov. 11. 1864.

DEAR SIR,

I have been considering the question of the *colour* of *Alice's Adventures*, and have come to the conclusion that *bright red* will be the best – not the best, perhaps, artistically, but the most attractive to childish eyes. Can this colour be managed with the same smooth, bright cloth that you have in green?

Truly yours,
C. L. DODGSON

Ch. Ch. Oxford,
Nov. 20. 1864.

DEAR SIR,

I fear my little book *Alice's Adventures in Wonderland* cannot appear this year. Mr Tenniel writes that he is hopeless of completing the pictures by Xmas. The cause I do not know, but he writes in great trouble, having just lost his mother, and I have begged him to put the thing aside for the present. Under these circumstances what time should you advise our aiming at for bringing out the book? Would Easter be a good time, or would it be better to get it out before then?

I liked the specimen of red cloth you sent. I have not yet seen the *Children's Garland*, but will look at it.

Believe me yours truly,
C. L. DODGSON

Three pages from Alice's Adventures Under Ground

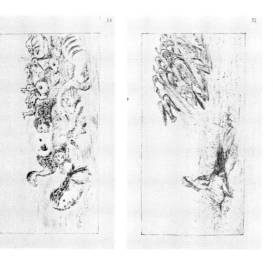

Ch. Ch. Oxford,   **Alice**

Dec. 16. 1864.

DEAR MR MACMILLAN,

I sent you off yesterday the whole of my little book in slip. It is the only complete copy I have, and I will call for it next week – on Tuesday, most likely. I hope you may not think it unfitted to come out under your auspices.

Believe me yours truly,

C. L. DODGSON

Five

Macmillan's did not think the book 'unfitted', though they may not have approached this children's story by an unknown Oxford clergyman with any great enthusiasm. When they sent Dodgson a specimen volume in May, 1865, he liked 'the look of it exceedingly'. He was now anxious to get the book published as quickly as possible, because his 'young friends . . . are all grown out of childhood so alarmingly fast'. Tenniel had checked his last proofs of the drawings by June 18th; 2,000 copies were printed off by the Clarendon Press by the end of June; and by July 4th, 1865 – three years to the day since the famous river expedition to Godstow – a special vellum-bound copy had been sent to Alice at the Deanery. Dodgson spent that day in London, where he met Alice with her father and sisters at the Royal Academy. If she had received her copy by then, she would no doubt have thanked him prettily, but Dodgson makes no mention of it in his diary.

Even now, there was still trouble in store for the long-delayed 'Alice'. The author went to Macmillan's on July 15th and 'wrote in twenty or more copies of "Alice" to go as presents to various friends'; but on July 20 he was compelled to call again on a less pleasant errand, in order to show Macmillan 'Tenniel's letter about the fairy-tale – he is entirely dissatisfied with the printing of the pictures, and I suppose we shall have to do it all again'. This drastic decision was, in fact, taken on August 2nd. The first edition was recalled after only forty-eight copies had been sold or (as was largely the case) given away. The printing was taken out of the hands of the Clarendon Press (to whom Dodgson in 1866 and 1867 paid £117 8s. 2d. in settlement for this and other work done for him by the Press) and given to Richard Clay; the type was re-set. The unbound sheets of the first edition were not, as the author originally intended, 'sold as waste paper', but were disposed of to Messrs. Appleton of New York who published them as the second (American) issue of the first edition in 1866. The true second edition of *Alice's Adventures in Wonderland*, printed by Clay, was published in November, 1865 (though it was dated 1866).

The story of these early issues and editions of 'Alice' is undoubtedly confusing. It has been necessary to tell it because its very complication has created a book-collectors' wonderland no less startling than that explored by Alice. An inscribed copy of the true first edition has fetched as much as £5,000; copies of the second edition have been priced up to £100 according to condition; and surviving copies of the Appleton issue have likewise been pursued as curiosities. Forgeries of the original title-page are not unknown.[83]

If Dodgson had deliberately set out to arouse the excitement of bibliographers, he could hardly have improved on the entirely fortuitous sequence of events that actually occurred. The most extraordinary thing is that it

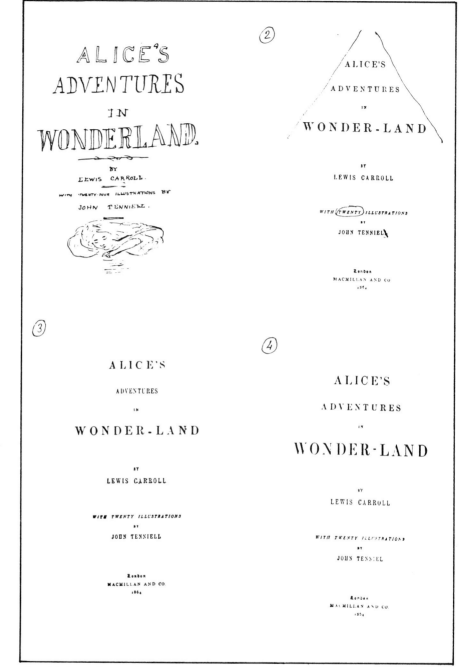

Trial title pages for Alice

should have been deemed necessary to withdraw the first edition at all. Dodgson wrote to Macmillan's on August 30th, 1865: 'If you have seen any of the new impression, I should be glad to know if the difference is *very* marked between it and the old, with regard to the pictures.' Whatever the publisher's opinion may have been, S. H. Williams, who compared the first and second editions, was at a loss to find the supposed defects of the first printing and actually thought that many of the woodcuts were sharper and better defined in the first edition than in the second, which was more lightly printed.[84]

Probably only someone as meticulous about the production of his books as Lewis Carroll would have bothered to have the whole work reprinted, though we must remember that the initial complaint came from Tenniel. However, it is gratifying to know that the author was entirely satisfied with the second edition when he received a copy of it on November 9th, 1865, considering it 'very *far* superior to the old, and in fact a perfect piece of artistic printing'.

Six

Dodgson was successful in recovering thirty-four of the issued copies of the first edition, and he presented them to a number of hospitals, including the Children's Hospital, Great Ormond Street, and the Oxford Infirmary.[85] If these books had been carefully locked up in cupboards they would in the long run have contributed most usefully to the revenue of the hospitals; but the majority probably fell to pieces in the hands of a long series of patients. Alice's vellum copy was also retrieved and exchanged for a new one – again a doubtful service, as it proved![86]

But it is a pleasure to revert, from the changes and chances of its printing, to the famous book itself. What sort of an impact did it make in a year that saw St Pancras Station completed and Lord John Russell as Prime Minister? The earliest recorded opinions of the first edition of *Alice in Wonderland* may be contained in two letters sent, apparently in August, 1865, to Dodgson's aunt Lucy Lutwidge by her friends Catherine Lucy Poole and F. M. Hartshorne. They are the more interesting as anticipating the eventual verdict of many other 'general readers'. Miss Poole said: 'The poetry caught my eye at once, and is just to my taste. . . . I had no idea Charles aspired to being a poet, but if he continues as he has begun, his hopes will be realised.' Miss Hartshorne was equally enthusiastic:

'I will add a little note to Lucy's letter to say how much I admire your nephew's book – the story is very clever & amusing and the opening lines are very charming. I hope the *real* "Alice" appreciates them as they deserve! We now remember seeing one of the illustrations (the Rabbit walking off after dropping his gloves and fan) in a publisher's illustrated catalogue & wondering what it could mean. The book is beautifully "got up" and with those excellent drawings is altogether most elegant. One could hardly have expected so much imagination and such graceful flowing lines from a mathematician; he must possess a great deal of poetic talent besides, & he proves that they are not incompatible one with another. I wish we had anything as pretty to send you in return.'[87]

The notices that 'Alice' received when it was sent out for review in November, 1865, tended to agree with the verdict of these two ladies. The *Reader* called it 'a glorious artistic treasure . . . a book to put on one's shelf as an antidote to a fit of the blues', and the *Pall Mall Gazette* wrote that 'this delightful little book is a children's feast and triumph of nonsense'. On the other hand, the *Athenaeum* thought it a 'stiff, over-wrought story', and the *Illustrated Times* 'too extravagantly absurd'.[88] But in the long run reviews do not matter. What is important in the case of any new book is that it should be read and recommended by those whose opinions are valued. Lewis Carroll took care to see that, of the seventy presentation copies that were distributed, a proportion fell into the hands of people with some influence in the literary or artistic world. Christina Rossetti's acknowledgment can be quoted:

'A thousand and one thanks – surely an appropriate number – for the funny pretty book you have so kindly sent me. My Mother and sister as well as myself made ourselves quite at home yesterday in Wonderland, and (if I am not shamefully old for such an avowal) I confess it would give me sincere pleasure to fall in with that conversational rabbit, that endearing puppy, that very sparkling dormouse. Of the Hatter's acquaintance I am not ambitious, and the March Hare may fairly remain an open question. . . .'[89]

By February, 1866, her brother, D. G. Rossetti, had also read 'Alice'. He thought '"Father William" and Alice's snatches of poetry . . . the funniest things he had seen in a long time'.[90]

We really have no idea how *Alice in Wonderland* was received by Archdeacon Dodgson or the rest of the author's family. Langford Reed has said that 'at the outset the good man was absolutely flabbergasted by its success,'[91] but he gives no authority for this statement. Remembering the father's nonsense letter to his son quoted on page 35, we may doubt whether he disapproved of the character of the book, or was unduly surprised by it, though he may well have been astonished at its quality.

Seven

By comparing *Alice's Adventures in Wonderland* with the original manuscript of *Alice's Adventures Under Ground*, which was published in facsimile in 1886, we can easily see what changes were made between the two versions. At first glance, they do not seem to be considerable; the story remains roughly the same. A second glance shows that the additions were many and important, as indeed they were bound to be, considering that the final version is nearly twice the length of the earlier.

In the original manuscript, we must first grow accustomed to the unfamiliar idea of seeing Lewis Carroll's own illustrations in the place of Tenniel's. As the earnestness of the amateur draughtsman occasionally rises in them to a

Dodgson's original drawing: 'Then followed the Knave of Hearts, carrying the King's Crown on a cushion'

weird frenzy that is almost Blake-like in its intensity, this is an exciting rather than a disappointing experience; Carroll's drawings, lacking Tenniel's professional accomplishment, could never have assisted 'Alice' to a popular

Tenniel's version: 'Off with her head!'

success, but, unlike Tenniel's, they are the work of a poet and have a private anguish which is more moving than it is amusing. They represent a genuine artistic achievement which has never been properly appreciated. It is probable that he used his sister Henrietta as his own model for Alice.

Lewis Carroll's neat script is easy to read. We recognise immediately such favourite pieces as the parodies of Watts and Southey, 'How doth the little crocodile' and 'You are old, Father William', and the parody of 'Star of the Evening', 'Beautiful Soup'. But a closer look shows that 'Speak roughly to your little boy', 'Twinkle, twinkle little bat', ''Tis the voice of the Lobster', and 'Will you walk a little faster' – which are parodies of G. W. Langford, Jane Taylor, Watts and Mary Howitt respectively – do not appear in the first version. The Mouse's 'tail' is different, too. Instead of opening with 'Fury said to a mouse, that he met in the house', it begins:

> We lived beneath the mat
> Warm and snug and fat
> But one woe, & that
> Was the cat!

And of course Lewis Carroll found it very much easier to devise the twists of the tail in his own handwriting than when he had to do the same thing in print;

The Mouse's tail drawn by Dodgson and set in type

a proof for the first edition in Christ Church Library shows the 'tail' set out straight and stiff, vertically; beside it is a card on which each line of the type has been carefully arranged and pasted by Lewis Carroll to make the tail.

There are many other small differences between the two versions; the major additions are the chapters 'Pig and Pepper' and 'A Mad Tea-party' and the trial scene. The original version contains a reference to the expedition to Nuneham which Dodgson had made on a very wet day, with his sisters and Duckworth and the three Liddells, a fortnight before the famous trip to Godstow. This has gone; and so, too, has a passage at the end of the story which mentions 'an ancient city, and a quiet river winding near it along the plain'. The general tendency in the alterations is away from parochial allusions and mere child's play towards what Falconer Madan has called 'more advanced and reasoned ingenuity'[92] – the result being a book that has kept the affection of children and won the admiration of adults.

Nevertheless, many allusions to people and things that were familiar to the young Liddells remain firmly embedded in the book. Dodgson himself was the Dodo (presumably a confession that when he stammered his name came out as 'Do-Do-Dodgson'), Duckworth was the Duck, Lorina was the Lory, Edith was the Eaglet – and Alice, of course, was Alice. The three little girls in the Dormouse's story, Elsie, Lacie and Tillie, are only the three Liddells in another disguise: Elsie stands for L. C., the initials of Lorina Charlotte; Lacie is an anagram of Alice; and Matilda (Tillie) was a family nickname for Edith. The lessons discussed by the Mock Turtle and the Gryphon are coloured by the children's experiences at the hands of Miss Prickett and several masters and mistresses who tried to teach them 'extras', including the Quadrille. 'Twinkle, twinkle little bat' is supposed to refer to Professor Bartholomew Price, who was nicknamed 'Bat', and the Mad Hatter is similarly alleged to have been inspired by Theophilus Carter, once a servitor of Christ Church and later a furniture dealer in the High.

But, though many contemporary references that might have amused the Liddells are undoubtedly preserved in 'Alice', it is highly dangerous to read too many allusions and hidden meanings into the book. Dodgson – who drew so much, even perhaps the Mouse's tail and Humpty Dumpty's fall, from subconscious memories of his childhood – did not construct his characters from observation, except in the most general sense; as he himself said, his ideas were wont to 'come of themselves'.[93] Even the Mad Hatter identification, which was established long before Dodgson died,* must be considered suspect. Bishop Strong, for instance, whose comments on Dodgson were always most intelligent, did not believe in it:

'One is often told that this or that particular person was the original from which the Hatter or some other character in the books was drawn. People say this, I think, because they cannot imagine that so simply convincing a character as the Hatter can have failed to exist in the world of fact, and because they cannot believe that anyone could have invented it. I do not think Dodgson observed people enough to construct his characters in that way. It will be remembered that he himself said that the last line of the "Hunting of the Snark" occurred to him by itself, and that the poem was written to explain it. I am sure that this was much more like the way he went to work than the other.'[94]

*See *supra*, p. 63.

How Dodgson's observations of people took animal form

If this convincing explanation of Lewis Carroll's method is accepted, we need not spend very long examining some of the far-fetched interpretations of character and incident in *Alice in Wonderland* that have been published. It is one thing to suggest that Dodgson may have been influenced by *The Water Babies* (though he can only have read the book when his own was far advanced), or that he may have named his 'caucus-race' after the manoeuvres of political or university elections; it is another thing to identify the Duchess with Bishop Wilberforce or the Cat with Cardinal Wiseman.[95] When we remember that Dodgson altered a passion-flower in *Through the Looking-Glass* to a tiger-lily, because of 'the sacred origin of the name', and repudiated the idea that the final scene of that book was based upon the triumphal conclusion of *Pilgrim's Progress*, 'saying that he would consider such trespassing on holy ground as highly irreverent'[96] – then, surely, it is not to be credited for a moment that he would have used either of the 'Alice' books as the vehicles of religious controversy?

Important specific influences on the 'Alice' books may be reduced to Edward Lear's nonsense verses and perhaps *The Water Babies*. The present writer has a personal theory that Dodgson may have got some hints from Chapter XI (Book I) of George Eliot's *The Mill on the Floss* (published in 1860) – 'Maggie Tries to Run Away from her Shadow'. But his originality remains unquestionable.

Alice in Wonderland owes its unique place in our literature to the fact that it was the work of a unique genius, that of a mathematician and logician who was also a humorist and a poet. It broke new ground because it was in no sense a goody-goody book but handled childhood freshly and without sententiousness. The outstanding achievement is the creation of a Dream World that is never for a moment unconvincing. If we must look, in the 'Alice' books, for any didactic Victorian message, perhaps we may find in them, as Peter Alexander has suggested, some such general warning as: 'Pay attention to the language you use but not too much attention. Remember that words were invented to refer to things.' The nearest parallel to the humorous method of Lewis Carroll is probably that of the Marx Brothers, whose dialogue not only has many verbal similarities with his, but who also, like him, assert one grand false proposition at the outset and so persuade their audiences to accept anything as possible.[97] It is as foolish to look for sustained satire in the one as in the other. Both have been based largely on a play with words, mixed with judicious slapstick, and set within the framework of an idiosyncratic view of the human situation; their purpose is entertainment. Lewis Carroll has one transcendent advantage – with his limpid prose he paints the colours of poetry.

The Freudian or psycho-analytical interpretation remains. For those who accept it, who see Charles Dodgson – with some justice – as a strongly repressed individual, and who apply the doctrine cautiously, not with prurience but with love and understanding, it may have its uses. It cannot touch the merit or detract from the achievement of 'Alice'. Indeed, Sir Herbert Read believes that 'such significance only adds to the value of such literature. . . . From our point of view, Lear is a better poet than Tennyson, Lewis Carroll has affinities with Shakespeare.'[98]

Alice, the Victorian child, still walks modestly forward with her patrician dignity and courage – through her own dream-adventures, through the applause, through the controversy: herself the simple answer, as she was the inspiration, for it all. In de la Mare's words, 'she wends serenely on like a quiet moon in a chequered sky'.[99]

Eight

The book that had begun its existence so unpropitiously soon showed that it was destined to live. But its progress was gradual rather than spectacular. In March, 1866, Dodgson told Macmillan that he had hoped for a larger sale, 'but perhaps unreasonably', and, when the idea of printing another 3,000 was mooted in August of that year, he was somewhat alarmed. However, he was pleased and surprised to find that after two years he had made a profit of £250 on his original expenditure of £380, which had included the illustrations. About 159,000 copies of 'Alice', in various editions, were printed in Great Britain during his lifetime, and by 1911 Macmillan's figure had advanced to 733,750 with the appearance of cheap editions. The book has subsequently gone on selling steadily, both in England and America, and since the expiration of the copyright in 1907 has brought profits to dozens of different publishers all over the world.

The price of the 1865 'Alice' was seven shillings and sixpence, reduced to six shillings for the second edition of 1866. Dodgson expressed his desire for a cheaper edition as soon as February 15th, 1869, when he wrote to Macmillan: 'My feeling is that the present price puts the book entirely out of the reach of many thousands of children of the middle classes, who might, I think, enjoy it (below that I don't think it would be appreciated).' And he added: 'The only point I really care for in the whole matter (and it *is* a source of very real pleasure to me) is that the book should be enjoyed by children – and the more in number, the better.' Yet he did not get his half-crown cheap edition until 1887, and on this question was presumably guided by Macmillan's advice.

Despite natural doubts as to her suitability for translation, 'Alice' soon crossed the channel, to France and Germany in 1869 and to Italy in 1872:

Alice, assise auprès de sa sœur sur le gazon, commençait à s'ennuyer de rester là à ne rien faire . . .

Alice fing an sich zu langweilen; sie sass schon lange bei ihrer Schwester am Ufer und hatte nichts zu thun . . .

Alice cominciava a sentirsi mortalmente stanca di sedere sul poggio, accanto a sua sorella, senza far nulla . . .

The emigrations inevitably worried the author, who, here as elsewhere, required of himself and others the strictest attention to detail. 'The mouse's tail had better be set up in an upright column to begin with,' he wrote to Macmillan of the French version in 1867, 'it is not worth while to take the trouble of zig-zagging it, till the words are definitely decided on.' Bill the Lizard also demanded consideration, because his name is not acceptable to continentals. He came through all right in French – '"Ah!" se dit Alice, "c'est donc Jacques qui va descendre"' – but he got into the German proofs as Bill. On October 22nd, 1868, Dodgson was writing to Macmillan: 'I think there will be no more to alter than the name of the Lizard, which I wanted changed from "Bill" to some German name. It occurs 20 or 30 times in the book, but I think the Printer might be trusted to attend to the corrections. . . .' Bill became

'Wabbel', not to English eyes an improvement.

Much more serious was the case of Father William, who sailed into French with 'Vous êtes vieux, Père Guillaume', but could not be allowed to take such a thoughtless plunge into German. This was, after all, a somewhat ribald song which might seriously have offended the Kaiser – and so we find a dignified compromise: 'Ihr seid alt, Vater Martin'. There were other doubts about the German proofs – 'By the way,' wrote Dodgson to Macmillan, 'will they be able to print the pictures properly in Germany? The proofs sent are very hideous.' He need not have worried about this, because the reproductions of the woodcuts in the first German edition were excellent.

The Italian translation has the distinction of being the first to alter the lettering in Tenniel's drawings, which in the French and German versions remained in English. 'DRINK ME' on the bottle was replaced by 'BEVI'. The Mad Hatter's hat, 'In this Style 10/6', was labelled 'Prezzo fisso L. 12'.

A very English little girl had set out on a long journey that was to bring her into the homes of many other children all over the world. Her creator Charles Dodgson watched her distant progress with some astonishment from his rooms at Christ Church, where life was not quite so amusing as in Wonderland; where mathematics had to be taken seriously; and where lizards were called Bill, and not Jacques or Wabbel or Tonio.

'You are old, Father William,'
the young man said . . . from
Alice's Adventures in
Wonderland

One

Frederick Locker once wrote a little essay, which he published in a book called *Patchwork*, about a Victorian drawing-room of the sixties. The room had gold wall-paper, sumptuous hangings and a brand-new, 'aggressive' crimson and orange carpet of velvet pile. There were humming-birds stifling under glass shades and magnificent paper-knives and smelling-bottles in velvet cases. There were books on the inlaid tables, 'depressing books – Books of Beauty, Views in the Holy Land, and Gems from our Poets, all elaborately bound'.

The mid-Victorian drawing-room was something so solemn and formidable that one could no more have contemplated disturbing its settled complacency than one would have thought of brawling in a cathedral. But, as Locker sat in this uncompromising drawing-room awaiting the return of his friends, he felt the urge to write down some verses. Discovering a large glass inkstand, he carried it cautiously and guiltily across the room to his chair. As he reached the middle of the room, the lower part of the inkstand, containing the ink, became detached from the top part which he was holding, and fell to the floor, 'rolling over and over, along the wretched crimson and orange velvet pile, and emptying its ample contents as it rolled'.

Although Locker's agony and embarrassment have no place in this biography, they may serve to suggest something of the terrifyingly respectable and conventional atmosphere into which *Alice in Wonderland* was born. The original illustrated manuscript was introduced into just such a drawing-room at the Christ Church Deanery, and it was surely on just such an inlaid table that Alice Liddell's vellum-bound copy must eventually have lain.

If 'Alice' lacked the explosive force of Locker's inkstand, the book carried the same radical challenge to complacency. Is it surprising that the critics should have been divided, and that relatively few first opinions should have been recorded? 'I want it to be a *table*-book,' Dodgson had written in one of his earliest letters to Macmillan's, but, though he had taken enormous pains over the printing and binding, *Alice in Wonderland* was never in danger of settling down with the Books of Beauty and the Views in the Holy Land.

The book was much too readable, and too often in the hands both of children and grown-ups, to be in danger of such a fate. The most remarkable thing about 'Alice' is that, though it springs from the very heart of the Victorian period, it is timeless in its appeal. This is a characteristic that it shares with other classics – a small band – that have similarly conquered the world. We best understand the importance of this factor when we compare 'Alice' with Kingsley's *The Water Babies*, which is cluttered up with Victoriana of all kinds and, even after rigorous pruning, can never be emancipated from the sixties.

But, though 'Alice' cannot 'date', its author is held fast in his period. The more paradoxical and irresponsible his humour, the more does it emphasise the earnestness of the shy Victorian clergyman whose frigidity could repel those who did not know him well and whose eccentricity grew with the success of his book. 'One of my tutors', wrote a Junior Student of Christ Church, E. K. Jupp, to his younger brother in 1868, 'is the man who wrote *Alice in Wonderland*. He looks something like the "Hatter", a little like the "Cheshire Cat" – most like the "Gryphon".'[100]

Two

'Alice', as we have seen, had required a long period of incubation, nearly three

'The King's argument was, that anything that had a head could be beheaded . . .' from Alice's Adventures in Wonderland

and a half years from the date of its inception in that summer of 1862 until it was well and truly published at the end of 1865 (though in a sense Lewis Carroll had been writing it much longer, ever since he was a little boy). Dodgson did not write much else of a humorous nature during these years, but he did produce his contribution to the Jowett controversy already mentioned, and his *Dynamics of a Particle*, which contains some entertaining parodies of Euclid as well as an extended reference to the famous contest between Gathorne-Hardy and Gladstone for the University seat in 1865. He also published his over-elaborate game of 'Croquet Castles', requiring ten balls, ten arches and five flags, which he had worked out with the young Liddells in the Deanery garden. His mathematical work was vigorously pursued and he brought out several pamphlets, among them the *Enunciations of Euclid* (1863) and the *Guide to the Mathematical Student* (1864). He continued to publish books and pamphlets on his special subjects, either anonymously or under his own name, at regular intervals throughout the rest of his life.

Dodgson's contributions to mathematics were not of lasting importance. As Bishop Strong has pointed out, [101] Dodgson's innate originality of mind was the chief danger in his mathematical books, as also in his writings on logic. He read comparatively little of the works of other mathematicians or logicians, preferring to evolve his theories out of his own mind. This method had its advantages, no doubt, yet it not only gave him a lot of unnecessary trouble but deprived him of the chance of escaping avoidable mistakes. In fact, he handled scientific matters in the same way as he dealt with conversational language, and the method was never likely to produce – nor did it produce – a mathematical achievement of comparable value, in its own line, to *Alice in Wonderland*. His work was useful, up to a point, for his own generation, but has not proved sufficiently distinctive to interest his posterity.

It has been Dodgson's misfortune that the best of his mathematical work should have been devoted to Euclid, for whom he had an unbounded admiration. *Euclid and his Modern Rivals* (1879) is by far the most approachable of his mathematical books for the general reader; though it appeared under the name of C. L. Dodgson, it is spiced with the wit more usually found in Lewis Carroll, and the dialogues, which are the strength of the 'Alice' books, are effectively handled in this very different context. Dodgson's edition of *Euclid I and II* was also of considerable value to education at the time of its appearance in 1882, and went through eight editions within a few years. But it is not used nowadays, for the simple reason that Euclid as such has almost completely disappeared from English teaching. Everyone has gone on to other forms of geometry, and hardly anyone now pays attention to the formal kind of work associated with Euclid.[102]

Three

Any mention of Dodgson's mathematical works is sure to bring one particular story to the minds of many people – a beguiling anecdote that refuses to die, though it is quite untrue – the story that Queen Victoria was so delighted with *Alice in Wonderland* that she asked to see the author's next book, and was therefore sent, presumably, the *Condensation of Determinants* (1866) or its sequel of 1867, *An Elementary Treatise on Determinants* (which incidentally gave its author 'more trouble' than anything he had ever written up to that time). Dodgson allowed this story to go unchallenged for many years, perhaps while he debated with himself whether it would be proper to contradict it, but eventually, in 1896, he did add the following postscript to his 'Advertisement' at the beginning of *Symbolic Logic*:

'I take the opportunity of giving what publicity I can to my contradiction of a silly story, which has been going the round of the papers, about my having presented certain books to her Majesty the Queen. It is so constantly repeated, and is such an absolute fiction, that I think it worth while to state, once and for all, that it is utterly false in every particular: nothing even resembling it has ever occurred.'

It is, however, true that Queen Victoria knew *Alice in Wonderland* and that she enjoyed it. She may well have seen the vellum-bound copy of the 1865 'Alice' which Dodgson presented to her daughter Princess Beatrice at the age of eight (he later replaced it by an 1866 copy, also in vellum). Walter de la Mare has related[103] how, not long after the appearance of 'Alice', a little girl of three and a half was seated on a footstool by the fire looking at Tenniel's pictures, while her aunt talked to the Queen, who was still in deep mourning for the Prince Consort, and her ladies at an adjacent tea-table. When the Queen asked the girl what she was reading, she got up, carried the book over to her Majesty, and pointed to the drawing which shows Alice swimming in the flood of her own tears. Looking into the Queen's face, she asked with the devastating directness of childhood: 'Do you think, please, *you* could cry as much as that?'

The profound hush that followed was broken only by the Queen's reply, which de la Mare's informant had forgotten, 'though it was so ardent a tribute to Carroll', he says, 'that even Dodgson might have welcomed it'. And the next day a locket, with a design of intertwined horse-shoes in coral and seed pearls and with a miniature portrait of the Queen within, was sent to the little girl by special messenger from Windsor.

Probably de la Mare is right in thinking Dodgson, if he had known of this incident, would have been gratified. Like the majority of Victorians, he was an ardent patriot and a loyal follower of the doings of the Royal Family. When the Prince of Wales came up to Christ Church as an undergraduate in 1859, he tried very hard to persuade him to sit for his photograph, but without success. Eventually he met the Prince and 'apologised for having been so importunate about the photograph', whereupon the Prince 'said something of the weather being against it'. However, the Prince admired his photographs of the young Liddells and gave him his autograph instead. [104]

They met again in 1863, when the Prince and Princess of Wales visited an Oxford bazaar. Dodgson detested bazaars, and only a strong compulsion would have got him there. The Prince bowed and made a remark about a picture – 'I don't know whether he knew me', commented Dodgson. The Liddell children were trying to sell some white kittens, and Alice was shy of offering hers to the Princess, so that Dodgson intervened on her behalf, being rewarded with the reply: 'Oh, but I've bought one of those kittens already' ('the only remark *she* is ever likely to make to me'). In October, 1864, he succeeded in photographing her brother, Prince Frederick of Denmark, and thought him 'a much brighter specimen of royalty than his brother-in-law'; his failure with the Prince of Wales evidently still rankled.

Prince Leopold, youngest son of Queen Victoria, photographed by Dodgson

That Dodgson took the trouble to record these royal trivialities in his diary shows that his shyness did not prevent him enjoying exalted company, and that he was indeed, though mildly and inoffensively, a bit of a snob. He arranged for some of his photographs to be shown to the Queen and was gratified when Lady A. Stanley wrote to say that the Queen admired them very much and that they were 'such as the Prince would have appreciated very highly and taken much pleasure in'. Walking through the Park at Windsor in the summer of 1865, he met the Queen driving in an open carriage and was pleased to receive 'a bow from her all to myself'. This was the nearest that he got to personal contact with his Sovereign. He would have appreciated the honour, accorded to Martin Tupper, of being received at Court, but it did not come his way.

Dodgson's loyalty nevertheless embraced more than a hint of mischievous irreverence – a paradox typical of that '*very* rebellious mind'. When he took Alice Liddell to see the illuminations in Oxford in celebration of the marriage of the Prince and Princess of Wales, there was one that particularly caught her fancy, in which the words 'May they be happy' appeared in large letters of fire. The next day Dodgson drew a caricature for her; underneath the phrase 'May they be happy' appeared two hands, holding very formidable birches, with the words 'Certainly not'.[105]

He more than once pretended, for the amusement of little girls, that he and the Queen were in correspondence. After he had given a photograph of himself to Maggie Cunnynghame in April, 1868, he wrote to her: 'As a great secret (please don't repeat it), the Queen sent to ask for a copy of it, but as it is against my rule to give in such a case, I was obliged to answer – "Mr Dodgson presents his compliments to her Majesty, and regrets to say that his rule is never to give his photograph except to *young* ladies." I am told she was annoyed about it, and said, "I'm not so old as all that comes to!" and one doesn't like to annoy Queens. . . .'[106]

We find a similar strategy being employed to entertain Minnie, Ella and Emmie Drury, whom he first met in 1869. It was for their mystification that he concocted, in a disguised hand, the note which is here reproduced in facsimile: 'Dear Mr Dodgson, I hope you will be able to come to our Garden Party on Friday afternoon. Yours truly Victoria R.'[107]

Perhaps Dodgson solaced himself in this way for his failure to receive any actual invitation of that kind. He must also have comforted himself – at about the same time – by getting on familiar terms with the Queens in *Through the Looking-Glass*.

Above: *Dodgson's 'fake' letter from Queen Victoria, purporting to invite him to a garden-party.* Right: *And the Queen cried 'Faster! Don't try to talk!'*

Four

But it was artists, not royalty, whom – next to children – Dodgson really liked best. He became personally acquainted with the leading Pre-Raphaelite painters, including Rossetti, Millais, Holman Hunt and Arthur Hughes (whose 'The Lady of the Lilacs' he bought to hang in his room at Oxford), and on his journeys to London he lost no opportunity of meeting them or visiting their studios. With Rossetti he was on good terms from the date of his first introduction to him by Alexander Munro, the sculptor, in September, 1863, when Rossetti showed him 'some very lovely pictures, most of them only half finished', and promised him the use of his romantic house and garden in Cheyne Walk, Chelsea, for taking photographs. Having already enjoyed 'Goblin Market', Dodgson was equally pleased with its author Christina Rossetti, when he met her, too, a week later; and he secured excellent photographs of her and her mother and brothers, taken either singly or in groups.

Dodgson's taste in painting was academic and conservative. Although he does express admiration in his diary for several of Rossetti's later poetic canvases, he reserves his highest praise for an early unfinished work, 'Found', which is one of Rossetti's few attempts at 'Pre-Raphaelite' moralising in the

The Rossetti family, 7 October, 1865: Dante Gabriel, Christina, Mrs Rossetti and William Michael. Photographed by Dodgson

Florence Bickersteth

John Everett Millais

Above: *Florence Bickersteth, daughter of the Bishop of Ripon.* Below: *John Everett Millais, the Pre-Raphaelite painter. Both photographed by Dodgson*

Above: *John Ruskin and Holman Hunt in the garden of Coniston.* Left: *Ruskin and Rossetti*

manner of Millais and Holman Hunt. Dodgson did not come across this picture until after Rossetti's death, when it was included in a memorial exhibition at the Burlington Gallery. He thought the expression on the man's face 'one of the most marvellous things I have ever seen done in painting'.[108]

With Millais his experience was rather the opposite. Dodgson took the same view as Dickens of the early 'Christ in the House of his Parents', which he thought 'full of power, but hideously ugly' (Diary, June 13th, 1862). But when he first visited Millais on April 7th, 1864, with an introduction from Holman Hunt, he liked him very much, and he was also greatly taken with his three daughters, especially Effie, whom he immediately recognised as the original of 'My First Sermon'. Anecdotal pictures of that kind were much to Dodgson's taste, and his acquaintance with Millais continued on a note of sustained admiration; the 'Boyhood of Raleigh' he thought the 'cleverest thing' in the Academy exhibition of 1872.

Arthur Hughes became a close friend; the diary records a 'splendid walk' with him in that year in the country around Albury and Shere, and Gernsheim reproduces delightful photographs of Hughes and his son and daughter. But earnestness and piety made Holman Hunt the ideal painter for a Victorian clergyman; he and Dodgson kept up a mutually respectful acquaintance over many years. 'Christ in the Temple' Dodgson thought 'about the most wonderful picture I ever saw',[109] and in 1883 Hunt told him: 'It was very kind of you to write to me the other day the story of the poor old woman in the International Exhibition in connection with the picture of "The Light of the World", and I assure you that I feel gratified to think that any work of mine can make so deep an impression upon another fellow being as this seems to have made upon her. . . . It was a beautiful subject which I was quite unworthy to do.'[110] Dodgson felt a similar interest in the work of Thomas Heaphy, and discussed with him, through an ear-trumpet, Heaphy's devout investigation of the origin of the traditional likeness of Christ.

The spare clerical figure of Dodgson was a welcome visitor in the studios of these and other artists. He won their friendship primarily as a fellow-artist in photography; it was only later, and incidentally, that they knew him as Lewis Carroll. In these artistic friendships of the sixties, Tom Taylor of *Punch*, benevolent but ponderous ('His hand was heavy, though his heart was kind'), was often the intermediary. It was to Taylor that Dodgson owed not only his introduction to Tenniel but also an *entrée* to the home of the Terrys which brought him his friendship with Ellen Terry – one of the most important in his life* – and it was to busy influential Taylor that he turned in January, 1866, when he wanted advice about an abortive drama which he tentatively entitled *Morning Clouds*.

A visit to *Little King Pippin*, the Drury Lane pantomime, in January, 1866, inspired Dodgson's only serious attempt at play-writing. He was attracted by the acting of a youth called Percy Roselle and sketched the plot of a domestic drama, in which he hoped Roselle might take the part of a boy stolen away from his widowed mother (whom he trusted would be played by Ellen Terry). One of the more poignant scenes was to show the boy passing – all unknowing – the house where his lost mother lived. Those inside would recognise his voice singing, and open the window, but too late. . . . However, all was to end well, with the death of the villain; and finally two children, reunited, were to

*See Chapter X.

Arthur Hughes.

*Arthur Hughes
Oct. 12. 63*

*Tom Taylor
Oct. 3. 1863*

Top: *Arthur Hughes's son Arthur, photographed by Dodgson.* Middle: *Arthur Hughes, the artist, and his daughter Agnes.* Below: *Tom Taylor, editor of Punch*

Charlotte McGouge

May 8th 1866

sing their grandfather to sleep. The audience might perhaps have been asleep already; for *Morning Clouds* does not sound very promising and suggests sentimental affinities with the more 'stagey' parts of *Sylvie and Bruno* rather than with the 'Alice' books.

Tom Taylor proved encouraging at first; Dodgson went so far as to elaborate his synopsis and to write some passages of dialogue. But Percy Roselle was not available, and Taylor and Miss Terry eventually decided the idea was not practicable. 'The public taste demands more sensation', Dodgson noted tersely in his Diary. One may regret the failure of *Morning Clouds*, nevertheless; for Dodgson's use of dialogue and understanding of the theatre indicate that he had a play in him somewhere which never came to the footlights.

The workings of a theatre fascinated him no less than his glimpses of artists' studios. There is a long account in his Diary of a visit 'behind the scenes' at the Haymarket Theatre in 1867 while a children's entertainment called *Living Miniatures* was being given. He sat in the prompter's box, wandered about in the wings, noted that the snow-storm was made by a man on a tall pair of steps with a basket of cut-up paper, and observed especially the enjoyment of the children and the care taken of them. This was the beginning of a persistent interest in child-actors, whose claims – and those of their managers, when deserving – he was quick to defend.

Thus Dodgson's very full life continued, art and photography vying for his spare-time recreation with the theatre and the society of children. His academic work did not get lighter, and conscience drove him to take an increasingly contentious part in the affairs of his college and university. At the beginning of 1864 he was engaged in a 'rather disagreeable correspondence' with Dean Liddell – not an easy man to argue with – about elections to Junior Studentships in mathematics at Christ Church, the upshot being that he declined to act as an assessor; and soon afterwards he resigned his office of Public Examiner in Mathematics in the University, justifying himself in a printed letter to the Vice-Chancellor. His main objection here was to the institution of the new 'Fourth Class' which he thought would lower the status of those working for 'Honours' and reduce the standard both of classical and mathematical education at Oxford. But he threw himself all the more ardently into his usual round, and declared that the Michaelmas Term of 1864 had been 'a harder-worked term than I have had for a long time'.

Oxford had its gentler uses. Celebrities were not to be found exclusively in London: in June, 1866, he had the pleasure of meeting Charlotte Yonge, at lunch with Professor Bartholomew Price, and of getting her likeness into one of his photograph albums. Mrs Gatty was another literary lady of his acquaintance, and for *Aunt Judy's Magazine*, which she edited, he wrote, in 1867, a little fairy-tale called 'Bruno's Revenge' which formed the nucleus of the subsequent *Sylvie and Bruno*. It was a story not without charm or humour, but suffered from the boy-fairy Bruno's tiresome habit of baby-talk, deployed to disconcerting extent in the later novel. Lewis Carroll was never very happy with boys, either in real life or (as Bruno and the attempted sketch for Percy Roselle shows) on paper. But Mrs Gatty did well to encourage him to produce more children's stories, saying, 'You may have great mathematical abilities, but so have hundreds of others. This talent is peculiarly your own, and as an Englishman you are almost unique in possessing it.'[111]

Some of 'Bruno's Revenge' was written late on a June night of 1867 – or, rather, in the early morning – while Dodgson listened to the music from a ball at the Corn Exchange, drifting in at his windows. He was not tempted to 'join the dance', but for once, at the end of a summer term, his mind turned to the prospect of a holiday outside his own country.

'What matters it how far we go?' his scaly friend replied.
'The further off from England the nearer is to France.
There is another shore, you know, upon the other side. . . .'

Five

Dr H. P. Liddon, a splendid preacher, later Canon of St Paul's, who accompanied Dodgson on this journey in 1867, was – one must hasten to emphasise – not at all a 'scaly friend', but on the contrary a thoroughly unselfish, kind-hearted, humorous man: an ideal companion for a journey. He was at this time a fellow Student of Dodgson's at Christ Church. They did not agree in all things – Liddon once wrote, 'I have never been inside a theatre since I took Orders in 1852, and I do not mean to go into one, please God, while I live'[112] – but they got on very well on the whole.

Dr H. P. Liddon, photographed by Dodgson

The two went to Russia together. Dodgson noted in his Diary of July 11th, 1867, that he had received his passport, that Liddon had said he could go abroad with him, and that they had decided on Moscow: 'Ambitious for one who has never yet left England.' It certainly was ambitious, and Russia may well seem a surprising choice for a first trip abroad. Probably the question 'What matters it how far we go?' came from Liddon, who had already travelled extensively on the Continent and would have been ready for fresh fields.

In retrospect, however, Russia appears an uncannily appropriate choice for Dodgson's only journey abroad. We may regret that he never saw Rome or Athens, but we cannot deny that in making straight for Moscow in the year 1867 he showed a prophetic grasp of essentials that was worthy of the author of *Alice in Wonderland*.

Dodgson's preparations for the journey were minute; he had made an exact science of packing, and like the White Knight thought it 'as well to be provided for everything'. They crossed from Dover to Calais on July 13th – a 'smooth trip of ninety minutes'. Both Dodgson and Liddon kept diaries during the weeks that followed. It is a pity that Dodgson's journal is not included in the two volumes of his diaries published in 1954, for it is in some respects more interesting and more carefully considered than his usual chronicles. The journal has, however, been published in America, and is included in R. L. Green's *The Works of Lewis Carroll* (Hamlyn, 1965); and from it we gain an immediate and typical impression of Dodgson travelling through Belgium, interesting himself at once in a little girl in the railway carriage, making a drawing of her, and kissing her 'Bon soir'.[113] They stopped in Brussels and again in Cologne, where Liddon noted that 'Dodgson was overcome by the beauty of Cologne Cathedral. I found him leaning against the rails of the Choir, and sobbing like a child. When the verger came to show us over the chapels, he got out of the way. He said that he could not bear the harsh voice of the man in the presence of so much beauty.'[114] They saw the picture galleries of Berlin and the Cathedral of Danzig, and then – by way of Koenigsberg, where Liddon was taken ill – they came to St Petersburg.

The churches of St Petersburg and the enthusiastic worshippers that
thronged them made a deep impression on the two English clergymen. The
hard-bargaining cab-drivers of the city were another object of fascinated
study. On July 29th Dodgson recorded the following intricate negotiations
with the driver of a droshky:

Myself. Gostonitia Klee – (Klees Hotel).
Driver (utters a sentence rapidly of which we can only catch the words)
      Tri groshen – (Three groshen = 30 kopecks)
M.   Doatzat kopecki? (20 kopecks?)
D.   (indignantly) Tritzat! (30)
M.   (resolutely) Doatzat.
D.   (coaxingly) Doatzat pait? (25?)
M.   (with the air of one who has said his say, and wishes to be rid of the
      thing) Doatzat. (Here I take Liddon's arm, and we walk off together,
      entirely disregarding the shouts of the driver. When we have gone a
      few yards, we hear the droshky lumbering after us: he draws along-
      side, and hails us.)
M.   (gravely) Doatzat?
D.   (with a delighted grin) Da! Da! Doatzat! (and in we get).

The travellers pushed on through Moscow to the furthest point of their
tour, Nijni Novgorod (later renamed Gorky), where they visited the famous
fair and heard the muezzin cry from the Tartar mosque. 'Towards the end it
rose gradually till it ended in a prolonged, shrill wail, which floated overhead
through the still air with an indescribably sad and ghostlike effect,' wrote
Dodgson; 'heard at night, it would have thrilled one like the cry of the
Banshee.' Then they returned to Moscow to present an introduction from
Prince Orloff, whom Liddon had met at Oxford, to Bishop Leonide, one of
the Suffragan Bishops of Moscow.

Bishop Leonide proved a most hospitable and intelligent companion,
cordially disposed towards the English Church, and at this point the tour
of Dodgson and Liddon became something of a goodwill mission from the
English clergy to their Russian Orthodox brethren. With Bishop Leonide,
they went to the Troitska monastery, about forty miles from Moscow, and
had an interview with Archbishop Philaret, the conversation between him
and Liddon being conducted through an interpreter. 'The Metropolitan
entered warmly into English Church matters,' wrote Liddon, 'and into the
circumstances of Roman Catholicism in England', and could not understand
Newman acknowledging 'anything so baseless in ecclesiastical history as the
Pope's claim of Supremacy'. Liddon reported the interview to Bishop Wilberforce and to Bishop Hamilton of Salisbury, urging them to write letters
congratulating Philaret on the fiftieth anniversary of his consecration as
bishop. Altogether, the envoys from Oxford played a useful part in im-
proving Anglo-Russian relations, though in this respect Liddon was the main
agent. Dodgson remained the conventional tourist – a little too much so,
perhaps, for Liddon's taste. When Dodgson made a drawing of the Russian
College at Eriniyo, Liddon commented drily: 'In this way we lost three-
quarters of an hour.'[115]

They returned by way of Breslau, Dresden and Paris. At Breslau Dodgson discovered the playground of a girls' school and thought it 'a very tempting field for a photographic camera', but of course he had not got his elaborate apparatus with him, and therefore could do nothing about it. The Russian girls had proved disappointing. 'After the Russian children, whose type of face is ugly as a rule, and plain as an exception,' he wrote, 'it is quite a relief to get back among the Germans with their large eyes and delicate features.' In Dresden he spent a long time before the Sistine Madonna, which not surprisingly enchanted him. In Paris they visited the Exhibition of 1867, to which the Society of Arts had been so diligent in sending parties of English 'artisans' – and Dodgson went twice to the theatre, Liddon abstaining.

The two months' tour had been a success, but Dodgson was pleased to get back to England, and described his return in one of his more poetic descriptive paragraphs, which though rare could be melodious and nostalgic (there are others at the end of *Alice in Wonderland*):

'. . . I remained in the bow most of the time of our passage, sometimes chatting with the sailor on the look-out, and sometimes watching, through the last hour of my first foreign tour, the lights at Dover, as they slowly broadened on the horizon, as if the old land were opening its arms to receive its homeward bound children – till they finally stood out clear and bold as the two light-houses on the cliff – till that which had long been merely a glimmering line on the dark water, like a reflection of the Milky Way, took form and substance as the lights of the shoreward houses – till the faint white line behind them, that looked at first like a mist creeping along the horizon, was visible at last in the grey twilight as the white cliffs of old England.'

Dodgson never left England again. He rarely referred to his Russian journey in later life. Though he had observed its incidents with humour and curiosity it seems not to have touched him vitally, but if anything to have deepened his patriotic insularity. In future, Sandown or Eastbourne were to be fully satisfying; and he never achieved a trip to the Holy Land with his camera that he had contemplated as early as 1856. His mind went abroad to strange places; the name of Lewis Carroll travelled the world; but C. L. Dodgson was content with the Oxford and the England he knew.

Six

The year 1867 was summed-up in Dodgson's Diary as 'A year of great blessings and few trials, of much weakness and sin: yet I trust I have learned to know myself better, and have striven (yet how feebly and ineffectually) to live nearer to God.' The year 1868 was destined to be remembered by him as a year of sadness and change.

It did not begin unpropitiously. Dodgson read *Our Mutual Friend*, 'one of the cleverest Dickens has written', went up to London in April to hear Disraeli and Gladstone speak in the House of Commons, and enjoyed himself as usual at the theatre and in artists' studios. He published an entertaining letter to the Senior Censor of Christ Church on the provision of opportunities at the New Museum for mathematical calculations, in which he poked fun at his own subject by suggesting 'a very large room for calculating Greatest Common Measure' and 'a piece of open ground for keeping Roots and practising their extraction'. The year also saw the appearance of two anonymous ciphers, a squib on the Woodstock election, and a pamphlet on the Fifth Book of Euclid. But his busy, methodical life was interrupted in June by the death of his father, which he described years afterwards as 'the greatest blow that has ever fallen on my life'.

Archdeacon Dodgson's illness was short and his death sudden. The circumstances were similar to those of Mrs Dodgson's death, and again the eldest son failed to reach Croft Rectory from Oxford in time. He went into the darkened room 'to take yet another look at the dear calm face, and to pray for strength', and he afterwards remembered the framed text, illuminated by one of his sisters, which hung in that room and which he said would always have for him 'a sadness and a sweetness of its own': 'Then are they glad, because they are at rest; and so he bringeth them into the haven where they would be.'[116] The lines are inscribed on the tomb of Archdeacon Dodgson and his wife in the shadow of Croft church.

Archdeacon Dodgson, Lewis Carroll's father

The death of his father not only revealed conclusively to his son how much he had depended on him but also brought Dodgson new responsibilities for the welfare of his sisters. He spent seven weeks at Croft, and in that time discussed with them where the new family home should be. The sisters decided at last that they would like to live in the neighbourhood of Guildford, and Dodgson, travelling there in August, soon discovered two houses that might suit them – one in Merrow, the other 'The Chestnuts', 'close to Guildford with a splendid view'. It was 'The Chestnuts' that was chosen.

The Chestnuts, Guildford

Now that more than a century has passed since 1868, it seems a little astonishing to find Dodgson describing this house in Castle Hill as 'close to Guildford', for it is now beyond question near the centre of the Cathedral city – a formal detached red-brick house with large square sash-windows, rather like an old-fashioned doll's house in shape. The fact that there are no windows at either of the sides heightens this illusion, and so does the steep narrow staircase which runs up the centre of the house. There is a long drawing-room on the ground-floor with windows at both ends, a small but pleasant garden, and (as Dodgson said) a delightful view over the Wey Valley from the front. The amenities were greatly increased when the Guildford Council purchased the adjacent Castle estate in 1885 and opened the grounds to the public.

'The Chestnuts' had probably been built in the eighteen-forties, though it might be thought earlier, for it has a late Georgian air. The house is not marked on a large-scale map of 1839 but appears in a water-colour of 1865. One of the gate-posts is now distinguished by a very attractive plaque, designed by Graily Hewitt in memory of Lewis Carroll and incorporating Alice, the White Rabbit, the Red King, Humpty Dumpty and the Cheshire Cat.*

The Dodgsons left Croft Rectory, after twenty-five years, on September 1st, 1868, and had moved into 'The Chestnuts' before the beginning of November. Henceforth it was to the house at Guildford that Lewis Carroll turned for his 'home'. At Christmas he was nearly always there.

Dodgson's sitting-room at Christ Church

*The plaque was unveiled by the Marquess of Crewe on May 24th, 1933, and paid for out of the profits of the Lewis Carroll Centenary celebrations at Guildford in the previous year.

Seven

At the same time that his sisters went into 'The Chestnuts', Dodgson took possession of new rooms at Christ Church which were to be his for the rest of his life. He first occupied this spacious apartment, which had formerly belonged to Lord Bute, at the end of October, 1868. The rooms, in the north-west corner of Tom Quad, are unusually imposing among the quarters of Oxford dons and have an interior staircase communicating to an upper floor. The entrance is into a dark passage, with doors leading to a dining-room, a pantry and a small bedroom (bleakly equipped in Dodgson's day with a 'japanned sponge bath'). The passage leads on into a large high sitting-room – cold in winter – with windows looking out over St Aldate's and the Archdeacon's garden. The sitting-room has a further amenity in the shape of two small turret-rooms on the St Aldate's front – more curious, perhaps, than valuable, but useful for amusing young visitors.

Upstairs (these were the arrangements of 1953) we find another bedroom, a box-room, a bath-room, and a cubby-hole which Dodgson turned into a photographic dark-room. Even here was not his furthest; for he eventually obtained permission to build a studio on the roof – an erection that can hardly have been sightly and has long been removed; he first used it in October, 1871.

Although he became increasingly abstemious and eventually almost gave up eating lunch altogether, it would be a mistake to suppose that Dodgson possessed no interest in food. It will be remembered that the contents of the bottle which Alice drank had 'a sort of mixed flavour of cherry-tart, custard, pineapple, roast turkey, toffy, and hot buttered toast', and that the taste of a Snark was 'meagre and hollow, but crisp: Like a coat that is rather too tight in the waist, with a flavour of Will-o-the-wisp' – all evidence, surely, of a discriminating palate? His little dining-room at Christ Church holds memories of many dinner-parties, some of them quite elaborate, though the dishes were always placed on squares of cardboard, as he considered mats an unnecessary extravagance. In his diary, luncheons and dinners were recorded by a small diagram, showing the names of the guests and the places they occupied; he also kept a *menu* book, so that the same people should not be given the same dishes too often. After a dinner-party of eight in May, 1871, he wrote promptly to his publisher, Macmillan, to report 'an invention of mine' (which does not seem to have been proceeded with). This was a plan of the table with the names of the guests in the order in which they were to sit, and brackets to show who was to take in whom; one to be given to each guest. He tabulated its advantages:

'1 It saves the host the worry of going round and telling every gentleman what lady to take in.
2 It prevents confusion when they reach the dining-room (the system of putting names round on the plates simply increases the confusion, though it would work well *with* this plan).
3 It enables everybody at table to know who the other guests are – often a very desirable thing.
4 By keeping the cards one gets materials for making-up other dinner-parties, by observing what people harmonise well together.'

Dodgson's study was simply but comfortably furnished with a large Turkey carpet, one or two arm-chairs, a crimson-covered couch and settee, and a dining-table and writing-table of mahogany. No visitor could fail to detect that its occupant was diligent and methodical. Manuscript boxes abounded, more than twenty of them – neatly labelled – being assembled in a special stand. The room also contained what was described after Dodgson's death as a 'pine nest' of twelve drawers, as well as a pine reading stand with a cloth cover – this presumably being the 'standing desk' at which he often liked to write. Letter scales and weights, quantities of stationery, shelves full of books, and a terrestrial globe filled much of the remaining space. When he was correcting exam papers at midnight, the scene must have been all too reminiscent of that described by Dodgson at the opening of *Euclid and his Modern Rivals*. Minos is there discovered ' seated between two gigantic piles of manuscripts. Ever and anon he takes a paper from one heap, reads it, makes an entry in a book, and with a weary sigh transfers it to the other heap. His hair, from much running of fingers through it, radiates in all directions, and surrounds his head like a halo of glory, or like the second Corollary of Euc. I. 32.'

The pictures that hung in Dodgson's rooms were mostly of little girls, and usually had some personal association for him, either with the subject or the painter. There was a sprinkling of religious and fairy pictures, a plaster bust of a child, and one or two stock Victorian engravings, such as 'Samuel' and 'The Order of Release'.[117] (If we could accept Reynolds's dictum that 'the virtuous man alone has true taste', we should be quite satisfied.) Perhaps the most interesting of the *objets d'art* in the sitting-room was a set of William de Morgan's famous tiles, which Collingwood says that Dodgson liked to explain by reference to *Alice in Wonderland* and *The Hunting of the Snark*.

The tiles, which figure largely in recollections of his later years, made their appearance only a decade before Dodgson's death. They were set around the fireplace and depicted a large ship (in three sections) and a number of more or

Left: *Tiles from the De Morgan Potteries, formerly on Dodgson's fireplace at Oxford.* Right: '*Little birds are dining*' *from* Sylvie and Bruno Concluded

Little Birds are dining
   Warily and well
   Hid in mossy cell :
Hid, I say, by waiters
Gorgeous in their gaiters—
   I've a Tale to tell.

Little Birds are feeding
   Justices with jam,
   Rich in frizzled ham :
Rich, I say, in oysters
Haunting shady cloisters—
   That is what I am.

Little Birds are teaching
   Tigresses to smile,
   Innocent of guile :

less fabulous creatures, some of which Dodgson interpreted for the benefit of his child-friends as the Lory, the Dodo, the Fawn, the Eaglet, the Gryphon and the Beaver. In the intervals between these subjects, a tile showing a group of weird birds was repeated.

'Called on Mr William de Morgan and chose a set of red tiles for the large fire-place', Dodgson wrote in his diary of March 4th, 1887. This indicates that the tiles were not made to his order but were taken from de Morgan's stock, Dodgson making what he considered an appropriate selection. They did not, of course, play any part in inspiring the 'Alice' books or *The Hunting of the Snark*, but – in the opinion of one of Dodgson's child-friends, Enid Stevens – the intermediate tiles may have suggested the 'Little birds are dining' verses in *Sylvie and Bruno Concluded*. The tiles remained in position until about forty years ago when they were swept away, rather unnecessarily, to reveal the original fireplace; and with them went a plain green paper on canvas which covered the walls in Dodgson's time.

Lewis Carroll was always interested in fireplaces. One of his poems was 'Faces in the Fire'. The chessmen in *Through the Looking-Glass* became involved with the fire-irons, and Tweedledee wore a coal-scuttle in battle. It dawns on us eventually that 'Sir Pokurranshuvvle', a character in his *Useful and Instructive Poetry*, written at thirteen, is none other than 'Sir Poker-and-shovel'. The domestic hearth was an important part of his life.

The de Morgan tiles were re-made into a screen, which was placed in the old room to remind visitors of the remote Carrollian days – days as distant as the elaborate 'gaselier' which used to hang in the centre, and the numerous oil stoves (with their adjacent thermometers) which were set about the room to combat draughts,[118] as distant as the whirr of the mechanical toy called 'Bob the Bat' darting about on his elastic, the sound of the 'orguinette' and the musical-boxes, or the smell of collodion from the dark-room upstairs.

Alice with Tweedledum and Tweedledee in Through the Looking-Glass

Through the Looking-Glass

One

'It will probably be some time before I again indulge in paper and print. I have, however, a floating idea of writing a sort of sequel to "Alice", and if it ever comes to anything, I intend to consult you at the very outset, so as to have the thing properly managed from the beginning.'

Thus Lewis Carroll to Macmillan's on August 24th, 1866, nine months after the successful launching of *Alice in Wonderland*. But he did not propose to start writing his new story until he had obtained a satisfactory illustrator, and he found this difficult. Tenniel was the obvious choice, but Tenniel had thought Dodgson very fussy over *Alice in Wonderland*, and (though that book had vastly increased his reputation) he declared at first that he could not afford the time to illustrate its sequel. Consequently we find Dodgson, in January, 1867, calling on Richard Doyle to ask him whether he would undertake it. Nothing came of this plan, and another year elapsed, while the idea continued to 'float'. By April, 1868, Dodgson was getting anxious, and in that month he made another approach to Tenniel, who still remained adamant and saw no chance of being able to do the drawings till 1870, 'if then'. Dodgson thereupon enquired of Sir Noel Paton, whose work he greatly admired, to see whether he could illustrate the book – which he was now calling *Looking-Glass House*. Paton pleaded ill-health, and urged, very properly, that 'Tenniel is *the* man'. W. S. Gilbert was momentarily considered; then a final desperate plea to Tenniel at last brought his consent, and on June 18th, 1868, Dodgson wrote gratefully to him 'accepting his kind offer to do the pictures (at such spare times as he can find) for the second volume of "Alice"'.

It was not until now that Dodgson systematically embarked on the writing of the book. Much material was ready to his hand. He searched his files and cuttings for poems that might be worked into the story, and two of his most notable discoveries were 'Jabberwocky', which we have seen was begun in 1855, and 'Upon the Lonely Moor', the parody of Wordsworth published in *The Train* in 1856, which formed the basis of the White Knight's song and largely determined the character of that remarkable creation. Whether 'The Walrus and the Carpenter', written in the metre of Hood's 'Eugene Aram', had also long been in existence must remain a moot point*; but Dodgson was able to draw on Halliwell-Phillips's collection of nursery rhymes for 'Tweedle-dum' and 'Tweedledee', 'The Lion and the Unicorn', and several similar ingredients. Above all, he still had his memories of many stories told to the young Liddells which had not found their way into *Alice in Wonderland*, particularly 'the ones to do with chessmen' which dated from the period when the children were excitedly learning to play chess.[119] Dinah, incidentally, was a recollection of Alice's cat.

The chapter called 'The Garden of Live Flowers' appears to have been influenced by Tennyson's 'Come into the garden, Maud'. All the flowers mentioned by Tennyson are there introduced by Lewis Carroll – with the exception of the passion-flower, which he changed to a tiger-lily so as to avoid any possible wounding of religious susceptibilities. Again, the 'Wool and Water' chapter embodies a piece of observation very well known to Oxford men, and still verifiable by a visit to the little shop on the opposite side of St Aldate's from Christ Church, the interior of which was used by Tenniel as a

*See *supra*, p. 71.

Alice's Shop, St Aldate's, Oxford

'I only hope the boat won't tipple over!' Drawing by Ralph Steadman

background for his drawings of the old Sheep (Plate p. 148).

But perhaps the most important single inspiration for *Through the Looking-Glass* came from a meeting with a little cousin named Alice Raikes which probably took place during August, 1868, while Dodgson was staying at his uncle Skeffington Lutwidge's house in Onslow Square, London – at a time when Tenniel's reluctant collaboration had just been obtained and when the new book will have been much in Dodgson's thoughts. Alice Raikes met him walking in the common garden at the back of the Onslow Square houses. After Dodgson had heard that her name was Alice, he said that he was very fond of Alices and invited her into his uncle's house.

The room they entered had a tall mirror standing in one corner. Dodgson gave his cousin an orange and asked her which hand she held it in. When she replied 'The right', he asked her to stand before the glass and tell him in which hand the little girl in the mirror was holding it. 'The left hand', came the puzzled reply. 'Exactly,' said Dodgson, 'and how do you explain that?' Alice Raikes did her best: 'If I was on the *other* side of the glass,' she said, 'wouldn't the orange still be in my right hand?' Years later she remembered his laugh. 'Well done, little Alice,' he said. 'The best answer I've had yet.'[120]

Alice Raikes learned later that Dodgson acknowledged his debt for that answer – and we should think of her whenever we look at Tenniel's drawing of Alice kneeling on that period mantelpiece between the clock and the artificial flowers in their glass covers (the most truly Victorian picture in either of the 'Alice' books).

Two

While *Through the Looking-Glass* was in its early stages, Dodgson was correcting proofs of what he described to Alexander Macmillan in January, 1868, as 'a small volume of verses, most of them reprints from Magazines, but the first and longest quite new. . . . My idea is to do all for it that type and paper will do, and to use broad leads – I think none but the best poetry will stand close printing and cheap paper.' His anticipations were modest, and he asked that only 'a *very* small number should be printed' and hoped 'no better fate for it than that it should get out of print and require a 2nd Edition'.

Below: *One of A. B. Frost's illustrations for 'The Trysting' in* Phantasmagoria

This book was *Phantasmagoria*, issued in January, 1869, which took its title from a long poem describing the unhappy predicament of an inexperienced little ghost. Among the best of the other humorous poems were 'Hiawatha's Photographing' and 'Poeta Fit, non Nascitur', both already published in magazines, and there were also a number of serious poems included as Part II. Dodgson had hoped for a frontispiece from George du Maurier, but did not get it.

Phantasmagoria achieved no sensational success, but the trade subscribed 300 or 400 copies, and 1,600 in all were printed. Meanwhile *Alice in Wonderland* was selling steadily, 3,000 copies being bought between June, 1868, and the end of the year. Thus encouraged, Dodgson worked on its sequel, and was able to send the first chapter of *Behind the Looking-Glass, and What Alice Saw There* (as he now provisionally entitled it) to Macmillan on January 12th, 1869. Henceforth proofs went to Tenniel from time to time, though it was not until a year later that he produced rough sketches for about ten of the pictures.

A title-page designed in 1870 for *Looking-Glass House* can be seen in the Huntington Library, Los Angeles. The first mention of *Through the Looking-*

Glass, a title suggested by Liddon, appears in the Diary of June 25th, 1870. The text was finished by the beginning of January, 1871, and was all in type by January 13th, when Dodgson noted: 'The volume has cost me, I think, more trouble than the first, and *ought* to be equal to it in every way.'

Dodgson's correspondence with Alexander Macmillan and his colleague G. L. Craik inevitably advanced in complexity as the sale and fame of *Alice in Wonderland* increased, and as such difficult questions as American rights and editions had to be faced. It was never a normal relationship between author and publisher because Dodgson kept control of the financial outlay and of the production of his books at every stage. He was almost fanatically anxious to secure artistic perfection and the best possible printing for his readers. The patience of Macmillan's in the face of a continuous stream of detailed enquiry and sometimes pedantic admonition is something to admire.

A letter to Macmillan of April 15th, 1870, concerning an early attempt at a title-page for *Through the Looking-Glass*, is typical of many others:

'My title page hasn't had fair play yet – as the printer doesn't follow out my directions. I want the large capitals to have *more below the line than above*: nearly twice as much. In the corrected copy I sent the A & F have slipped a little lower than I meant: the others are about right.

Secondly, the "AND" ought to be half-way between the two lines, and not (as they have printed it) nearer to the upper line.

Thirdly, the 3 lines of title ought to be closer together, and not so close to the top of the page.

Fourthly, the comma and full-stop ought to be set lower.

All the above faults I have endeavoured to remedy in the corrected copy I enclose.

I send an uncorrected one with it that you may see the difference.'

The main production difficulties of *Through the Looking-Glass* centred in the most famous item in the book, 'Jabberwocky'. As early as January 24th, 1869, Dodgson was telling Macmillan: 'I want to have 2 pages of "reverse" printing in the new vol. – such as you must hold up to the looking-glass to read'; and he went in great detail into the technical means by which the whole of 'Jabberwocky' might be printed on these pages. A week later, however, he had 'pretty nearly settled in my own mind that it will be too troublesome for the reader to have 2 pages of "reverse" type to make out, and that we had better limit it to one or 2 stanzas (with perhaps a picture over them to fill the page) and print the rest of the ballad in the usual way'. Dodgson was right about this, and, as everyone knows, the reverse type was confined to the first verse of 'Jabberwocky'.

A far more serious question was whether Tenniel's horrific picture of the Jabberwock should be used for the frontispiece, as had originally been intended. Dodgson was anxious not to frighten his young readers, and drew up a circular letter in the early months of 1871:

'I am sending you, with this, a print of the proposed frontispiece for *Through the Looking-Glass*. It has been suggested to me that it is too terrible a monster, and likely to alarm nervous and imaginative children; and that at any rate we had better begin the book with a pleasanter subject.

Above and opposite page top: '*In another moment Alice was through the glass . . .*'

So I am submitting the question to a number of friends, for which purpose I have had copies of the frontispiece printed off.

We have three courses open to us:

   (1) To retain it as the frontispiece.
   (2) To transfer it to its proper place in the book, (where the ballad occurs which it is intended to illustrate) and substitute a new frontispiece.
   (3) To omit it altogether.

The last-named course would be a great sacrifice of the time and trouble which the picture has cost, and it would be a pity to adopt it unless it is really necessary.

I should be grateful to have your opinion, (tested by exhibiting the picture to any children you think fit,) as to which of these courses is the best.'[121]

According to Collingwood, the jury to which Dodgson submitted this problem consisted of 'about thirty of his married lady friends'. In thirty nurseries therefore the infants chosen for the experiment will, presumably, have been confronted by the Jabberwock as he came whiffling through the tulgey wood – and their unguarded reactions will have been precisely noted in decibels. The jury of matrons must have voted in favour of the second of Dodgson's three courses. At all events, the monster was displaced from the frontispiece in favour of the less disturbing White Knight, the Jabberwock appearing in his appropriate place in the first chapter.

Three

Throughout the year 1871 the publication date of *Through the Looking-Glass* advanced and receded according as Tenniel worked on or temporarily laid aside his drawings; not until November 1st could Dodgson write in his diary that '*Alice Through the Looking-Glass* is now printing off rapidly'. Tenniel played a part in shaping the text as well as the illustrations, for it was by his advice that a projected episode introducing a wasp in a wig was omitted, and that Alice in the railway carriage was made to catch at the goat's beard which 'seemed to melt away as she touched it'. But the strain of drawing for Lewis Carroll proved too great for him, and a later invitation to illustrate another of his books was met by a resolute refusal: 'It is a curious fact,' wrote Tenniel, 'that with *Through the Looking-Glass* the faculty of making drawings for book illustrations departed from me, and, notwithstanding all sorts of tempting inducements, I have done nothing in that direction since.'[122]

The publication of *Through the Looking-Glass* was attended by none of those extraordinary misadventures which had befallen the first edition of *Alice in Wonderland*. Though dated 1872, it was published in time for Christmas, 1871, and was very well received. The *Athenaeum* of December 16th made full amends for its hostile criticism of *Alice in Wonderland* and wrote: 'It is with no mere book that we have to deal here . . . but with the potentiality of happiness for countless children of all ages.' One of the hundred copies that Dodgson distributed went to Henry Kingsley, who said that he received it in bed and would not stop reading until he had finished it. He thought it better than its predecessor, indeed 'the finest thing we have had since *Martin Chuzzlewit*'; reading it was 'like gathering cowslips in springtime'.[123]

Macmillan's began by printing 9,000 copies, but soon found that they had underestimated the demand and proposed to print another 6,000 immediately. Henry Kingsley, in the letter just quoted, said: 'I lunch with Macmillan habitually, and he was in a terrible pickle about not having printed enough copies the other day.' Dodgson's reaction, however, was characteristically conscientious. He had been worrying as usual about the pictures, and especially about a complaint of Tenniel's that there had been 'inequality' in their printing, which Dodgson attributed to 'the pressing between sheets of blank paper in order to dry for binding'. On December 17, 1871, he wrote to Alexander Macmillan:

'I have now made up my mind that whatever be the *commercial* consequences, we must have no more artistic "fiascos" – and I am stimulated to write *at once* about it by your alarming words of this morning. "We are going on with another 6,000 *as fast as possible*." My decision is, we must have *no more hurry*: and *no more sheets must be pressed under blank paper*. It is my *particular desire* that all the sheets shall in future be "stacked" and let to dry naturally. The result of this may possibly be that 6,000 will not be ready for sale till the end of January or even later. Very well: then fix that date in your advertisement: say that "owing to the delay necessary to give the pictures their full artistic effect, no more copies can be delivered until the end of January".

You will think me a lunatic for thus wishing to send away money from the doors; and will tell me perhaps that I shall thus lose thousands of would-be purchasers, who will not wait so long, but will go and buy other Christmas-books. I wish I could put into words how entirely such arguments go for nothing with me. As to how many copies we sell I care absolutely nothing: the one thing I *do* care for is, that all copies that *are* sold shall be artistically first-rate.'

After this, all went well with *Through the Looking-Glass* until 1893, when it was in its sixtieth thousand. The reproduction of the drawings was then thought to be unsatisfactory, and efforts were made to suppress the edition. Dodgson issued a leaflet asking those who possessed copies of the edition to return them to Macmillan's, when they would receive new copies in exchange.

Four

Through all the painstaking and, it may be thought, ultra-punctilious letters to Macmillan's, shines one clear fact – that literature was enriched by another children's classic, and that henceforth 'Alice' would sparkle as a double-star. *Through the Looking-Glass* has never caught up the lead in sales and popularity that *Alice in Wonderland* had already won, but it is doubtful whether children or grown-ups make any marked distinction between the two books, considering them rather as two parts of the same story. Indeed, if it is a question of a comparison of characters, the Looking-Glass team, with the White Knight (capt.), Tweedledum and Tweedledee, the Walrus and the Carpenter, the Jabberwock, Humpty Dumpty and the Red and White Queens might conceivably outplay Father William (capt.), the White Rabbit, the Duchess, the Cheshire Cat, the Mad Hatter, the March Hare, the Dormouse and the Mock Turtle, who would be among those selected to represent Wonderland. Alice remains the essential common factor – Alice, as Lewis Carroll himself described her, 'loving and gentle . . . courteous to *all*, high or low . . . trustful, ready to accept the wildest impossibilities with all that utter trust that only dreamers know; and lastly, curious – wildly curious, and with the eager enjoyment of Life that comes only in the happy hours of childhood'.[124]

It is not often that an author produces such a successful sequel to a best-seller as Lewis Carroll did; there is no better method, however, of proving that success is not a flash in the pan. The new 'Alice' was eagerly awaited by countless homes, and did not disappoint them. Mrs Vivian Hughes in her delightful *A London Child of the Seventies* (1934)[125] describes how the book came to one typical household. '*Alice in Wonderland* we all knew practically by heart,' she wrote, 'and one of the red-letter days of my life was a birthday when I received from my father *Through the Looking-Glass*. I got through the morning somehow, and then buried myself in it all the afternoon, my pleasure enhanced by the knowledge that there was a boring visitor downstairs to whom I ought to be making myself agreeable. . . . As I handle the book now I live over again that enchanted afternoon.' There is an echo of that rapture in Violet Markham's autobiography published in 1953: '"Alice" was in a class apart. It is proverbial that all admirers of Lewis Carroll go through life finding ever deeper and more appropriate applications of his words.' And two of her three instances come from *Through the Looking-Glass*.

The *Oxford English Dictionary* (1933) recognises two words as having been introduced into the language by the Jabberwock poem. They are 'chortle', which, the Dictionary says, has 'some suggestion of *chuckle*, and of *snort*, and 'galumph' (perhaps some reminiscence of *gallop*, *triumphant*) – 'To march on exultantly with irregular bounding movements.' A good many other strange words which the poem brought into general use – e.g. 'Whiffling', 'burbled', 'beamish', 'slithy' – turn out, on investigation, to be inspired revivals of Lewis Carroll's rather than direct inventions.

'Jabberwocky' has been translated into several languages, including Latin and Greek (a German version is given in Appendix C). It is surprising that, despite the difficulties, more translators of *Through the Looking-Glass* as a whole have not come forward. It was not until 1923 that it went into German as *Alice in Spiegelland*, and in 1933 into French; in 1949 André Bay's translation appeared, *La Traversée du miroir et ce qu' Alice trouva de l'autre coté*. The latter is only one indication, however, of a new interest in Lewis Carroll that has been discernible in France since the nineteen-forties, and partial translations both of 'Wonderland' and 'Looking-Glass' by Jacques Papy were included in Henri Parisot's study of 1952. The book appeared on the London stage in its own right in 1954, in a dramatisation by Felicity Douglas.

Through the Looking-Glass, being based informally on a game of chess and 'hammered-out' as an intellectual process more than *Alice in Wonderland*, lends itself much less to Freudian theorising. The Freudians, indeed, derive their conclusions mainly from the early spontaneous chapters of 'Wonderland'. But some of the characters in Tenniel's drawings, especially in the 'Looking-Glass', have suggested political caricature (a plausible idea only in so far as Tenniel was a *Punch* cartoonist with the features of Gladstone and Disraeli constantly before him), and there have been many other conjectures.

It is not surprising that such an unusual *tour de force* as the 'Alice' books should have aroused enormous curiosity and stimulated a minute examination of the text, an occupation harmless enough so long as it was treated humorously and taken not too seriously – as in the parallel case of Sherlock Holmes. 'Nonsense' lends itself particularly to an endless search for hidden meanings. But when we are told, as we have been told in *The White Knight* by Alexander

L. Taylor (1952), that the books are laced throughout with intentional references to religious and academic controversy, the joke has gone too far. One might as well carry the search for direct meanings and allusions into the charmingly nonsensical letters that Dodgson wrote to his child-friends.

The 'Alice' books may be explained as the original work of a mathematician and logician, interested in the precise meaning of words, who was at the same time a genius of invention and poetic imagination with a love for children and a gift for entertaining them. There are, certainly, a few passing references to contemporary Oxford matters that might have amused the young Liddells, but such satire as there is in the books is based mainly on a general observation of human nature rather than on the exploitation of actual circumstances. Inspiration came in bits and pieces, as Bishop Strong and Dodgson himself have indicated. That Dodgson did have a lot of contemporary controversy whirling in his mind while he wrote the 'Alice' books is undeniable; and Mr Taylor has indicated some of the embittered circumstances of the time. But they remained in the background, were assimilated by the mind of an artist, and transmuted unconsciously into a work of genius. Dodgson's care to change the passion-flower into a tiger-lily is proof enough of his view that adult susceptibilities were not the concern of a fairy-story.

Five

In the years during which *Through the Looking-Glass* was in course of writing or production, one or two incidental happenings may be noted. At Christmas, 1869, Dodgson became involved in some elaborate amateur theatricals organised by his sisters' Guildford neighbour, the diplomatist and author W. W. Follett Synge, and acted the part of a doctor in charades before an audience that included 'Mr and Mrs A. Trollope'. With his habitual enthusiasm for all local happenings, he threw himself as readily into the Guildford occasion as he had into similar excitements at Croft and wrote a characteristic account of the evening disguised as No. 9999 of *The Guildford Gazette Extraordinary*. This pamphlet is one of Lewis Carroll's rarest publications; the introduction to the 'Gazette' is given as Appendix B.

In the following June (1870) Follett Synge was Dodgson's guest at Oxford for Commemoration, and went with him to see the Installation of the new Chancellor of the University, Lord Salisbury. Dodgson obtained introductions to Lord and Lady Salisbury and took a successful photograph of the future Prime Minister with his two sons in the costume they wore as his train-bearers. This was not one of the occasions on which Dodgson regretted being identified as Lewis Carroll; indeed he wrote in his diary of June 25th: 'I fancy "Wonderland" had a great deal to do with my gracious reception.' Thereafter he was often Lord Salisbury's guest at Hatfield; he shared with his host a common taste in Conservatism and humour; the snobbish side of Dodgson delighted in the association. Dodgson several times stayed at Hatfield for New Year festivities, when there was usually a large party of children in the house, Princess Alice being among them on one occasion. He was always called upon to tell stories and more than once recited embryo chapters of *Sylvie and Bruno*. This he eventually found rather a strain, and at the end of 1875 he 'declined to undertake my usual role of story-teller in the morning' and expressed the hope in his diary that he had 'broken the rule of being always expected to do it'. Shortly afterwards his visits to Hatfield seem to have temporarily lapsed, but the Salisburys took care to remove any suspicion that may have lurked in his mind that he had been invited purely as an entertainer. In 1878 Lady Salisbury wrote him the following note:

DEAR MR DODGSON,
  Though you have foresworn children's parties perhaps grave old folks may tempt you. Will you come on Dec. 19 for a few days and be old and serious.
                              Yours very truly,
                                 G. SALISBURY
Dec. 2.[126]

Apparently this invitation was not accepted. Perhaps Dodgson did not find Lady Salisbury in all respects quite grave enough! When in 1873 he went with her and a party to a pantomime, he left them before the end, 'as they *would* stay for the harlequinade' (which Dodgson had already seen and pronounced 'very coarse').

The bachelor life continued, a busy life full of interest, and lived unselfishly – as is shown by Dodgson's visits in 1871 to the death-bed of an old carpenter at Oxford. Did he ever fall in love, and was his failure to marry a disappointment to him? This large question requires a separate chapter.

'. . . The soul of the first Alice looked out at her eyes with such a quality of re-presentment, that I became in doubt which of them stood there before me, or whose that bright hair was; and while I stood gazing, both the children gradually grew fainter to my view, receding, and still receding, till nothing at last but two mournful features were seen in the uttermost distance, which, without speech, strangely impressed upon me the effects of speech: "We are not of Alice, nor of thee, nor are we children at all. The children of Alice call Bartrum father. We are nothing; less than nothing, and dreams. We are only what might have been, and must wait upon the tedious shores of Lethe millions of ages before we have existence, and a name" – and immediately waking, I found myself quietly seated in my bachelor armchair, where I had fallen asleep. . . .'

CHARLES LAMB ('Dream Children: A Reverie')

One

These lines of Lamb's have a permanent significance for the case of any ageing bachelor who dreams dreams, and their phrasing is so strange and indeed uncanny in its coincidence that they may be thought to suggest Charles Dodgson's predicament with particular vividness. It is so probable as to be almost certain that a man who loved children as much as Dodgson did must, at some time, have thought of the unborn children who might have been his; and it is likely, too, that he may have associated with that thought, however fleetingly and poetically, the best-loved of all his child-friends, Alice Liddell, whom he had seen grow from infancy to womanhood, and who had been present continuously to his imagination during that period. Such would be no more than human nature. But it certainly does not follow that Dodgson was 'in love' with Alice in an adult sense. There are many considerations and circumstances to suggest that this was not the case.

Dodgson's character was exceedingly complex. He had disciplined himself so thoroughly and cultivated his self-control so successfully that he might well have been mistaken by those who met him for a person of great steadiness with a restricted inner life. In fact, however, this surface control disguised a precarious balance and much inner tension, which showed itself in occasional outbursts of irritability. He was one of those perplexing beings who are at once self-centred and unselfish, richly endowed emotionally but at the same time emotionally immature. A paradox himself, it is not surprising that the strange dichotomy of his character should have revealed itself (in his writing) in subtle changes of significance, and in statements no sooner made than they were abruptly reversed.

He was a man who carried his childhood with him; the love that he understood and longed for was a protective love. He had a deep instinctive admiration for women, yearning for their sympathy and often finding it. But it is probable that he could not reconcile in himself love and desire, and likely that he avoided problems of adult love and intimacy in his own life because he knew that he was pulled in two different ways (ambivalence is the modern term), and that in any close relationship something compelled him to seek distance and detachment.

To live such a lonely life – although he came to recognise, probably rightly, that it was the best life for him – must have required great courage. Dodgson was indeed a very brave man. Outwardly he was reconciled to his lot. 'So you have been for twelve years, a married man,' he wrote to his friend F. H. Atkinson in 1884, 'while I am still a lonely old bachelor! And mean to keep so, for the matter of that. College life is by no means unmixed misery, though married life has no doubt many charms to which I am a stranger.'[127] Inwardly there were moments of anguish and depression, though there is reason to believe that towards the end of his life the burden lifted.

Between the years 1860 and 1862, Dodgson wrote several poems of a romantic melancholy that show clearly enough that he pined for the love that was denied him. They may be poetic exercises of imaginary application, but the pervading mood is too insistent to allow them to be explained away on that account. Thus in the poem 'Three Sunsets' he shows that he was aware of the dangers that lie in wait for those

> Who let the thought of bliss denied
>   Make havoc of our life and powers,
> And pine, in solitary pride,
>   For peace that never shall be ours,
> Because we will not work and wait
> In trustful patience for our fate.

In another poem, 'Stolen Waters', he warns himself and others of the perils of temptation ('I kissed her on the false, false lips'), receives from 'a clear voice singing' the counsel 'Be as a child', and shows that he understood already how he must work out his destiny:

> And if I smile, it is that now
>   I see the promise of the years –
> The garland waiting for my brow,
>   That must be won with tears,
> With pain – with death – I care not how.

In 'Faces in the Fire' he again anticipates his own solitary future and writes of some idealised 'true love'

> That might have been my own, my dear,
> Through many and many a happy year –
> That might have sat beside me here.

('Faces in the Fire' appeared in *All the Year Round* in 1860, and Dodgson quite cheerfully bought a copy of *Pickwick Papers* with the proceeds.[128])

Two

These melancholy and very personal poems were collected in Part II of *Phantasmagoria* and reappeared in the little book called *Three Sunsets* which was published in the month after Dodgson's death. They were there interspersed with some exceedingly arch and not unprovocative drawings of naked little girls ('fairies') commissioned by him from his friend Gertrude Thomson. Though they are totally unrelated to the text, Miss Thomson's 'fairies' unintentionally provide a running commentary on the poems. We shall refer to them again later.*

The book *Three Sunsets* leaves a sad impression, which was recognised by

*See Chapter XIV.

Dodgson's biographer S. D. Collingwood when he wrote the following passage:

'One cannot read this little volume without feeling that the shadow of some disappointment lay over Lewis Carroll's life. Such I believe to have been the case, and it was this that gave him his wonderful sympathy with all who suffered. But those who loved him would not wish to lift the veil from these dead sanctities, nor would any purpose be served by so doing. The proper use of sympathy is not to weep over sorrows that are over, and whose very memory is perhaps obliterated for him in the first joy of possessing new and higher faculties.' [129]

This well-meant paragraph has been the starting-point of any number of wild conjectures by later writers who have scented the possibility of hidden love-affairs. They have wondered, not unnaturally, what Collingwood had in mind. Fortunately these doubts can now be set at rest, for Collingwood's cousin Menella Dodgson asked him that very question at the time of the Lewis Carroll centenary, and received the following reply, which was dated February 3rd, 1932:

'Nothing I have read in L.C.'s diaries or letters suggested – to the best of my memory – that he had ever had any affaires de cœur.

I *think* that Aunt Fanny once told me that it was the family's opinion that Uncle Charles had had a disappointment in love, and that they thought (or she also thought) that the lady in question was Ellen Terry.

I don't think I ever had the *complete* diary, though possibly Uncle Wilfred had it.*

The "shadow" I hinted at had no other basis than what I had heard from Aunt Fanny. When Ellen Terry was just growing up – about 17 – she was lovely beyond description . . . and it is highly probable that he fell in love with her; he may even have proposed to her. Whereas, in regard to the Liddells it was *Alice* who was undoubtedly his pet, and it was his intense love for her (though she was only a child) which pulled the trigger and released his genius. Indeed it is quite likely that Alice's marriage to Hargreaves may have seemed to him the greatest tragedy in his life.'

It seems clear from Collingwood's statement that the only reason why he wrote about 'the shadow of some disappointment over Lewis Carroll's life' was that he believed him to have been in love with Ellen Terry. Dodgson's eldest sister Frances Jane ('Aunt Fanny') is generally admitted to have been the most balanced in her judgment of all his brothers and sisters – so that there was good reason for Collingwood to pay attention to her view; at the same time she never had a love-affair of her own, so that her ideas on this subject were probably vague. Collingwood himself was the soul of honesty, but perhaps not entirely reliable in his opinions. This much having been said, there obviously remains every justification for reconsidering Lewis Carroll's long friendship with Ellen Terry in the new light thus thrown upon it.

*Here Collingwood was mistaken, for his biography includes quotations from all the volumes of the diary which have since disappeared.

Three

Dodgson first saw Ellen Terry on June 16th, 1856, when, as a young man of twenty-four, he went to the Princess's Theatre to see Charles Kean and Mrs Kean in *A Winter's Tale*. 'I especially admired the acting of the little Mamillius, Ellen Terry,' he wrote in his diary, 'a beautiful little creature, who played with remarkable ease and spirit.' Ellen Terry was then eight years old, and this was her first appearance on the stage. She admits in her autobiography that as Mamillius she was 'really a sweet little thing'.[130]

Thereafter Dodgson watched for her appearances on the stage. 'Puck was very cleverly acted by the little Ellen Terry', he wrote after another visit to the Princess's Theatre on December 16th, 1856. In the next year a performance at the same theatre by her sister Kate as Ariel gave him great pleasure, and in January, 1858, he again saw 'the beautiful little Ellen Terry' both as Puck and as 'Goldenstar' in a pantomime, when he thought her 'the most perfectly graceful little fairy I ever saw'. The gap in the diaries means that we have no further reference to Ellen Terry until July 21st, 1863, a time when Dodgson was eagerly seeking fresh subjects for his camera. He then noted that 'Mr Tom Taylor knows the Misses Terry, and speaks very highly of them: I think I must try to get *them* also as sitters'. On July 24th he observed that 'Miss Ellen Terry is beginning to look, and act, just like Miss Kate'.

In the meantime G. F. Watts had also noticed the Terry sisters, had thought that he would like to paint them and had got in first with his request. Tom Taylor, the universal go-between, brought them to Watts's studio at Little Holland House and they sat for his famous picture of 'The Sisters'. Clement Scott has well suggested the contrast between Kate, the 'pure English beauty', and Ellen, 'ideal, mystical and mediaeval'. Watts, who was three times Ellen's age, felt immediately attracted to her; Ellen, flattered by the admiration of the great man, was advised that she had the chance of making 'a good match'; and on January 20th, 1864, when she was still only fifteen years old, she was married to him at St Barnabas, Kensington.[131] The marriage not surprisingly proved a failure, and they were soon separated, though not formally divorced until 1877.

'The Sisters' by Watts

What might have happened if Ellen Terry had sat to Dodgson for a photograph before she sat to Watts for a painting must remain an interesting conjecture. But in fact Dodgson was left to admire 'a beautiful head by Watts of Mrs Watts (Miss Ellen Terry)' in the Royal Academy of 1864, and only met her for the first time in the following December. Throughout the year he tried to get a chance of photographing her and called several times at the Terrys' home at 92 Stanhope Street. After a conversation with Tom Taylor he decided on 'not going to call, as I had intended, at Little Holland House'; and one assumes that he had been warned of the impending separation. At long last, on December 21st, 1864, he found in the drawing-room at Stanhope Street, 'to my delight, the one I have always most wished to meet of the family, Mrs Watts'. He was 'very much pleased' with what he saw of her – 'lively and pleasant, almost childish in her fun, but perfectly ladylike'. The gaiety of the two sisters he thought might have been partly assumed, doubtless to cover the dispiriting domestic situation, but he pronounced them both charming.

Henceforth Dodgson was reckoned to be on regular visiting terms with the large Terry family, as he was with Kate Terry's family after her marriage to Arthur Lewis. In April, 1865, he heard Mrs Watts 'play and sing', and in July

Ellen Terry by Watts

*Ellen Terry, photographed by
Dodgson in 1865*

spent two days with them all, photographing them singly and in groups. His photograph of Ellen Terry, inscribed by her 'Truly yours Ellen Alice Watts' (Alice was clearly a name that he could not hope to escape), is included by Helmut Gernsheim in his book. On this occasion and again later he persuaded her to play 'Castle Croquet' with him and her sisters – an ordeal obviously destined to be undergone by Alices. In the following year he took a second and very charming photograph of her at an open window, which is reproduced on the opposite page.

During 1866 Dodgson saw Ellen Terry often, both on and off the stage. They became very good friends, and we have noted that he designed for her his abortive drama *Morning Clouds** – though she found it impossible to be encouraging about its chances. In 1867 he saw less of her, and by going to live with E. W. Godwin in the country in 1868 she exiled herself for six years not only from Lewis Carroll but also from many of her other friends.

A Victorian clergyman might perhaps have been expected to disapprove of Ellen Terry's elopement without benefit of clergy, but Dodgson never allowed the shadow of conventional morality to dim his devotion to her for one moment. When she returned to the stage in 1874 he was back in his old place in the stalls, and thought her acting in *The Wandering Heir* 'simply *wonderful*'. He thought her 'wonderful' again in *New Men and Old Acres* in 1877, though there was a touch of compassion in his comment: 'The gush of animal spirits of a light-hearted girl is beyond her now, poor thing!' She moved him nearly to tears in *Olivia* in 1878, and in 1879 he found her Ophelia 'simply perfect'.

Not until June 18th, 1879, did he renew the friendship which had been interrupted for twelve years – he meticulously noted in his diary the date of their last meeting, May 11th, 1867. She then seemed to him 'as charming as ever'; and he approved of her second husband Charles Kelly and of her two children. He did not allow their friendship to lapse again so long as he lived. Only a few months before his death he went over from Eastbourne to Winchelsea to visit her, and watched her in the garden with one of his child-friends, Dolly Rivington, 'swinging, side by side, in hammocks'. A last memory of one who, like himself, could never grow old.

Four

It will be noticed that, though Ellen Terry recurs as a theme of delight throughout Dodgson's life from 1856 onwards, the actual period which held even the possiblity of any romantic feeling between them was short, namely from December 21st, 1864, until May 11th, 1867. He was thirty-two when they met; she nearly seventeen and, as Collingwood has observed, very lovely. But she was, in the eyes of the Law and the Church, a married woman, and Collingwood's conjecture that he might have proposed marriage to her can surely be dismissed as unthinkable. This does not dispose of the question whether he fell in love with her. Gordon Craig anyway had his own idea of men who proposed marriage to his mother: 'How could anyone in his kind senses,' he once wrote, 'ask such a dear madwoman in marriage – really, a joke's a joke. . . . Is it customary to marry visions – to espouse harmonies – to be tied to Fairy Queens?'[132] The question expects the answer No, but it is pertinent to add that of all the famous Victorians the one most likely to fall in love with a Fairy Queen was Lewis Carroll.

*See *supra*, p. 139.

Among the many women whom he knew throughout his life there is not one who can have been nearer Dodgson's artistic ideal than Ellen Terry. This was true of her at any age, but especially true of her at seventeen, when after nine years of stage experience she was far from being a woman of the world and was indeed still half an innocent child. Nor is it far-fetched to suppose that, after less than a year of unreal marriage at Little Holland House, she felt hurt and puzzled to find herself back in Stanhope Street, and may have looked on the admiring, intelligent and shyly sympathetic young clergyman who found her there as a friend in need. Not for nothing did Graham Robertson call her 'the Painter's Actress' – and Dodgson had an eye for pictures. Ellen Terry wrote, as she talked, with many underlinings or italics – and Dodgson himself was fond of underlinings. When we are told that his sister believed that he was in love with Ellen Terry, we cannot but wonder whether she was right.

If our reading of Dodgson's character has been correct, his love for Ellen Terry, assuming it existed, was no more likely to have found physical expression than his love for any other woman: that was his tragedy. It was not a love that was likely to have been put into writing.

The original letters that he wrote to her do not appear to have survived – they are not in the Ellen Terry Museum at Smallhythe – but Langford Reed was able to see some of them when he was preparing his book about Lewis Carroll which was published in 1932, and has quoted passages which show no more than a friendly affection. There are other excerpts in Ellen Terry's autobiography. The letters refer mainly to theatrical matters; they are all later than the period 1864–7. Langford Reed also quotes one remark of Dodgson's, from a source that the present writer has not succeeded in tracing, which is rather more provocative: 'I can imagine no more delightful occupation than brushing Ellen Terry's hair!'[133]

What Dodgson's feelings for Ellen Terry may have been in the year or so that followed their first meeting, and whether at that particularly unhappy stage of her life her eyes may have given him a little encouragement, are likely to remain matters of conjecture. 'He was as fond of me as he could be of anyone over the age of ten', she wrote in her autobiography.[134] Ellen Terry, for her part, had a genuine affection for her friend, but that she ever entertained any warmer feeling for him is improbable. 'She loved once, and that without criticism – only once', declared Gordon Craig.[135]

When Dodgson wrote to point out that a little girl whom he took to see her in *Faust* had said of the scene where Margaret begins to undress, 'Where is it going to stop?' – and when he went on to suggest that she should alter her playing of that scene, she was understandably angry. 'I thought you only knew *nice* children', she replied scathingly.[136] But as a rule their correspondence was entirely harmonious, and Ellen Terry was exceedingly considerate to the little girls whom Dodgson brought to her plays. He kept some of her letters. This is a typical note, undated:

Tuesday.

Oh, Patience! I never wore yellow and sky-blue as a combination in my life! The Juliet dress I *think* you mean was the *first* one – 'twas yellow satin – pearl trimming – yellow big *real* daisies in the hair and natural leather (yellowish) shoes. 'Twas not a pretty dress but prettier than the one you describe. Please this is a quick little scrawl for your little friend. I mean to answer *your* letter when Beatrice is *developed* (I mean I'll send you the lady photographed). If

you *only* would give up going to morning performances!! I saw you in front on Sat. morning and was so sorry for you. The play was never acted worse. Thursday and Friday nights the plays are always acted far and away better, and the whole thing goes better differently. I trust this will arrive in time to stay the little girl from wearing pink or pea-green shoes (coloured photographs are never to be relied upon). Ted and Edie are out or they would send their love with mine. I will write *properly* very soon. Yours most sincerely,
ELLEN TERRY.

A letter of 1883 shows that Ellen Terry accepted Dodgson's advice on her playing of the church scene in *Much Ado About Nothing*. She signed that letter 'with affection', and concluded another letter in the following year with 'Dear Mr Dodgson, I hope you are very well and happy. . . . We all send our love.'[137]

These were only the natural expressions of a warm-hearted woman, used to the affection and admiration of men. That Lewis Carroll may at one period have been in some sense in love with her is a suggestion that cannot be disproved. No other woman of his time could have satisfied so completely the ideals of the artist and the man of the theatre in him.

Five

The idea that the author of *Alice in Wonderland* should have fallen in love with Ellen Terry at seventeen will hardly strike any reader as completely improbable. More scepticism may be felt about the theory, which has been developed by Mr A. L. Taylor with every refinement of ingenuity in his book *The White Knight*, that Dodgson 'fell in love', in the adult sense, with Alice Liddell.

Dodgson first met Alice when she was four and he was twenty years older; he had already shown that he enjoyed the company of little girls and that he was particularly successful at entertaining them. Throughout her childhood he stood to her in the position of a kind and protective uncle. He loved her as a child – she became his 'ideal child-friend' – and she inspired the books by which he will be always remembered. It has often happened that men have made successful marriages with women younger than themselves whom they have known in girlhood – Dodgson's brother Wilfred, for example, married a girl who was twelve years his junior, to whom he had been attracted since she was thirteen; but this would not have involved such a strain as the change to a romantic relationship from an avuncular relationship that had subsisted since Alice was four, nor was the disparity between the ages so great.

We cannot dismiss the likelihood that, in seeking the society of little girls while still a young man in his twenties, Dodgson was compensating himself, in part, for his inability to form friendships with women of his own age. Children were an escape from sex rather than any sort of conscious satisfaction of it, but they gave him the affection he needed and helped him to fulfil the Platonic and protective love which was characteristic of his nature. The romantic poems of 1860–2 were written while Alice Liddell was between seven and ten years old. The poem 'Faces in the Fire' of 1860, which imagines an old man looking back on his friendship with a growing girl and lingers over the 'might have been' of such a relationship, draws its material, surely, not only from Alice Liddell but from all the children Dodgson had admired –

including perhaps that 'beautiful little creature' Ellen Terry – and indeed from the very spirit of childhood which he understood so well. It suggests that he had a foreboding that he would never marry, but no more than that. In its nostalgia for the past it is an extension of the poem 'Solitude' which he wrote as early as 1853.

It is tempting to interpret the White Knight's parting from Alice as Dodgson's poetic comment on the loss of this ideal child-friend. The White Knight asks Alice to wave her handkerchief until he gets to the turn of the road: 'I think it'll encourage me, you see.' 'Of course I'll wait,' is Alice's reply, 'and thank you very much for coming so far – and for the song – I liked it very much.'

After they have shaken hands, the White Knight rides slowly away into the forest.

'It wo'n't take long to see him *off*, I expect', Alice said to herself, as she stood watching him. 'There he goes! Right on his head as usual! However, he gets on again pretty easily – that comes of having so many things hung round the horse –' So she went on talking to herself, as she watched the horse walking leisurely along the road, and the Knight tumbling off, first on one side and then on the other. After the fourth or fifth tumble he reached the turn, and then she waved her handkerchief to him, and waited till he was out of sight.

'I hope it encouraged him', she said, as she turned to run down the hill. . . .

To see in this particular passage a little allegory – perhaps entirely unconscious – of Lewis Carroll's farewell to Alice as a child, is a conjecture that may be forgiven (though it remains no more than a conjecture). Dodgson advanced on his solitary way, taking some hard knocks but always managing to get up again and to keep going forward; his many interests and ceaseless activity helped him – he had 'so many things hung round the horse'. But Lewis Carroll's fantasies are capable of such varied interpretation that to search them further for evidence that he was 'in love' with Alice Liddell is an unprofitable and necessarily an inconclusive task.

His relations with her parents were strained – so much is clear. Mrs Liddell tore up all the letters that he wrote to Alice when she was a small girl; 'I cannot remember what any of them were like, but it is an awful thought to contemplate what may have perished in the Deanery waste-paper basket', Alice herself recorded many years later.[138] Can we infer anything from this? There was no one better qualified to answer that question than Alice's son, Caryl Hargreaves,* who kindly gave the author the following opinion:

'I do not think that Dodgson was ever "in love" with my mother in the sense in which that phrase is generally used. I don't think Dodgson was ever in love with anyone, that is to say, contemplated marriage, which is what I think is generally meant in this connection.

My grandmother certainly did not discourage the friendship when the girls were children, but perhaps when they became of marriageable age she was overcome by Victorian ideas. It might not have been approved of by Oxford in the 1870s for the marriageable daughters of the Dean to go about with an unmarried don of the Dean's college.'

*Caryl has nothing to do with Carroll. He was named after a character in a novel which his aunt happened to be reading at the time of his christening.

Mrs F. B. Lennon in her biography[139] states that Caryl Hargreaves told Professor J. E. Zanetti 'that Mrs Liddell "hated" Carroll.' Hargreaves could not, in fact, remember any such conversation and did not wish any such opinion to be attributed to him. There must have been some misunderstanding. Dodgson, he felt, was perhaps not the kind of man who would particularly have interested his grandmother, and she may have thought him rather eccentric, but Hargreaves added: 'I cannot imagine my grandmother *hating* him: it is *far* too strong a word.' Dodgson retained no hard feelings for Mrs Liddell; he inscribed a copy of *Alice's Adventures Under Ground*, the facsimile of the original manuscript, 'To Her, whose children's smiles fed the narrator's fancy and were his rich reward, from the Author, Xmas, 1886'.[140]

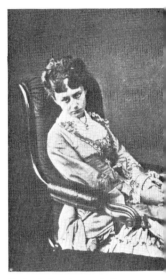

Alice Liddell grew up into a young woman whose artistic and intellectual ability was well above the average, yet it is doubtful for many reasons that she could have made a happy marriage with Dodgson. Unlike him, she came of an aristocratic family (Dean Liddell's grandfather was a baronet and the Liddells were descended from the barony of Ravensworth); and she was perfectly content with a country life and county society. It is unlikely that she ever considered Dodgson for a moment as a possible husband. She married (though not till 1880) Reginald Hargreaves, a few months younger than she, who went to Christ Church as an undergraduate from Eton. He was about as different from Lewis Carroll as any man could be: in the front rank as a shot, a fine cricketer who played for Hampshire, a good golfer, and very proud of his trees – some of them the tallest in England – on the Cuffnells estate in Hampshire which he inherited.

'The children of Alice call Bartrum father.' The Hargreaves had three sons, of whom two were killed in the 1914–18 war. If 'Faces in the Fire' were to be considered as in any way anticipating Alice Liddell's future, which is not admitted, one verse in the original poem would have been prophetically accurate.

Dodgson's last photograph of Alice, 1870

> 'Tis now a matron with her boys,
> Dear centre of domestic joys;
> I seem to hear the merry noise.

But it was such a bad verse that Dodgson removed it when the poem was reprinted in 1869.

Six

Dodgson saw comparatively little of Alice Liddell after she was fourteen, but she remained in his thoughts. When *The Wonderland Quadrilles*, a set of piano pieces by C. H. R. Marriott, were published in 1871, he suggested that they should be dedicated not to him but 'To Alice'. In his own dedication of *Through the Looking-Glass* he wrote of Alice:

> I have not seen thy sunny face,
>   Nor heard thy silver laughter;
> No thought of me shall find a place
>   In thy young life's hereafter –
> Enough that now thou wilt not fail
> To listen to my fairy-tale.

Although the copy of *Through the Looking-Glass* that went to her in December of 1871 was bound in morocco, he had long been endeavouring to arrange something even more distinctive for her. 'I want to have the presentation copy of the "Looking Glass" (I mean the one for Miss A. Liddell) bound with an oval piece of looking-glass let into the cover. Will you consult your binder as to whether the thing is practical?' he wrote to Macmillan's on April 15th, 1870. Apparently it wasn't; but the thought was typical of his abiding sense of gratitude for the source of his inspiration.

That Dodgson's interest in the Liddell girls did not pass unnoticed by the undergraduates of Christ Church is evidenced by a curious squib in verse entitled *Cakeless* which was written by the Rev John Howe Jenkins, then an undergraduate of the House, and published in 1874. The British Museum copy has a note in pencil: 'Printed at Oxford by Mowbray, The edition suppressed, The author rusticated'. It is strange that this lively little satire has not hitherto attracted the attention of Lewis Carroll's biographers.[141]

Cakeless has two main purposes; the first is to ridicule Mrs Liddell and her alleged endeavours at matchmaking for her daughters, the second to show that Dodgson was unpopular in the College and disliked by some of his colleagues in the Senior Common Room. Its plot, which concerns a triple marriage of Ecilia, Rosa and Psyche, daughters of Apollo (Dean Liddell) and Diana (Mrs Liddell), may well have been inspired by the wedding of their eldest daughter Lorina to W. B. Skene, of Hallyards and Pitlour, Fife, on February 7th, 1874. Diana tells the 'chorus of drunken satyrs' that after this triple marriage they need 'look no more for any "perpendiculars"' (i.e. standing receptions at the Deanery), and the satyrs sing:

> Apollo was a worthy peer,
> His daughters cost him many a frown;
> Diana held them all too dear,
> But Fife he brought the market down.

The suggestion here, obviously, is that Skene (Fife) – a Fellow of All Souls – was not quite the bridegroom that Mrs Liddell would have chosen for Lorina.

A pencil note in the British Museum copy of *Cakeless* describes Diana as 'Fond of hunting for husbands for daughters'. It is she who opens the play by greeting Apollo with the words: 'Great partner, art thou sad? I bring good cheer.' To them enters their daughter Ecilia – duly identified in the British Museum copy as Alice – who declaims:

> Mother, it always has been your behest
> That truth and confidence are ever best.
> You always wished that I should marry one
> Or Prince, or peer, or else a member's son.
> The last have I at length securely trapped,
> And in the toils of courtship firmly wrapped.
> I trust my father will his favour show,
> And let me with this handsome stranger go.

DIANA. Surely Yerbua's not the happy man?
ECILIA. He is, he is! he loves me all he can.
DIANA. My blessings on you, daughter! would that she

Who's gone before had made a match like thee!
Apollo! one would deem you whelmed with grief.
APOLLO. I've lost my daughter!
                    (*Aside*) What a blest relief!

Yerbua presumably stands for Aubrey Harcourt, of Nuneham Park, Stanton
Harcourt, only son of Edward William Harcourt and Lady Susan Harriett,
only daughter of the second Earl of Sheffield. He was born in the same year
as Alice, 1852, and was, as one would expect, educated at Eton and Christ
Church: a thoroughly eligible suitor for Mrs Liddell's daughters. It may be
that the linking of his name with Alice's in this undergraduate satire of 1874
is intended to suggest that he was then paying court to her; but his choice
eventually fell on the third daughter Edith, who died with tragic suddenness
in 1876, aged twenty-two, soon after the announcement of their engagement.

It was doubtless the author's intention that the allusions in *Cakeless* should
not always be capable of exact interpretation. Apollo's daughter Rosa
announces that she has 'trapped a noble lord of high degree', while Psyche
declares that she has 'trapped a Prince, the youngest of his race'. Rosa may
suggest Rhoda, the Liddell's fourth daughter, but neither she nor Violet the
fifth daughter were of marriageable age in 1874.

Rosa's bridegroom, Rivulus, may be identified as Lord Brooke, who was up
at Christ Church at about this time and who eventually succeeded his father
as the fifth Earl of Warwick. When he returns thanks to Apollo's toast after
the wedding, he apologises for his father's absence because he has to rebuild
'our noble hall' which had been damaged by fire: there was a disastrous fire at
Warwick Castle in 1871.

Psyche's 'catch' is the biggest of the lot. Her bridegroom, Regius, is
obviously intended for Queen Victoria's youngest son, Prince Leopold,
another contemporary undergraduate of Christ Church, whom Dodgson
photographed in 1875. Regius's excuse for the absence of his parent from the
wedding is given, not very grammatically, in the words 'Today doth
Buckingham *ma mère* contain.'

At the beginning of Act II of *Cakeless* we find the 'Wedding company
settled in church. Among them may be seen, Agonistes, Dutch Skipper, and at
some little distance, Kraftsohn, biting his nails'. Agonistes and Dutch Skipper
probably stand for the Rev E. F. Sampson and the Rev H. S. Holland, both
dons of Christ Church, while Kraftsohn is obviously Dodgson. No sooner has
the service begun than we read: 'KRAFTSOHN (*interrupting*): I do protest against
this match, so let me speak'. And a pencil note in the margin of the British
Museum copy runs: '– dgs-n had been rejected'.

APOLLO. (*irate*)
        Strip, strip him, scouts!
        This is the knave we seek.
KRAFT   By circles, segments, and by radii,
        Than yield to these I'd liefer far to die.

The scouts advance, 'throwing their "perquisites" at the head of KRAFTSOHN,
who takes refuge in the cloisters'. But the further trials of Kraftsohn, otherwise
Dodgson, as described in *Cakeless*, will be best related in the next chapter, where

we shall have an opportunity of considering some of his incursions into college controversy which inspired the rest of the satire.

As a specimen of undergraduate wit, *Cakeless* is competent and mildly entertaining. In its local references, however, it is obviously so provocative that the author could hardly have hoped to escape punishment. As he read it, the face of Dean Liddell must have grown more than usually grave. No wonder the edition was suppressed and John Howe Jenkins sent down.

Seven

The evidence provided by *Cakeless* must be handled with caution. So far as we can accept it, there is confirmation here of Mrs Liddell's snobbery and of her match-making propensities, already implied by other sources. In *The Vision of the Three T's* Dodgson wrote of 'The Gold-fish, which is a species highly thought of, and much sought after in these parts, not only by men, but by divers birds, as for example the king-fishers' (a passage said to have given offence at the Deanery).[142] 'You always wished that I should marry one Or Prince, or peer, or else a member's son,' Ecilia reminds her mother in *Cakeless* – and this attitude would have told against Dodgson, despite his advancing fame as Lewis Carroll.

Dodgson's protest against the wedding might, however, be thought merely to typify his reactionary views on college affairs in general. Nor can the pencilled comment '– dgs-n had been rejected', though presumably contemporary, be taken very seriously, for it is just the sort of remark that might have been made frivolously by a member of Christ Church who had observed at a distance Dodgson's long association with the young Liddells, without appreciating his motives and idiosyncrasies or the avuncular nature of his affection for little girls. It was alleged, entirely without foundation, at the time of his centenary in 1932, that he had been in love with one of Alice's younger sisters; and we have seen that he was once even suspected of designs on the governess, Miss Prickett.

It is just possible (though most unlikely) that Dodgson might have made a happy marriage with a brilliantly clever girl like Ethel Rowell, who shared his interests in logic and mathematics, who understood that side of his mind, and who at the age of twenty went into mourning for him when he died.* But in the crucial period of Dodgson's life no Miss Rowell came upon the scene, and, threading the maze of speculation once again, we still find only two women at the centre of it – Alice Liddell and Ellen Terry.

That he loved them both in some sense need not be doubted. His love for Alice crystallised and consecrated his love for children. As she passed out of childhood, it became clear that neither her family background nor her own interests offered any reliable foundation for adult love. Just at that time he met Ellen Terry – at seventeen half woman and half child – whose radiant character and genius stirred all his artistic sensibilities. Here perhaps came his one clear romantic call – it was not one that he could attempt to answer. As the years went by, the news of Alice's marriage may yet have brought him a pang, as Collingwood suggests, for he was not without jealousy.

In his memories of these two very different beings lies the nucleus of his disappointment; he regretted not only the 'might have been' of those relationships, but the inherent dichotomy of his character that made it impossible for

*See *supra*, p. 20.

him to resolve the dilemma of sexual love. Several books in his library with titles like *The Ways of Women* and *Physical Life of Women* show that he had a deep curiosity about the opposite sex. That he felt a man's normal temptations we know from his introduction to *Pillow Problems*, where he wrote of 'unholy thoughts, which torture with their hateful presence the fancy that would fain be pure'.

The normal answer, however, was not for him. Dr M. J. Mannheim, after studying specimens of the handwriting, has come to this conclusion:

'He could not love except in a protective way. He would not have been able to combine love with sexual desire. That preoccupied him, but he remained frightened of his unconscious. He had a strong need to be loved, but marriage unless with a very inferior woman appears improbable, though one cannot be dogmatic about such a problem. His past-fixation was too great for him to come to terms with reality or the reality of a woman.'

In the end probably all was for the best. The security of the Oxford life proved an ever-increasing attraction; it was after all, as he said, 'by no means unmixed misery'. Renunciation brought compensations in the form of work well done – he was not without happiness of a kind. His sadness was not entirely personal, but came partly, as with many sensitive people, from the realisation that life itself is sad. To offset depression he had the Christian revelation of hope and love, which meant much to him. 'A working life is a happy one', he wrote in his diary of February 14th, 1871, 'but oh that mine were better and nearer to God!'

It was preferable that Lewis Carroll should have been a busy bachelor than an unhappy husband.

Towards the Snark

Through the Looking-Glass had consolidated the triumph of *Alice's Adventures in Wonderland*; as the sales of both books advanced, the fame of Lewis Carroll increased proportionately. The proprietor of that pseudonym not only found himself in possession of a comfortable income, but was also able to enjoy the agreeable luxury of worrying over the exploitation of his success.

Ch. Ch.
Nov. 26/72.

Dear Mr Macmillan,

Will you kindly, with all reasonable expedition on receipt of this, engage a couple of copying-clerks, and have *all* the speeches in 'Alice' and the 'Looking-Glass' written out, with the names of the speakers, and such directions as 'Enter the White Rabbit', 'Exit the Red Queen', in the ordinary dramatic form, *and get them registered as two dramas*, with the same names as the books – I am told that is the only way to retain a right to forbid their being represented by any one who may choose to dramatise them. I trust to you to get it all done in such a way as will satisfy the requirements of the law. Please put in *all* the speeches.

In haste,
Very truly yours,
C. L. Dodgson.

The dramas were duly registered, but five years later Dodgson discovered that he had overestimated the effect of this precaution and that he was unable to interfere with an adaptation projected by the Elliston family. He gave permission for an entertainment based on *Alice in Wonderland* at the Polytechnic in 1876 and for the dramatisations which were published by Kate Freiligrath-Kroeker in 1880 and 1882, and took a special interest, as we shall see, in Savile Clarke's operetta of 1886. There were many musical settings of the songs from both books.

Dodgson seems to have taken the normal and understandable pleasure of an author in seeing his work made available to an ever-increasing audience. Thus on March 17th, 1876, when he was asked by Routledge's to allow some of his poems to appear in an anthology, he wrote to Macmillan's:

'I don't think our views quite harmonise. *You* take the publisher's view, doubtless, that it might injure the sale of the book. But really I don't feel much fear of that. And as to anything of mine being included among (respectable) collections of Nursery Rhymes, it is a classical position I have not hitherto aspired to. I should rather like, than otherwise, to be represented in a *good* collection of such things.'

So far as his personal identification with Lewis Carroll was concerned, however, the position was infinitely complicated. He obviously took great pleasure in being known as Lewis Carroll to his many child-friends, and was most lavish in presenting them with copies of his books. We have seen, moreover, that he felt no qualms that his authorship of *Alice in Wonderland* should have facilitated his introduction to Lord Salisbury. At times one is reminded of Oscar Wilde's epigram: 'There is only one thing in the world worse than being talked about, and that is not being talked about.' But during the last twenty years of his life he did show an almost morbid determination to avert any attempts at 'lionisation', and his progressive withdrawal from social life was foreshadowed as early as May 26th, 1872, when he wrote in his diary that he had refused an invitation to luncheon 'for the two-fold reason that I do not go out on Sunday and that I do not go out to luncheon'.

Dodgson's place in the life of Christ Church was not, in the years of his fame, entirely comfortable. For many years his colleagues had known him as a shy and unobtrusive person whose hidden potentialities they could be excused for disregarding. Suddenly, on the strength of two small fantasies, they found him enjoying a popular fame which they knew could never be theirs. They were surprised, and perhaps one or two of them were slightly resentful. Dodgson remained as modest and shy as before, but, for some strange reason which they could not quite understand, he now belonged not only to Christ Church but also to the world. It was the old situation of the prophet who is not without honour save in his own country; its echoes lingered at Christ Church long after Lewis Carroll's death.

The situation was not made any easier by the firm and uncompromising line taken by Dodgson in College affairs.[143] He first battled against the Canons on behalf of the Students, urging their right to a larger share in the government of the College, and then made effective ridicule of many reforms sponsored by Dean Liddell and the Governing Body; in his humorous satires he did not spare his personal friends. His conscientious punctiliousness, in many ways so honourable, made him seem pedantic and even selfish when it was expressed in perpetual complaints against the College servants. He showed little interest in the undergraduates or their activities, and it was difficult for his colleagues to restrain a feeling of impatience at the troops of little girls that made their way so often to his rooms. W. Tuckwell, an observer from New College, saw the dark side: 'Austere, shy, precise, absorbed in mathematical reverie, watchfully tenacious of his dignity, stiffly conservative in political, theological, social theory, his life mapped out in squares like Alice's landscape, he struck discords in the frank harmonious *camaraderie* of College life.'[144]

Despite all this, it is true to say that many members of the Senior Common Room looked beneath the surface, loved what was best in the man and would have confessed their Christ Church days much the poorer without him. One greater than Tuckwell, Professor York Powell, who knew Dodgson from the early seventies onwards, has described the simplicity of his Oxford life, the hard work nearly all day 'with the barest apology for lunch', the walk in the afternoon, the dinner in hall and chat with a friend in his room afterwards, followed by more work till he went to bed. 'He wanted all his time for his work, he said, and he often told us he found the days too short.' York Powell has crystallised his dominant memories into an affectionate paragraph:

'The quiet humour of his voice, a very pleasant voice, the occasional laugh, – he was not a man that often laughed, though there was often a smile playing about his sensitive mouth, – and the slight hesitation that whetted some of his wittiest sayings, – all those that knew him must remember; but his kindly sympathies, his rigid rule of his own life, his unselfish love of the little ones, whose liegeman he was, his dutiful discharge of every obligation that was in the slightest degree incumbent on him, his patience with his younger colleagues, who were sometimes a little ignorant and impatient of the conditions under which alone Common-room life must be in the long run ruled, his rare modesty, and the natural kindness which preserved him from the faintest shadow of conceit, and made him singularly courteous to every one, high or low, he came across in his quiet academic life, – these his less-known characteristics will only remain in the memories of his colleagues and contemporaries. Dodgson and Liddon long made the House Common-room a resort where the weary brain-worker found harmless mirth and keen but kindly wit. Liddon, on his days, was a fine talker, full of humour and observation, an excellent mimic, a maker of beautiful and fine-coloured phrase, a delightful debater. Dodgson was a good teller of anecdote, a splendid player at the game of *quodlibet*, which St Louis commended as an after-dinner sport, a fantastic weaver of paradox and propounder of puzzle, a person who never let the talk flag, but never monopolised it, who had rather set others talking than talk himself, and was as pleased to hear a twice-told tale as to retail his own store of reminiscence . . .'.[145]

Dodgson was remembered in Christ Church as a wit; it would have been surprising to hear otherwise. York Powell describes him as 'an exceptionally good after-dinner speaker', on the rare occasions when he could be persuaded to speak. But those of his verbal witticisms that have been recorded read somewhat mechanically and bear some sense of strain – he needed the leisure of pen and paper to develop his humour. It was a condition that he himself analysed mercilessly. 'It sounds like a horse,' Alice thought to herself in the railway train, and a small voice, close to her ear, said, 'You might make a joke on that – something about "horse" and "hoarse", you know.' Or again, 'I was in a wood just now,' said Alice, 'and I wish I could get back there!' 'You might make a joke on *that*,' said the little voice, 'something about "you *would* if you could", you know.' Dodgson sometimes listened to the little voice.

Left: Alexander (Xie) Kitchin, photographed by Dodgson in the 1850s. Right: Vere Bayne by Dodgson

His friend Vere Bayne, in his perfunctory diary, with its frequent entries

'Walk with Dodgson', set down some of his friend's jokes. One of these, a photographer's quip, has been often quoted: 'How do you attain to excellence? Take a lens and place Xie [Kitchin, one of his girl friends] in front of it.' Another may be less familiar: '"Our relations are becoming rather strained", as the Spanish Inquisitor said, after he had ordered his second cousin to be set on the rack.' [146] 'Heard this evening [October 22nd, 1870] the last new joke of the author of *Alice in Wonderland*', wrote Edward Lee Hicks in his diary. 'He (Dodgson) knows a man whose feet are so large that he has to put on his trousers over his head.'[147] None but the masters of conversation can survive such cold-blooded re-examination, yet this was good talk at the time. It does perhaps remind us that Dodgson occasionally suggested jokes for *Punch*.

He was a born inventor, whose aids to memory, methods of calculating and other helpful devices tumbled into his mind at all hours. 'While undressing,' says the Diary of November 30th, 1875, 'thought of a process (which I worked out next day) for finding angles from different sines and cosines.' He continually devised puzzles and was a master of the anagram. The following note to Francis Paget can be dated to the period of the trial of the Tichborne Claimant (1873–4) whose defending counsel Edward Vaughan Kenealy was subsequently disbarred:

MY DEAR PAGET,
  'Ah! we dread an ugly knave!' There! I thought it out last night after getting into bed. It is a correct anagram for 'Edward Vaughan Kenealy.'

Yours &c.,

C. L. D.[148]

Two

Between 1872 and 1874 Dodgson published anonymously three small satirical pamphlets on Oxford controversies which were eagerly bought and read in Oxford and caused much local amusement, as well as some irritation to those most directly attacked. The pamphlets were *The New Belfry of Christ Church, Oxford* (1872), *The Vision of the Three T's* (1873) – both concerned with Christ Church affairs – and *The Blank Cheque* (1874), which ridiculed a proposal to authorise the building of the new Examination Schools before any plan or estimate had been prepared. These three pamphlets, together with three earlier pamphlets on Oxford matters were reissued in 1874 as *Notes by an Oxford Chiel*.[149]

The 'New Belfry' and the 'Three T's' were aimed straight at Dean Liddell and at the work which he had inspired and was supervising on the buildings of Christ Church. Dodgson's relations with the Dean had long been uneasy; it is not surprising that after this open declaration of war they did not improve. Liddell had already carried through considerable alterations to the Deanery and to the Cathedral, but a thorough 'restoration' of the Cathedral was not begun until 1870. Among the many changes, that which particularly incensed Dodgson was the removal of the bells from the church to a new and hideous temporary wooden structure provided for them above the Hall staircase. His rejoinder was the 'New Belfry', and it was at once apparent from the opening paragraph that he had produced a minor *tour de force*: 'The word "Belfry" is derived from the French *bel*, "beautiful, becoming, meet", and from the German *frei*, "free, unfettered, secure, safe". Thus the word is strictly equivalent to "meat-safe", to which the new belfry bears a resemblance so perfect as almost to amount to coincidence.'

Dodgson pursues the joke for fifteen pages. 'What traveller is there,' he asks, 'to whose lips, when first he enters that great educational establishment and gazes on this its newest decoration, the words do not rise unbidden – "Thou tea-chest"?' Referring to 'the impetus given to Art in England by the new Belfry', he reports:

'The idea has spread far and wide, and is rapidly pervading all branches of manufacture. Already an enterprising maker of bonnet-boxes is advertising "the Belfry pattern": two builders of bathing machines at Ramsgate have followed his example: one of the great London houses is supplying "bar-soap" cut in the same striking and symmetrical form: and we are credibly informed that Borwick's Baking Powder and Thorley's Food for Cattle are now sold in no other shape.'

He gives a dramatic dialogue between the Dean, Canons and Students, and the 'mad Architect', which includes the following parody sung by the Treasurer and Chorus:

> Five fathoms square the Belfry frowns;
>   All its sides of timber made;
> Painted all in greys and browns;
>   Nothing of it that will fade.
> Christ Church may admire the change –
> Oxford thinks it sad and strange.
> Beauty's dead! Let's ring her knell.
> Hark! now I hear them – ding-dong, bell.

The pamphlet ends with a reminiscence of the work of an earlier member of Christ Church, Martin Tupper.

In the following year the argument was continued with the 'Three T's' – the Tea-chest, the Trench (an 'improvement' at the south-east corner of Tom Quad) and the Tunnel, the new double-arched entrance to the Cathedral. This pamphlet took the form of a parody of Walton's *Compleat Angler*, ingeniously done but rather too long for its substance and showing signs of labour. A reference to Gold-fish and King-fishers was mentioned in Chapter X as having offended the Deanery; but the best thing in the 'Three T's' is the classic parody of Sheridan: 'Here's to the Freshman of bashful eighteen!' Dodgson followed this up with an entirely serious pamphlet of 'Objections, submitted to the Governing Body of Christ Church, Oxford, against certain proposed alterations in the Great Quadrangle'. He was successful in one of his three objections – that to a proposed grass slope which was to take the place of the terrace wall. The next year he sent a letter to the *Pall Mall Gazette* protesting against the extravagance of the Dean's schemes, and especially against an abortive proposal to erect cloisters in Tom Quad.

C. P. Snow's novel *The Masters* painted a rather depressing picture of the childish intrigues and jealousies to be found in learned Common Rooms, but a study of the inner life of Christ Church in Liddell's day would suggest that he did not exaggerate. Witty as they are, there is a certain immaturity about Dodgson's pamphlets which continues to surprise; this elaborate local satire might have been expected from an undergraduate of twenty but scarcely from a man of forty. One views with some sympathy the attempt of the disgraced undergraduate author of *Cakeless* in 1874 – mentioned in the last chapter – to take him down a peg.

Dean Liddell's annoyance at the satire on himself and Mrs Liddell in *Cakeless* must have been somewhat assuaged by the hearty determination with which his 'foeman' Kraftsohn (Dodgson) is pitched into during the latter half of that pantomime. It will be remembered that, after protesting at the wedding of Apollo's daughters, Kraftsohn is pursued into the cloisters. Apollo's henchman Romanus* then pronounces sentence:

Take him through trench and tunnel to the chest,
Nor ever leave the cursed fiend at rest.
Leave him in Wonderland with some hard-hitting foe,
And through the looking-glass let him survey the blow;
Confine him in the belfry, not in Peck,
And make him sign at pleasure your blank cheque.

Kraftsohn is locked in the belfry by the scouts, and this so pleases Apollo-Liddell that he forgets to be angry when his wife tells him the wedding-cake has not arrived:

Bother the cake! yonder within the chest
My foeman Kraftsohn bites his nails at rest.

Act III of *Cakeless* shows Kraftsohn in the belfry, still 'biting his nails with rage', and soliloquising:

Ah, tea-chest! thou thy slanderer dost repay
For all the calumnies that he did ever say;
List to the captive's stifled moan,
Take the unhappy pilgrim home.
Ah, scouts! a pamphlet I will surely write
Which with a serpent's tooth will keenly bite.
Your perquisites, your pilferings I'll betray,
And turn to hellish night your garish day.

Romanus now decrees the final stage of Kraftsohn's punishment, immersion in 'Mercury' (the pond in the centre of Tom Quad at Christ Church):

Pinch him and pull him and turn him about,
Through bricks and through mortar the foe of the scout;
Whelm him deep in the plashing sea
Where the crocodile lives and the kedgeree.
KRAFTSOHN: My fate is sealed; my race is run,
My pilgrimage is wellnigh done.
Farewell to pamphlets and to angles round!
I seek a shore where Euclid is not found.

*I cannot attempt to identify Romanus among Dean Liddell's supporters, though the suggestion may be that he was a classical scholar.

Enter by Mercury's brink Romanus with his two attendants bearing Kraftsohn between them. They plunge him in.

ROMANUS: Full fathoms five e'en now he lies,
Of his bones are segments made.
Those circles are that were his eyes.
Nothing of him that doth fade
But doth suffer a sea-change
Into something queer and strange.
Goldfish hourly ring his knell.
     Ding-dong.
Hark! now I hear them, ding, dong, bell.

It will be noticed that the choice of another adaptation of Ariel's song to end *Cakeless* is a deliberate reference to Dodgson's parody in the 'New Belfry', which has already been quoted, and that the selection of goldfish to ring his knell is an allusion to that passage in the 'Three T's' which particularly stirred the Deanery.

Three

Dodgson showed great consideration for all animals – in his case a logical extension of his love for children and part of his sympathy for all weaker nature. One emphasises this particulary, because in England animals seem often to have been more thought about than children. Dodgson loved children more than animals; he seems never to have had a dog or cat of his own, but whenever he noticed an animal in distress he was deeply concerned. Thus when he saw a kitten in the street with a fish-hook in its mouth he took the trouble to carry it to a doctor to have the hook extracted; on another occasion he persuaded the owner of some horses to have their bearing-reins taken off. Mice in his rooms were caught in a White-Knightly trap of his own invention which could be immersed in water so as to give them a quick death, and when the ancient Common Room cat at Christ Church had to be destroyed he wrote to Sir James Paget for his advice:

'It seems a shame to occupy your time and attention with so trivial a matter as a pet-cat: but all the modes you suggest, except the poisoned meat, would be unsuitable. To shut it up in a cage would produce an agony of terror: and the same may be said of the hypodermic injection (which would have to be done by a stranger, I suppose), and, most of all, of the journey to London. Is there no kind of poison which would *not* involve the risk of being vomited, and which would produce a painless sleep? My own idea would have been to give *laudanum*, (I don't know what quantity, say a drachm) mixed with some meat or fish – Would not this do?'

When *Alice in Wonderland* had its first public representation at the Polytechnic in 1876, much of it being presented by 'dissolving views', Dodgson vetoed a verse in a song in which the drowning of kittens was humorously treated. And to a friend who had lost a pet dog he wrote: 'You have certainly given to *one* of God's creatures a *very* happy life through a good many years – a pleasant thing to remember.'[150]

It was inevitable that with this sensitivity Dodgson should have been worried about vivisection ('I am afraid that man vivisects', he once remarked when he passed a distinguished professor in Oxford[151]), and his anxiety was heavy on him in 1875, when he followed up a letter in the *Pall Mall Gazette* with an article in the *Fortnightly Review* which was reprinted as a pamphlet: *Some Popular Fallacies about Vivisection*. He did not advocate its total abolition, but argued its evil effect on the operator and wished to see it more carefully restricted by law, though the pamphlet, as Falconer Madan points out, 'fails to be fully effective from the juxtaposition of pitiless logic with warm and generous sentiment'.[152] In 'Fame's Penny-Trumpet', an unusually bitter poem of 1876, he continued the attack with less subtlety.

Four

Out of this atmosphere of controversy and contention which surrounded Dodgson in the early eighteen-seventies, there now emerged one of his most widely appreciated masterpieces, that Odyssey of the Nonsensical, *The Hunting of the Snark*:

> And when quarrels arose – as one frequently finds
>   Quarrels will, spite of every endeavour –
> The Song of the Jubjub recurred to their minds
> And cemented their friendship for ever!

Holiday's illustrations for
The Hunting of the Snark

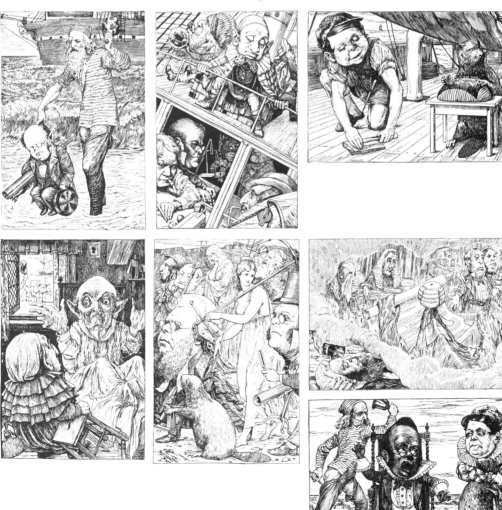

It is a plausible conjecture that some of the imagery of the 'Snark' was drawn from his pamphlets on the Christ Church controversies, that the Snark's fondness for bathing-machines, which he believed added 'to the beauty of scenes – a sentiment open to doubt', may have been inspired by the ungainly shape of the New Belfry, and that the Beaver's apprehension in the presence of the Butcher owed something to Dodgson's horror of vivisection. To search the poem for hidden meanings or an intentional allegory is as much a waste of time in the case of the 'Snark' as it is with the 'Alice' books. 'I'm very much afraid', wrote Dodgson himself, 'that I didn't mean anything but nonsense!' – and it is probably just for this reason that he succeeded in writing the longest and best sustained nonsense poem in the language. There are many other poems written with profound intellectual pretension that may seem nonsensical enough to many readers, but this is one of the few poems of deliberate nonsense that is an addition to our literature. Dodgson was delighted to adopt any helpful interpretations:

'. . . words mean more than we mean to express when we use them; so a whole book ought to mean a great deal more than the writer means. So, whatever good meanings are in the book, I'm glad to accept as the meaning of the book. The best that I've seen is by a lady (she published it in a letter to a newspaper), that the whole book is an allegory on the search after happiness. I think this fits in beautifully in many ways – particularly about the bathing-machines: when the people get weary of life, and can't find happiness in towns or in books, then they rush off to the seaside, to see what bathing-machines will do for them.'

The detail of the 'Snark' was 'hammered-out', but the poem owes its magical quality to sheer poetic inspiration and it is by this element that, like 'Jabberwocky' (with which it has an affinity emphasised by the use of many of the same words), it transcends mere comic verse. The last line of the whole poem, 'For the Snark *was* a Boojum you see', came suddenly into Dodgson's mind as he was walking at Guildford in July, 1874, and a few days afterwards he composed the whole of the final stanza. He did not, he said, know what it meant at the time – or later – but 'at odd moments during the next year or two, the rest of the poem pieced itself together.'[153] The process was one of creative intuition; like the best of modern art, the 'Snark' was both obscurely instinctive and sharply intellectual.

Into the making of the poem come the figures of Gertrude Chataway,* a little girl Dodgson first met at Sandown in 1875, and Henry Holiday, who, despite Ruskin's forebodings, created some not unsatisfying illustrations. By the time Dodgson met Gertrude in September, 1875, the 'Snark' was far advanced, but she encouraged him to push on with it and was rewarded by a dedication in verse. Dodgson rejected a drawing by Holiday of the actual Snark (or Boojum), thinking rightly that it was best to leave the monster to imagination. For the benefit of the curious, Holiday's conception shows an unpleasant fat face with small eyes, a large mouth and a vast double-chin.[154]

Dodgson told Macmillan's that he wanted the 'Snark' to be advertised for publication on April 1st, 1876 – 'Surely that is the fittest day for it to appear?' – but several presentation copies bear the inscribed date March 29th. In the course of his correspondence with his publishers over the book, he made

*See *infra*, p. 209.

an excellent suggestion on February 6th, 1876 (more practical, it must be admitted, than many he inflicted on them) which has an important place in the history of the book-wrapper or 'dust-cover', which up till then had always consisted of plain paper:

'When you have got the lengthways title cut for the back of the book, I want you to print it (or the same words in ordinary type, which would do just as well) on the paper wrapper. The letters had better slope a good deal, so as to be easily read as the book stands upright. The advantage will be that it can stand in bookstalls without being taken out of paper, and so can be kept in cleaner and more saleable condition.*

I should like the same thing done for "Alice" and the "Looking-Glass" for the future – and even those on hand, which are already wrapped in plain paper, might be transferred into printed covers. . .'

Falconer Madan says in his 'Handbook' that the 'Snark' was not 'written primarily for children', but Dodgson told Macmillan's on February 3rd, 1876, with reference to a rejected design for the cover by Holiday: '*That* would have done beautifully for a volume of poems meant for aesthetic adults. *This* book is meant for children.' He further emphasised the point by inserting in every copy of the 'Snark' sold in the first few weeks a new pamphlet, very different in tone, called 'An Easter Greeting to Every Child who loves "Alice"', which was later reprinted in editions of other books of his. 'No need to leave off putting them in the moment Easter-day is past', he wrote to Macmillan's.

The poem received mixed reviews and did not sell particularly well at first. Dodgson asked the publishers at the beginning of 1877:

'How has the "Snark" sold during the Xmas Season? That, I should think, would be a much better test of its success or failure than any amount of sale at its first coming out. I am entirely puzzled as to whether to consider it a success or a failure. I hear in some quarters of children being fond of it . . .'

There was soon no doubt that the 'Snark' was a success, though not on the scale of the 'Alice' books; its appeal has been rather to adults than to children. By 1908 it had been reprinted seventeen times, and the many subsequent issues include several American editions.

Looking through the poem again, one notices that, like the 'Alice' books, it is most carefully organised. The strange Odyssey gains cumulative effect from its telling. The 'nonsense', in the sense of intellectual wit, thus becomes the least part of it. Indeed, there is something weirdly impressive and moving about the whole expedition. In the concluding stanzas Lewis Carroll reached a flight of instinctive poetry that was more common to his prose – and which may lead us on to another chapter.

---

*The sloping letters were eventually used on the spine of the book, but not on the wrapper. (*The Library*, 5th ser., Vol. 26, No. 2, pl. vi).

Lewis Carroll as a Poet

Lewis Carroll was undoubtedly a poet, even though he never made poetry a serious vocation or struck Bohemian and histrionic attitudes and even though much that he wrote does not rise above a level of accomplished humorous verse. We feel that it was a true poet who, as a boy at Croft, scribbled those lines on the wood-block which he hid under the floor-boards –

> And we'll wander through
> the wide world
> and chase the buffalo –

and we understand that it was a poet who wrote the opening chapters of *Alice in Wonderland* and who imagined the gardeners painting the rose tree or the episodes of Alice and the Fawn, the White Knight, and the Sheep in the little dark shop. He was, indeed, perhaps most poetic when he wrote in prose, and we must think of the 'Alice' books, with their harmonious and unforced blending of prose and verse, as being primarily a poetic achievement.

G. K. Chesterton did not allow for this when he wrote that 'Edward Lear was greater than Lewis Carroll; at least, he could do what Lewis Carroll could not do. Lewis Carroll's nonsense was merely mathematical and logical. Edward Lear's nonsense was emotional and poetical.'[155] Chesterton sadly underestimated the author of 'Alice'. In the 'Alice' books Lewis Carroll did what Edward Lear could not do – he created a sustained poetic fantasy on a considerable scale, and this has put him in a higher class than Lear, despite the fine music of Lear's rolling lines.

In Lewis Carroll's work as a whole there is both emotion and poetry. It is true that we never find in it such a romantic landscape as Lear's 'great Gromboolian plain' and 'the Hills of the Chankly Bore'. Carroll had no feeling for the broad effects of landscape and was content with miniatures:

> In winter, when the fields are white,
> I sing this song for your delight –
>
> In spring, when woods are getting green,
> I'll try and tell you what I mean.
>
> In summer, when the days are long,
> Perhaps you'll understand the song:
>
> In autumn, when the leaves are brown,
> Take pen and ink, and write it down.

There is music in his verse, which many composers have interpreted in different ways, but it is music for a string quartet rather than for a full orchestra:

> In a Wonderland they lie,
> Dreaming as the days go by,
> Dreaming as the summers die:
>
> Ever drifting down the stream –
> Lingering in the golden gleam –
> Life, what is it but a dream?

There is the same wistful nostalgia in the lines which he wrote for the dream-music of his friend C. E. Hutchinson of Brasenose:

> When midnight mists are creeping,
>   And all the land is sleeping,
> Around me tread the mighty dead,
>   And slowly pass away.
>
> Lo, warriors, saints, and sages,
>   From out the vanished ages,
> With solemn pace and reverend face
>   Appear and pass away.
>
> The blaze of noonday splendour,
>   The twilight soft and tender,
> May charm the eye: yet they shall die,
>   Shall die and pass away.

These are both little pieces for muted strings which succeed in capturing what was for Lewis Carroll a recurrent mood. He went further, perhaps, when his nonsense took him on wilder flights, as in ''Twas brillig and the slithy toves' or the concluding verses of *The Hunting of the Snark*:

> 'It's a Snark!' was the sound that first came to their ears,
>   And seemed almost too good to be true.
> Then followed a torrent of laughter and cheers:
>   Then the ominous words 'It's a Boo –'
>
> Then, silence. Some fancied they heard in the air
>   A weary and wandering sigh
> That sounded like – 'jum!' but the others declare
>   It was only a breeze that went by.
>
> They hunted till darkness came on, but they found
>   Not a button, or feather, or mark,
> By which they could tell that they stood on the ground
>   Where the Baker had met with the Snark.
>
> In the midst of the word he was trying to say,
>   In the midst of his laughter and glee,
> He had softly and suddenly vanished away –
>   For the Snark *was* a Boojum, you see.

Then, silence

It is a climax that is faithfully reproduced in Louis Aragon's French:

> Au milieu du mot qu'il essayait de dire
> Au milieu de son rire et de sa joie
> Doucement soudainement il s'était évanoui
> Car le Snark était un Boojum voyez-vous.[156]

Lewis Carroll's other long poem, *Phantasmagoria*, has never had the popularity of the 'Snark', yet his achievement in creating a sympathetic character of a worried little ghost deserves attention:

My father was a Brownie, Sir;
   My mother was a Fairy.
The notion had occurred to her,
The children would be happier,
   If they were taught to vary.

The notion soon became a craze;
   And, when it once began, she
Brought us all out in different ways –
One was a Pixy, two were Fays,
   Another was a Banshee. . . .

The poem, for all its flippancy, does not disguise, but perhaps serves to emphasise, a persistent interest in the supernatural which is demonstrated in the following extract from a letter (December 4th, 1882), to Langton Clarke:

'. . . That trickery will *not* do as complete explanation of all the phenomena of table-rapping, thought-reading, etc., I am more & more convinced. At the same time I see no need as yet for believing that *dis*embodied spirits have anything to do with it. I have just read a small pamphlet, the first report of the "Psychical Society", on "thought-reading". The evidence, which seems to have been most carefully taken, excludes the possibility that "unconscious guidance by pressure" (Carpenter's explanation) will account for all the phenomena. All seems to point to the existence of a natural force, allied to electricity & nerve-force, by which brain can act on brain. I think we are close on the day when this shall be classed among the known natural forces, & its laws tabulated, & when the scientific sceptics, who always shut their eyes, till the last moment, to any evidence that seems to point beyond materialism, will have to accept it as a proved fact in nature.'[157]

As with many other writers of light verse, including Praed, Lewis Carroll was furthest from poetry when he wrote most seriously. His 'serious' romantic poems are conventional exercises lacking originality and inspiration, and carrying little more than biographical interest. The 'Song of Love' from *Sylvie and Bruno* is almost painfully sincere but at the same time cloyingly sweet and sentimental:

The name of the secret is love

Say, whose is the skill that paints valley and hill,
   Like a picture so fair to the sight?
That flecks the green meadow with sunshine and shadow,
   Till the little lambs leap with delight?
'Tis a secret untold to hearts cruel and cold,
   Though 'tis sung, by the angels above,
In notes that ring clear for the ears that can hear –
   And the name of the secret is Love!

   For I think it is Love,
   For I feel it is Love,
For I'm sure it is nothing but Love!

The last three lines, which one can imagine chanted knowingly by an amateur chorus of elves, with coy little movements of the head from side to side, are particularly distressing. Preferable in their simplicity are these verses in 'Christmas Greetings from a Fairy to a Child':

> We have heard the children say –
>   Gentle children, whom we love –
> Long ago, on Christmas-Day,
>   Came a message from above.
>
> Still, as Christmas-tide comes round,
>   They remember it again –
> Echo still the joyful sound,
>   'Peace on earth, good-will to men'.

It is surprising that the writer of these lines did not produce hymns for children, a congenial task, one would suppose, which he might have done well.

As we have seen, Lewis Carroll read widely in English poetry; his library contained most of the earlier masters, as well as contemporaries such as Rossetti, the Brownings, Swinburne, and, of course, Tennyson. His collection of light verse was particularly comprehensive and included Hood, Locker, Patmore, Leigh Hunt, Praed, Calverley and W. S. Gilbert (whose *Bab Ballads*, which he owned in the first edition of 1869, probably influenced *The Hunting of the Snark*). His catholicity is attested by the presence of works by Tupper and Alfred Austin. But a paragraph from a letter to Alexander Macmillan of August 22nd, 1886, will best show his continuing interest in poetry and the soundness of his conservative taste:

'You never made a more judicious present than when you gave me your "Golden Treasury" Wordsworth. It is a real delight to me: so handy, so well printed, and so well selected – containing pure gems *only*. I should like a copy of "Scotch Song". And won't you give the world a "Golden Treasury" Burns? Also a vol. of "Lake Poets" would be very acceptable. I would take for it Coleridge, Keats, Hood (serious poems only, or *perhaps* admitting the "Ode to Rae Wilson") and Hartley Coleridge. I don't know if Hood ever actually lived in the Lake Country, but he would suit the others very well. His "Haunted House" ought by no means to be omitted, long as it is.'

From childhood he was in the habit of reading poetry critically for any signs of obscurity or confusion of thought. As early as 1845, he included in *Useful and Instructive Poetry* an entertaining Shakespearean skit in which he imagined that the sleeping King in *Henry IV*, Part II (Act IV, Sc. iv), could overhear his son's soliloquy and was able to take him up on several points of detail. He developed a sharp eye for anything that he thought precious or pretentious and more than once satirised affectation, especially in 'Poeta Fit, non Nascitur', in which a boy is made to ask his grandfather, 'How shall I be a poet?' and is advised to 'learn to look at all things with a sort of mental squint':

> 'For instance, if I wished, Sir,
>   Of mutton-pies to tell,

Should I say "dreams of fleecy flocks
　　Pent in a wheaten cell"?'
'Why, yes,' the old man said: 'that phrase
　　Would answer very well.'

The boy was further urged to 'mention no places, names or dates', to be 'consistently obscure', to fill up with 'Padding' and to reserve a 'great Sensation-stanza' to be placed towards the end.

Then proudly smiled that old man
　　To see the eager lad
Rush madly for his pen and ink
　　And for his blotting-pad –
But, when he thought of *publishing*,
　　His face grew stern and sad.

No one would expect original poetry from a critic who set himself determinedly against experiment, and in fact the serious poems in which Lewis Carroll argued around the old dilemma of love and conscience are as formal and academic as a picture by Alma Tadema. The sea! – that at least should have drawn poetry, one might have hoped, from such a confirmed sea-side visitor as Lewis Carroll. But what do we find?

Pour some salt water over the floor –
　　Ugly I'm sure you'll allow it to be:
Suppose it extended a mile or more,
　　That's very like the Sea.

And as for sand, the inference of 'The Walrus and the Carpenter' is not in its favour:

They wept like anything to see
　　Such quantities of sand:
'If this were only cleared away,'
　　They said, 'it *would* be grand!'
'If seven maids with seven mops
　　Swept it for half a year
Do you suppose', the Walrus said,
　　'That they could get it clear?'
'I doubt it', said the Carpenter,
　　And shed a bitter tear.

The lines are immortal; and in 'The Walrus and the Carpenter' one detects again – in the fate of the oysters – that ruthless element which, as in 'Jabberwocky' and the 'Snark', so often accompanies Lewis Carroll's higher flights. A strain of parody is present in most of his best verse, though not all of it has the sublimity of the parodies in the 'Alice' books, which are vital re-creations superseding such originals as Southey's 'You are old, Father William' and Wordsworth's 'Resolution and Independence'. Often he was content, as perhaps the best of our parodists, to do the job on hand supremely well and to leave it at that. Thus Longfellow was easy game:

> From his shoulder Hiawatha
> Took the camera of rosewood,
> Made of sliding, folding rosewood;
> Neatly put it all together.
> In its case it lay compactly,
> Folded into nearly nothing;
> But he opened out the hinges,
> Pushed and pulled the joints and hinges,
> Till it looked all squares and oblongs,
> Like a complicated figure
> In the Second Book of Euclid.

*A. B. Frost's illustrations for
'Hiawatha's Photographing'*

This he perched upon a tripod—
Crouched beneath its dusky cover—
Stretched his hand, enforcing silence—
Said, " Be motionless, I beg you ! "
Mystic, awful was the process.

All the family in order
Sat before him for their pictures :
Each in turn, as he was taken,
Volunteered his own suggestions,
His ingenious suggestions.
First the Governor, the Father :
He suggested velvet curtains
Looped about a massy pillar ;
And the corner of a table,
Of a rosewood dining-table.
He would hold a scroll of something,

Hold it firmly in his left-hand ;
He would keep his right-hand buried

(Like Napoleon) in his waistcoat ;
He would contemplate the distance

With a look of pensive meaning,
As of ducks that die in tempests.
  Grand, heroic was the notion :
Yet the picture failed entirely :
Failed, because he moved a little,
Moved, because he couldn't help it.
  Next, his better half took courage ;
She would have her picture taken.
She came dressed beyond description,
Dressed in jewels and in satin
Far too gorgeous for an empress.
Gracefully she sat down sideways,
With a simper scarcely human,
Holding in her hand a bouquet
Rather larger than a cabbage.
All the while that she was sitting,
Still the lady chattered, chattered,
Like a monkey in the forest.
" Am I sitting still ? " she asked him.
" Is my face enough in profile ?
Shall I hold the bouquet higher ?
Will it come into the picture ? "
And the picture failed completely.
  Next the Son, the Stunning-Cantab :
He suggested curves of beauty,
Curves pervading all his figure,
Which the eye might follow onward,
Till they centered in the breast-pin,
Centered in the golden breast-pin.
He had learnt it all from Ruskin
(Author of " The Stones of Venice,"
" Seven Lamps of Architecture,"

" Modern Painters," and some others) ;
And perhaps he had not fully

Understood his author's meaning ;
But, whatever was the reason,

All was fruitless, as the picture
Ended in an utter failure.

Next to him the eldest daughter :
She suggested very little,

Only asked if he would take her
With her look of " passive beauty."
  Her idea of passive beauty
Was a squinting of the left-eye,
Was a drooping of the right-eye,
Was a smile that went up sideways
To the corner of the nostrils.
  Hiawatha, when she asked him,
Took no notice of the question,
Looked as if he hadn't heard it ;
But, when pointedly appealed to,
Smiled in his peculiar manner,
Coughed and said it " didn't matter,"
Bit his lip and changed the subject.
  Nor in this was he mistaken,
As the picture failed completely.
  So in turn the other sisters.
  Last, the youngest son was taken :
Very rough and thick his hair was,
Very round and red his face was,
Very dusty was his jacket,
Very fidgety his manner.
And his overbearing sisters
Called him names he disapproved of :
Called him Johnny, " Daddy's Darling,"
Called him Jacky, " Scrubby School-boy."
And, so awful was the picture,
In comparison the others
Seemed, to one's bewildered fancy,
To have partially succeeded.
  Finally my Hiawatha
Tumbled all the tribe together,

(" Grouped " is not the right expression),
And, as happy chance would have it

Did at last obtain a picture
Where the faces all succeeded :

Each came out a perfect likeness.
  Then they joined and all abused it,
Unrestrainedly abused it,
As the worst and ugliest picture
They could possibly have dreamed of.
" Giving one such strange expressions—
Sullen, stupid, pert expressions.
Really any one would take us
(Any one that did not know us)
For the most unpleasant people ! "
(Hiawatha seemed to think so,
Seemed to think it not unlikely).
All together rang their voices,
Angry, loud, discordant voices,
As of dogs that howl in concert,
As of cats that wail in chorus.
  But my Hiawatha's patience,
His politeness and his patience,
Unaccountably had vanished,
And he left that happy party.
Neither did he leave them slowly,
With the calm deliberation,
The intense deliberation
Of a photographic artist :
But he left them in a hurry,
Left them in a mighty hurry,
Stating that he would not stand it,
Stating in emphatic language
What he'd be before he'd stand it.
Hurriedly he packed his boxes :
Hurriedly the porter trundled
On a barrow all his boxes :

Or Sheridan, who was adapted to Oxford life so neatly and gaily:

> Here's to the Freshman of bashful eighteen!
>   Here's to the Senior of twenty!
> Here's to the youth whose moustache can't be seen!
>   And here's to the man who has plenty!
>   Let the man Pass!
>   Out of the mass
> I'll warrant we'll find you some fit for a Class!

Or Goldsmith, whose 'Deserted Village' gave Carroll a framework for his defence of the Oxford Parks against the encroaching games-players, and helped him to his solitary and unfriendly reference to cricket:

> Amidst thy bowers the tyrant's hand is seen,
> And rude pavilions sadden all thy green;
> One selfish pastime grasps the whole domain,
> And half a faction swallows up the plain;
> Adown thy glades, all sacrificed to cricket,
> The hollow-sounding bat now guards the wicket;
> Sunk are thy mounds in shapeless level all,
> Lest aught impede the swiftly rolling ball;
> And trembling, shrinking from the fatal blow,
> Far, far away thy hapless children go.

In all his parodies Lewis Carroll shows the master's touch. Although he apparently never attempted to make the acquaintance of his rival in nonsense, Edward Lear, it is pleasant to note that he was an admirer of C. S. Calverley, his closest competitor in parody and acrostic, and that the two were in correspondence in the autumn of 1872. 'Thanks for mention of London address,' Lewis Carroll wrote to him on October 27th of that year, 'when I have time, I will copy you out one or two other acrostics, which exist only in M.S., as you pay me the compliment of admiring the printed one.'[158] On November 8th he wrote again to suggest 'an idea . . . of guessing well-known poems as acrostics, and making a collection of them to hoax the public'. Calverley replied that he had been on the point of suggesting the very same idea and followed it up by interpreting Kirke White's 'To an early Primrose' in the form of an acrostic. He also sent Dodgson a Shakespearean sonnet, the initial letters of which formed the name William Herbert, and 'April, or The New Hat' which was a double acrostic.[159]

The masters are happily observed thus exchanging their little masterpieces. Before Christmas in 1872 Lewis Carroll found an opportunity of calling on C. S. C. in London, but he does not tell us in his diary anything about that interview. Perhaps, apart from their dexterous play with words, the pair had little in common – and Dodgson may even have come up against Calverley's hearty enjoyment of beer and tobacco.

In all that belonged to a versifier's ingenuity Lewis Carroll excelled, and he also had in reserve quite a big stick for his opponents in controversy, which he brought out for the benefit of the vivisectionists and 'original researchers' in 'Fame's Penny-Trumpet':

> Blow, blow your trumpets till they crack,
> Ye little men of little souls!
> And bid them huddle at your back –
> Gold-sucking leeches, shoals on shoals!

This is not the richest invective, though it does remind us that Lewis Carroll was latterly an admirer of Rudyard Kipling, but it is a relief to observe that he could occasionally let off steam. The ending of his 'Elections to the Hebdomadal Council' of 1866 is also vigorously sarcastic over the attempts to remove a Conservative majority on the Council:

> Then, then shall Oxford be herself again,
> Neglect the heart, and cultivate the brain –
> Then this shall be the burden of our song,
> 'All change is good – whatever is, is wrong –'
> Then Intellect's proud flag shall be unfurled,
> And Brain, and Brain alone, shall rule the world!

Lewis Carroll's pen might have been of great use to the Conservative party if he could have spared the time to write political verse for the newspapers, for he was swift and deft to make his points in rhyme. An interesting example of his impromptu skill was revealed by Professor Duncan Black when he discovered, in 1952, a mass of papers in the Christ Church Treasury relating to Dodgson's period of office as curator of the Senior Common Room.

Among them were some lines written by Lewis Carroll on the back (which in those spacious days was always left blank) of a *Punch* cartoon from the issue of February 1st, 1862. The lines were a reply to some unsigned verses, published on an adjacent page and headed 'The Shepherd of Salisbury Plain', which attacked the Bishop of Salisbury, Walter Kerr Hamilton, a high churchman, who had proceeded against the Rev Dr Rowland Williams of Broadchalke near Salisbury for expressing views considered by the Bishop to be contrary to the doctrine of the Church of England. In the end Dr Williams, after lengthy legal argument, appears to have succeeded in retaining his living until his death in 1870. Lewis Carroll's pertinent defence of the Bishop's point of view, headed 'Sequel to "The Shepherd of Salisbury Plain"' can now be published for the first time:

> But supposing this sheep, when he entered the fold,
> Had solemnly taken a vow
> To shape all his bleats to one definite mould,
> Pray what can be said for him now?
> Must the rules we hold binding in business and trade
> Be ignored in the Church's domain?
> And need promises never be kept that are made
> To the Shepherd of Salisbury Plain?
>
> Though freedom of bleat is withholden from none
> Of the flock, be his wool black or white,
> Yet the freedom of breaking your promise is one
> To which few would insist on their right.

So, my friend, without wishing to charge upon *you*
The quibble your verses maintain,
I but say, would that all were as honest and true
As the Shepherd of Salisbury Plain!
Audi alteram partem.[160]

Ultimately, however, we must leave this accomplished versifier – who has, after all, many equals – and in our final analysis of Lewis Carroll as a poet return to the world of musical nonsense which he subdued so thoroughly and made his own. It was not he who introduced nonsense to nineteenth-century English literature – that honour belongs to Sydney Smith – and to weigh Lewis Carroll in the scales against the delightful Edward Lear would be an invidious task where both are indispensable. Yet it was Lewis Carroll, with his logician's equipment and his rare understanding of the mind of childhood, who really won us our freedom of the world of nonsense (a freedom that, like most freedoms, has been abused) and it is the purity of this art – 'almost unique', as Edmund Wilson has said, 'in a period so cluttered and cumbered'[161] – that has ensured his survival.

For this we have honoured him excessively and thus unkindly, Chesterton thought, by turning 'Alice' into a 'national institution, an educational classic'. There is a degree of truth, and some danger, here. 'This day ye shall remember before God all those His servants' – thus runs a prayer read in Liverpool Cathedral in 1932 – 'who write what many read, especially His servant, Charles Lutwidge Dodgson, sometime deacon in the church of God, through whom the healing power of mirth has been vouchsafed; and ye shall bless the name of the Lord Most High for every delight of the imagination which makes us friends of God in this world of wonder.'[162] Lewis Carroll would have been embarrassed, no doubt, by this and other signs of our respect. It is not his fault if 'Alice' is now 'a part of education'. We have, perhaps, made rather too much of him, humour being important to the English; foreigners will forgive us, however, because Lewis Carroll has enriched their imagination as well as ours. 'Car le Snark était un Boojum voyez-vous.'

The spirit of the man who wrote at twenty-three:

I dreamt I dwelt in marble halls,
And each damp thing that creeps and crawls
Went wobble-wobble on the walls,

was overlaid with the passing of the years but continued to shine even out of the disappointing confusion of his latter-day *Sylvie and Bruno*. He gave us there the original verse-epigram which has been called the 'Waterford':

He thought he saw a Banker's Clerk,
Descending from a bus:
He looked again, and found it was
A Hippopotamus:
'If this should stay to dine,' he said,
'There won't be much for us.'

He showed in 'The Three Badgers':

How blest would be
A life so free –
Ipwergis-Pudding to consume,
And drink the subtle Azzigoom.

He made us contemplate the dangerous possibilities of bird-life:

Little Birds are playing
Bagpipes on the shore,
Where the tourists snore:
'Thanks!' they cry. ''Tis thrilling
Take, oh, take this shilling!
Let us have no more!'

At such moments a Lewis Carroll who was past fifty touched hands with his younger self. In the long run, the polished writer of humorous verse takes his place in the English tradition; the nonsense-poet who made his own rules remains always fresh. That achievement of Lewis Carroll's is distinct and unchallengeable.

As Man to Man

'Please keep a look-out among illustrated books,' wrote Dodgson to G. L. Craik of Macmillan's on November 25th, 1876, 'and let me know if you see any artist at all worthy of succeeding to Tenniel's place. I should *much* like to write one more child's book before all writing-power leaves me.'

That, too, was the fervent hope not only of Macmillan's but of eager admirers of Lewis Carroll all over England and beyond. Alas, the years went by – and no new child's book appeared. We know that the work was 'on the stocks', and had been, in a manner of speaking, since the story 'Bruno's Revenge' appeared in *Aunt Judy's Magazine* in 1867. After *Through the Looking-Glass* was out of the way, Dodgson told more chapters of the new 'child's book', which he was already calling *Sylvie and Bruno*, to the children at Hatfield in 1873 and 1875. The 'Elveston' of the book was probably modelled on Hatfield, 'the Earl' on Lord Salisbury, and 'Lady Muriel' on one of his daughters.[163]

But *Sylvie and Bruno* never advanced systematically, as the 'Alice' books had done. Dodgson was in a dilemma from the first, because he was determined to break away from the pattern of his previous children's tales and apparently had no very clear plans for doing so. Thus we find him accumulating a great mass of material over many years, 'all sorts of odd ideas, and fragments of dialogue, that occurred to me – who knows how? – with a transitory suddenness that left me no choice but either to record them then and there, or to abandon them to oblivion', as he put it in his ultimate preface. This was not a propitious way of writing a book, but, without any clear inspiration, it was, as he said, 'the best I can do'. When *Sylvie and Bruno* eventually did appear, in 1889, it was not surprisingly a disappointment.

Meanwhile, Dodgson was rapidly losing that supremely lucid 'writing-power' of his in the persistent accumulation of other day-to-day interests, in studying anatomy with the help of a set of bones that his colleague Barclay Thompson had ordered for him; in his photography, which he continued until 1880; in a revived interest in drawing which showed itself in pains-taking copies from casts and child-models (there is a drawing of a cast of a foot in a sketch-book owned by the Dodgson family which indicates how hard he tried); in a new-found zeal for issuing pamphlets on voting and elections; and of course in his chronic mania for inventing puzzles such as *Word-Links* (1878), its sequel *Doublets* (1879) – which he suggested, unsuccessfully, should be advertised at 'Price Five Groats' – and *Mischmasch* (1882). His correspond-ence with his publishers alone must have taken a disproportionate amount of his time, because it is full of tentative proposals that failed to mature, besides recurrent requests for the purchase of theatre tickets – for which he was prepared to reward the office-boy with a shilling (later raised to half a crown), though if Mr Macmillan's son was the messenger he declined 'to offer *him* a shilling!' In the forty-second thousand of *Through the Looking-Glass* he discovered that both the Kings had been omitted from the chess-diagram; he had tried to prove to 'two little friends' at Eastbourne 'that it ends in a *real* check-mate in which, as I tried it on a recent copy, I need hardly say I signally failed'. And, in addition to all such topics in his letters to Macmillan's, he was involved in argument over the trade-terms for his books and in protesting that the booksellers took too large a share of the profits.* No wonder that the embryo *Sylvie and Bruno* lost all cohesion.

Out of the welter appeared *Euclid and his Modern Rivals* in 1879. The *World* and *Figaro* both announced that he was doing 'a burlesque Euclid', but he did not think it worth while contradicting them, though he remarked to Alexander Macmillan: 'I am just the last person in the land who would think of so dishonouring the great mathematician!' He did not expect 'any sale, to speak of', felt sure 'the total result will be a loss', and printed only 250 copies of the first edition. The news that these had been sold was 'as welcome as it is unexpected'. He did not print any more copies, however – wisely as it proved – but in 1885 published a Supplement and a second edition.

Euclid and his Modern Rivals appeared under the name of 'Charles L. Dodgson, M.A., Senior Student and Mathematical Lecturer of Christ Church, Oxford'. As Falconer Madan has said, it is 'one of the outstanding examples of serious argument cast in an amusing style, designed to prove that for elementary geometry a revised Euclid is better than any proposed modern substitute'.[164] The dramatic dialogue is very well done, and the book is important because it shows more clearly than anything else that Dodgson and Carroll cannot be separated into different compartments.

Dodgson followed it up in 1882 with his edition of *Euclid, Books I and II*, valuable in its day, which went through eight editions by 1889. The following year saw the appearance of a pamphlet on *Lawn Tennis Tournaments: The True Method of Assigning Prizes with a Proof of the Fallacy of the Present Method*. Dodgson exposed the very rough justice of the usual method of conducting tournaments, but the elaborate system he devised could only, one suspects, be satisfactorily operated for a tournament at a Mathematicians' Summer School, and shows the same impracticability for general purposes as his ideas on elections. 'Let it not be supposed,' he wrote, 'that, in thus proposing to make these Tournaments a game of pure skill (like chess) instead of a game of mixed skill and chance (like whist), I am altogether eliminating the element of luck, and making it possible to predict the prize-winners, so that no one else would care to enter.' But even this mild consolation has not served to recommend his method, which would have turned every club scorer into a chartered accountant.

In 1883 Dodgson published a new collection of his verse called *Rhyme? and Reason?* which was largely taken from the humorous part of *Phantasmagoria* but included *The Hunting of the Snark* and a few poems that had not hitherto been published or collected. The chief interest of the book lay in the sixty-five new drawings by A. B. Frost, the American illustrator, whom Dodgson had engaged after some preliminary discussions with Walter Crane (whose drawings for Mrs Molesworth's *The Cuckoo Clock* had pleased him). Walter

A. B. Frost's illustrations for 'Ye Carpette Knyghte' and 'Size and Tears'

---

*After an attempt to regulate the discount allowed on the sale of his books, Dodgson wrote a pamphlet on *The Profits of Authorship* (1884) which has not survived, but from which Collingwood quotes a passage (pp. 227–8): 'The publisher contributes about as much as the bookseller in time and bodily labour, but in mental toil and trouble a great deal more. I speak with some personal knowledge of the matter, having myself, for some twenty years, inflicted on that most patient and painstaking firm, Messrs Macmillan and Co., about as much wear and worry as ever publishers have lived through. . . .' This cannot have been far from the truth. But almost the only rebuke, and that a mild one, which I have discovered in looking through Macmillan's letters to Dodgson is contained in a letter from G. L. Craik of October 25th, 1883: 'It does add very largely to our labour to discuss wordy detail in writing. I notice that the letters written by you touching on the arrangement concluded in our last agreement covered thirty pages of your writing. Just think how impossible it would be to carry on any business at this rate' (Dodgson Family Papers).

Crane, besides being very fully occupied, thought Dodgson 'a most particular person' – and Dodgson, for his part, did not entirely admire Crane's 'rather thick wood cut sort of line'.[165] Frost, though occasionally vulgar, proved successful with 'Phantasmagoria' and 'The Three Voices'. But he lacked Tenniel's delicacy and was not the man Dodgson was seeking for *Sylvie and Bruno*. 'If only he could draw a pretty child, he might do my next book,' he wrote in his diary of August 17th, 1883, 'but there seems little hope of it.'

Rhyme? and Reason? – for many years the standing collection of Lewis Carroll's verse – was in its eighth thousand in 1901. It sold better from the first than the author had anticipated. 'Peccavi!' he told Craik of Macmillan's. 'It *was* my doing I admit, that so few "R and R" were printed: and your firm advised a larger number. I am sorry if anyone is put to inconvenience.' And then he went on to express his hope once again that

'No risk may be run of the execution being deteriorated by hurrying the work. Whether we have more copies ready by Christmas, or Easter, or any other time, is a matter to me of no importance at all, compared with having printing, binding etc., all of *first-class* quality. Please secure *that*, at any rate, whatever else we miss.'

Two

Just as nothing was too much trouble to Dodgson so far as his work or his books were concerned, so, equally, he would go to any pains for a generous motive that appealed to him. We notice this in countless small ways. At Guildford he was once seen to enter a shop, buy some cakes, and distribute them to seven hungry little ragamuffins in the street.[166] In 1880 he 'worked off' with his 'electric pen' thirty copies of a circular about the presentation of a testimonial to the Christ Church cook. In 1881 he made a special expedition to pick fritillaries for a little girl who wanted to paint them, and sent them to her in a tin box wrapped in wet cotton-wool. The number of copies of his books that he presented to children's hospitals must have run into many hundreds, if not thousands, but he also sent out circulars to the hospitals asking whether they would like to have the books. And when he was dissatisfied with the production of an edition he took care to see that it was distributed with discrimination – as was the case with the sixtieth thousand of *Through the Looking-Glass* in 1893, when he offered copies 'to Mechanics' Institutes, Village Reading-Rooms, and similar institutions, where the means of purchasing such books are scanty'.[167]

Collingwood says that several times, when he was asked to lend money, he replied: 'I will not *lend*, but I will *give* you the £100 you ask for.'[168] He was always generous to his own family, but there is no better example of the extent to which he was prepared to help others than a circular which he distributed in 1883 on behalf of his friend T. J. Dymes. The copy quoted is addressed in ink to 'Dear Mrs Neate', and is headed 'Ch. Ch. Oxford. Dec. 21. 1883':

'Having a strong prejudice against "begging-letters", I begin this letter with the assurance that it is not one. I ask for no help in money: but I am sending this to all my friends, far and near, in hopes that from some of them may come information or advice, that may be serviceable to a friend of mine who is in great distress.

My friend is an Oxford Graduate, who took a Third Class in Classics. For a good many years he was in the Tea Trade, but as it turned out very unremunerative, he took, some 8 years ago, an under-mastership in a Boys' School.

To detail the circumstances, under which he left the School, would involve the reputations of others, and I do not think I need do more than give you my assurance that, to the best of my belief, they were in no way discreditable to him, but that he was the victim of gross injustice, having had promises of a gradually increasing income, which were never fulfilled. He has a wife and 8 children (one son and seven daughters), and the meagre income on which he began work at the School (and which never rose) was not enough to live on. After exhausting most of his private resources, he found himself, a few months ago, in a state of insolvency, and was on the point of being sold up by certain creditors, to whom he had given a Bill of Sale on his furniture. Friends came forward to subscribe, and I lent him a sum of money, by means of which he got a release (on paying 5s in the £) from those creditors, and I now hold a Bill of Sale on the furniture.

He has been seeking (but so far in vain) work as an under-master, and no doubt all of the family, capable of work, would be willing to work rather than continue dependent on the charity of relations. . .'

Dodgson goes on to cite testimonials to Dymes and to give details of the capabilities of the others of his family who were old enough to work. And, in order to make every possible use of his circular, he adds a postscript about an entirely different matter:

'If you have any friends in London, who have children, and who would like them to have lessons in drawing at their own house, would you kindly refer them to me for further information? A young lady-artist, a friend of mine, gives lessons in this way, and I should be very glad to find her some more pupils.'[169]

This is all so admirable that it speaks for itself. But love, in Dodgson's case, as he remarked in one of his poems, was 'bitter-sweet'; and the best way of understanding his character (so far as it can be understood), and of appreciating how his alternating moods made him liked and disliked in turn, is perhaps to follow one impression by another entirely different. In 1879 he had staying with him at Christ Church the editor of *Vanity Fair*, T. Gibson Bowles. Bishop C. M. Blagden

'Saw him in Common Room with him, and then the two walked across the quadrangle to Dodgson's rooms. An hour or two later, Strong, who had been to see the Junior Censor, found Bowles sitting disconsolately on the stairs. When he asked what he was doing there he found that Bowles, returning to Dodgson's rooms, had said very humbly: "I suppose that I couldn't have a pipe here, could I?" and was met with the answer: "You know that I don't allow smoking here. If I had known that you wanted to smoke, I would have ordered the Common Room Smoking Room to be got ready for you." So he went out on to the cold dark stairs, and fortunately fell in with Strong, who carried him off to his rooms in Peckwater and entertained him for the rest of the evening.'[170]

The explanation for this particular incident may be found in Dodgson's horror of tobacco, but similar *brusqueries* from him were not uncommon.

Three

As Dodgson's income grew with the fame of 'Alice' – and G. D. Leslie painted 'Alice in Wonderland' (a lady reading to a child) for the Royal Academy, and Stanley Leathes contemplated his *Alice's Wonderland Birthday Book* – Dodgson found his enthusiasm for the mathematical lectureship at Christ Church growing steadily less. In 1880 he accepted a cut of £100 in his salary, at his own suggestion, and in 1881, secure in his life fellowship, he resigned the lectureship altogether. He had never much enjoyed the work, and now he confided to his diary of July 14th that his chief motive for continuing it had been to provide money for others, that he had long been able to retire, and that he hoped by more book-writing to make up even the £300 a year he would lose. On October 18th he noted: 'I shall now have my whole time at my own disposal, and, if God gives me life and continued health and strength, may hope, before my powers fail, to do some worthy work in writing – partly in the cause of Mathematical education, partly in the cause of innocent recreation for children, and partly, I hope (though so utterly unworthy of being allowed to take up such work) in the cause of religious thought. May God bless the new form of life that lies before me, that I may use it according to His holy will!' On November 30th he nevertheless delivered his last lecture with regret: 'There is a sadness in coming to the *end* of anything in Life. Man's instinct clings to the Life that will never end.'

Now, if ever, one might have hoped that Dodgson would have used his opportunity to make *Sylvie and Bruno* a worthy successor to the 'Alice' books. But he seems not to have enjoyed his life of leisure, with no settled occupation apart from that of a free-lance writer, as much as he had expected. Only a year later, on December 8th, 1882, he accepted the onerous post of Curator of the Senior Common Room – admitting some misgivings, but in the hope that 'it will take me out of myself a little, and so may be a real good. My life was tending to become too much that of a selfish recluse.'

Dodgson succeeded his friend Vere Bayne, who had been Curator for twenty years and who had laid in so much sherry that Dodgson calculated that it would last – at that rate – for three hundred years. At least, that is what Barclay Thompson told M. E. Sadler,[171] and from the same source we learn that, 'Using this Dodgsonian calculation, Barclay moved at a C.R. meeting that there should be a wine committee. This was carried. Bayne resigned. Dodgson came over to Barclay in a corner of C.R. and said that he (Dodgson) would never become stiff and autocratic like Bayne. Dodgson was elected Curator. In a fortnight he had become "clothed with brief authority" and was angrily irritable at any suggestion of change. He drew up a long list of rules. Quickly he himself broke them. . . .'

Dodgson was not an 'easy' character to deal with in college affairs, but apparently John Barclay Thompson (who later removed the Thompson and became known as John Barclay) was even more difficult. Dodgson's version in his diary of December 8th, 1882, of the circumstances of his election as Curator does not confirm Barclay Thompson's account in all particulars.

According to the diary, Dodgson defended his old friend Bayne against implied charges of obstinacy and extravagance. As for the wine committee, it was already in existence, but fresh powers were given to it. To attempt to allocate blame for their disagreements as between Dodgson and Barclay Thompson would be a tedious and unprofitable task. What is certain is that they quarrelled, probably more than once. The following extracts from Dodgson's letter-books supply an account of one of these quarrels – a trivial and unnecessary squabble, in which Dodgson eventually conceded that all the right may not have been on his side:

Ch. Ch. Nov. 1, 1883.

DEAR THOMPSON,

I am sorry you do not approve of my having altered the order for Liqueurs which was agreed on at the Wine-Committee Meeting – I can assure you my simple wish is to do what is most for the interests of C.R. (e.g. if I had ordered the 12 'Green Chartreuse' agreed on, I fear it would have been wasted money, and that it would not have been consumed) and where what seems their interest clashes with the letter of any rule, I take the responsibility of breaking that rule.

Believe me,
Very truly yours
C. L. DODGSON.

J. B. Thompson, Esq.

Ch. Ch. Nov. 2/83.

DEAR THOMPSON,

I can only repeat that I am sorry you do not approve of my conduct as Curator: but please don't think me disrespectful if I beg to be excused discussion. Most truly, I am very busy – in many other ways than with wine-business – and have a distracting lot of correspondence.

Let me earnestly beg, however, that no difference of *views* may affect our *personal* friendship, and that the 'odium theologicum' may have no place in C.R. matters or between Ch. Ch. men.

Always truly yours,
C. L. DODGSON.

P.S. As you object to getting those 2 liqueurs from the 'Army & Navy', and as *I* can't get them there, not being a member, I am ordering some from Snow & Co.

Ch. Ch. Nov. 3/83.

DEAR THOMPSON,

'Second thoughts are best', and mine are that you were right in objecting to so many Liqueurs being bought for C.R. . . .[172]

The argument slides off in another direction, and we shall not pursue it here. But another extract from the letter-books, this time of June 3rd, 1886, shows that these disputes were not infrequent: 'Common Room chooses to break *its* promises,' wrote Dodgson on that occasion to J. A. Stewart, '*I* choose to keep *mine*.'[173] Perhaps the truth was not always quite so simple.

In their domestic concerns these eminent scholars often showed themselves testy and small-minded. But such a large house-keeping job as Dodgson had taken on would have tried the patience of most men, and Dodgson did it systematically and well, bringing order to what had been a chaotic system of accountancy and establishing the use of ledgers. His chief concern was the upkeep of the wine-cellar, but he was also responsible for servants' wages, for the purchase of coals, groceries, stationery, newspapers, and indeed generally for anything that affected the welfare and comfort of what is virtually a large club. The collection of Common Room papers discovered by Professor Duncan Black in 1952 made it possible to illustrate the range of his activity for the first time.[174] No wonder that the spontaneity of the story-teller flew out of the window while his desk was covered with tradesmen's catalogues and order-forms.

He soon made a careful map of the wine-cellar, dated February 5th, 1883, and a cardboard liqueur measure with different markings for Green Chartreuse and Dry Curaçoa. Notices, either printed or in his own round hand, continually followed one another on the Common Room board: 'The Curator of C.R. requests you to put a cross against your name, if you mean to breakfast here tomorrow.' 'A desire having been expressed that a better *quality* of wine should be supplied as "Champagne A" (though not accompanied by any expression of willingness to pay a higher *price*), the Curator has procured samples, which Members are invited to taste, in Common Room, at . . . o'c.' 'In view of the fact that the price of Tea has gone down considerably, though Messrs Twining have for many years made no alteration in their charges, the Curator has procured samples from Messrs Cooper, Cooper and Co., made up in quarter-pound packets. . . .'

The letter-books show a wide range of subject-matter. Those young animals, the undergraduates, occasionally cast their shadows across the civilised living of the Senior Common Room. Thus Dodgson wrote to a colleague, Robert Faussett, on February 27th, 1883:

Reverend Robert Godfrey Faussett, 1827–1908, photographed by Dodgson

'Would you kindly look at the C.R. w.c's, which much need repairing and re-painting, and which Telling* thinks is a matter for the "House" to undertake. They were considerably damaged, years ago, by riotous undergraduates, and have never been put into good order since. They are certainly very shabby and one would almost be ashamed to take a guest there.'

And to another colleague, R. E. Baines (the Reader in Physics) on July 1st, 1889:

'You threw me into no small difficulty, yesterday, when your friend, Mr Blunt, brought me word of your wish that the Henley Crew should *somehow* be enabled to buy, and take with them, a bottle of Brandy from the C.R. Cellars. Of course it was *quite* out of the question to let any one, not being a Member of C.R., buy from our Cellars. I didn't feel called upon to *give* them a bottle: they are not so poor that they can't buy their own provisions! To let them buy it, through the Curator, would be a very awkward precedent. The only way I could think of to gratify your wish, and yet not get C.R. into a "fix", was to tell Mr Blunt (who expressed the perfect readiness of the crew to pay for the Brandy) that he had better pay *you*: and I then sent an order to Telling to

*The Common Room manservant.

deliver to the bearer a bottle of Brandy, & charge it to *you*. Even *that* is against Rules: but it is an exceptional occasion; so I will ignore it.'

There were even more solemn occasions, such as that which required the dispatch (April 14th, 1887) to M. E. Sadler, the Steward, of

'a formal representation to you as to the very inferior cookery now prevalent. During the last 10 days or so we have had
    (a) Beefsteak almost too tough to eat.
    (b) Mashed potatoes that were a mere sop.
    (c) Portugal onions quite underboiled and uneatable.
    (d) Yesterday I ordered (for the last time: I shall not again) baked apple-
         dumplings. Their idea of that dish seems to be this "take some apples:
         wrap each in the thinnest possible piece of pastry; bake till nearly black,
         so as to produce the consistency of – say pasteboard."
    (e) Cauliflowers are *always* sent with no part soft enough to eat except the
         tops of the flowers. This the Cook defends, & seems to think no one
         ever expects to eat more: he explains that, if boiled till the stalks are
         eatable, the flower would be overboiled. All I know is that everywhere,
         except here, cauliflower is a very nice vegetable, & eatable as a whole.
         Here only 5% is eatable, & that absolutely flavourless.
    (f) Potatoes (boiled) are *never* "mealy", as cooked here.
However these last two are chronic grievances. We never get boiled potatoes, or cauliflowers, properly cooked in Hall.
    I don't think I'm remarkably fastidious as to cookery, but I may say that I should think very poorly of a London restaurant (with dinners (say) at 2/- a head) that supplied such cookery. . . .'

Needless to say, Dodgson's relations with the tradesmen were impeccably correct:

Ch. Ch. Common Room,
Oxford.
Dec. 24/89.

Mr Dodgson has given directions to return to Messrs Snow the box of Portugal fruit.

He would have thought it hardly necessary to point out that the Curator, whose duty it is to try to procure the *best* goods he can for Common Room, cannot possibly accept *presents* from any of the tradespeople concerned.

He thinks it only fair to warn Messrs Snow that any repetition of such attentions may seriously affect their position as wine-merchants dealt with by Common Room.
Messrs Snow & Co.

He had always liked marmalade – did not Alice pass a jar labelled 'ORANGE MARMALADE', disappointingly empty, on her fall down the rabbit-hole? – so that it is not surprising that, when Dodgson's brother's family started to produce home-made marmalade, he should have done his utmost to recommend it to his colleagues. Eventually the following notice appeared on the Common Room Board:

TO ALL LOVERS OF ORANGE
MARMALADE

The Curator's brother (who has a large family and several pupils) makes it on a large scale, and could supply some for the use of Members of C.R., if any let the Curator know that they desire it. He finds it very good, and it can also be guaranteed as absolutely genuine, and not, as is the case with much supplied in shops, largely composed of Vegetable-Marrow. C.R. would probably be able to supply it at 10*d*. (possibly 9*d*.) for a 1 lb. jar.
Feb. 23. 1890.*

Four
Dodgson discussed the problems of his office humorously in *Twelve Months in a Curatorship* (1884) which was followed by a Supplement and by a Postscript, in which he proposed six 'Rules for the Wine-Committee', designed to avoid future difficulties. Apparently one of the chief troubles was that it was almost impossible to get the Wine-Committee to assemble. In 1886 he produced a further instalment of reflections, *Three Years in a Curatorship*, in which he considered the ventilation, lighting and furnishing of the Common Room under the heading 'Airs, Glares and Chairs'. Two leaflets of the same year dealt with the question of who should pay rent for the rooms used by the Common Room; and the discoveries made at Christ Church in 1952 included the first known copy of a confidential circular, intended for the Governing Body and headed 'Remarks on Report of Finance Committee', which is a thorough and useful examination of the finances of Christ Church in 1886.[175]

As the years went on, Dodgson chafed more and more at the obligations and restrictions of the Curatorship. He attempted to resign in May, 1889, after proposals of his for the use of the Drawing Room when required in the evenings, and for the payment of £1 to the servant to compensate him for his trouble, had been rejected. Swiftly Dodgson rushed into print in the third person:

During the six years that have elapsed since Common Room did him the honour of electing him, he has constantly tried to act fairly and handsomely towards all with whom, as Curator, he has had to deal. Now for the first time he finds himself called upon to act, on behalf of Common Room, in a very different spirit – a spirit which he feels to be entirely unworthy of the large and wealthy Club whose business he transacts.

Having tendered his resignation, he was persuaded to withdraw it after a unanimous resolution 'to leave all questions of wages in the hands of the Curator'. When a propitious occasion did at last come for his retirement, in favour of T. B. Strong, three years later, he said farewell gracefully with a circular that was among the papers discovered in 1952[176]:

For Members of Common Room only.
MEETING OF COMMON ROOM.
Thursday, March the 3rd, 1892, at 1.30 p.m.

*Fortunately the recipe has not perished. Thanks to the generosity of Menella Dodgson, I can testify that Dodgson's advocacy was based on more than family loyalty, and that it is excellent marmalade.

'Nonumque prematur in annum.'
'*And let him be oppressed until the ninth year.*'

It is my earnest wish to be permitted to resign, at this next Audit-Meeting, the office of Curator, with which Common Room did me the honour of entrusting me nine years ago.

It is an office very pleasant to the holder, from some points of view: and, for my own part, though I cannot say that the being thus placed 'en evidence', in our evening gatherings, has at all added to my enjoyment in attending them, yet I have thoroughly enjoyed the opportunities thus afforded me, by the frequent practice of placing a guest next to the Curator, of coming into contact with many interesting strangers, and of doing what I could to make their visits enjoyable to them.

But it is also an office which entails on its holder a very considerable expenditure of time, and of work which, though not needing severe efforts of thought, is almost as tiring to the brain as if it did. This time and trouble I find myself, year by year, (as the disproportion becomes more and more glaring between the remaining years of life and the work that I long to complete during those years), less and less able to spare.

Still, so long as it did not appear that a successor could readily be found, I have gladly, though at some personal inconvenience, continued to give my services to my friends, who have shown to me such unvarying kindness.

Now, however, that I have reason to believe that this obstacle to my retirement no longer exists, I entreat to be allowed to resume the position of an ordinary Member of Common Room, from which I most reluctantly emerged, and to which I shall most gladly return.

And, if a certain resemblance be traceable, between my poor services as Curator and the branches of a coral-spray cast up by the sea, in the waywardness and grittiness that both so remarkably display, I may apply to myself the words, in which a living Poet has told us how

> 'every breaker, how supreme soe'er
> The wealth its individual bosom bear,
> Impelled by no poor egotist desires,
> To the community of waves retires
> Wholly as undistinguished as before,
> When it has cast its corals on the shore'.
>
> C. L. DODGSON, *Curator.*

Feb. 13, 1892.

It was a disarming farewell, in which Dodgson showed that he could recognise and laugh at his own 'grittiness', and that he bore no grudge against his critics in the Common Room. But he was so pleased to be escaping that he could not fail to be genial. 'The sense of relief, at being free from the burdensome office, which has cost me a large amount of time and trouble, is very delightful', he wrote in his diary of March 4th, 1892. He still found energy to collect 'as a Curatorial parting gift' a booklet of Common Room resolutions and statistics, *Curiosissima Curatoria*. The sad thing, from the point of view of posterity, is that this man of genius should have chosen to spend nine years of his life doing a job that could have been tackled by any competent administrator; housekeeping statistics will not nourish a Wonderland, and *Sylvie and Bruno* was no more than a Curator's egg.

Five

A batch of about fifty letters from Dodgson to M. E. Sadler, Steward of Christ Church from 1886 to 1895, help to fill out the day-to-day picture of Dodgson's college life.[177] Among them is one to Sadler's predecessor Arthur Acland. They show Dodgson to have been continually complaining about something or other, and though his grumbles were wrapped in a wry humour, their cumulative effect must have been very trying. One can imagine the hard-pressed Steward crying, 'Oh dear, Dodgson again!' whenever he saw that distinctive and all too clear handwriting.

As might have been expected from the references in *Cakeless*, Dodgson's chief preoccupation was with the inefficiency of the College servants. The messengers were always apparently clearing the letter-box at the wrong hours, to the detriment of his huge correspondence. In snowy weather he feared that his letters or parcels would get wet, and proposed that the House should

Page of a letter of February, 1881, from C. L. Dodgson to Arthur Acland when Steward of Christ Church

for our Messengers —
firstly, for their own health
& comfort in such weather,
a set of waterproof capes
with high collars —
Secondly, for the security of
our letters & parcels, a
set of deep
baskets (as more
easily carried
when loaded
than square ones)
with waterproof
covers —
Yours hydrophobically
C L Dodgson

'provide for our Messengers – first, for their own health & comfort in such weather, a set of waterproof capes with high collars – secondly, for the security of our letters & parcels, a set of deep baskets (as more easily carried when loaded than square ones) with waterproof covers'.

Other complaints concerned 'a dangerous effluvium, caused by some defect of drainage'; large puddles at the entrance to Tom Quad; breakage of his glass and china; the bad lighting of his staircase; alleged overcharging of meals sent to his rooms – and then there was the alarming occasion in 1886, when the chimney of the Scout's room (underneath his) caught fire:

'I hope you will not only inspect the premises, but have a full investigation as to *who* is responsible for the occurrence, & whether we are liable to its recurrence at any moment – perhaps when we are all in bed. The scout here, & his assistant are, I should think, stupid enough & forgetful enough to cause any amount of accident: &, if ever Ch. Ch. *is* partly burned down, I think the odds are in favour of *this* staircase being the one to begin it!'

In 1891 the age-old joke of the window-cleaner at the bedroom window hit him with peculiar force:

'On Saturday morning, just after I had got out of bed, a ladder was reared against the bedroom window, & a man came up to clean it. As I object to performing my toilet with a man at the window, I sent him down again, telling him "you are not to clean it *now*", meaning, of course, that *that* window was to be left till I was dressed. Instead of moving away the ladder to the next windows (my smaller sitting-room) they went away, and have not returned. So the bedroom-window, the 2 windows of the sitting-room, & the window of the pantry, are not yet cleaned. They are ready to be cleaned at any time, whether I am here or not, with the single exception that I object to the bed-room window being cleaned while I am dressing.'

One must sympathise with Dodgson: his austere bedroom was very small and afforded little opportunity for taking cover. Alice was once in a similar difficulty when the White Rabbit tried to get in at her window. 'That you wo'n't', she thought, and she put her hand out of the window, 'made a snatch in the air', and was rewarded by the sound of 'a little shriek and a fall, and a crash of broken glass'. At Christ Church it was safer to write a note to the Steward.

From the pile of complaining letters, we may take two more, almost at random. In November, 1886, it was the milk delivered for breakfast that worried him – not that he got too little, but that he got too much. One morning he measured it and found it was 'more than $\frac{9}{10}$ of a pint'. 'Now *half* a pint is ample supply for me. If I am only *charged* for $\frac{1}{2}$ a pint, of course there is nothing to complain of, even if they chose to leave me a gallon! But I fear that, if I get *more* than I pay for, somebody else must get *less* than *he* pays for'.

Then there was the matter of the installation of electric bells in Dodgson's rooms (1888). He realised that, in case of fire or illness, he might have difficulty in calling attention to his plight. Sadler suggested a bell that would ring in the porter's bedroom until it was stopped; but this provoked Dodgson to some characteristic reflections:

'(1) If it didn't wake him at first going off, it wouldn't do so by *continuity* of sound, which is as somniferous as silence: it is the sudden *change*, from sound to silence, or from silence to sound, that *wakes*. A miller will sleep sound while the mill is going: but wakes if it stops.

(2) It would limit our power to *one* kind of signal. Now it might be very desirable to institute a *code* of signals (by different numbers of rings in) for various purposes (e.g. one kind to mean "Fire!").'

A code of rings! How the eternal boy in Dodgson must have rejoiced at the thought, and how he must have longed to devise a really elaborate code and get it printed! But this seems to have been one of the 'rare items' that Madan was never able to list (too many long faces in the porter's lodge, perhaps, at the thought of having to distinguish – in the middle of the night – between a chimney-fire and an attack of synovitis).

These letters catch many aspects of Dodgson and hold them to the light: his punctiliousness and integrity; his selfishness that was mixed up with thought for others – the messengers should have high collars to their waterproofs, and someone was paying too much for too little milk; the modesty and chastity displayed in the window-cleaning incident; the scientific approach to the problem of rousing the sleeping porter. . . . And there is another little note, this time to Mrs Sadler, that is very typical of the later Dodgson – 'Many thanks: but kindly excuse me – I'm not an at-homely man.' Not 'at-homely' in the social sense, certainly; but, in his home at Christ Church, very much the proud householder.

What are little girls made of?
Sugar and spice, and all that's nice.

One

The asperities and the civilities, the plottings and plannings of a college oligarchy consumed only a part of Dodgson's time. What he enjoyed most, in his later life as in his youth, was the society of children – and he took care continually to replenish his store of child-friends, whom he met on train journeys (where he entertained them with puzzles drawn from his black bag), or at the sea-side (where he carried a useful stock of safety-pins), or in the homes of those of his friends who were parents.

Children always brought out the best in him. He once wrote movingly[178] of 'the awe that falls on one in the presence of a spirit fresh from God's hands, on whom no shadow of sin, and but the outermost fringe of the shadow of sorrow, has yet fallen'. As a grown man, he recognised 'the bitter contrast between the haunting selfishness that spoils his best deeds and the life that is but an overflowing love – for I think a child's *first* attitude to the world is a simple love for all living things'; and he believed that 'the best work a man can do is when he works for love's sake only, with no thought of name, or gain, or earthly reward.' In *Alice in Wonderland*, and in the many inimitable letters to his child-friends collected by Evelyn Hatch, there is persuasive evidence in favour of this contention.

But, for Dodgson, children were almost exclusively little girls. It would be

'To me (boys) are an unattractive race of beings' – Dodgson. Photograph of Angus Douglas, circa 1865, by Dodgson

a mistake to suppose that he could not get on with boys when he tried; one or two examples of successful friendships with them, especially in earlier days, have been mentioned in this book, and his nephew S. D. Collingwood has testified that 'on the few occasions on which I have seen him in the company of boys, he seemed to be thoroughly at his ease'.[179] When the boys were prepared to enjoy his puzzles (and perhaps in this respect they were less tolerant than little girls), all went well; he made paper pistols for them, too, that went off with a considerable crack*; if the boy was somewhat advanced, precocious, artistic, Dodgson would appreciate his company. 'He was one of us,' wrote Bert Coote, then a juvenile actor, 'and never a grown-up pretending to be a child in order to preach at us . . . his sense of the theatre was extraordinary.'[180] Only one letter to a little boy is included in Miss Hatch's collection, and that was written to an unidentified 'Bertie' (probably Bert Coote again). It is a valiant attempt by Dodgson to put himself, for once, in the place of a boy, and is all about soldiers, which were not a congenial subject for him. Even here he could not resist adding at the end, with an almost audible sigh: 'Have you any sisters? I forget. If you have, give them my love.'[181]

As boys admire 'Alice' no less than girls, Dodgson's preference for their sisters could lead to a sad little episode like the following, described by Mrs Alice Collett[182]:

'My father, James Owen, had been a Junior Student of Christ Church and knew the mathematical don, Mr Dodgson. Once when I was about five I was travelling with my parents and a young brother, a little older than myself, when my father caught sight of Mr Dodgson on Guildford platform. "Come in here, Dodgson," he called, and to our great delight he came. Then followed a journey I shall never forget and a time which might have been boring became entrancing. For kind "Lewis Carroll" took me on his knee and told me stories and drew pictures for me. I had the luck to be called Alice and to have a quantity of fair hair, so he took a fancy to me, while my poor brother, who knew "Alice" almost by heart, gazed at its author with adoring eyes but had no notice taken of him.'

If Dodgson did not, on the whole, get on well with boys, it is a natural corollary that he should not usually have been at his happiest with men. And of his general aversion to boys there is overwhelming evidence. 'To me they are not an attractive race of beings (as a little boy, I was simply detestable),' he wrote to one correspondent, 'and if you wanted to induce me, by money, to come and teach them, I can only say you would have to offer more than £10,000 a year!'[183] 'I am fond of children (except boys)', he told another.[184] 'Boys are not in my line: I think they are a mistake: girls are less objectionable,' he wrote to the headmaster of Marlborough, Dr G. C. Bell.[185] And when S. G. Owen endeavoured to interest him in the sons of his colleague H. L. Thompson when they happened to meet him on his staircase at Christ Church, he replied, 'I don't like little boys,' and went into his room and shut the door.[186]

As a voluntary uncle, enjoying pleasure without responsibility, he could choose his own nieces – and there was no limit to their number. The thought that he might have married and had sons of his own opens up a disastrous

---

*He learned this trick from Francis Epiphanius ('Piffy'), son of Coventry Patmore, at Hastings on October 8th, 1890: see *The Diaries of Lewis Carroll* (1954), p. 480.

prospect; it may not be far-fetched to suppose that this was an additional consideration that weighed in the balance with him against matrimony and helped to keep him single.

Two

Dodgson's friendships with little girls were of two kinds: the first, and most numerous, came to an end at about the age of fourteen or fifteen. 'Usually the child becomes so entirely a different being as she grows into a woman, that our friendship has to change too: and *that* it usually does by gliding down, from a loving intimacy, into an acquaintance that merely consists of a smile & a bow when we meet!' he wrote to Edith Blakemore on February 1st, 1891.[187] The loving child became no more, as Praed put it, than 'Mrs Something Rogers'. But there were other friendships, such as those with Edith Blakemore herself and with Gertrude Chataway, which survived the crucial date and continued until the end of his life.

In general, the course of Dodgson's friendships with little girls has been adequately chronicled by S. D. Collingwood and their quality attested by Evelyn Hatch's selection of his letters. Isa Bowman, one of his favourites,

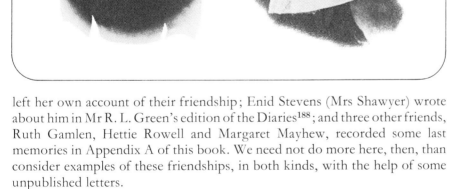

Two studies of Isa Bowman: left, as herself; right, as Alice in Wonderland

left her own account of their friendship; Enid Stevens (Mrs Shawyer) wrote about him in Mr R. L. Green's edition of the Diaries[188]; and three other friends, Ruth Gamlen, Hettie Rowell and Margaret Mayhew, recorded some last memories in Appendix A of this book. We need not do more here, then, than consider examples of these friendships, in both kinds, with the help of some unpublished letters.

Dodgson was in the habit of spending part of his summer holiday at one of the south-coast watering-places. From 1873 to 1876 he stayed at Sandown. In 1877 he began a series of visits to Eastbourne which continued until his death. On July 31st of that year he went for the first time to a lodging-house at 7 Lushington Road, kept by Mr Dyer (who worked in the post office) and his wife, where he had 'a nice little first floor sitting room with a balcony, and bedroom adjoining'. Mrs Dyer was 'a good motherly creature', as he told Gertrude Chataway, and 7 Lushington Road – a small, semi-detached house, conveniently placed for the sea, with a broad road in front of it and a little garden at the back – was to be his summer home for the next twenty years. In 1896 he loyally accompanied the Dyers when they moved to 2 Bedford Well Road, a humbler house further from the sea, with marshland and open country at the back, which in 1952 was the abode of a chimney sweep. The only letter to Mrs Dyer that the present writer has seen is business-like in tone:

Ch. Ch. Oxford. Oct. 21/82.

DEAR MRS DYER,

I see that I wrote '1' for '12' in your bill, so that I still owe you 11*s*. I enclose a postal order for 12/6. If you send me 1/4 change, we shall be right. Also please return the enclosed, signed.

Yours very truly,
C. L. DODGSON.

P.S. Would you please put the three bottles of sherry that I left, *lying down*, as the corks get so dry if they are kept standing. Did Mrs Richards send for the desk?[189]

At Eastbourne, Dodgson worked hard at his books, attended such theatres and concerts as were available – and of course went to church on Sundays, took very long walks, and spent a good deal of time on the beach. It was there that, on a summer evening in 1877, he met one of the first and best-loved of his Eastbourne friends, Agnes Hull, a very pretty, lively child, the daughter of a London barrister. By 1879 he was calling her 'My darling' – and making a joke about it – and in a postscript to a letter of January 15th, 1880, he tried very hard to persuade her to give him a certain present (one wonders whether he got it):

'Every time I pack that black bag of mine, I feel the want of one or two little bags, of strong brown holland, to put the little things into, & keep them from wandering all over the bag, & playing hide & seek among the larger things. For instance, it would be *very* convenient to have a bag 6 inches square, with two tapes, drawing contrary ways, so that the mouth would draw up tight and not come open easily. If I bought such a bag, it would have a certain value: if it were given me, it would be ten times more valuable: but if it were *made for me*, by some child that I loved, and if she marked it with her name or initials, so that I might always remember who it was from, it would be a treasure I should like to keep all my life.'

When the Hulls left Eastbourne that year (1880), Dodgson wrote: 'Aggie Darling, I'm quite too low-spirited to write much. Why *did* you all go away so soon? Lushington Road is awfully dull. . . .'

It is clear that, half in play and half in earnest, these friendships could grow rather intense, and as the girls neared an age of maturity they may have been slightly disturbing to both parties. The following letter is not one of those published by Evelyn Hatch:

My Darling Aggie,

Oh yes, I know quite well what you're saying – 'Why ca'n't the man take a *hint*? He might have *seen* that the beginning of my last letter was meant to show that my affection was cooling down!' Why, of course I saw it! But is that any reason why *mine* should cool down, to match? I put it to you as a reasonable young person – one who, from always arguing with Alice* for an hour before getting up, has had good practice in Logic – haven't I a right to be affectionate if I like? Surely, just as much as *you* have to be as unaffectionate as *you* like. And of course you mustn't think of *writing* a bit more than you *feel*: no, no, *truth* above all things! (Cheers – Ten minutes allowed for refreshment). I came up to town on Monday with Mr Sampson† (some of you have met him at Eastbourne) to see 'The Cup' & 'The Belle's Stratagem', & on Tuesday I made a call or two before going back to Guildford, & passed 'High St, Kensington'. I had turned it (half) over in (half of) my mind, the idea of calling at 55. But Common Sense said 'No. Aggie will only tease you by offering you the extremity of her left ear to kiss, & will say "This is for the *last* time, Mr Dodgson, because I'm going to be sixteen next month!"' 'Don't you know', said Common Sense, 'that *last times* of anything are very unpleasant? Better avoid it, & wait until her sixteenth birthday is over: then you'll be on shaking-hands terms, which will be calm & comfortable'. 'You are right, Common Sense', said I. 'I'll go & call on other young ladies. . . .'

Drawings by Dodgson
Left: *Beatrice, 23 September, 1876.* Top right: *May Mileham, 14 June, 1885.* Below: *Charlotte Neal and Edith Morley, Sandown, 8 September 1874*

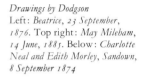

*Her elder sister.   †Rev E. F. Sampson of Christ Church.

In another unpublished letter, written from Oxford on May 21st, 1881, the danger dissolves in laughter. It is·worth printing for its own sake:

MY DARLING AGGIE,

(I had better say at once, candidly, that I don't expect more than 'My dear Mr Dodgson' & 'yrs truly' in reply). The fact is, now they are charging a guinea a stall for 'Othello', *I can't afford your price*. I know what it cost to extract the first 'darling' out of you, for you were honest enough to tell me. It cost – well, I won't say how many shillings, but it cost *a stall at the Lyceum*. Now, it is possible that, if I promised you a ticket for 'Othello', I might get a 'darling darling' in reply, but *one may buy sweets too dear*. For example, *I never give 3/6 for a stick of barley-sugar.* The moral is obvious.

Besides, is *bought* affection worth much, after all? I doubt it.

I send a copy of the last bill I have had to pay in that way. I think I shall give up that kind of barley-sugar now. (Miss Wiggins is a very nice girl – She lives somewhere in London, but I forget the exact address.)

Always your loving friend,

C. L. DODGSON.

Mr C. L. Dodgson Dr to Miss Amelia Wiggins

	£	s.	d.
To smiling at you when we met in the street ..	Copy of Tennyson's Poems.		
To pretending to be amused at a joke of yours [N.B. I wasn't]	A work-box.		
To listening with interest to a story of yours. [N.B. I was awfully bored]	A writing-desk.		
To beginning a letter to you 'My darling Mr Dodgson' & ending it 'Your loving A –' [N.B. All humbug]	A stall at the Lyceum.		
Received			
A. Wiggins.	£50	0	0

The end of that friendship came, as Dodgson seems to have half-feared it would, when a last kiss broke the spell; but he was delighted to receive an affectionate letter from Agnes Hull after that, and in his reply signed himself: 'Always your loving old friend (& mean to be so till you are "fair, fat, and forty").'[190]

Three

Dodgson once said that children were 'three-fourths of my life',[191] but he was not unique among Victorian clergymen in his romantic interest in little girls (for it is plain that, if they were something less than sweethearts to him, they were considerably more than daughters). The Rev Francis Kilvert, who lived from 1840 to 1879, showed much the same preoccupation, and, what is more, he wrote about it very frankly in his remarkable diary. If Dodgson had treated his diary as a confessional, as Kilvert did, it seems probable that he must have written in the same vein; but Dodgson was more circumspect, and his diary was consequently duller.

Coates, 1857. Photographed by Dodgson

Katie Brine.

ALEXANDRA

Madeline Catherine Parnell

Effie Millais

Dymphna Ellis.

Katie Brine, granddaughter of
Dr Pusey

Madeline Catherine Parnell, niece
of Mrs Longley

Xie Kitchin as 'A Chinaman'

Effie Millais, daughter of John
Millais

Amy Hughes, daughter of Arthur
Hughes

Dymphna Ellis, daughter of the
Rector of Cranborne

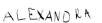

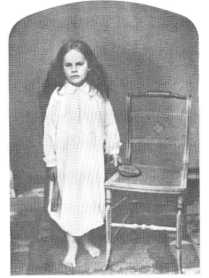

AliceConstance

Zoe Strong

Effie Millais

Polly Terry

*Alice Constance Westmacott,
daughter of the sculptor, Richard
Westmacott*

Alie Murdoch

All photographs by Dodgson

Irene MacDonald

*Mr and Mrs Millais with their
two daughters*

*Zoe Strong, a relative of
Dr T. B. Strong, Dean of Christ
Church*

*Marion and Florence, sisters
of Ellen Terry*

We should remember that it was the custom in those days for honorary uncles to kiss honorary nieces more freely than is now the case. 'Shall I confess', wrote Kilvert in his diary, 'that I travelled ten miles today over the hills for a kiss, to kiss that child's sweet face.' Dodgson might have gone to the same lengths; one lady, who was taken out by him as a child, has told the present writer that she was rather surprised to be kissed by him in the middle of a performance in a theatre. As their daughters approached the 'dangerous age', some mothers grew understandably cautious, and Dodgson's diary for 1880 records that he kissed a girl in that year whom he thought to be fourteen but who turned out to be seventeen; when he wrote a 'mock apology', the mother replied sternly: 'We shall take care it does not recur.'

If Dodgson had been less conscientious he would of course have said nothing about this incident. But henceforth he became extra-punctilious, and when necessary he took pains to get permission in advance. The following letter is not one that Ethel Rowell included in her charming article on Dodgson in *Harper's Magazine* (February, 1943):

Ch. Ch. Oxford
June 25/95.

Dear Mrs Rowell,

The being entrusted with the care of Ethel for a day is such a great advance on mere acquaintanceship, that I venture to ask if I may regard myself as on 'kissing' terms with her, as I am with many a girl-friend a great deal older than *she* is. Considering that – she being 17 and I 63 – I am quite old enough to be her *grandfather*, I hope you won't think it a very out-of-the-way suggestion. Nevertheless, if I find you think it wiser that we should only shake hands, I shall not be *in the least* hurt. Of course, I shall, unless I hear to the contrary, continue to shake hands only.

Very truly yours,
C. L. Dodgson.[192]

He had always been hyper-sensitive, and the slightest rebuff (real or imagined) with regard to his girl friends was now enough to put him on the defensive. One of the artist families with which he was friendly was that of E. M. Ward, the historical painter, and after Ward's death in 1879 he continued to visit Mrs Ward, who was herself an artist, and her daughters and son Leslie ('Spy' of *Vanity Fair*). Mrs Ward quoted a few of his letters in her 'Reminiscences' (1911), but she left certain passages unpublished – which is something that a biographer of Lewis Carroll learns to expect, for often not the least revealing passages in his correspondence sprang from the continual misunderstandings and trivial grievances that bedevilled his personal relations. Thus, in 1895, when he sent his love to Mrs Ward's daughters, and did not receive the response he hoped for, he wrote: 'Will you kindly forgive the liberty I took, but now see to have been over bold, in sending so affectionate a message to your daughters?' After Mrs Ward had hastened to reassure him, he was happy again:

'*Please* don't imagine that I felt (or feel) as if I had anything to "forgive" in your previous letter! I simply thought (as I had, or believed I had, sent my "love" to your girls) that the reply, "my girls join in very kindest regards", was, tho' perfectly friendly, one that showed I had worded my message too strongly, & had better modify it in future. But now, after your second kind letter, I shall *not* modify it! On the contrary, I send them my love again – second edition, revised, enlarged, and with notes & marginal references!'[193]

Four

Throughout his life Dodgson saw girls' clothes getting more and more uncomfortable; they were at their worst in the seventies and eighties, with their bustles, bows and tight-lacing. He hated all this, especially the tight boots and high-heeled shoes with pointed toes, and any other devices that tended to make children old before their time. One of the things he admired most about Gertrude Chataway was that she was allowed to 'run in and out of the sea in little bathing pants and a fisherman's jersey, a thing quite unheard of in those days'.[194]

It is rather curious that this voluminous dress for little girls should have coincided with a popular fashion for presenting them artistically with nothing on. The Christmas card designed by W. S. Coleman and reproduced below is typical of the taste of the late seventies, which persisted into the twentieth century, and is further instanced by Gertrude Thomson's drawings for *Three Sunsets*. And of course, despite Victorian convention, similar effects

Typical Christmas card (left) *of the 1870s, designed by W. S. Coleman.* Right: *Drawing by E. Gertrude Thomson from* Three Sunsets

might occasionally have been observed on a deserted stretch of coast. Francis Kilvert, another bachelor clergyman, walking from Shanklin to Sandown in 1875, found a subject for a rhapsody:

'One beautiful girl stood entirely naked on the sand, and there as she half sat, half reclined sideways, leaning upon her elbow with her knees bent and her legs and feet partly drawn back and up, she was a model for a sculptor, there was the supple slender waist, the gentle dawn and tender swell of the bosom and the budding breasts, the graceful rounding of the delicately beautiful limbs and above all the soft and exquisite curves of the rosy dimpled bottom and broad white thigh.'

Dodgson did not express himself so frankly in his diary, but his appreciation was no less. 'I *wish* I dared dispense with *all* costume,' he wrote to Harry Furniss about his illustrations for *Sylvie and Bruno*; 'naked children are so perfectly pure and lovely . . .'.[195]

Now it is probable that the secret of Dodgson's remarkable success in photographing little girls was due to his, in a sense, 'falling in love' with his sitters. 'Unless I fall in love with my subject I don't make a successful picture,' said a later photographer of children, Marcus Adams, 'which,' he added, 'is why I don't choose to photograph the ladies.'[196] If child-photography is therefore a somewhat emotional business, one might have had reason to feel apprehensive for Dodgson as he embarked, in the late seventies, on the new venture of photographing little girls in the nude. It was to be his final fling as a photographer.

The development was not surprising. He had, after all, photographed them in nearly every other possible costume, and he approached the climax by way of various kinds of *déshabille*. He was most punctilious about considering his subjects' feelings. On May 23rd, 1880, he wrote to Mrs Chataway, 'I don't think I will suggest taking her [a girl called Dulcie] in a night-gown (as Gertrude wished) – she is too shy & self-conscious for it – not a genuine *child*, like Gertrude.'[197] He did, however, photograph other children in night-gowns, and during 1879 and 1880 he made a number of nude studies; some of these were of one of Leighton's models, whom Gertrude Thomson brought to Oxford. He proposed to Mrs Chataway that he should photograph her daughter in the nude, using the expression 'Eve', but it does not appear that permission was granted.[198]

Dodgson's artistic interest was genuine, but he was on dangerous ground. Probably Mr R. L. Green is right in assuming that hostile reactions from mothers whom he approached at this time led to his abandoning photography after 1880. This was certainly a difficult year for him (it was the year in which he was rebuked for kissing the girl of seventeen!).

We know from Margaret Mayhew's (Mrs Davies's) reminiscences (Appendix A) that her mother objected to a proposed photograph of her eldest daughter Ruth. (It is a curious coincidence, by the way, that Francis Kilvert was another admirer of the charming daughters of A. L. Mayhew, for many years chaplain of Wadham.) Dodgson did not forget the incident, and long afterwards wrote a cautious letter to Mrs Mayhew before embarking on his friendship with her youngest daughter Margaret:

Ch. Ch.
Feb. 29, 1896.

Dear Mrs Mayhew,

When, several years ago, it seemed desirable that your children should forget all about me & my photography, which was not to your liking, I imagined that our acquaintanceship had come to an end – not, I hope, with any angry feeling on either side, but simply extinguished as no longer desirable to keep up.

Now, however, that chance has made me acquainted with your little Margaret, I see no reason, unless you desire it, to repel the friendship she is ready to offer. That you allowed her to keep the book I sent her is a sort of sign that you do not object. However, in *writing* to her, I think it best to send the letter to *you* – leaving you free either to hand it on, or to destroy it & tell her nothing about it, whichever you think best.

Believe me

Very truly yours,

C. L. DODGSON.[199]

Fortunately for Margaret, her mother raised no objection to her friendship with Lewis Carroll. The episode of the forbidden photograph was closed. The last mention of those unfortunate 'nude studies' is in Dodgson's Instructions to his Executors:[200]

'Please erase the following negatives: I would not like (for the families' sakes) the possibility of their getting into other hands. They are best erased by soaking in a solution of washing soda. 2175 – 2176 – 2180 – 2441 – 2444 – 2447 – 2457 – 2462 – 2463.'

The year 1880 was in many ways a sad one for Dodgson, to whom all endings were painful. On September 4th his 'dear aunt' Lucy Lutwidge (opposite) died; she had been a second mother to all the Dodgsons since they had lost their own. A few days later Alice Liddell was married to Reginald Hargreaves; she had postponed her marriage for many years, partly because her husband was in no hurry, and partly because the tragic death of her sister Edith in 1876 had seriously affected her. That Dodgson found the news depressing is probable; whatever our views on his 'love life', Alice's marriage must have come as a reminder that happy days were irrevocably past and that spring had turned to autumn. He does not refer to it in his diary.

Lucy Lutwidge, Dodgson's aunt and 'second mother', photographed by him

Five

As we have seen, the majority of Dodgson's child-friendships came to an end rather abruptly. But not all. There were some girls who, as he told Edith Blakemore in 1891, were 'rather the exception among the hundred or so of child-friends who have brightened my life'. It looked at one time as if his friendship with Gertrude Chataway would be no different from the rest. 'So sorry you are grown-up,' he wrote to her in 1878, and to her mother in 1880 he said, 'I wonder when I shall, or whether I ever shall, meet my (no longer little) friend again! Our friendship was very intense while it lasted – but it has gone like a dream. . . .'[201] Indeed, all these friendships had something dream-like about them.

The friendship with Gertrude Chataway was, however, revived by a visit of Dodgson's to the Chataways at Rotherwick in 1886; and in 1890, when he heard that Gertrude was not well, he wrote her a most interesting letter from Eastbourne:

'. . . Do you think a visit to the Seaside (Eastbourne) could benefit you? And, if so, will you come & be my guest here for a while?

I put that question *first*, advisedly: I want you just to get over the shock of so outrageous a proposal a bit: & then you can calmly consider what I have to say in defence of asking a young lady of your age to be the guest of a single gentleman. First, then, if I live to next January, I shall be 59 years old. So it's not like a man of 30, or even a man of 40, proposing such a thing. I should hold it quite out of the question in either case. I never thought of such a thing myself, until 5 years ago – then, feeling I really had accumulated a good lot of years, I ventured to invite a little girl of 10, who was lent without the least demur. The next year I had one of 12 staying here for a week. The next year I invited one of 14, quite expecting a refusal, *that* time, on the ground of her being too old. To my surprise, & delight, her mother simply wrote "Irene may come to you for a week, or a fortnight. What day would you like to have her?" After taking her back, I boldly invited an elder sister of hers, aged 18. She came quite readily. I've had another 18-year-old since, & feel quite reckless now, as to ages: &, so far as I know, "Mrs Grundy" has made no remarks at all.

But have I had any one who is *grown-up*? (as I presume *you* are, by this time). Well, no, I've not actually *had* one here, yet: but I wrote the other day to invite Irene's eldest sister (who must be 23 by this time) & she writes that she can't come this year "but I shall love to come another time, if you'll ask me again!"

I would take moderately good care of you: & you should be middling well fed; & have a doctor, if you needed it; & I shouldn't allow you to talk, as that is evidently not good for you. My landlady is a good motherly creature, & she & her maid would look after you well.

Another point I may as well touch on, the cost of coming. There has been a difference among my child-guests, in that respect. Some – I fancied, when I began the paragraph, that there had been one, at least, whose railway-fare I had *not* paid. But I find there was none. (You see, I travelled from London *with* most of them, so it was natural to pay: though in some cases perhaps they *could* have afforded it themselves: but there were certainly *some* who couldn't have come at all, unless I had said beforehand "*I* will pay the journey expenses".) Therefore (with no fear that I shall offend you by so doing) I make the same offer to you.

Now *do*, my dear child, get your parents to say "yes" (I mean, supposing sea-air is good for you); & then say "yes" yourself; & then tell me whether you would be competent to travel down here alone, or if I had better come to escort you.

At present there is, lying on the sofa by the open window of my tiny sitting-room, a girl-friend from Oxford, aged 17. She came yesterday, & will perhaps stay a week. After she is gone, if *you* could come for a week or longer, I should love to have you here! It would be like having my Sandown days over again!'[202]

In its combination of would-be sophistication and complete innocence, this letter is reminiscent of the opening sentence of Daisy Ashford's *The Young Visiters*: 'Mr Salteena was an elderly man of 42 and was fond of asking peaple to stay with him. He had quite a young girl staying with him of 17 named Ethel Monticue. . . .' The description of Mr Salteena as 'an elderly man of 42' inevitably recalls Dodgson, who had long been in the habit of over-stressing his age, particularly on occasions such as this. In other respects Dodgson did not particularly resemble Mr Salteena; he was, in fact, younger in spirit, and it will be remembered that Mr Salteena 'was not very adicted to prayers'. There is, however, a significant comparison to be drawn between *The Young Visiters* and *Alice in Wonderland*, the former showing an extraordinary fusion of precocity and inspiration, the latter representing a precocious emotion recollected in tranquillity for the benefit of other children. Any reader who studies both books will often be struck by the identity of outlook.

Gertrude Chataway came to stay at Eastbourne, but not until 1893, when Dodgson pronounced it 'a really delightful visit'. Gertrude thought that any misunderstandings he may have had with other girls came about because they did not like 'to be treated as if they were still ten years old. Personally I found that habit of his very refreshing'.[203] In the meantime he had had many other young guests to stay at Eastbourne, though not all parents were ready to give their permission, as Ruth Gamlen (Mrs Waterhouse) shows in Appendix A. 'Mrs Grundy' was still a force to be reckoned with. 'Dear May Miller was engaged to dine with me,' thus runs an Eastbourne diary entry of August 14th, 1894, about one of two sisters; 'but Mrs Miller wrote to say there was so much "ill-natured gossip" afloat, she would rather I did not invite either girl without the other.'

From Dodgson's point of view all this fuss was most unreasonable; at the same time, the caution of parents was perfectly understandable. Even Dodgson's sister, Mary Collingwood, was constrained, in 1893, to write him a letter on the subject of his girl-guests, which he pronounced 'most kind and sisterly'. In his reply he said:

'The only two tests I now apply to such a question as having some particular girl-friend as a guest are, first, my own conscience, to settle whether I feel it to be entirely innocent and right, in the sight of God: secondly, the parents of my friend, to settle whether I have their *full* approval of what I do. You need not be shocked at my being spoken against. *Any*body, who is spoken about at all, is *sure* to be spoken against by *some*body: and any action, however innocent in itself, is liable, and not at all unlikely, to be blamed by *somebody*. If you limit your actions in life to things that *nobody* can possibly find fault with, you will not do much. . .'.[204]

The children who were lucky enough to stay with Dodgson and really get to know him well – either at Eastbourne or in rooms which he engaged for them at Oxford – were conscious, as Isa Bowman put it, of a 'love and reverence' for him that 'nearly became an adoration'.[205] Enid Stevens, who was not allowed to stay with him, regretted later that 'days of close intercourse with one who, however whimsical his mind, was one of the few genuine scholar-saints were denied me because the saint was male and I was a little girl'.[206]

Sylvie and Bruno

15

One

Between April, 1880, and March, 1885, Dodgson contributed a series of ten mathematical problems, in the form of short stories, to Charlotte M. Yonge's women's magazine, the *Monthly Packet*. The resulting volume, *A Tangled Tale* (1885), is one of his most tantalising books. The problems are ingeniously woven into the stories, and obviously afforded much thought for the readers of the *Monthly Packet* (whose attempted solutions are published at the end); but the book is tantalising for another reason – because it shows once again that Dodgson was a master of narrative and dialogue, and makes us regret that he did not write more light fiction, similar in kind but without *arrière pensée*. There are many passages in *A Tangled Tale* to rival the landlady's reply to the question 'Does the cat scratch?' –

From left to right: *'Balbus was assisting his mother-in-law to convince the dragon'*; *'But the Captain put aside the suggestion with a wave of the hand'*; *'Why do they say "Bamboo" so often?'*; *'He remains steadfast and unnerved'*. By A. B. Frost for A Tangled Tale

The landlady looked round suspiciously, as if to make sure the cat was not listening. 'I will not deceive you, gentlemen,' she said. 'It *do* scratch, but not without you pulls its whiskers! It'll never do it,' she repeated slowly, with a visible effort to recall the exact words of some written agreement between herself and the cat, 'without you pulls its whiskers!'

The master had lost none of his skill, but one laments that so much good writing was employed only, as he put it in his preface, like 'the jam of our early childhood', in an attempt to conceal a mathematical medicine. Although academically a failure as a teacher, Dodgson always remained a teacher at heart, even with his child-friends, and he could now rarely bring himself to write without some didactic purpose. *A Tangled Tale* was a success within its chosen limits, but it leaves the reader longing for the undiluted jam of 'Alice'. It is an interesting book for another reason, because, being published under the name of Lewis Carroll it emphasises – much in the same way as the humour of *Euclid and his Modern Rivals* (which was signed by Charles L. Dodgson) – that there is no sense in trying to split the author's character into two, with Dodgson on one side of the line and Carroll on the other.

'Many thanks for a long series of notices, condemnatory of "Tangled Tale",' wrote Dodgson to Macmillan on March 27th, 1886. 'I feel rather tempted to send a few of them to Miss Yonge (at whose request it was written) and say "and this blighted reputation I owe to your baneful influence!" Spite of this chorus of blame, it is selling pretty well, don't you think?' The book went into a second edition in 1886 but could hardly have been expected to go further.

Throughout 1886 Dodgson was struggling with the details of the facsimile edition of his original illustrated manuscript of *Alice's Adventures Under Ground*. The idea of publishing it had occurred to him early in 1885, and he had at once asked permission of Mrs Hargreaves, whom he called 'my ideal child-friend' ('I have had scores of child-friends since your time, but they have been quite a different thing'). Mrs Hargreaves consented, and the manuscript was safely photographed, but before the photographer had delivered all the zinc-blocks (for which he had been paid) he absconded, and Dodgson had to take out a summons against him. This entailed 'the new and exciting experience of being put into the witness-box, and sworn, and cross-examined by a rather savage magistrate's clerk, who seemed to think that, if he only bullied me enough, he would soon catch me out in a falsehood!'[207] After this, the negatives required for the missing blocks were surrendered, the work was placed in safer hands, and all went smoothly.

Dodgson wrote to Mrs Hargreaves on July 15th, 1885:

'Whether the publication will be a source of gain, or not, it is impossible to say: but if it is, I hardly like the idea of taking the whole profits, considering that the book is now *your* property, & I was thinking of proposing to send half of them to *you*. But a better idea has now occurred to me, which I now submit for your approval: it is to hand over the profits to Hospitals and Homes, *for Sick Children*.'[208]

After Mrs Hargreaves had gladly agreed, Dodgson wrote again to say that

'it is very pleasant to think that you are thus connected with the fac-simile edition. Of the existence of the original you were of course the chief, if not the only, cause. You shall have the original back again in (I hope) exactly the state in which I received it, and (of course) one of the earliest copies of the fac-simile. May I also have the pleasure of presenting one to your eldest daughter (even if she be *not* an "Alice" – which I think unlikely)?'[209]

Dodgson never had the pleasure of presenting a copy to Alice's daughter, because her three children were all sons. The manuscript went back to her, and remained in her possession until it was sold in 1928 for £15,400, eventually reaching the British Museum, twenty years later, through American generosity. But the manuscripts from which 'Alice' and *Through the Looking-Glass* were set up by the printer have never been discovered; they must be a favourite day-dream for any book-auctioneer.

The facsimile was published in the usual red cloth and gilt edges, to match the other 'Alices'. 'But we cannot have medallions,' Dodgson told Macmillan; 'my drawings are too bad for that.' He changed his mind sufficiently to allow his drawing of the Mock Turtle to appear in a medallion on the back; the front cover was filled with some fanciful lettering of his own design.

Alice's Adventures Under Ground was ready for Christmas, 1886; but Dodgson was much preoccupied then with several other matters – the first, a collection of poems with the unpromising title *Bumble-Bee Bogo's Budget*, which he had promised to see through the press for his Guildford friend W. W. Follett Synge; the second, his own book *The Game of Logic*, which was unsuccessfully printed by Baxter of Oxford and had to be entirely reprinted by Clay; the third, the first important theatrical production of *Alice in Wonderland*, by Savile Clarke, which was put on at the Prince of Wales' Theatre, on December 23rd. He wrote a new stanza of 'The Walrus and the Carpenter' for the play, added parts for the 'Ghosts' of the 'First and Second Oysters', and expanded ''Tis the voice of the lobster' from six lines to sixteen (in which form it has since appeared in all later editions of the book).

The Game of Logic was another of Dodgson's attempts to disguise a didactic dose with helpings of jam – the dose in this case being formal deductive logic and the jam consisting of a board and counters and many humorous examples. 'Besides being an endless source of amusement (the number of arguments, that may be worked by it, being infinite),' he declared in his preface, 'it will give the Players a little instruction as well.' He enjoyed himself, and worried Macmillan's, by carefully choosing the quality of the cardboard and the colours of the counters – red and grey – which were to be put into a special envelope and enclosed in each copy. Macmillan's then had the job of counting the counters: 'I am having a lot more counters sent to you. They are invoiced 21,200 grey and 14,750 red. The former lots were called 1,000 of each, and I retained 120 red and 150 grey. So that you ought to have, now, 15,630 red and 22,050 grey: i.e. enough red for 3,900 copies and enough grey for 4,400 copies.' This must have been one of the hazards of publishing that Macmillan's took care not to encounter again; for when Dodgson later expanded his game into *Symbolic Logic* an announcement said that an envelope containing counters and diagrams could be had for an extra threepence ('by post 4d.').

The present writer, being quite incapable of testing the game's suitability for children, persuaded his friend Marghanita Laski (who copes with these things very well) to try it out with her family. This is Marghanita Laski's report:

'Children are always intrigued by a book that has something detachable to be played with, and in *The Game of Logic* it is the stiff white envelope with the coloured counters inside that immediately attracts them. "It's an intelligence-test!" mine said instantly when they saw the general idea of what they had to do, and the one that likes intelligence-tests was agog to get going, while the other had to be cajoled to start. But for a generation trained in intelligence-tests, there was nothing foreign about the conception.

Lewis Carroll's approach assumed much more patience than the modern child expects to be asked for. "Underline the word that is different", is all the introduction that the modern test is likely to need, where *The Game of Logic* begins with five pages of closely, if nicely, printed prose. The explanations of the Propositions that "Some new Cakes are nice", "No new Cakes are nice", and "All new Cakes are nice" are best annotated by an adult, and the eleven-year-old – the one who doesn't like intelligence-tests – was saying impatiently "Can't we cut all this and get on with the game?" long before I'd finished explaining. But the nine-year-old was excited; to many children, logic is strangely satisfying at about nine.

On page six, we took a red counter out of the envelope, and placed it in a certain position on the smaller square printed as frontispiece, and we were easily able to deduce that Some new Cakes were nice. With enthusiasm we moved on to a grey counter and the discovery that No new Cakes were nice, and then we all took quite a long time over the Double Propositions that No Cakes were new, and All new Cakes were nice. There was a *very* difficult point on page ten when Mr Carroll asked us whether the Proposition "The Cake you have given me is nice" was Particular or Universal, and the eleven-year-old couldn't see it mattered anyway, was this a game or wasn't it? But page thirteen, with the need to interpret seven possible variations of counter-position excited everyone; it was just like reading a code.

But after page thirteen, there was no pretending that this was a game for children any more – at least, Mr Carroll could go on pretending, but we could not. The small square was left behind, and though we were still coping with cakes, our counters now had to be placed in any variants of sixteen different positions on a far more complicated diagram. We managed to get them into a position that read "No new Cakes are wholesome", but after that, Mr Carroll dropped – one can hardly say like a hot cake – these excessively qualitative edibles, and began talking in algebraic symbols. And not only were these totally devoid of interest, they were TOO DIFFICULT. True, by the end of section one, Mr C had relented to the extent of allowing us to interpret *abc* and *def* as wise old men and reckless foolish gamblers, but it was too late. *The Game of Logic* had swum out of our ken.

I think – I hope – that the other seventy-five pages of the book were meant for post-graduate university students, for I gave up when my children did.

We played the game a second time at their insistence, and a third time at mine. After that, it went into the bookshelf, and was brought out only for adult guests. As a game, it's really fun for a child only once, because no variation is possible, and without a live Mr Carroll at one's elbow, one's capacity comes to a dead stop at the same point every time. Which means, I suppose, that it's a very fair test of intelligence.'

Two

After *The Game of Logic* had been finally disposed of in February, 1887, Dodgson wrote two theatrical articles for the *Stage* and a letter for the *St James's Gazette* defending the employment of children in theatres, and then busied himself with his *Curiosa Mathematica*, Part I, a highly technical examination of Euclid's 12th Axiom, which appeared in 1888 and had gone into a fourth edition by 1895. More interesting to most people, however, was *The Nursery Alice* – a project which had been on the stocks for some time and was launched in 1889.

In *The Nursery Alice* Dodgson presented a retelling of 'Wonderland' in shortened and simplified form for children below the age of five, with twenty of Tenniel's illustrations, enlarged and coloured to excellent effect. Gertrude Thomson provided a coloured cover (Plate p. 226) which is more acceptable than most of her work, and the whole venture was a distinct success, Dodgson showing that he knew just what was wanted. The first ten thousand copies were condemned – we might almost have expected it: 'The pictures are *far* too bright and gaudy, and vulgarise the whole thing,' Dodgson told Macmillan's. But he was very pleased with the second edition, and the book was in its eleventh thousand when the author died.

Dodgson took one of his mathematical notebooks and turned it round to make a list of those to whom he wished to send copies of *The Nursery Alice*. Many old friends were remembered – Mrs Hargreaves, of course, Tenniel, Duckworth, Christina Rossetti, Princess Alice. . . . Besides Mrs Hargreaves' name, he added 'morocco' for the binding, then crossed it out – well, one

Cover of The Nursery Alice

couldn't go on for ever.[210]

Dodgson's didacticism was well served by *The Nursery Alice* – better than it would have been by his abortive scheme for a bowdlerised edition of Shakespeare for girls which occupied him earlier in the eighties.

Three

The incessant labours of the amateur publisher and the Common Room Curator (were they, after all, only a form of delaying tactics now that he felt his inspiration had begun to fail?) could no longer postpone the writing of *Sylvie and Bruno*.

In November, 1886, ten years almost to the day since he had announced to Macmillan's his wish 'to write one more child's book', he informed them that Harry Furniss had consented to provide the drawings and that he thought of publishing it in 1888. 'But I should be glad to get parts of it set up in slip, as I am a little nervous about the risk of the M.S. being destroyed by fire: and I could never *remember* it all.' One is suddenly reminded of the coil of rope that Hans Andersen carried about with him, in case there should be a fire at any of the hotels he stayed at.

The writing of *Sylvie and Bruno* began to suffer from a handicap from which Dodgson had hitherto been remarkably free – that of intermittent ill-health. He was feeling the effect of many years of strain, brought on by the rigorous discipline of his life and by continual over-work. Unfortunately, his self-discipline did not extend to going to bed early, and like many bachelors he often worked into the small hours. He seems to have been unable to relax and, in an effort to keep himself well, increased his physical exercise to a point of excess. Walks of more than twenty miles were common for him – in May, 1881, there is a diary note of a walk of twenty-seven miles – and it becomes increasingly obvious that he had got into a vicious circle, and, moreover, was probably not eating enough to keep up his strength. In 1882 he made several excursions on a tricycle called the 'Velociman' – and was soon designing improvements for its steering, so that the rider could 'lean the way you want to turn, which is instinctive and safer as to upsetting'. He also suggested to the maker of the tricycle, an Oxford man named Charsley, that 'there should be means of locking the machine, so that it will stand on a hill', and a method of changing speed (Diary, June, 1882). He bought one of the early typewriters, and towards the end of his life a 'Whiteley' exerciser – and in these experiments closely followed the scientific spirit of the age.

Like all those who read medical books, he was quick to diagnose his own symptoms. A spell of ill-health in June, 1881, he put down to 'an attack of "vasical catarrh" with fever as a secondary'. On his fifty-first birthday he noted: 'I cannot say I feel much older at 51 than at 21!' but in July, 1883, he recorded 'a sort of ague, with cystitis'; he had 'two miserable feverish nights, in a state between waking and sleeping, and worrying over the same idea (something about Common Room ledgers) over and over again'. For some time he lay on his sofa reading novels, including Miss Thackeray's *Old Kensington* ('lovely writing').

It was very unusual for Dodgson to abandon himself to fiction in this way, for he made a great point of diversifying his reading. In fact, he understood that the mind must be trained and dieted no less than the body. There is a passage, distinctly reminiscent of Mrs Eddy, in his little-known but characteristic paper 'Feeding the Mind', in which he assumes that it might be possible to take the mind to the doctor and have its pulse felt:

'Why, what have you been doing with this mind lately? How have you fed it? It looks pale, and the pulse is very slow.'

'Well, doctor, it has not had much regular food lately. I gave it a lot of sugar-plums yesterday.'

'Sugar-plums! What kind?'

'Well, they were a parcel of conundrums, sir.'

'Ah, I thought so. Now just mind this: if you go on playing tricks like that, you'll spoil all its teeth, and get laid up with mental indigestion. You must have nothing but the plainest reading for the next few days. Take care now! No novels on any account!'[211]

'Feeding the Mind' was a lecture that Dodgson delivered for W. H. Draper, Vicar of Alfreton, in September, 1884. He had another attack of 'a feverish cold of ague-type' while he was staying at Alfreton on that occasion, but the local doctor then pronounced him 'a thoroughly healthy man'.

So indeed he probably was, physically speaking. But W. H. Draper, recalling Dodgson's 'nervous, highly strung manner as he stood before the little room full of simple people' to talk on 'Feeding the Mind', put his finger on the reason for much of the ill-health that he experienced. The occasional sleeplessness, and the intermittent attacks of migraine during which he saw 'moving fortifications' (he first recorded such an attack in 1885) were clearly of nervous origin, and the other maladies from which he suffered in the late 'eighties – such as boils, eczema, cystitis and synovitis – are not uncommon in persons of his constitution when under strain. Synovitis more than once condemned him to his sofa and to courses of bandages and iodine. He consulted a homoeo-pathic doctor in 1888 and was told that his spleen was out of order. In February, 1891, he fainted at the end of morning chapel and found himself an hour later lying on the floor of the stalls with his nose bleeding.

This doleful recital will make it clear that Dodgson's health provided many obstacles to the writing of *Sylvie and Bruno*. But he made good progress on the book during 1887, and, as was often his practice, read something by Anne Isabella Thackeray (Mrs, afterwards Lady, Ritchie) to get himself 'into tune'. The following letter to Mrs Ritchie not only contains a tribute to the writer whom he appreciated so highly in his later years, but gives such a compre-hensive account of his own life at this time that it is worth quoting in full:

Ch. Ch. Oxford.
Oct.24/87.

My Dear Mrs Ritchie,

You will, I fear, have long ago given me up as a hopeless correspondent, who is so ungrateful as not even to notice the very kind invitation (written Jan. 13, more than 9 months ago!) to come & dine, & sleep, & renew old acquaintance 'any day after Jan. 16th'. But it has never been out of my memory for long together: again & again I have been going to write – & again & again it has been 'there is so-and-so that really *ought* to be done today, & the letter has waited so long that another day ca'n't matter'. And the days, even now, still answer to your definition: none can deny that they are 'after Jan. 16th'! Dear

Mrs Ritchie, if you'll kindly regard the invitation as not, even *yet*, wholly extinct, I would like to come *very* much, & could do so almost at any time. My life is of that happy kind that I am not tied to *any* times or seasons (except an occasional College Meeting, or University voting, that I feel bound to attend) as I gave up lecturing some years ago, in order to have some portion of my life, before bodily powers begin to fail, to complete a quantity of book-writing that I have *projected*, and feel that I ought if possible to complete. Every one, I suppose, feels more fitted for some *one* line of work than for all others – & *there*, most likely, lies the work that God means him to do: & that is what I feel about these uncompleted books: it is the work I am more fit (or rather less unfit) for than for other kinds.

I had nearly 4 months at Eastbourne this summer, working (often 6 hours a day) at one single book (a story, but for rather older readers than 'Alice') which is still far from completion. Perhaps at Christmas, 1888, I *may* have the pleasure of sending you a copy: I cannot predict yet. I had with me a copy of 'Five Old Friends &c' (not that I hadn't read it all before) in order to read a bit, now & then, before beginning to write, & so get my ear into *tune*. Not that I want to imitate your style (I don't believe in any one imitating any one else), however much I admire it: but to read such English sets my fancy *going*, so to speak: till sometimes the sentences come almost too quick for me to write them down.

It will be a great pleasure to make the acquaintance of your husband (whom I don't think I have ever met) & of your children. I once saw the little girl, when about a year old, I think, when I called on you in – Young Street, wasn't it? – somewhere in Kensington. Now that I'm an old man, I am declining, universally, invitations to dinners or for visits: & I have even given up *calling* on friends. But every law has its exceptions.

Yours very sincerely

C. L. DODGSON.[212]

He did not get on so well with the book at Oxford as he had at Eastbourne, and on December 10th recorded that he had 'been so busy, in Common Room work etc., that I have only done *one* new sentence of my story-book. But today I wrote three MS. pages, the substance of which I have had in my head for some time.' So the book gradually took shape – or, rather, increased in size, for shape is not the word to use for something essentially formless. He was continually in correspondence with Harry Furniss about the illustrations. Furniss, a masterly if sometimes rather vulgar draughtsman, showed extraordinary patience in coping with a flood of exasperating criticism and eventually produced drawings that did for *Sylvie and Bruno* all that an illustrator could possibly have done. 'I put up with his eccentricities', he wrote of Dodgson in his autobiography:

'I put up with a great deal of boredom, for he was a bore at times, and I worked over seven years with his illustrations, in which the actual working hours would not have occupied me more than seven weeks, purely out of respect for his genius. I treated him as a problem, and I solved him, and had he lived I would probably have still worked with him. He remunerated me liberally for my work; still, he actually proposed that, in addition, I should partake of the profits; his gratitude was overwhelming.'[213]

'He thought he saw an elephant, That practised on a fife . . .' from 'The Mad Gardener's Song'

THE MAD GARDENER'S SONG

HE thought he saw an Elephant,
    That practised on a fife:
He looked again, and found it was
    A letter from his wife.
"At length I realise," he said,
    "The bitterness of Life!"

PETER AND PAUL

"PETER is poor." said noble Paul,
  "And I have always been his friend :
And, though my means to *give* are small,
  At least I can afford to *lend*.
How few, in this cold age of greed,
  Do good, except on selfish grounds !
But I can feel for Peter's need,
  And I WILL LEND HIM FIFTY POUNDS ! "

Yet still he got the old reply,
  "It is not quite convenient ! "

The Fourth arrived, and punctual Paul
Came, with his legal friend, at noon.
"I thought it best," said he, "to call :
One cannot settle things too soon."
Poor Peter shuddered in despair :
  His flowing locks he wildly tore :

Ah, Paul, a single five-pound-note
  Would make another man of me ! "
Said Paul, "It fills me with surprise
  To hear you talk in such a tone :
I fear you scarcely realise
  The blessings that are all your own !

"You're safe from being overfed :
  You're sweetly picturesque in rags :
You never know the aching head
  That comes along with money-bags :

And people sneered at one so poor,
  I never used my Peter so !
And when you'd lost your little all,
  And found yourself a thing despised,
I need not ask you to recall
  How tenderly I sympathised !

"Then the advice I've poured on you,
  So full of wisdom and of wit :
All given gratis, though 'tis true
  I might have fairly charged for it !

*How Furniss met Dodgson's
eccentricities: Drawings for*
Sylvie and Bruno

Four

Sylvie and Bruno was published in December, 1889, and its successor *Sylvie and Bruno Concluded* in December, 1893, both being of four hundred pages with forty-six illustrations by Harry Furniss. It was, in fact, a very large work – each volume, as Lewis Carroll hopefully emphasised in the advertisements, containing 'nearly as much as the two "Alice" books put together', and therefore providing a good return for seven shillings and sixpence. But books, unlike groceries, are not in the long run valued by their weight; and unfortunately this was not 'the best butter'.

A lengthy and apologetic preface is seldom an encouraging approach to any book. *Sylvie and Bruno* and its sequel are each preceded by rambling addresses of a kind that a clergyman might make from the steps of the chancel, beginning with a few observations of local interest (i.e. details of the composition of the book) and then branching off into good works and moral reflections of all kinds – the need for a Child's Bible or for a *Shakespeare for Girls*, the hazard of sudden death coming to someone unprepared for it, the insincerity of elaborate church services and the self-conceit thereby engendered in choir-boys (a subject which Dodgson now approached from the same low-church evangelical standpoint as Martin Tupper).

These prefaces warn us of what is coming. The artist has not been snuffed out, but he has been overlaid by the moralist. The fairy-tale is there, and with it some entertaining fantasy in prose and verse that is quite in the old vein and has a life of its own when detached from its context; but Dodgson, the didactic moralist, has attempted to marry with it a conventionally 'uplifting' period novel, and the experiment is disastrous to the book as a whole. The contrast extends to Furniss's illustrations, which alternate between whimsical but not unpleasing fancies reminiscent of Thackeray or Doyle and uncompromisingly realistic drawings typical of the Victorian society novel.

And yet the book remains one of the most interesting failures in English literature. It is certainly unique; no one but Dodgson could have written it; nothing like it will be produced again. Many people will say 'Thank goodness for that'. Others will still undertake the difficult task of reading it, in order to see how a late Victorian clergyman sought to combine his genius for a children's story with the overriding need to deliver his conscience and preach the gospel of love. Those who will get most from *Sylvie and Bruno*, and will be likely to remember it with tolerant affection, will be those who have approached both Lewis Carroll and his period with sympathy rather than scepticism, and have tried to reconcile the hidden conflicts of the man and the time.

The book has a further significance not usually credited to it. Dodgson was determined to get away in *Sylvie and Bruno* from the pattern of the 'Alice' books, and in his attempt he had the interesting idea – really only an extended examination of the sleeping-waking problem which had occupied him since childhood – of introducing 'fairies' into human situations, and of postulating that man may go through three stages in relation to the supernatural: the ordinary state of 'no consciousness'; the mixed or, as he called it, the 'eerie' state ('in which, while conscious of actual surroundings, he is *also* conscious of the presence of Fairies'); and a form of trance, or dream-state. This is discussed in the preface to the second volume. The theory is demonstrated in the book, so that the course of the story is not surprisingly difficult to follow. But here *Sylvie and Bruno* may have had an influence on later writers. Within twenty-five years of his death, Dodgson could have seen – on that same stage of the Haymarket Theatre on which he had visited the cast of *Living Miniatures* in 1867 – such plays as Maeterlinck's *The Blue Bird* and Barrie's *Mary Rose*, in which similar material, handled with equal seriousness but more subtlety, was greatly assisted by Norman O'Neill's music. These plays would have interested Dodgson enormously. They might have made him realise that, even in *Sylvie and Bruno*, he tended towards a theatrical presentation; and he would have appreciated the help of music in his transitions.

Sylvie and Bruno bears the same relation to Lewis Carroll's earlier works, *mutatis mutandis*, as *Finnegan's Wake* to the more intelligible earlier productions of James Joyce. It is worth giving some time to it, though not too much, as the honourable experiment of a remarkable mind. The songs and poems can be enjoyed for their own sake, and so can such episodes as the visit to Dogland, the 'Outlandish Watch', and the 'hunting-down of the scholars' in Chapter XII. To some readers the mawkish baby-talk of Bruno may be the greatest single bar to enjoyment.

The first volume of *Sylvie and Bruno* had reached its thirteenth thousand by Dodgson's death; *Sylvie and Bruno Concluded* was not so successful. If Dodgson was upset, he hid his disappointment; he had long ago given up reading reviews. 'I am quite satisfied that its small sale is not at all due to insufficient advertising,' he wrote to Macmillan's on May 24th, 1894, 'and that more advertising would have done no good. . . . Don't do any more *extra* advertising – it seems to be only throwing money away. I did not know the reviews had been unfavourable. If the reviewers are right the book does not deserve to sell: if they are wrong, it will gradually get known by people recommending it to their friends.' His brother Edwin Dodgson gave *Sylvie and Bruno* a further lease of life by preparing an abridged version, omitting the heavier passages, which was published in 1904.

Five

In earlier years Dodgson had intermittently enjoyed the fame of Lewis Carroll, and sometimes seemed to welcome the opportunity that it afforded him of

The Pig-Tale

He knew the consequence must be
That he would never get his fee—
And still he sits, in miserie,
   Upon that ruined Pump!

making the acquaintance of distinguished people. To the end of his life, he never lost pleasure in revealing himself to children as Lewis Carroll, and he gave away inscribed copies of his books in unusual numbers. But, after a very brief experience of fame, he took a poor view of the pleasures of a hunted lion, and became morbidly obsessed with the determination to escape every kind of avoidable attention. In this warfare he felt no scruples. Edward Bok, the American journalist, went for a walk with him and stayed to lunch, but was told quite flatly: 'You are not speaking to "Lewis Carroll".'[214] Requests for autographs were similarly rebuffed, often with the help of his typewriter or of Christ Church colleagues who wrote third-personal letters on his behalf.

A large 'fan mail', as we should now call it, poured in upon him both at the office of Macmillan's and at Christ Church. Whenever a letter arrived at Oxford addressed to 'Lewis Carroll' he was deeply disturbed at the evidence that his disguise had been pierced. So far as possible, he got Macmillan's to send his replies, and when he was interested he took trouble over them:

'Will you kindly inform Mr A. Silver, of 84 Brook Green, that Mr Lewis Carroll has no objection to his using Tenniel's pictures for the wall-paper which he proposes to design. Please add the suggestion that the *longer* the paper can be made, before the pattern repeats itself, the better: the thing has been already tried once, but the pattern repeated itself in about 2 yards of length, so that, even in a small room, the same picture would recur many times, with a very tedious effect. 20 yards of length, before the pattern recurs, would be none too long.'

(October 14th, 1888.)

After hearing the 'Phonograph' in 1890, Dodgson wrote in his diary: 'It is a pity that we are not fifty years further on in the world's history, so as to get this wonderful invention in its *perfect* form.' But in some ways he was very fortunate to have lived when he did. If he had lived fifty years later, he might have been compelled to desperate manoeuvres on the promenade at East-bourne, and even to the wearing of dark glasses. It was lucky for him that he escaped the era of the press photographer; otherwise we should have seen, at regular intervals, snapshots of a nervous clerical figure in a top-hat, caught in a corner of Tom Quad, looking extremely annoyed and warding off the camera with a mass of Common Room papers. So much evidence of his extreme distaste for 'lionising' has been published that it is unnecessary to repeat it here, but some unfamiliar letters in this vein may be quoted. No publisher would ever have succeeded in securing the presence of Lewis Carroll at one of his sherry parties; the following quotation comes from a letter to Alexander Macmillan of May 9th, 1879:

'Many thanks for your kind intimation of the days of your "receptions" in Bedford Street: but (how many "buts" there are in life!) I fear that in such an assembly it would be almost impossible to preserve an incognito. I cannot of course help there being many people who know the connection between my real name and my "alias", but the fewer there are who are able to connect my face with the name "Lewis Carroll" the happier for me. So I hope you will kindly excuse my non-appearance.'

The second quotation is from a letter to F. H. Atkinson of December 10th, 1881:

'. . . As to my photo, I must still beg to be excused. Possibly your book of poetry has not brought on you all the annoyances of one who, having been unlucky enough to perpetrate two small books for children has been bullied ever since by the herd of lion-hunters who seek to drag him out of the privacy he hoped an 'anonym' would give him. I have really had *much* persecution of that sort, since I wrote *Alice's Adventures in Wonderland* & *Through the Looking-Glass*, & I so much *hate* the idea of strangers being able to know me by sight that I refuse to give my photo, even for the albums of relations.'[215]

The third is from a letter to Mrs Richards of December 11th, 1885:

'. . . I think I may venture to beg you not to send him [some admiring stranger] to me: it *can* only be as a "lion" he wants to know me, & a lion is the *one* animal I *do'n't* want to be regarded as. It is hard work sometimes – "choking off" the lion-hunters! Some people have a mania for the thing. You might offer him an introduction to Mr Bradlaugh, which I should think would be *much* more in his line!'[216]

Finally, there is the following letter to his sister-in-law Isabel Dodgson, wife of his brother Skeffington, which shows that he remained adamant even to requests from his own family:

7 Lushington Road,
Eastbourne.
July 31/90.

My Dear Isa,

I fear the only answer I can give to your question is that I have the greatest possible objection to my name appearing in any collection of autographs whatever; & I shall be much obliged to your friend (I do not remember ever meeting any one of the name) if he will abandon his intention of so including it. The whole tribe of autograph-hunters & celebrity-hunters are distasteful to me, & cause me a good deal of worry. As an instance, I have just been told by my landlady here that a 'gentleman' called, in my absence, & said he wished to see me to ask some questions about my books. Finding that I was out, he gave no name, but said he would 'look in another time'. I have no doubt he is a lion-hunter, & probably an autograph-hunter as well. I told her to tell him, when he calls again, that I have nothing to say to him about any books at all, that I acknowledge no connection with them, and that I decline to see him.

It is strange to me that people *will not* understand that, when an author uses a 'nom-de-plume', his object is to *avoid* that personal publicity which they are always trying to thrust upon him.

There! You've brought upon your head a regular showerbath of indignation: but it *is* a worry, you will allow.

With love to you both, & to Irene, I am

Your affectionate brother,
C. L. Dodgson.[217]

What would have happened if the visitor had called to discuss, not the 'Alice' books, but *Euclid and his Modern Rivals* by Charles L. Dodgson, is not indicated: such a contingency was apparently thought so unlikely that it could be disregarded. The year 1890, in which this letter was written, seems to have brought Dodgson's 'shower-bath of indignation' to the point of overflowing, for in the same year he had the following extraordinary circular printed at Oxford:

'Mr Dodgson is so frequently addressed by strangers on the quite unauthorised assumption that he claims, or at any rate acknowledges the authorship of books not published under his name, that he has found it necessary to print this, once for all, as an answer to all such applications. He neither claims nor acknowledges any connection with any pseudonym, or with any book that is not published under his own name. Having therefore no claim to retain, or even to read the enclosed, he returns it for the convenience of the writer who has thus mis-addressed it.'[218]

This may be thought to carry dissimulation beyond all reasonable bounds; perhaps the circular was not much used, for examples of it are rare. Considering that his own income, and the generous help that he was able to give members of his family, were entirely founded on books published under a pseudonym, it was really rather absurd of him – one hesitates to use a stronger word – to issue such a sweeping disclaimer; the circular shows scrupulous accuracy being carried away by a passionate longing for privacy. (In June, 1890, Dodgson asked Macmillan's for 'slightly better terms for myself. I am obliged to look to L.S.D. a little, as the calls on me, relatively to my income, are enormous.' As an instance of how Dodgson relied on his royalties from Macmillan's, there is a diary entry of October 1st, 1894, stating that, as he had received £500 less than he had expected, owing to the failure of *Sylvie and Bruno Concluded*, he did not see how he could give his 'usual family gifts next year', though a letter to Macmillan's of April 15th, 1895, shows that the particular difficulty was partially overcome.)

Farquharson Sharp's *Dictionary of English Authors* (1897) indicates that Dodgson carried his private war into the field of reference books, but in the last year of his life an entry slipped into *Who's Who* that one presumes he never saw, and which would surely have horrified him if he had. He is there entered under 'Carroll, Lewis', with a cross-reference from Dodgson; a mixed selection of his books is provided which includes both pseudonymous works and works issued under his own name; and his address is actually given as Christ Church, Oxford. This was the first edition of *Who's Who* in its present form. Messrs A. and C. Black[219] say they believe that 'quite a number of eminent persons did not at first respond to the invitation to supply details', that in some cases 'the entries were made up editorially from such information as was generally available', and that the time factor may have prevented the entries being submitted to the subjects concerned. 'Had Mr Dodgson lived another year he would have received a printed proof of the entry as it appeared in 1897.' He was at least spared that shock.

One

It is well to choose a sunny day to look at the famous portraits of Christ Church, for the magnificent hall with its dark panelling needs the light filtered through the lofty windows to illumine Kneller's Locke, Romney's Wesley or Millais' Gladstone. Around the high table which symbolises the centre of college life hang three portraits of men whom Lewis Carroll knew very well. There is Watts's tribute to Dean Liddell, dominating and austere; Orchardson's clever study of his successor Dean Paget, with his thin, ascetic yet humorous features; and a theatrically posed portrait by Orpen of Paget's successor, Dean Strong. Such prominence would not have been coveted by C. L. Dodgson. More than a hundred feet, indeed the whole length of the hall, away from these dignitaries hangs Herkomer's posthumous portrait of Lewis Carroll, representing him with restraint and taste. But its place, though withdrawn, was well chosen. Beside the doorway, it modestly commemorates a life spent in the service of the House, but hints also at a name known far beyond. Enquiring visitors can see the portrait of the author of 'Alice' without any loss of time, and, after a quick glance at the fan-tracery outside, get on to other essential sights of Oxford.

Dodgson, naturally enough, nowhere expressed his opinion in writing of Dean Liddell's decision to retire at Christmas, 1891; Collingwood says that this came as 'a great blow' to him, but, as their relationship had been consistently antagonistic, it is much more likely that it came as a great relief. Francis Paget was a close personal friend, and Dodgson registered in his diary the hope, which was fulfilled, that he would be the new Dean.

There are signs that Dodgson was a much happier, a more contented man in the nineties than he had been for a long time. Dr M. J. Mannheim has studied specimens of his handwriting of 1888 and of 1895, and he has observed a contrast between them which is almost as striking in its way as that between the letters of 1844 and 1852 which we considered in Chapter IV. Dr Mannheim found that the letter of 1888 was depressed, hesitant, full of tension, but that by 1895 much of this 'ambivalence' had disappeared. Vitality and interest in reality had greatly increased. Dodgson was apparently going on his way with considerable perseverance and self-assertion. There are traces, in the handwriting of 1895, of dogmatism, and even of pomposity, but the anxious doubt of 1888 had yielded to confidence and renewed certainty.

What do we find in the facts of his life that might explain such a change? The eighties had certainly been a time of difficulty. They began with Alice Liddell's marriage; with the trouble over his photography and the abandonment of his hobby; with a fuss about a kiss – indications, perhaps, that 'the old Adam' had not been entirely conquered. Dodgson gave up his lectureship, and soon afterwards threw himself into the duties of the Curatorship, which proved a prolonged source of worry. *Sylvie and Bruno* was a chaotic mass of manuscript that he had yet to subdue.

By 1895, or earlier, however, the situation was much more encouraging. He had finally come to terms with his sex life; as 'an old man' he found happiness in fatherly friendships with girls, and had acquired the courage to defy 'Mrs Grundy'. *Sylvie and Bruno* was out of the way; so, too, was that tiresome Curatorship. Dean Liddell had given place to the friendly Paget in the Deanery.

All this tends to support Dr Mannheim's conclusions. The layman's eye must confirm them, too, when it compares Dodgson's often weak and faintly smudgy handwriting of the eighties with the stronger and more confident script of the nineties. One may also here mention the curious fact, noticed by Mr Warren Weaver,[220] that up to about 1871 Dodgson practically always used black ink, then for twenty years largely employed purple ink, and finally, after about 1891, reverted to black ink. What, if anything, the psychological significance of this may be is something that the present writer cannot hope to estimate; but it is a fact that the 'purple period' tended in Dodgson's life to depression and unhappiness.

Two

The nineties began propitiously with the publication on July 2nd, 1890, of one of Dodgson's most charming inventions – 'The Wonderland Postage-Stamp Case' (Plate above). This is a practical joke in the best sense. It consists of an interior holder with pockets for stamps of eleven different values between a halfpenny and a shilling. Thus far its purpose is strictly utilitarian; but the holder slips into a cover, and both are decorated with coloured pictures after Tenniel – so that Alice holding the baby is transformed, by pulling out the holder, into Alice holding the pig, and on the other side the Cheshire Cat (complete) turns into the Cheshire Cat's valedictory grin. It is Lewis Carroll's innocent little gift to the naughty nineties, and has kept its freshness while parts of the *Yellow Book* have gone sour.

Accompanying it was a miniature pamphlet: 'Eight or Nine Wise Words about Letter-Writing'. Dodgson wrote so many letters that he had plenty of advice to give, and all of it is useful and entertaining. The envelope should be addressed and stamped first of all, he urged. '"What! Before writing the *letter*?" Most certainly.' He considered this a form of insurance against 'the hurried wind-up – the wildly-scrawled signature – the hastily-fastened envelope, which comes open in the post – the address, a mere hieroglyphic – the horrible discovery that you've forgotten to replenish your Stamp-Case – the frantic appeal, to every one in the house, to lend you a Stamp – the headlong rush to the Post-Office, arriving, hot and gasping, just after the box had closed – and finally, a week afterwards, the return of the Letter, from the Dead-Letter Office, marked "address illegible"!'

The inventor obviously enjoyed everything to do with his Stamp-Case and wrote about it gaily: 'Postage-Stamp-Cases may be divided into one species, the "Wonderland". The title is entered at Stationers' Hall: the two Pictorial Surprises, and the "Wise Words", are copyright.' He took pains to explain how it worked and to ensure that no purchaser could fail to realise that the baby turned into a pig: 'If *that* doesn't surprise you, why, I suppose you wouldn't be surprised if your own Mother-in-law suddenly turned into a Gyroscope!' The Case, he emphasised, was not intended to be carried about in the pocket. Many people seldom used any stamps except 'Penny Stamps for Letters, Sixpenny-Stamps for Telegrams, and a bit of Stamp-edging for cut fingers,' and for them a purse or pocket-book sufficed. No, he had designed his Case for those, like himself, who wanted extra stamps for parcels and foreign letters, and it was meant to be kept at home with the writing-materials. He gently mocked the Pears' Soap advertisements (a great source of amusement in the nineties): 'Since I have possessed a "Wonderland Stamp-Case", Life has been bright and peaceful, and I have used no other. I believe the Queen's Laundress uses no other.'

Dodgson's practice of addressing the envelope before writing the letter was similar to the method of calculation he employed in his *Pillow Problems*, published in 1893 as Part II of *Curiosa Mathematica*. For nearly all of these he wrote the answer first, then the question and solution. The first edition of *Pillow Problems* has the sub-title: 'Thought out during Sleepless Nights'. In consequence he received many sympathetic letters, so that for the second edition he substituted 'Wakeful Hours' for 'Sleepless Nights', explaining that he had never suffered from insomnia, but that when he failed to sleep it was usually because of 'luxurious idleness in the preceding day'. It is clear, however, that he did not regularly sleep well.

He was greatly occupied with games and puzzles during the last years of his life. In 1890 he published 'Circular Billiards', an esoteric game of billiards for that fabulous piece of furniture, a circular table with cushions but no pockets or spot. In 1891 he conducted a series of competitions in *The Lady* to launch another new game with the fantastic title 'Syzygies', which was really an extension of an earlier and simpler game of his called 'Doublets' – the idea being to link two words by a series of other words which have certain letters in common. Walrus, for example, is turned into Carpenter by the intervening links, peruse and harper. 'Syzygies' was published in 1893 with another game, 'Lanrick', played on a chess or draughts board.

Towards the end of his life Dodgson, in the character of Lewis Carroll, was drawn into closer contact with his readers than before, and apparently enjoyed addressing them by means of advertisements and leaflets. It is as if the clergyman who never had a parish of his own felt a pastoral urge to speak to his flock. When the sixtieth thousand of *Through the Looking-Glass* failed to come up to his expectations in 1893, he drafted a leaflet promising to exchange any copies of the edition that were returned to Macmillan's, and offering to send the rejected copies to mechanics' institutes, village school libraries, etc. Couched in the third person, the same announcement appeared in the personal column of *The Times* on Saturday, December 2nd, 1893. The last sentence is perhaps the most interesting: 'He takes this opportunity of announcing that, if, at any future time, he should wish to communicate anything to his readers he will do so by advertising in the 'Agony' Column of some of the daily papers on the first Tuesday in the month.' (Tuesday was Dodgson's 'lucky day'.)

A search through the personal columns of *The Times* has revealed only one further insertion, that on Tuesday, March 6th, 1894, in which, after a renewal of his offer regarding *Through the Looking-Glass*, the advertisement continues:

'He takes this opportunity of giving his readers the rules for "Co-operative Backgammon", which he thinks will prove a novel and interesting variety of the game. (1) Each player throws three dice; with two he moves for himself, and with the third for his adversary. (2) If no one of the three dice is available for the adversary, a player may use any two he likes; otherwise he is bound to leave, as third die, one which will be available for the adversary.'

Other friendly items of 'parish gossip' can be found in the advertisement pages at the end of Dodgson's books. Thus in 1893 his readers learned that they could buy *The Nursery Alice* at 'only just over cost price' because 'the colours came out a little too bright', and that Tom Hood's *From Nowhere to the North Pole* could not possibly have influenced *Alice's Adventures in Wonderland* because it was published nine years later. In an author's note to a new edition of 'Alice' at Christmas, 1896, he responded to enquiries by putting on record 'a fairly appropriate answer' to the Mad Hatter's riddle: 'Why is a raven like a writing-desk?' 'Because it can produce a few notes, though they are *very* flat; and it is never put with the wrong end in front.' He may have felt this rather feeble, and he excused himself by explaining it was 'merely an afterthought: the Riddle, as originally invented, had no answer at all'.

In a prospectus for *Symbolic Logic*, Part I, of 1896 – a development of his *Game of Logic*, and the last book of Lewis Carroll's to appear in his life-time – he boosted his new work with great vigour. 'As to *Symbolic Logic* being *dry*, and *uninteresting*, I can only say, *try* it!' It is pleasant to be able to record that enough people did try *Symbolic Logic* to send it into four editions in the year of publication. It was in the advertisement at the beginning of *Symbolic Logic* that, as we have seen, Dodgson corrected the 'silly story' about 'my having presented certain books' to Queen Victoria.

Three

Apart from very occasional visits to London or to friends further afield, Dodgson's life in the nineties was spent at three points (as he might have expressed it) in a straight line – Oxford, Guildford, Eastbourne. It is perhaps not the least evidence of the strengthened confidence and determination of his last years that he should now have made a new reputation for himself, as a preacher, in all three towns.

This success was not easily won. Probably only fellow stammerers can appreciate the courage that Dodgson needed to face the ordeal of speaking in public. He wrote in his diary of February 1st, 1894, that reading the

Dodgson's house at Eastbourne

lesson was 'too great a strain on the nerves to be tried often', and on the subject of preaching he had opened his heart to Edith Blakemore in a letter written three years earlier (February 1st, 1891). 'A sermon would be quite formidable enough for me, even if I did *not* suffer from the physical difficulty of hesitation,' he said, 'but with *that* super-added, the prospect is sometimes almost too much for my nerves.' He described how he had undertaken to preach at Guildford at Christmas, 1890, and said that as the day drew nearer he felt so 'entirely despondent' that he went to the curate's house to ask him to bring a sermon with him 'in case I should feel unequal to preaching'. 'Luckily for me,' he continued, 'he wasn't at home; and I didn't go again, but made up my mind to face it, & make the best of it.' No one could understand, thought Dodgson, what a 'drawback in life hesitation sometimes is . . . *any* public speaking is generally formidable to me'.[221]

Knowing that each sermon was a battle, in which victory was a matter of touch and go, we must feel a great admiration for Dodgson. The choir-boys at St Mary's, Guildford, did not, of course, understand what was involved and took a different view. One of those who sat in the Guildford choir under him, Amos Chalcraft, told the present writer in 1952 that they were rather sorry when he preached because he took so long about it. He hesitated particularly badly at the beginning of his sermons, said Mr Chalcraft, but got on better later. He remembered Dodgson as 'very frail' and his cassock as 'green with age'! 'The most terribly thin-looking man I ever saw,' said Mr Chalcraft; 'he looked as if he could have done with a good dinner.' The sharp eyes of youth thus summed up the effect of a habit of lunching on biscuits and a glass of sherry, followed perhaps by a strenuous walk.

Yet, although he made no robust impression, it seems that Dodgson was, on the whole, happy and reasonably well in his last years. 'To say I am quite well "goes without saying" with me', he wrote to Mary Brown on August 31st, 1894. 'In fact, my life is so strangely free from all trial and trouble that I cannot doubt my own happiness is one of the talents entrusted to me to "occupy" with, till the Master shall return, by doing something to make other lives happy.'[222] He put the same point more flippantly to another friend on January 1st, 1895: 'Go carefully through the list of bankruptcies; then run your eye down the police cases; and, if you fail to find my name anywhere, you can say to your mother in a tone of calm satisfaction, "Mr Dodgson is going on *well*".'[223] With *Alice in Wonderland* selling an average of 4,800 copies a year, and *Through the Looking-Glass* 3,000, he was able to help others financially – for he kept little for himself – but he thought also of his preaching as a form of service to his fellow men. When his brother Skeffington invited him to preach at Alfrick, Worcester, in 1893, he replied: 'I am glad to take opportunities of saying "words for God", which one *hopes* may prove of some use to somebody. I always feel that a sermon is worth the preaching, if it has given *some* help to even *one* soul in the puzzle of Life.'[224]

He preached his first Eastbourne sermon on September 10th, 1893, and in his last year spoke more than once at children's services there, telling an allegory called 'Victor and Arnion' which he might have published if he had lived. At Oxford he preached regularly at services for college servants for several years (knowing what he thought of some of the 'Scouts', it is obvious that this was an opportunity he would not have missed for anything!). After a time his sermons were no longer requested for these services. This was not intended as any reflection on his sermons, but it made him diffident about accepting an invitation from the newly appointed Vicar of St Mary's, Oxford, the Rev H. L. Thompson, to preach at a special service for undergraduates.

Ch. Ch., Oxford.

Dec. 2/96.

My Dear Thompson,

Your letter causes me to write, *now*, a letter I had meant to keep waiting till your installation as Vicar of S. Mary's.

That you may not misunderstand it, I begin by saying that to preach the sermon to undergraduates, which you propose I should do, would be, to me, a privilege to be most deeply thankful for. But it is not a matter in which one's own feelings should be regarded, till the question has been settled what is *best* to be done, in the spiritual interests of others.

Please regard what I now tell you as confidential.

When the Services for College Servants began here, I was asked to help; and I generally preached a sermon every Term, at the request of Warner,* who has throughout been the principal actor in the affair, & has done, I am sure, *great* good, in organising & maintaining the services.

Whether my sermons were at all worth preaching, or worth listening to, is a question *I* am of course wholly unfit to discuss – and which I had much rather *not* discuss. So I will simply state the fact that my help ceased to be asked for, nearly 3 years ago. I held my peace, for there are *two* things I dread doing – & I don't know which I dread most. One is, the declining to preach when invited to do so: this feels to me like a wanton throwing away of an opportunity, that perhaps God meant me to take, of doing something, however trivial, in His service. The other is, the offering when not invited. This feels like a deliberate courting of failure (for I generally feel, on the eve of such an attempt, as if a failure were nearly *certain*).

However, I did venture, after all that long interval, to name the matter to my dear friend the Dean. It is obvious how difficult he would have felt it to say 'your sermons were not thought to be worth hearing', & how gladly he would name any other sufficient reason. The reason he gave was that it was wished to make the services more *parochial*, so that preachers had been invited who were used to *parish* work (in which I have had next to no experience).

But the possibility of the *other* reason existing *also* makes me write this, to suggest that, before asking any help from me, you should talk to Warner (without telling him you have received this letter). You can easily learn from him (and need not repeat to me) *all* his reasons. And you will then be able to judge for yourself whether or not to renew your application to me. I hope and pray that you may do what is *best* for your congregation.

Sincerely yours,

C. L. Dodgson.[225]

The upshot of this heartfelt, characteristic letter, and of any enquiries that may have followed it, was that Thompson did 'renew his application' to Dodgson, and that he twice preached to undergraduates at evening services at St Mary's, Oxford, in 1897 – on March 7th and on October 24th. He had his own

*Canon William Warner, Senior Student and Tutor of Christ Church.

way of speaking, seemed to forget the audience in his anxiety to explain his point clearly, and moved all who heard him by the force of his sincerity. One observer has recorded his impression that 'he thought of the subject only, and the words came of themselves. Looking straight in front of him he saw, as it were, his argument mapped out in the form of a diagram, and he set to work to prove it point by point, under its separate heads, and then summed up the whole.'[226] The second of these two sermons was against belief in Eternal Punishment, and Canon H. E. Hone, who was one of the undergraduates who heard it, says: 'It made a great impression on me – not so much the matter of it but the sincerity, earnestness and humility of the man who preached it.'[227]

Four

The Rev C. L. Dodgson swings round the corner briskly in his short tails, turn-down collar, white tie and top-hat; out from Tom Quad into St Aldate's on the way to visit some friends in North Oxford; out through Castle Arch into Quarry Street on the way to St Mary's, Guildford; out from his Eastbourne lodgings on the way to the promenade, with his head thrown back to breathe the sea air. More tired than he knew, gaunt, and to strangers aloof and remote, he still walks erect with the spring of the young man who climbed the cliff-side at Whitby forty years before. And now, in the nineties, he walks before the eyes of those like Ruth Gamlen, Hettie Rowell and Margaret Mayhew who contribute their recollections at the end of this book – or of one like Lord Simon whose severe exterior concealed (as in Dodgson's case) a warm heart, and whose precise logical brain made him one of Dodgson's few undergraduate friends.

The memories of the children who knew him are singularly consistent and uniformly happy; to his young friends he was always sympathetic. But even they may have felt – and still more their elders who caught a sharp rebuke about Sunday observance, jesting on sacred subjects, or bad taste in the theatre – that he belonged already to the past. Hettie Rowell's sister Ethel, whose memories were quoted in the first chapter of this book, saw him thus, for a moment, as a survivor from stricter and more formal days:

'I was walking along our little street toward our house when I caught sight of him standing at the door, waiting to be let in: a tall figure in a morning coat, a tall hat, very tall and with a broad, curved brim. He held himself stiffly, one shoulder slightly higher than the other; in his almost overemphasised erectness there was an old-fashioned seriousness, an air of punctiliousness, a breath of the past and of the passing which touched me even then with a quick, sharp pang of apprehension and almost of pity, a breath which now sings itself for me in the age-old song of Thomas Hardy's "An Ancient to Ancients". . . .

It seemed to me as I approached that he dwarfed our house, made the old high doorstep with the big chip out of it look very poor, and I was frightened by a certain incongruity in his presenting himself *at all* at our door, in his coming down our street to see us like this. I was within an ace of turning back and running away, but it was he who turned and saw me, and at once all was well. He held out a hand, and with the words "Is your mother at home?" he was inside the low dining-room in which we mostly sat.'[228]

Dodgson may have called to discuss with Mrs Rowell the possibility of his

Left and right: *Two drawings of Dodgson by H. Furniss from Some Victorian Men*

Above and opposite: *photographs of Dodgson in his forties and fifties. The one above is probably a self-portrait*

243

nieces lodging with her in term-time while they attended the Oxford High School. Miss Hettie Rowell describes that episode (Appendix A), and the following letter to Mrs Rowell (March 21st, 1897) shows Dodgson's uncompromising objection to their staying in any house in which undergraduates lived. Undergraduates to him were, indeed, a species almost *ferae naturae* (despite his praise of them quoted on page 78):

'It is scarcely *my* "decision", that my nieces had better not come to your house. Their parents would never think of allowing them (even if it were possible) to lodge in any of the many houses where *undergraduates* are taken; & I fear your son must be reckoned under the same heading.

I say "even if it were possible", as to undergraduates: for of course it would *not* be possible. All such lodgings have to be licensed by the Delegates of Lodging-houses: & they would never permit such an arrangement. Where there are young men who are *not* undergraduates, of course the *Delegates* could not interfere. *Parents & guardians* would be the chief obstacle – as I think you will find them to be in the case of *all* High School girls.'[229]

Two months later, when he escorted Hettie Rowell back to her home after she had dined with him at Christ Church, they talked of happiness, and Dodgson mentioned his belief that it was usually realised in retrospect. On May 23rd, 1897, he copied out for her some lines by Margaret Fuller, Marchioness Ossoli, which, coming from him in the last year of his life, have a special poignancy:

Lines by Margaret Fuller Ossoli. 23/5/97

Let me but gather from the earth one full-grown fragrant flower:
Within my bosom let it bloom through its one blooming hour:
Within my bosom let it die, and to its latest breath
My own shall answer 'Having lived, I shrink not now from death'.
It is this niggard halfness that turns my heart to stone;
'Tis the cup seen, not tasted, that makes the infant moan;
For once let me press firm my lips upon the moment's brow;
For once let me distinctly feel 'I am all happy now';
And Love shall seal a blessing upon that moment's brow.[230]

These lines, so suggestive of the White Queen's more prosaic 'jam tomorrow and jam yesterday – but never jam *to-day*', must have been pondered over by Dodgson; he did not copy them out for Hettie Rowell, we may be sure, without reflecting that they had an application for his own life. Was it a 'niggard halfness' in him that sometimes seemed to 'turn his heart to stone'? And did he ever, after his childhood, know a time when he could say 'I am all happy now'? It is something, at least, that he may have realised his happiness in retrospect.

When one of his last child-friends, Margaret Mayhew, joined with another girl, Ethel Harland, to send him an invitation in 1896, he replied to 'My dear Margarethel', and, when he came to his signature, said 'Of course I have to divide myself in two, when writing to a *double* friend!'[231]

Here, for once, is the authentic split-man so beloved of the psychologists.

The split, be it noted, is horizontal, not vertical. A vertical division between Carroll and Dodgson cannot, on examination, be sustained. But the horizontal division, between the happy boy at Croft Rectory and the earnest mathematician who never grew to full maturity, was something real; his intimations of Wonderland were, as it were, photographed on his mind before he was fourteen, and were retained there long after academic discipline had cast him outwardly in the mould of the Victorian don.

Five

Towards the end of his life Dodgson often contemplated death, and saw it approaching without fear. He wrote to one of his sisters in 1896:

'It is getting increasingly difficult now to remember *which* of one's friends remain alive, and *which* have gone "into the land of the great departed, into the silent land". Also, such news comes less and less as a shock, and more and more one realises that it is an experience each of *us* has to face before long. That fact is getting *less* dreamlike to me now, and I sometimes think what a grand thing it will be to be able to say to oneself, "Death is *over* now; there is not *that* experience to be faced again".'[232]

Yet at the close of the year 1897 Dodgson did not wish to die. He was busy that autumn with his sermons, and, after coming to Guildford for his usual Christmas holiday on December 23rd, he worked hard at the second part of his *Symbolic Logic*, which he thought of also as 'work for God'.

On January 5th, 1898, he received a telegram telling him of the sudden death of his brother-in-law, the Rev C. S. Collingwood. He greatly wished that he could go to Southwick, near Sunderland, for the funeral, but he was already ill himself, and could only write by return to send his sister and her sons 'my love and *deep* sympathy'. 'With a feverish cold, of the bronchial type, and the risk of ague (a form my colds usually take), Dr Gabb forbids me to risk it.' It was typical of him that he should have added the sentence: 'You will very likely be in need of some ready money: so I enclose £50 "on account".'[233]

This was not his last letter. He wrote at least one more, to his nephew, which has not hitherto been published. In its anxiety for his family it is characteristic, but it is also curiously moving in view of what was to come:

My Dear Stuart,

I have sent you a message, of love and sympathy, through your mother. This note is on a business-matter that will not wait.

When my dear Father died in 1868, we gave almost 'carte blanche' to the undertakers, without any stipulations as to *limit* of expense – the consequence was a *gigantic* bill – so large, that we had great difficulty in getting the authorities at Doctor's Commons to sanction such extravagance.

If I had the thing to do again, I should say to the undertaker 'Now that you know *all* that is required, I wish you to give me a signed promise that your charges *shall not exceed a stipulated sum*.' I should then take the advice of experienced friends as to whether the limit named was a reasonable one; and, if they said 'no', I should apply to another undertaker.

You and your mother will have to live with the strictest economy: you have no money to throw away.

Your aff^te uncle
CHARLES L. DODGSON[234]

Within a week bronchial symptoms had developed; he went to bed. As Collingwood says, 'his breathing rapidly became hard and laborious, and he had to be propped up with pillows. A few days before his death he asked one of his sisters to read him that well-known hymn, every verse of which ends with "Thy Will be done". To another he said that his illness was a great trial of patience. . . . He seemed to know that the struggle was over. "Take away those pillows," he said on the 13th, "I shall need them no more".'[235] The spirit was willing, indeed eager to finish *Symbolic Logic*; the tired body could go no further.

'Life, what is it but a dream?' The mind, perhaps, had returned to Daresbury parsonage ('What a long letter I've written. I'm twite tired') or to the garden at Croft Rectory, where the dream began – to the excitement of the railway game, to the small pages of *Useful and Instructive Poetry*, to the thimble, the glove and the left-hand shoe hidden beneath the floor-boards, to the mysterious words on the wood-block:

> And we'll wander through
> the wide world
> and chase the buffalo.

It had been a strange adventure; the wide world had been full of delights and dangers, the chase exhausting. We who have followed Lewis Carroll's life know that all sweeping judgements must be put aside; that for each moment of brusqueness there was a touch of kindness, that always beside the pedant stood the generous, imaginative friend. The sensitive boy from the Rectory, with his genius and his principles, was allotted no easy task in life. More than once the balance had trembled; he had found the courage to keep it true.

Above all, he had kept faith with the children, the Alices, the Ellens and all the rest. He had loved them as children, had hopelessly longed for them as women; but in the final test it was love that conquered; he had not failed his own early vision in the garden. He had passed on to children the special gift that only he could give; he had created a whole new mythology for the world; and for his reward he had been loved more than most men, and is still loved.

Lewis Carroll died at half-past two on the afternoon of January 14th, 1898. And Dr Gabb came slowly down the steep, narrow staircase of the square red house at Guildford to speak the words that say everything: 'How wonderfully young your brother looks!'

Map by Gwen Meux of Boulder, Colorado, showing the places where Dodgson lived and visited and the characters from his books that came to life in those places

Children playing on the Alice in Wonderland Memorial, Central Park, New York, 18 September, 1959

**Last Memories
of Lewis Carroll**

Appendix

One   By Viscount Simon (1873–1954).

It was very odd that Lewis Carroll, or rather Mr Dodgson of Christ Church, should have taken any special interest in me, but as a Freshman I may have attended some of his mathematical lectures, and we must have conversed, because he invited me to dine and I several times had the good fortune to be his guest at the House.

He did not like strangers to treat him as the author of Lewis Carroll's books. Do I not remember that when the first number of a weekly illustrated paper called *Black and White* appeared they published an indignant letter which Mr Dodgson had written to the Editor from Oxford, refusing the invitation to write for them a contribution 'by Lewis Carroll'? I suppose they would have paid handsomely for such an article, but the effect of his letter protesting that they should *assume* he was the author of *Alice in Wonderland* must have resulted in giving the paper an interesting paragraph for nothing.

At the dinner table he liked to 'quiz' his neighbours with occasional conundrums with a mathematical air, which I at any rate found very entertaining. Here are two of them which I recall to have been posed in my hearing on these occasions.

1. A man wanted to go to the theatre, which would cost him 1*s*. 6*d*., but he only had 1*s*. So he went into a Pawnbroker's shop and offered to pledge his shilling for a loan. The Pawnbroker satisfied himself that the shilling was genuine and lent him 9*d*. on it.

The man then came out of the shop with 9*d*., and the Pawnbroker's ticket for 1*s*. Outside he met a friend to whom he offered to sell the Pawnbroker's ticket and the friend bought it from him for 9*d*. He now had 9*d*. from the Pawnbroker and another 9*d*. from the friend and so was able to go to the theatre.

'The question is', said Lewis Carroll, 'who lost what?'

I remember much discussion round the table and I modestly advanced the answer that the friend lost 6*d*. as he had to repay the loan to the Pawnbroker in order to recover the shilling. Lewis Carroll turned to me and said: 'My young friend, your answer is not indeed right, but it does you the greatest credit, for it shows that you are so ignorant of the ways of Pawnbrokers that you think they do their business for nothing!' I had not allowed for the fact that the Pawnbroker charged interest.

2. Take two tumblers, one of which contains 50 spoonfuls of pure brandy and the other 50 spoonfuls of pure water. Take from the first of these one spoonful of the brandy and transfer it without spilling into the second tumbler and stir it up. Then take a spoonful of the mixture and transfer it back without spilling to the first tumbler.

'My question is,' said Lewis Carroll, 'if you consider the whole transaction, has more brandy been transferred from the first tumbler to the second, or more water from the second to the first?'

The answer, of course, is easy enough to work out, for the spoonful of the mixture will consist of 1/51 parts of brandy and 50/51 parts of water, so on the whole transaction 50/51sts of brandy has been transferred from the first tumbler to the second, and 50/51sts of water from the second tumbler to the first. But Lewis Carroll then observed that it was quite unnecessary to work out these fractions. You started with a tumbler containing 50 spoonfuls of brandy and at the end this tumbler still contained 50 spoonfuls, neither more nor less. Whatever it had lost in brandy it had gained in water, and as there had been no spilling the quantities were equal.

Lewis Carroll took special pleasure in concocting rather absurd but very elementary questions of this kind, and there are many more elaborate posers in one of his mathematical books called *Pillow Problems*, e.g. A girls' school, consisting of X pupils goes a walk *en crocodile* every day, the girls walking Y abreast. How many days can they take this dull exercise without any girl walking more than once next to the same girl? The complication, of course, is that if they walk more than two abreast, a girl on the outside would only have *one* other girl next to her, but a girl in the middle would have *two*.

The truth about Lewis Carroll is that he was always engaged in genially pulling somebody's leg and he did this very amusingly by propounding a comic mathematical problem to a non-mathematical mind. That at least was the side of him which he showed to me at occasional dinner parties, and I think he found the Canons of Christ Church easy meat!

His parody of Euclid's third 'Postulate' is a good example of his wit. That Postulate runs: 'Let it be granted that a circle can be described about any centre at any distance from that centre.' He transformed this into: 'Let it be granted that a controversy can be raised about any subject at any distance from that subject.' How true that is!

Two   By Mrs A. T. Waterhouse (née Ruth Gamlen)

I first met Mr Dodgson in 1892 at a tea party given by Mrs Stevens in Crick Road for a few little girls. I was nine years old – nearly ten. We were playing in the garden in an aimless sort of way when Enid Stevens, about my age, told me that perhaps Mr Dodgson was coming. 'He's an old clergyman,' she said, 'but he's really Lewis Carroll.' Now I knew my 'Alices' very well and I knew that Lewis Carroll lived in Christ Church and that that was not his real name, but to be told that he was an old clergyman was rather disconcerting; even if he had written *Alice in Wonderland* he would probably spoil the party. However, in a very short time Mrs Stevens brought Mr Dodgson into the garden, an old clergyman certainly but not at all the decrepit old creature I had so hastily imagined. He stood at the door leading from the house into the garden, a very upright old man with nearly white hair, wearing the long, old-fashioned clerical coat and the turn-down collar and white tie so often worn by old dons in orders at that time. He had a pale, clean-shaven face and his thin mouth seemed almost quivering with delight at the prospect of playing with four or five little girls. The party soon became Mr Dodgson's party. We all went indoors to have tea. He talked delightfully, and I remember how exasperating it was to be asked whether I would like another piece of cake when I was trying so hard to hear what he was saying at the other end of the table. After tea we went back into the garden and Mr Dodgson asked us what we would like to do – should we play croquet or would we like him to tell us a story? Now I hated playing croquet and quickly and fervently begged for a story, so we all sat round him on the garden-seat and he recited the nonsense verses and told us stories out of *Sylvie and Bruno*.

Shortly after this party my mother had a letter from Mrs Stevens to say that Mr Dodgson would like to see more of her little girl. If Mr and Mrs Gamlen would like him to make friends with her he suggested that Mrs Gamlen might perhaps like to go for a walk with him so that she might make his acquaintance. I need hardly say that my parents were delighted to fall in with this plan, and my mother and Mr Dodgson went for a walk round the Parks one day to their mutual satisfaction. And so I became one of Mr Dodgson's little girls.

He brought me a present one day soon after this walk, a copy of *Alice's Adventures Under Ground* in facsimile of his handwriting with his own illustrations. I was enchanted. 'How lovely,' I cried, 'and it's my birthday.' 'Oh dear, that won't do at all,' said Mr Dodgson. 'I don't approve of birthdays and I never give birthday presents and so I can't give you this book.' I must have looked very disappointed. 'Never mind,' he said, 'you shall have it as an *un*-birthday present and that will make it all right,' and that is what he wrote with my name inside the book with his fountain pen, out of which the ink seemed to flow like black cream.

One day I was invited to dine with Mr Dodgson in his rooms. This was a very great treat. He fetched me. We walked to Christ Church. We dined and we talked and at nine we went up on to the roof and waited till Tom rang one hundred and one times and then he took me home. It was a very enjoyable party. Mr Dodgson showed me so many things – so many treasures and contrivances – of which I only remember the tall desk, and the file in which he kept all his menus, so that no little girl dining with him should ever have the same dinner twice. He told me a great many stories about the funny little girls he had met upon the beach at Eastbourne, and after dinner we had a most confidential talk about illustrators, how obstinate and tiresome they were, more especially Holiday who had given him infinite trouble over *The Hunting of the Snark*. And he showed me his rooms – two floors at the N.W. corner of Tom Quad, all except the sitting-room very bare and austere, and the dark room where he had developed his photographs. Another evening we looked at quantities of photographs of his young friends.

Mr Dodgson took me to London one day, and after this he was very anxious that I should spend a few days with him at Eastbourne. He would arrange for me to stay in the house of three old ladies, friends of his, and he would look after me in the day time. My parents were quite firm in not allowing me to go away with him, and I was not at all disappointed. The old ladies sounded formidable, and tho' I liked Mr Dodgson very much I did not want to be with him all day long.

Then there was the episode of the little pantomime actress. You know that Mr Dodgson was very fond of little girls who went on the stage and did not drop them when they grew up. At this time he was much interested in the little Bowman girls, all on the stage, and more especially in Isa, who had been playing in a pantomime. He invited Isa to visit him in Oxford and in order that there should be no ill-natured gossip about her visit he arranged for her to stay in the house of an old lady who, my mother said, was gossip's very fountain-head, so associating her with Isa's visit and stopping all chatter at its source. And having invited Isa to Oxford he was very anxious that I should meet her, but of course she was on the stage and he was afraid that my parents might object. You must remember that this was in the eighteen-nineties when actresses occupied a very different position to what they do now and that Mr

Dodgson was always extremely careful in observing social conventions. So in order that my parents might see for themselves what a very nice little girl Isa was he invited them to meet her at dinner. This was a quite unnecessary precaution on Mr Dodgson's part for my parents would have been only too glad that I should know this little friend of his, but of course they were delighted to go. Later my mother said that as a dinner party it had not been a very great success, but she and my father had enjoyed it and been very much amused. You can see it all – Mr Dodgson never very happy in the society of grown-ups, the poor shy little girl of twelve, and my parents (both of them very good company) doing their best to make themselves agreeable. It was a proof of Mr Dodgson's infinite kindness to a child that he should have gone through what must have been a tiresome ordeal on her behalf. After this introduction I was invited to meet Isa Bowman, though Mr Dodgson much disliked entertaining two children at the same time. I must confess that she caused me bitter disappointment. Here was a child who had spent whole weeks flying about in gorgeously beautiful transformation scenes in a pantomime and had nothing whatever to say about her wonderful experiences. She was so shy and silent that she made me feel shy too and I am afraid that the tea-party was no more of a success than the dinner, but I am almost sure that Isa came to tea with me one day and we got on much better.

Now, as presents of books and letters and invitations came from Mr Dodgson, my father, who was an amused on-looker at this friendship, used to say: 'This is all very well while it lasts, but a day will come when he will drop you like a hot potato.' And sure enough it did. I think that a game that Mr Dodgson had invented and that he was anxious that I should play was the beginning of the end, an elaborate game played with pieces on a board. I was not at all a clever little girl and I thought it very dull and tiresome, but other more intelligent children apparently liked it. I can remember no more invitations after this, but one day a parcel containing a book came addressed in Mr Dodgson's handwriting. I tore it open. It was *Symbolic Logic*, a silly book to my young mind, no story but rather like Mr Dodgson's talk only not so amusing. It was a parting present.

Three   By Miss H. L. Rowell

I knew Mr Dodgson only during the last four years of his life. It was early in 1894 that he first called on my mother and quickly established friendly relations with the whole family, especially with my sister Ethel, whom he had previously met, and whose unusual ability attracted him, so that he soon began to give her lessons in elementary logic in his rooms at Christ Church. It was not, however, until two years had passed that my admiration and awe of him turned to a warmer feeling, and that there thus began a friendship which lasted until his death some eighteen months later.

At this time my sisters were all away, and my brother and I were the only children at home, and gradually it came about that Mr Dodgson would come fairly frequently to have tea with my mother and myself. He always asked to have tea in the dining-room so that, when it was finished, he could spread on the unused half of the table some puzzle or mathematical problem, with or without a solution, or so that we could continue some very elementary work in logic, in connection with the book he was then preparing for the press. This was varied by the telling of strange and wonderful tales or by the repetition of curious rhymes: these after-tea hours were never lesson-hours, but always amusing and stimulating, though at times demanding much concentration on my part.

Then came my first invitation to dinner with him, and, from this time onwards, very occasionally, such invitations would come, always emphasising that his dinner parties were morning dress and adding that he would call for me at $6\frac{1}{4}$ – so he wrote it. I think the happiest of such occasions was in the summer term of 1897. He fetched me, as usual, soon after six o'clock, and, on our way down the Corn Market, we called for one of his old friends, Lady – –, whose name I have forgotten, and who was staying in Oxford for a short visit. On the previous evening the Prince of Wales, afterwards Edward VII, had dined at Christ Church, and Mr Dodgson was seemingly as pleased as I was to begin dinner with turtle soup, soup left from the night before – my first experience of tasting such soup. Dinner finished as always with a small glass of Benedictine, and the talk turned for a moment at the end of the evening to *The Hunting of the Snark*, and finding I did not possess it, he gave me a copy, writing my name in it with his usual flourishes around the date.

On our way back along the Corn Market, I told him what a happy evening it had been for me, and he answered that happiness was nearly always realised only in retrospect, and the thought was not 'I *am* happy now', but rather 'I *was* happy then'. So we talked until I reached home.*

I remember, also, a later occasion, when I did *not* go to dinner with him as had been planned. I was then a schoolgirl of seventeen and hoping to enter a university in a year's time. It was discovered, too late, that on the day after that fixed for the dinner, an examination in German for girls going to a university was to be held at school, and that the girl with the highest marks was to receive a prize of £10 or £20 – I forget which – such money to be spent on books. My mother therefore decided that I should stay at home, work at my German, go to bed early and try to win the £20 prize. As I was rather sadly turning over the pages of some German book in the schoolroom upstairs, the door suddenly opened – it was 6.15 – and Mr Dodgson came into the room, greeted me, and then gave me a German grammar book with my name and the date written in it: whether it was a new book or one he had long possessed, I am unable to say, as I have, alas, lost the book. He was in the room a bare five minutes: I remembered that the walk from Christ Church to our house was just over a mile.

My memory turns to another incident in that summer of 1897. In the following September, the two nieces of Mr Dodgson were coming as pupils to the High School and had, therefore, to live in Oxford during term time. Mr Dodgson had, I think, always had an admiration and respect for my mother and he suggested that his nieces should board with us! He probably thought also that their coming would be of financial help to my mother. I was definitely opposed to the plan, and my mother was hesitant. Our house was old, three-storied and inconvenient: it has long since been pulled down. It was, however, finally agreed that they should come, but the arrangement was soon to be upset. One day, when we were sitting at tea, my brother and his two friends came into the house very noisily from school, and went to the little room opposite the dining-room, used by my brother as his study. My mother turned to

*Lewis Carroll copied out for her some lines by Margaret Fuller on this theme. See p. 244, *supra.*—D. H.

Mr Dodgson and made some remark about her son: Mr Dodgson's face fell, and he said, 'I had forgotten your son: it makes all the difference: what are your plans for him?' My mother explained that my brother was hoping to go to Queen's College in a year's time (this he did not do) but to live at home, and that one friend, Cyril Hurcomb, later Lord Hurcomb, was to go to St John's, while the second friend, Jack Drinkwater (he was Jack and not John until he was twenty!) was leaving Oxford that July. Mr Dodgson finished his tea almost in silence and soon left, saying he must reconsider the whole matter. In two days he wrote to my mother saying that he did not think it would be wise to send his nieces to live in a house where under-graduates would be coming in and out, and that he was very sorry indeed that he had forgotten my brother, and neglected to ask what were the plans for his future. This letter closed the incident: it was as though it had never been. I rejoiced at the decision – the schoolroom would still be my very own – and I do not think my mother was sorry.*

Looking back to the years when I knew Mr Dodgson I see him first as the celebrated author of 'Alice', quietly conscious of his world-wide fame, but putting on one side the name of Lewis Carroll, and remaining in himself, Mr Dodgson, the friend of children, a kindly, affectionate man, the inventor of many strange and ingenious puzzles, and the teller of many wondrous tales. Then I see him as an Oxford don of the eighties, rather than of the nineties, moulded and circumscribed by the conventions of the time and place, a moralist and a mathematician. Lastly, there is the lover of beauty, emotional and introspective, lonely in spirit and prone to sadness, a side rather guessed at than known. It is not for me to venture an opinion as to how far these differing elements of his personality made a harmonious whole man. I suggest, however, that, in his later years at least, the Oxford don and the moralist triumphed at times over the lover of beauty, but that the whimsical genius of the man who gave to the world *Alice in Wonderland* and *Alice through the Looking-Glass*, remained dominant to the end, and illumined his whole being. It was a high privilege for me, a schoolgirl, to be numbered among his friends during the last year of his life, and a great honour.

Four   By Mrs Arthur Davies (née Margaret Mayhew)
It is with a good deal of diffidence that I set down these very personal recollec-tions of such a unique character as Lewis Carroll. There are, I think, two reasons why they may be of interest, the first the rather strange way in which I was fortunate enough to be admitted to the company of Mr Dodgson's child-friends, and the second, my belief that I must have been one of the latest, if not the last, of that company.

I was the youngest of an ordinary Victorian family, an 'after-thought' I always considered myself, my three sisters being respectively seventeen, sixteen and eleven years, and my youngest brother five years older than me. How my three elder sisters became friends with Mr Dodgson I was never told, but I remember my mother telling me the cause of the abrupt ending of that friendship.

It is well known that Mr Dodgson was an ardent amateur photographer. My mother raised no objection to my youngest sister, aged about six or seven,

*A rather firm letter from Dodgson to Mrs Rowell on this matter is quoted on p. 244, *supra*.—D. H.

being photographed in the nude, or in very scanty clothing – I cannot now remember which – but when permission was asked to photograph her elder sister, who was probably then about eleven, in a similar state, my mother's strict sense of Victorian propriety was shocked, and she refused the request. Mr Dodgson was offended, and the friendship ceased forthwith.

Being so much the youngest in the family, I might have been rather a lonely child, but for a wealth of young friends and among them, a year or more my senior, a very pretty clever girl, Enid Stevens, who had long been a great friend of Mr Dodgson. In the kindness of her heart, she made up her mind that I should share this privilege with her. So she begged her mother to ask me to tea one day when Mr Dodgson was to be a guest at their house. Now I was very far from being either pretty or clever, and in addition was often very unsuitably dressed, but my friend's manoeuvre succeeded, and during the last two years of his life I spent some unforgettably wonderful hours in Mr Dodgson's company. But perhaps before I come to describe the really personal episodes in our friendship, I ought to mention one occasion which could not be termed happy. I must have seen Mr Dodgson out of doors, striding along, head in the air, in semi-clerical dress, his coat of the 'morning' or short-tails style, not the square-cut clerical frock coat; never wearing a 'dog-collar', but always a very low turn-down collar with a white tie, his top-hat well at the back of his head – reminding me of Tenniel's drawing of the Mad Hatter – but the first time I saw him at close quarters, indoors, was on a Sunday afternoon, when our headmistress, the well-known Miss Soulsby, had announced that Mr Dodgson would give an address in the High School Studio. I have no recollection of the subject of the talk, or whether it was announced beforehand, and was suitable for a child of twelve or thirteen, but my mother simply sent me along to hear it with a friend from the country who lived with us in term-time in order to attend the High School.

Now Mr Dodgson suffered from some impediment in his speech, a sort of stutter, and on this occasion he opened his mouth wide enough for his tongue to be seen wagging up and down, and in addition to this, carried away by the theme of his discourse, he became quite emotional, making me afraid that he would break down in tears. I submit that all this was enough to upset a young school-girl's powers of self-control, and I had difficulty in suppressing my giggles. I suppose, on our return home, we gave a truthful account of my behaviour, for I retain the impression that I was made to feel thoroughly ashamed of myself. I began by speaking of this little episode as one that could not be called happy, but I hasten to add that this was the only occasion during our friendship to which the term unhappy could be applied.

Having re-established contact with my family, Mr Dodgson never spoke to me of his earlier friendship with my sisters; but I have discovered that he remembered very clearly its abrupt ending. Through the kindess of Mr Hudson I have been able to read, for the first time, copies of three letters now in the Huntington Library, California, the last of which, addressed to my mother, shows how essentially kind and courteous and punctilious he was, and that he felt he must be careful in dealing with a lady of such strict Victorian principles. The perusal of it touched me very much.*

Tea in college with an ordinary undergraduate was quite an exciting event for a school-girl in those days. How much more so was a visit to Mr Dodgson's

*This is the letter published on pp. 218–19, *supra.*—D.H.

suite of rooms in the north-west corner of Tom quad, which he told you with pride had been occupied by members of the Royal family, when up at the House.

A very delightful custom of Mr Dodgson's was to commemorate any expedition with him by the gift of one of his books. I was given *Alice Through the Looking-Glass*, *The Hunting of the Snark* and *Sylvie and Bruno*. The first of these expeditions consisted in a walk and prowl round Magdalen College, followed by tea in his rooms, during the summer term of 1896. On this occasion I think there was one other youthful guest. The second was a year later, at the time of Queen Victoria's Jubilee celebrations. With three other guests – the friend to whom I owed so much, and two adults – I was invited to dine in his rooms. Dinner over, we went up on to the flat roof of that part of the College to wait till it was dark enough to sally forth to see the illuminations. We were, I suppose, only about thirty yards away from Tom Tower, and I shall never forget the start I gave when Tom struck the first note of nine o'clock, and how five minutes later we counted the hundred and one notes of the curfew bell. Then on a perfect summer's night followed a walk through the thronged streets, I feeling particularly safe on the arm of Mr Dodgson.

In October of the same year came perhaps the greatest treat, certainly the most intimate and personal, and, as it turned out, the last, namely an invitation to go to a matinée in London on a Saturday. I was provided with a book for the journey to Paddington, and Mr Dodgson even produced a little travelling set of a game which I somehow connect with the name 'Nine Men's Morris'. He told me he knew that girls liked driving in hansoms, so in a hansom I was taken to lunch with a friend of his, a Mrs Fuller, and then on to the Royal Court Theatre, Sloane Square, to see Martin-Harvey in a play called *The Children of the King*. We had seats in the middle of the front row of the stalls. Mr Dodgson told me that on one occasion the demand for tickets had been so great that the manager had put some chairs in front of his seats. The man was summoned forthwith, and I of course do not know what passed between them, but Mr Dodgson was promised that if ever such a thing happened again, his tickets would be transferred to the chairs. Back to Paddington, and so home, escorted to the front-door of my home, north of the Parks – and a far cry from Christ Church – by my friend and famous host. I think that must have been the last time that I saw him, for during the following Christmas holidays came the shock of the news of his death following on a sharp attack of influenza.

'The Guildford Gazette Extraordinary'

Appendix

[The following introduction to *The Guildford Gazette Extraordinary* is a characteristic and entertaining fragment of Lewis Carroll's 'best period'. *The Guildford Gazette Extraordinary* is exceedingly rare; the text has been taken from a copy discovered at Christ Church, Oxford, in 1952 by Professor Duncan Black, and inscribed on the cover: 'Common Room, Ch. Ch. from the Editor'. It is reproduced by permission of the Curator of the Senior Common Room, Christ Church.

The occasion of the publication of the *Gazette* was an amateur entertainment at Guildford, where Lewis Carroll was staying at his sisters' home, 'The Chestnuts', at Christmas 1869. He noted in his diary: 'Theatrical performance at Mr Synge's – very enjoyable. *The* treat of the evening, to me, was the "Dirge of Dundee", sung by Alice Shute, to the tune of "Ye Banks and braes"; unaccompanied, with a perfectly true and deliciously sweet voice.' It should be added that the majority of the performers were drawn from the families of Synge and Shute.]

THE GUILDFORD GAZETTE EXTRAORDINARY
'If I chance to talk a little wild, forgive me.' – *Shakespeare*.

No. 9999.   Dec, 29, 1869.

OPENING OF THE NEW THEATRE
(From our Special Correspondent, Mr Lewis Carroll)

It was towards the close of one of those days of dreamy and delicious languor for which Guildford is so justly celebrated. The unbroken calm of the weather had been pleasingly varied by an incessant hailstorm, and its sultriness subdued by a severe frost, and now the mellow shades of Evening were fast deepening into the brilliant obscurity of Night. At such a moment might have been observed (had there been light enough for the purpose, and any one present to observe) a small but resolute band of wayfarers (they numbered a poor thousand at most) wending their way in the direction of the new and spacious Theatre, just about to be opened for its great and long-to-be-remembered Inaugural Entertainment.

Of these travellers (for we must not yet desert the guidance of the great model of Romance-writing) one was older than the other – in fact, it might be said that several of them were older than several others – or, to state it in more general, though less poetical language, they were of various ages. And here, great G. P. R. James, farewell!* We quit thy guiding hand, and assume the pen of the antiquarian and the philosopher.

The earliest instance, afforded us by the annals of our beloved country, of an 'Entertainment' strictly so called, was given under most exceptional circumstances, and with an audience which appears to have consisted of Royalty pure and simple. The incident is embodied in the following lines of rude, yet pathetic, doggrel:

> Cheerful sang the monks of Ely,
> As Knut the King was passing by:
> 'Row to the shore, Knights,' said the King,
> 'And let us hear these Churchmen sing!'

*The style of the romances of George Payne Rainsford James (1799–1860) had already been parodied by Thackeray.—D. H.

Though the loyalty of an age, whose bards could thus dare to abridge the name of their sovereign (properly Kanute or Canute) into a monosyllable, to suit the exigencies of their verse, may fairly be called in question, yet we may not doubt that it was to the King's ear alone that the lay was addressed: for him alone were those monastic voices raised in harmony – voices which appear, by the way, to have been so low and weak (but whether from fast or feast deponent sayeth not) that the King was driven perforce to bring his boat to land, and moor it at the very feet of the mellifluous, but inaudible, ascetics.

Let us contemplate for a moment the simple condition of things indicated by this venerable tetrastich. Monks and Knights appear to have divided society; Music and War we may judge to have been their principal occupations: probably the two verbs most in use in those days were the simple, but most suggestive, monosyllables 'to sing' and 'to shoot'.

The few incidents that occurred between the reigns of Canute and Victoria are all so admirably recorded by the graphic pens of Hume and Macaulay, that we should but insult our readers were we to venture to depict them with our humbler goosequill.

We proceed, then, by a transition which we trust may prove as successful as it is sudden, to the consideration of the memorable epoch, Dec. 28, 1869. Those two simple verbs 'to sing' and 'to shoot' were perhaps, even at that late period, after the lapse of so many centuries, not wholly forgotten.

And both are appropriate to the Entertainment now to be recorded: for the 'singing', the mere mention of the 'Dirge of Dundee' will suffice for all who had the privilege of being present; while, if it be doubted how 'shooting' could find a place in such a scene, we can only say that if Cupid's darts were not flying thick as hail, it was not for want of bright eyes to rain them down – let each reader lay his hand upon his heart (if he happens to possess one) and make reply.

There is, however, we have reason to believe, some deeper allusion in these apparently simple phrases, than we have been able to fathom: for the following cabalistic phrase was on many a tongue during that eventful evening – that 'to have seen sing shoot, and to have heard shoot sing, was a treat well worth coming for'. We have devoted our whole intellectual energies, during several hours, to the task of grappling with this profound enigma, and are compelled at last to leave it, in all its original obscurity, to the sagacity of the reader.

The fact that the Inaugural Entertainment was to be given solely by amateurs lent an additional zest to the evening, and even if the enterprising Manager had not, with his usual liberality, given away orders of admission in almost reckless profusion, the house would still have been filled to overflowing. The reporters of the Press were alone excluded on this occasion, the Manager tersely remarking, that there would be 'press enough without them'.

Time would fail us to describe the decorations, and the many contrivances for the comfort of the audience, and we must content ourselves by briefly mentioning a most original feature in the arrangements – the abolition of pit, gallery and boxes; so that the whole house constituted one magnificent dress-circle. We append the programme of the performance.

[The remainder of the 16-page pamphlet is taken up with the text of the entertainment, interspersed with short comments by Lewis Carroll. It was mostly from the pen of W. W. Follett Synge and included an elaborate charade on the word Killiecrankie.]

Notes and References [C. = *The Life and Letters of Lewis Carroll*, by Stuart Dodgson Collingwood (Fisher Unwin, 1898).

W. *and* M. = *A Handbook of The Literature of the Rev C. L. Dodgson (Lewis Carroll)*, by S. H. Williams and Falconer Madan (Oxford, 1931).

LCH = *The Lewis Carroll Handbook*, a new version of W. *and* M. by Roger Lancelyn Green (Oxford, 1962).

G. = *The Diaries of Lewis Carroll*, edited and supplemented by Roger Lancelyn Green (Cassell, 1954).]

N.B. The greater part of the Dodgson Family Collection is now in Guildford Muniment Room. The surviving MS. volumes of Lewis Carroll's Diaries are in the British Museum.

1. Christ Church Library.
2. *Harper's Magazine*, February, 1943. 'To Me He was Mr Dodgson', by E. M. Rowell.
3. W. *and* M., p. 221; LCH, p. 275.
4. Harvard College Library.
5. I am most grateful to Mrs Audrey Skimming (*née* Fuller) for putting this scrapbook at my disposal.
6. Menella Dodgson kindly lent me her marked copy of the auctioneer's catalogue.
7. Preface to *The Lewis Carroll Centenary in London 1932*, pp. ix–x.
8. C., Chap. I, and G., Chap. I, give the best accounts of the family history and background.
9. C., p. 8.
10. G., p. 5.
11. Dodgson Family Papers.
12. Christ Church Treasury Papers.
13. G., p. 6.
14. B.M. Add. MSS., 40, 522, f. 205.
15. Ibid., f. 197.
16. Ibid., f. 371.
17. B.M. Add. MSS., 40, 522, f. 373.
18. G., p. 8.
19. *Northern Echo*, January 5th, 1932; G., p. 9.
20. See the Catalogue of the Harcourt Amory Collection of Lewis Carroll in the Harvard College Library, compiled by Flora V. Livingston (1932).
21. There is a copy of the plan at Croft Rectory. It was traced from the original by Philip Dodgson Jaques in 1950.
22. This box is now (1975) in Rottingdean Toy Museum.
23. The manuscript of *La Guida di Bragia* was sold at Sotheby's in 1951 for £110. The play was first published in the *Queen* magazine, 18 November, 1931, and reissued in a limited xerox reprint by Denis Crutch, 1972.
24. W. *and* M., p. xx. The friend's name is not given.
25. The manuscript of *Useful and Instructive Poetry* was sold at Sotheby's in 1953 for £220. It was published in 1954 by Geoffrey Bles with a selection of the illustrations and an introduction by Derek Hudson. It is now in the Alfred C. Berol Collection, New York University.

26. *C.*, pp. 12–14, p. 25.

27. *C.*, p. 26.

28. *C.*, p. 30. This passage seems to have been in Vol. III of the Diary, covering the last three months of the year 1855, which was available to Collingwood but has since disappeared.

29. *W. and M.*, p. xvii.

30. Dodgson Family Papers.

31. Harvard College Library.

32. Dodgson Family Papers. *G.*, p. 19.

33. *C.*, p. 29. The letter is dated December 18th, 1849.

34. *C.*, p. 340.

35. *G.*, pp. 28–9.

36. Dodgson Family Papers.

37. Ibid.

38. *Henry George Liddell, D.D.*, by the Rev Henry L. Thompson (1899), p. 149.

39. *C.*, p. 341.

40. Dodgson Family Papers; and see *The Lewis Carroll Picture Book*, pp. 215–16.

41. Dodgson Family Papers.

42. Harvard College Library.

43. *C.*, p. 53.

44. Collection of Mrs Frances Stockwell, Yarram, South Gippsland, Victoria, Australia.

45. Dodgson Family Papers.

46. *Lewis Carroll*, by Walter de la Mare (1932), p. 49; *The White Knight*, by Alexander L. Taylor (1952), pp. 17–19; *G.*, p. 61.

47. See *The Times Literary Supplement*, September 14th, 1951, and succeeding issues.

48. *C.*, p. 143.

49. *Supplement* to *W. and M.*, p. 3.

50. *C.*, pp. 214–16.

51. Ibid., p. 64.

52. Letter from Mr Charles Dougan to the author.

53. *W. and M.*, p. 212.

54. *Lewis Carroll: Photographer*, by Helmut Gernsheim (2nd edition, 1950), p. 36.

55. Ibid., pp. 28–9

56. *C.*, p. 365.

57. 'Alice's Recollections of Carrollian Days', by Caryl Hargreaves, *Cornhill Magazine*, July, 1932.

58. *C.*, p. 102.

59. Gernsheim, op. cit., 2nd ed., p. 122.

60. The fullest account of this visit to Farringford is given in a letter from Dodgson to his cousin William Wilcox. See *Strand Magazine*, May, 1901, and *W. and M.*, p. 195.

61. *C.*, p. 92.

62. Yale University Library.

63. Ibid.

64. Ibid.

65. Ibid.

66. Harvard College Library.

67. See *George MacDonald and his Wife*, by Greville MacDonald, (1924), pp. 301 and 342–3.

68. *C.*, pp. 83–5.

69. *A Selection from the letters of Lewis Carroll to his Child-friends*, edited by Evelyn M. Hatch (1933), pp. 22–5.

70. Alfred C. Berol Collection, New York University.

71. *C.*, p. 74.

72. *G.*, p. 150.

73. Christ Church Library.

74. See *Lewis Carroll: Correspondence Numbers*, by Warren Weaver (New York, 1940).

75. Dodgson Family Papers.

76. See *G.*, pp. 169–72.

77. H. L. Thompson, op. cit., p. 252.

78. *Cornhill Magazine*, July, 1932.

79. This account of the river expedition on July 4th, 1862, is derived from Collingwood's biography, from Lewis Carroll's diary, from his article '"Alice" on the Stage', from Canon Duckworth's reminiscences (the two last are both included in *The Lewis Carroll Picture Book*, 1899), and from 'Alice's Recollections of Carrollian Days' in the *Cornhill Magazine*, July, 1932. For the Meteorological Office's wet-blanket, see Gernsheim, op. cit., 2nd ed., pp. 122–4. I am also indebted to a personal letter from Mr F. R. G. Duckworth.

80. *The Lewis Carroll Picture Book*, p. 360.

81. *W. and M.*, p. 22.

82. Ibid., p. 18.

83. Ibid., pp. 17–24 and 225–36; *LCH*, pp. 27–33; and see *The House of Macmillan: 1843–1943*, by Charles Morgan (1943), pp. 79–80.

84. *W. and M.*, p. 226.

85. *G.*, Appendix B.

86. Macmillan Correspondence.

87. Dodgson Family Papers.

88. *G.*, p. 237.

89. Dodgson Family Papers.

90. Catalogue of the Harcourt Amory Collection, Harvard College Library.

91. *Life of Lewis Carroll*, by Langford Reed (1932), p. 46.

92. *W. and M.*, p. 111; *LCH*, p. 134.

93. *The Lewis Carroll Picture Book*, pp. 166–7.

94. *The Times*, January 27th, 1932.

95. See A. L. Taylor, op. cit., pp. 54–61.

96. *C.*, pp. 150–1.

97. See a most interesting paper by Peter Alexander, 'Logic and the Humour of Lewis Carroll', in *Proceedings of the Leeds Philosophical Society* (1951).

98. *The Philosophy of Modern Art*, by Sir Herbert Read (1952), 'Surrealism and the Romantic Principle'.

99. *Lewis Carroll*, by Walter de la Mare (1932), p. 55.

100. *The Lewis Carroll Centenary in London 1932*, edited by Falconer Madan (1932), p. 131.

101. *Cornhill Magazine*, March, 1898.
102. I am indebted to Professor C. A. Coulson, F.R.S., for his opinion of Dodgson's mathematical work.
103. Walter de la Mare, op. cit., pp. 43–4.
104. *C.*, p. 86.
105. *Cornhill Magazine*, July, 1932, p. 9.
106. Gernsheim, op. cit., p. 96.
107. I am grateful to Mrs Audrey Skimming for permission to reproduce the 'Queen Victoria' letter, and to Mr Helmut Gernsheim for drawing my attention to it.
108. *C.*, p. 225.
109. Dodgson Family Papers (letter to Mary Collingwood, April 19th, 1860).
110. Dodgson Family Papers.
111. *C.*, p. 109.
112. *Life and Letters of Henry Parry Liddon*, by J. O. Johnston (1904), p. 282.
113. See *Tour in 1867*, by C. L. Dodgson, Ch. Ch., Oxford, from the original manuscript in the collection of M. L. Parrish, Esq., Pine Valley, New Jersey (Philadelphia, privately printed, 1928).
114. J. O. Johnston, op. cit., p. 100.
115. Ibid., pp. 102–9.
116. *C.*, pp. 131–2.
117. Catalogue of the Sale, May 10th and 11th, 1898.
118. *Lewis Carroll*, by F. B. Lennon (1947), p. 162.
119. *Cornhill Magazine*, July, 1932, p. 5.
120. *G.*, p. 272. An account of this incident by Alice Raikes (Mrs Wilson Fox) appeared in *The Times*, January 22nd, 1932.
121. *W. and M.*, p. 44; *LCH*, p. 57.
122. *C.*, p. 146.
123. *C.*, p. 142, and see Catalogue of the Harcourt Amory Collection of Lewis Carroll (Harvard College Library).
124. *The Lewis Carroll Picture Book*, pp. 168–9.
125. Oxford University Press, 1934.
126. Dodgson Family Papers.
127. *C.*, p. 231.
128. Catalogue of Harcourt Amory Collection (Harvard College Library).
129. *C.*, p. 355.
130. *Ellen Terry's Memoirs* (1933), p. 18.
131. Ibid., pp. 50–2, etc.
132. *Ellen Terry and her Secret Self*, by Edward Gordon Craig (1931), p. 50.
133. *The Life of Lewis Carroll*, by Langford Reed (1932), p. 90.
134. Op. cit., p. 142.
135. Op. cit., p. 14.
136. *Ellen Terry's Memoirs*, p. 142.
137. Copies of these letters are in the Dodgson Family Papers. They were sold at Sotheby's in November, 1932.
138. *Cornhill Magazine*, July, 1932, p. 9.
139. Op. cit., p. 192.
140. Ibid., p. 192.
141. B.M. 11779 b. 5(3). See also *W. and M.*, p. 63.
142. *W. and M.*, p. 54; *LCH*, p. 70.

143. *W. and M.*, p. xiii.

144. *Reminiscences of Oxford*, by the Rev W. Tuckwell (1900), pp. 161–2.

145. *Frederick York Powell: A Life and a Selection from his Letters and Occasional Writings*, by Oliver Elton (1906), Vol. II., pp. 365–6.

146. Christ Church Library.

147. *Life and Letters of the Rt Rev. Bp Edward Lee Hicks*, edited by J. H. Fowler (1922), p. 25.

148. J. M. Thompson Collection.

149. *Notes by an Oxford Chiel* is reprinted in full as Chapter II of *The Lewis Carroll Picture Book* (1899).

150. *C.*, p. 174, and *The Lewis Carroll Picture Book*, pp. 357–8. The letter to Sir James Paget, dated May 1st, 1887, was in Christopher Hassall's Collection. It is addressed to 'Sir William Paget' – doubtless a slip of the pen, for Collingwood says that Dodgson consulted Sir James Paget on this as on other occasions.

151. *C.*, p. 166.

152. *W. and M.*, p. 65; *LCH*, p. 81.

153. *The Lewis Carroll Picture Book*, pp. 167–8, *G.*, p. 335, and *C.*, p. 173.

154. The drawing was reproduced in the *Listener*, June 29th, 1932, and in M. Gardner's *Annotated Snark* (Penguin, 1967).

155. See *A Handful of Authors* (1953) for Chesterton's essays on Lewis Carroll and Edward Lear.

156. *La Chasse au Snark: Une Agonie en Huit Crises* (The Hours Press, 1929).

157. Warren Weaver Collection, University of Texas.

158. Captain Hugh Calverley Collection, Toronto.

159. *C.*, pp. 152–6.

160. Christ Church Treasury Papers.

161. See *The Shores of Light* (1952) for Edmund Wilson's estimate of Lewis Carroll.

162. *Daily Express*, January 28th, 1932.

163. *G.*, p. 423.

164. *W. and M.*, p. 78; *LCH*, p. 96.

165. *G.*, p. 367.

166. *C.*, p. 388.

167. *W. and M.*, p. 143; *LCH*, p. 170.

168. *C.*, p. 325.

169. Berol Collection, New York University.

170. *Well Remembered*, by Claude Martin Blagden (1953), pp. 114–15.

171. *Michael Ernest Sadler*, by Michael Sadleir (1949), p. 95.

172. Christ Church Treasury Papers.

173. Ibid.

174. Ibid.

175. Professor Duncan Black did not mention this in his interesting account of the Common Room papers in *Notes and Queries*, February, 1953.

176. *W. and M.*, p. 137, say: 'No copy is known at present', and *G.*, p. 489, 'No copy of this seems to have survived', but *LCH*, p. 164, puts this right.

177. Michael Sadleir Collection. (1953).

178. Introduction to the facsimile of *Alice's Adventures Under Ground* (1886), p.v.

179. *C.*, p. 109.

180. *The Life of Lewis Carroll*, by Langford Reed, p. 95.

181. Evelyn M. Hatch, op. cit., pp. 119–20.

182. In a letter to the author.

183. Evelyn M. Hatch, op. cit., p. 177.

184. *C.*, p. 416.

185. *The Lewis Carroll Centenary in London 1932*, edited by Falconer Madan, p. 134.

186. Letter from J. M. Thompson to the author.

187. Berol Collection, New York University.

188. *G.*, pp. xiv–xvi.

189. Dr F. L. Pleadwell Collection, Honolulu.

190. The letters to Agnes Hull were in Cecil G. Keith's Collection in 1953, and I am indebted to him for some additional information.

191. To Arthur Girdlestone, quoted in *The Story of Lewis Carroll*, by Isa Bowman (1899), p. 60.

192. Miss H. L. Rowell Collection.

193. Letters of October 3rd and 6th, 1895. Author's Collection (1953).

194. *Memories of Lewis Carroll*, by A. G. Atkinson (reprinted from the *Hampshire Chronicle*, March 13th, 1948).

195. *The Confessions of a Caricaturist*, by Harry Furniss (1901), Vol. I, p. 106.

196. *Illustrated*, September 12th, 1953.

197. Berol Collection, New York University.

198. Ibid.

199. Huntington Library, San Marino, California.

200. Harvard College Library.

201. Berol Collection, New York University.

202. Ibid.

203. A. G. Atkinson, op. cit.

204. *G.*, pp. 501–2.

205. Isa Bowman, op. cit., p. 36.

206. *G.*, p. xxv.

207. *C.*, p. 237, and pp. 256–8.

208. Mrs Elizabeth Hartz Collection, Bernardsville, New Jersey. (1953).

209. Ibid.

210. Ibid.

211. *Feeding the Mind*, by Lewis Carroll, with a prefatory note by William H. Draper (1907), pp. 17–18.

212. Mrs Hester Thackeray Fuller Collection. (1953).

213. See *Confessions of a Caricaturist*, by Harry Furniss (1901), Vol. I, Chapter IV.

214. *Edward Bok: An Autobiography* (1921), p. 199.

215. Berol Collection, New York University.

216. Yale University Library.

217. Mrs Irene Jaques Collection.

218. *W. and M.*, p. 135; *LCH*, p. 155.

219. In a letter to the author.

220. See *Lewis Carroll: Correspondence Numbers*, by Warren Weaver, p. 16.

221. Berol Collection, New York University.

222. *C.*, p. 325.

223. *C.*, p. 394.
224. Mrs Irene Jaques Collection.
225. J. M. Thompson Collection.
226. *C.*, p. 76.
227. In a letter to the author.
228. *Harper's Magazine*, February, 1943.
229. Dr Lall G. Montgomery Collection, Muncie, Indiana.
230. Ibid.
231. Rear-Admiral A. Davies Collection.
232. *C.*, p. 330.
233. *G.*, p. 543.
234. Dodgson Family Papers.
235. For the last illness see *C.*, pp. 347–8 and 363–4.

A Select Bibliography

(Based on the bibliography in the 1966 reprint of *Lewis Carroll*, 'Writers and their Work' series, by permission of Longmans and the British Council. Publication London, unless stated otherwise.)

Bibliography:

A BIBLIOGRAPHY OF THE WRITINGS OF LEWIS CARROLL [CHARLES LUTWIDGE DODGSON, M.A.], by S. H. Williams (1924) – the pioneer bibliography, still of value.

A LIST OF THE WRITINGS OF LEWIS CARROLL . . . Collected by M. L. Parrish. Privately printed, Philadelphia (1928) catalogue of the collection of M. L. Parrish of Philadelphia, now in the Princeton University Library.

A HANDBOOK OF THE LITERA-TURE OF THE REV. C. L. DODGSON [LEWIS CARROLL], by S. H. Williams and F. Madan (1931) – for thirty years the standard bibliography. A supplement was issued in 1935.

THE LEWIS CARROLL HAND-BOOK. A new version of the preceding: revised, augmented, and brought up to date by R. L. Green (1962).

THE HARCOURT AMORY COLLECTION OF LEWIS CARROLL IN THE HARVARD COLLEGE LIBRARY, compiled by F. V. Livingston. Privately printed, Cambridge, Mass. (1932). 'Lewis Carroll's Periodical Publications', by R. L. Green. *Notes and Queries*, March 1954.

Collected Editions:

THE COLLECTED VERSE OF LEWIS CARROLL (1932) – with illustrations by Sir J. Tenniel, A. B. Frost, H. Holiday, H. Furniss, and the author.

THE COMPLETE WORKS OF LEWIS CARROLL, with an Introduction by A. Woollcott and the illustrations by John Tenniel. New York (1937) – incomplete but useful.

THE WORKS OF LEWIS CARROLL, ed. R. L. Green (1965).

Selections:

THE LEWIS CARROLL PICTURE BOOK, ed. S. D. Colling-wood (1899) – an entertaining miscellany. The sub-title reads: 'A Selection from the Unpublished Writings and Drawings of Lewis Carroll, together with Reprints from Scarce and Unacknowledged Work'. The selection includes some of his photographs and letters, and reminiscences of him. Re-issued as a paperback under the title *Diversions and Digressions of Lewis Carroll*, 1961.

FURTHER NONSENSE VERSE AND PROSE, by Lewis Carroll, ed. L. Reed, illustrated by H. M. Bateman (1926) – a sequel (hence the misleading title) to *Nonsense Verse: An Anthology*, compiled by the same editor.

ALICE IN WONDERLAND, THROUGH THE LOOKING-GLASS, ETC., with introduction by E. Rhys (1929) – useful selection of the works, including *Phantasmagoria, A Tangled Tale, The Hunting of the Snark*, and Carroll's own illustrations to *Alice*.

FOR THE TRAIN. Lewis Carroll's contributions to *The Train*, 1856–7. Preface by H. J. Schonfield (1932) – contains other excerpts from his other writings on the subject of trains.

THE RUSSIAN JOURNAL AND OTHER SELECTIONS, ed. J. F. McDermott. New York (1935). – The Russian Journal reprinted in *The Works of L.C.* (1965).

THE HUMOROUS VERSES OF LEWIS CARROLL, with illustrations by John Tenniel, ed. J. E. Morpurgo (1950).

Separate Works – juvenilia:

THE RECTORY UMBRELLA AND MISCHMASCH (1932) – the last two of Lewis Carroll's manuscript magazines, published in full with a foreword by F. Milner.

USEFUL AND INSTRUCTIVE POETRY [1845] (1954) – the earliest of the manuscript magazines, with an introduction by D. Hudson.

Separate Works (under the pseudonym 'Lewis Carroll'):

ALICE'S ADVENTURES IN WONDERLAND, with forty-two illustrations by John Tenniel (1865) – the author stopped the publication of the first edition because he was dissatisfied with its production, and in consequence barely more than a dozen copies have survived. There was a second edition in 1866. Apart from the Bible, few books have been more translated (in whole or in part) than *Alice's Adventures in Wonderland*. Only French, Italian, German and Danish complete translations appeared in the author's lifetime.

PHANTASMAGORIA AND OTHER POEMS (1869).

THROUGH THE LOOKING-GLASS AND WHAT ALICE FOUND THERE, with fifty illustrations by John Tenniel (1872) – translated into German, 1923, and French, 1949.

SOME POPULAR FALLACIES ABOUT VIVISECTION. Oxford (1875).

THE HUNTING OF THE SNARK, with nine illustrations by H. Holiday (1876) – translated into French by Louis Aragon, 1929.

AN EASTER GREETING TO EVERY CHILD WHO LOVES 'ALICE'. Oxford (1876).

DOUBLETS: A WORD-PUZZLE (1879).

RHYME? AND REASON? With sixty-five illustrations by A. B. Frost and nine by H. Holiday (1883).

A TANGLED TALE, with six illustrations by A. B. Frost (1885).

ALICE'S ADVENTURES UNDER GROUND (1886) – a facsimile of the original MS book (now in the British Museum) afterwards developed into *Alice's Adventures in Wonderland*, with thirty-seven illustrations by the author. Reissued, 1965.

THE GAME OF LOGIC (1886).

THE NURSERY 'ALICE' (1889) – contains twenty coloured enlargements from Tenniel's illustrations with the text 'adapted to nursery readers'. A delightful effort, too little known. Re-issued by Dover Books (Constable).

SYLVIE AND BRUNO, with forty-six illustrations by H. Furniss (1889).

CIRCULAR BILLIARDS FOR TWO PLAYERS (1890).

EIGHT OR NINE WISE WORDS ABOUT LETTER-WRITING (1890) – issued with the 'Wonderland Stamp Case' in a pink envelope containing both.

SYLVIE AND BRUNO CONCLUDED, with forty-six illustrations by H. Furniss (1893).

SYZYGIES AND LANRICK: A WORD-PUZZLE and a GAME FOR TWO PLAYERS (1893).

SYMBOLIC LOGIC: PART I. ELEMENTARY (1896).

THREE SUNSETS AND OTHER POEMS, with twelve drawings by E. G. Thomson (1898).

FEEDING THE MIND (1907) – a lecture delivered in October, 1884, with a prefatory note by W. H. Draper.

Separate Works (by C. L. Dodgson):

A SYLLABUS OF PLAIN ALGEBRAICAL GEOMETRY. Oxford (1860).

THE FORMULAE OF PLANE TRIGONOMETRY. Oxford (1861).

A GUIDE TO THE MATHEMATICAL STUDENT: PART I, PURE MATHEMATICS. Oxford (1864).

CONDENSATION OF DETER-MINANTS (1866).

AN ELEMENTARY TREATISE ON DETERMINANTS (1867).

THE FIFTH BOOK OF EUCLID. Oxford and London (1868).

EUCLID, BOOK V. Oxford (1874).

EUCLID AND HIS MODERN RIVALS (1879).

EUCLID, BOOKS I AND II, edited by Charles L. Dodgson, M.A. (1882).

LAWN TENNIS TOURNAMENTS (1883).

THE PRINCIPLES OF PARLIAMENTARY REPRE-SENTATION (1884).

SUPPLEMENT TO 'EUCLID AND HIS MODERN RIVALS' (1885).

SUGGESTIONS AS TO THE ELECTION OF PROCTORS. Oxford (1886).

CURIOSA MATHEMATICA PART I. A NEW THEORY OF PARALLELS (1888).

CURIOSA MATHEMATICA PART II. PILLOW-PROBLEMS (1893).

Separate Works (anonymous):
RULES FOR COURT CIRCULAR: (A New Game of Cards for Two or More Players.) Place of publication unknown (1860).
AN INDEX TO 'IN MEMORIAM' (1862) – suggested and edited by Dodgson but chiefly compiled by one or more of his sisters.
CROQUET CASTLES. Place of publication unknown. (1863) – an elaborate variation of the game of croquet for five players.
THE NEW METHOD OF EVALUATION AS APPLIED TO π. Oxford (1865).
THE DYNAMICS OF A PARTICLE. Oxford (1865).
CASTLE-CROQUET. Oxford (1866) – a revision of *Croquet Castles* for four players.
THE ELECTIONS TO THE HEBDOMADAL COUNCIL. Oxford (1866).
THE DESERTED PARKS. Oxford (1867) – a parody of Goldsmith's *Deserted Village*, attacking a proposal that the University Parks at Oxford should be used in part for College cricket grounds. The proposal was rejected.
THE OFFER OF THE CLARENDON TRUSTEES. Oxford (1868) – an amusing *jeu d'esprit* on the subject of providing opportunities at the New Museum for mathematical calculations.
THE NEW BELFRY OF CHRIST CHURCH. Oxford (1872).
THE VISION OF THE THREE T'S. Oxford (1873) – these two items are both skits on proposals for architectural alterations at Christ Church.
THE BLANK CHEQUE. Oxford (1874) – a clever fable, with the University as Mrs Nivers, based on a proposal to authorise the building of the new Examination Schools before any plan or estimate had been prepared.
NOTES BY AN OXFORD CHIEL. Oxford (1874) – reprints of six of Dodgson's anonymous Oxford pieces.
WORD-LINKS – a word-game. Oxford (1878).

MISCHMASCH – a word-game. Oxford (1882).
TWELVE MONTHS IN A CURATORSHIP: BY ONE WHO HAS TRIED IT. Oxford (1884).
SUPPLEMENT TO 'TWELVE MONTHS IN A CURATORSHIP'. Oxford (1884).
THREE YEARS IN A CURATORSHIP: BY ONE WHOM IT HAS TRIED. Oxford (1886).
A POSTAL PROBLEM. Place of publication unknown (1891).
CURIOSISSIMA CURATORIA. Oxford (1892).

Diaries and Letters:
TOUR IN 1867 BY C. L. DODGSON. Privately printed. Philadelphia (1928) – the diary of a trip to Russia in 1867 with Dr H. P. Liddon. From the MS in the Parrish Collection. Reprinted in *The Works of L.C.* (1965).
A SELECTION FROM THE LETTERS OF LEWIS CARROLL TO HIS CHILD-FRIENDS ed. E. M. Hatch (1933).
THE DIARIES OF LEWIS CARROLL, ed. R. L. Green. 2 vols. (1953).
Note. The originals of Dodgson's numerous letters to his publishers, Macmillans, were sold in London in 1957 and are now in the U.S.A.

Biographical and Critical Studies:
THE LIFE AND LETTERS OF LEWIS CARROLL (REV. C. L. DODGSON), by S. D. Collingwood (1898).
THE STORY OF LEWIS CARROLL, by I. Bowman (1899).
CONFESSIONS OF A CARICATURIST, by H. Furniss. 2 vols. (1901).
THE POETRY OF NONSENSE, by E. Cammaerts (1925).
'Lewis Carroll', by W. de la Mare (1932) – this essay originally appeared in *The Eighteen-Eighties*, ed. W. de la Mare, 1930.
'Alice's Recollections of Carrollian Days', by C. Hargreaves, *The Cornhill Magazine*, July 1932.
THE LIFE OF LEWIS CARROLL, by L. Reed (1932).
THE LEWIS CARROLL CENTENARY IN LONDON 1932, ed. F. Madan (1932).
'*Alice in Wonderland* Psycho-

Analyzed' by A. M. E. Goldschmidt, *New Oxford Outlook*, May 1933.
SOME VERSIONS OF PASTORAL, by W. Empson (1935) – contains an essay: '*Alice in Wonderland*: The Child as Swain'.
LEWIS CARROLL: CORRESPONDENCE NUMBERS, by W. Weaver. New York (1940).
THE HOUSE OF MACMILLAN (1843–1943), by C. Morgan (1943).
LEWIS CARROLL, by F. B. Lennon (1947) – rev. edition, 1962.
THE STORY OF LEWIS CARROLL, by R. L. Green (1949).
LEWIS CARROLL: PHOTOGRAPHER, by H. Gernsheim (1950). Dover edition (1969).
ARGUMENT OF LAUGHTER, by D. H. Munro. Melbourne (1951).
LOGIC AND THE HUMOUR OF LEWIS CARROLL, by P. Alexander. Leeds (1951) – reprinted from the *Proceedings of the Leeds Philosophical Society, VI.*
THE FIELD OF NONSENSE, by E. Sewell (1952).
THE WHITE KNIGHT: A STUDY OF C. L. DODGSON (LEWIS CARROLL), by A. L. Taylor (1952).
LEWIS CARROLL (*Poètes d'Aujourd'hui*), par H. Parisot, Paris (1952).
THE SHORES OF LIGHT, by E. Wilson (1952) – contains an estimate of Lewis Carroll.
A HANDFUL OF AUTHORS, by G. K. Chesterton (1953) – contains an estimate of Lewis Carroll.
'The Real Lewis Carroll', by R. L. Green, in *The Quarterly Review*, January 1954.
'The Griffin and the Jabberwock', by R. L. Green, *The Times Literary Supplement*, 1 March 1957.
'Lewis Carroll at the Seaside', by S. Godman, *The Times*, 27 July 1957.
'Lewis Carroll's First Publication', by R. L. Green, *The Times Literary Supplement*, 13 September 1957.
LEWIS CARROLL, by R. L. Green (1960).
DICHTUNG ALS SPIEL, by A. Liede. 2 vols Berlin

(1963) – contains studies of Edward Lear and Lewis Carroll.
THE ANNOTATED ALICE, ed. M. Gardner (1964).
ALICE IN MANY TONGUES: THE TRANSLATIONS OF 'ALICE IN WONDERLAND' by W. Weaver (1964) – a first-class pioneering work.
ALICIA IN TERRA MIRABILI, C. H. Carruthers (1964).
ALICIAE PER SPECULUM TRANSITUS, by C. H. Carruthers (1966) – fluent Latin translations of *Alice's Adventures in Wonderland* and *Alice Through the Looking-Glass.*
ALICE IN WONDERLAND, French and English texts. Ed. and tr. Jean Gattégno and H. Parisot. Paris, 1970.
LEWIS CARROLL: Cahier. Editions de l'Herne, Paris. Ed. Henri Parisot (1971).
ALICE IN WONDERLAND and other Carroll texts, with critical and biographical excerpts from various authors. Ed. Donald J. Gray. New York (1971).
ASPECTS OF ALICE. Ed. Robert Phillips (1972). – a valuable collection of varied critical pieces, 1865–1971.
LEWIS CARROLL: UNE VIE. By Jean Gattégno. Paris (1974). – the best French biographical study so far published.

Index

Acrostics, 190
Adams, Marcus, 218
Addinsell, Richard, 29
Alexander, Peter, 128
Alfreton, 228
Alfrick, Worcester, 239
'Alice', original: *see* Hargreaves, Mrs Alice Pleasance
Alice, Princess, 23, 157, 225
Alice's Adventures in Wonderland, story of *Alice's Adventures Under Ground* told for the benefit of Alice Liddell during boat trip from Oxford to Godstow (1862), 22, 113–15; other theories of origin, 71–3, 109–10; story committed to paper, 103, 115–16; advisers on publication, 117; title decided on, 119–20; publication delays and difficulties, 120–3; first edition (1865) recalled, 121; second edition (Nov. 1865) published, 121; comparison between first and second editions, 121–3; early opinions of, 123–4, 131; changes from original manuscript of *Alice's Adventures Under Ground*, 124–6; allusions to people and things, 126–8; Victorian message of, 128–9; copyright expires (1907), 129; timeless in its appeal, 131; Queen Victoria and, 132–3; no direct hidden meanings in, 156–7; popularity, 174; D.'s efforts to prevent exploitation, 174; not influenced by Tom Hood, 238; tributes to, 19, 23; Gladstone's opinion of, 24
Characters, artistic and commercial reproductions of, 29; incorporated on plaque at 'The Chestnuts', 144; comparisons with *Through the Looking-Glass*, 155–6
Collections of editions, 29
Dramatised versions, 29, 174, 180, 224
Facsimile edition of original version (1886), 124, 169, 223, 250
Film versions, 29, 31
First edition (1865), recalled; unbound sheets sold to Appleton's of New York, 121; published as American issue (1866), 121; prices offered for, 121; issued copies recovered and presented to

Alice's Adventures in Wonderland —Cont.
hospitals, 123
Illustrations, 29; author illustrates original version, 117, 124–5, 223; Tenniel agrees to illustrate published edition, 118; model for Alice, 119; in German and Italian editions, 130; use as design for wallpaper, 232
Manuscript from which the book was set up, never discovered, 223
Manuscript of original version (*Alice's Adventures Under Ground*), received by Alice Liddell (1864), 117–18; bought and resold (1928), 27, 223; presented to British Museum (1948), 27, 223
Musical versions, 29, 174
Sales and prices of editions, 27, 129, 152, 155, 239
Second edition (Nov. 1865), published, 121; prices offered for, 121
Translations, 29, 129–30, 156
'Why is a raven like a writing desk?' D.'s answer, 238
Alice's Adventures Under Ground, origins, 37, 113–18; changes made for publication as *Alice's Adventures in Wonderland,* 124–6; facsimile edition, original manuscript, and illustrations: *see under Alice's Adventures in Wonderland*
Alice's Wonderland Birthday Book, 198
All the Year Round, 108, 160
Alma Tadema, Sir Lawrence, 24, 188
America: *see* United States
Anagrams, 177
Aragon, Louis, 185
Artists, skits on pictures by, 56; D.'s friendships with, 135, 137
Ashford, Daisy, *The Young Visiters,* 220–1
Athenæum, 123, 154
Atkinson, F. H., 112, 159–60, 233
Attwell, Mabel Lucie, 29
Aunt Judy's Magazine, 139, 194
Austin, Alfred, 187

'B. B.', initials used by D., 70, 80
Badcock, Mary Hilton, 119
Baines, R. E., 200
Baldwin, Stanley, 28
Barclay, John: *see* Thompson, John Barclay
Barham, R. H., *Ingoldsby Legends,* 118

Barnard Castle, 83
Barrie, J. M., 28, 231
Bath High School, 24
Bay, André, 156
Bayne, T. Vere, 20, 25, 37, 106, 176–7, 198
Beatrice, Princess, 133
Beaumaris, Anglesey, 26
Behind the Looking-Glass: see Through the Looking-Glass
Bell, Dr G. C., 208
Bellot, J. R., 72
Bennett, Henry Leigh, 52
Besant, Sir Walter, 23
Black, Messrs A. & C., 234
Black, Prof. Duncan, 191, 200, 256
Black and White, 248
Blackmore, R. D., 23
Blagden, Bishop, 197
Blackmore, Edith, 209, 219, 239
Blank Cheque, The, 177
Blundstone, F. V., 28
Boat Race, Varsity (1856), 81
Bok, Edward, 232
Book-wrappers, D.'s suggestion for, 183
Booksellers, D. and their profits, 195
Bower, Dallas, 29
Bowles, T. Gibson, 197
Bowman, Isa, 209, 221, 250–1
Bradshaw's Railway Guide, skit on, 47
Brinklord Roman camp, 53
British Museum, 27, 223
Brontë, Emily, *Wuthering Heights,* 82
Brooke, Lord (later Earl of Warwick), 171
Brown, Fredric, *Night of the Jabberwock,* 42
Brown, Mary, 239
Browning, Robert and E. B., 187
'Bruno's Revenge', 139
Bull, Rev. Dr, 39
Bumpus, Messrs, 28
Bunin, Lou, 29
Bunyan, John, *Pilgrim's Progress,* 128
Burlington Gallery, 137
Burton, R. L., 78
Bute, Lord, 145
Butler, Samuel, *Hudibras,* 81

Cakeless, 170–2, 179–80, 204
Calverley, C. S., 81, 187, 190
Cameron, Julia Margaret, 86
Cammaerts, Emile, 77
Carnarvon, Lord, 64
'Carroll, Lewis', origin of *nom de plume,* 80–1
Carroll, Lewis: *see* Dodgson, Rev. Charles Lutwidge
Carter, Theophilus, 126

Castle Croquet (game), 132, 165
Chalcraft, Amos, 239
Charlesworth, Rev. G. Edward, 16, 45
Charlton Kings, 116
Charsley, 227
Chataway, Gertrude, 182, 209, 219–21
Cheshire Cat's 'We're all mad here', origins, 82
Chesterton, G. K., 184, 192
'Chestnuts, The' 19, 21, 28, 143–4, 256
Christ Church, Oxford, contemporaries of D. at, 23, 37, 63–4; D.'s father a scholar of, 36; living presented to D.'s father, 40–1; D. goes into residence (1851), 59; early days at, 61–4; dogs at, 61, 63; D. nominated to Studentship (1852), 68; reform in Fellowships and Scholarships, 68; D. made sub-Librarian, 74; quarters occupied by D., 77; D. defends against adverse criticism, 78; Liddell succeeds Gaisford as Dean (1855), 78; D. made 'Master of the House', 78; D.'s wish to retain Studentship, 103–4; in 1862, 112; D. declines to act as assessor at elections to Junior Studentships, 139; D. takes new rooms (1868), 145–7; effect of D.'s popular fame on life at, 175–8; firm action of D. in college affairs, 175; D.'s pamphlets, 'The New Belfry' and 'Three T's', 177–9, 180; D. accepts £100 cut in salary at own suggestion (1880), 198; D. resigns mathematical lectureship (1881), 198; D.'s service as Curator of the Senior Common Room (1882–1892), 198–203; difficulties with Wine Committee, 200–1; D. retires as Curator, 202–3; D.'s complaints and grumbles, 204–6; famous portraits at, 235; Paget succeeds Liddell as Dean (1891), 235; D.'s sermons to college servants, 239–40
'Christmas Greetings from a Fairy to a Child', 187
Circular Billiards (game), 237
Clarendon Press, 118, 121
Clarke, Langton, 186
Clarke, Savile, 29, 174, 224
Clay, Richard, 121
Coleman, W. S., 217
Coliseum, Albany Street, 102

College Rhymes, 96, 108
Collett, Mrs Alice, 208
Collingwood, Prof. B. J. (nephew), 28
Collingwood, Rev. C. S., 245
Collingwood, Mrs Mary Charlotte (sister), 38, 60–1, 69, 109, 221
Collingwood, Stuart Dodgson (nephew), biography of D., 25; *Lewis Carroll Picture Book*, 26, 258; D.'s complete Diary available to, 74, 103; on D.'s supposed love-affair, 161, 165; D.'s last letter to, 245–6; biography of D. cited, *passim*
Cologne Cathedral, 140
Comet, The, 50
Comic Times, 80, 84, 85
Condensation of Determinants, 132
Conundrums and problems, 248–9
Cooper, Sir Edwin, 28
Co-operative Backgammon (game), 238
Coote, Bert, 208
Cornhill, 25, 114
Court Circular (game), 107
Covent Garden Theatre, 82
Cowley-Brown, Rev. G. J., 63–4
Cowper, Lord, 64
Craig, E. Gordon, 165, 166
Craik, G. L., 21, 153, 194, 195, 196
Crane, Walter, 23, 195–6
Crawshay, Florence, 87
Cremer's toy-shop, 102
Crimean War, 75, 78
Crockett, S. R., 23
Croft, Yorkshire, D.'s father appointed to living, 40–1; description of Rectory, 42–3; D.'s drawing and verse, 43; relics of Dodgson children found under floor-boards (1950), 44–6, 184, 246; D. returns to (1849), 55, 58, 59; Church of St Peter, 58; 'Jabberwocky' composed at, 76–7; D. teaches in Sunday School, 79; D. conducts baptisms at, 79; D.'s father and mother buried at, 143; Dodgsons leave after twenty-five years, 144; mentioned, 85, 87, 95, 157, 245, 246
Croquet Castles (game), 132, 165
Cuddesdon, 106
Cundall, Joseph, 96
Cunnynghame, Maggie, 134
Curiosa Mathematica, 225, 237

Daily Chronicle, 19–20

Daily Dispatch, 109
Daily Mail, 19
Daily News, 19
Daily Telegraph, 19
Dane, Clemence, 29
Daresbury, Cheshire, 28, 34, 38–40, 43, 59, 87, 246
Davies, Mrs Arthur: *see* Mayhew, Margaret
Davies, Sir Walford, 29
de la Mare, Walter, 25, 28, 71, 129, 133
Denman, Edith, 17
de Morgan, William, 146–7
Derwent House School, Carshalton, 24
Dickens, Charles, *David Copperfield*, 53; quoted, 78; and Millais picture, 137; *Our Mutual Friend*, 142; *Martin Chuzzlewit*, 154; *Pickwick Papers*, 160
Disney, Walt, 29, 31
Disraeli, Benjamin, 142, 156
Dodgson, Caroline Hume (sister), 38
Dodgson, Rt Rev. Charles, Bishop of Elphin, 34
Dodgson, Capt. Charles (grandfather), 34
Dodgson, Archdeacon Charles (father), ancestry, 34; character, 35–6; nonsense letter to D., 35, 124; D. influenced by, 35; at Daresbury, 38–9; list of children, 38; appointed to living of Croft (1843), 40–1; life at Croft Rectory, 42, 44, 45; disapproval of theatres, 47; gives D. grounding in mathematics, 50; Dr Tait's letter to, 55; High Churchman, 58, 68; death of wife (1851), 59; letter to D. (1852) quoted, 68; Canon Residentiary at Ripon, 74; photograph sent to D., 78; proposes personal saving system to D., 104; opinion of 'Alice' not recorded, 124; death (1868), 143
Dodgson, Rev. Charles Lutwidge (Lewis Carroll) (*see also under names of persons, books and subjects throughout index*), birth (1832), 34; ancestry, 34; childhood years at Daresbury, 35–8, 39; family moves to Croft (1843); life at Croft Rectory (1843–6), 42–50; edits and illustrates manuscript family magazines, 47–50, 56–8; anticipations in childhood of later works, 49–50, 77; at Richmond Grammar School, 50–2;

unhappy years at Rugby School (1846–9), 52–6, 58; attacks of whooping-cough and mumps, 55; back at Croft (1849), 55, 58; goes into residence at Christ Church, Oxford (1851), 59; death of mother, 59; abiding reverence and love for his mother, 59–60, 66; undergraduate days at Oxford, 61–73; Boulter Scholarship, 68; Second in Classical Moderations, First in Mathematics (1852), 68; nominated to Studentship at Christ Church, 68, 104; reading-party at Whitby (1854), 69–73; first published works, 70; First Class in Final Mathematics and B.A. (1854), 73; sub-Librarian of Christ Church; given Bostock Scholarship (1855), 74; writes first verse of 'Jabberwocky' (1855), 76; quarters at Christ Church, 77–8; defends Christ Church against adverse criticism, 78; duties at Christ Church (1855), 78; 'Master of the House' and M.A., 78; contributes to *Comic Times* (1855), 80; and *The Train* (1856), 80–1; fall while skating, 81; reluctance to leave Oxford, 103, 104; doubts about taking Holy Orders and doing parochial work, 103–5; decides to take Deacon's Orders, 104–6; ordained (1861), 106; first book, *A Syllabus of Plane Algebraical Geometry* published (1860), 107; industry as author, 107; edits *College Rhymes*, 108; tells story of *Alice's Adventures Under Ground* during boat trip to Godstow (1862), 112–15; commits story to paper, 115–16; illustrates original manuscript, 117–18, 124–5; decides on title for publication, 119–20; publication difficulties and delays, 120–3; *Alice's Adventures in Wonderland* published (1865), 123–4; as Dodo in *Alice*, 126; publishes mathematical works, 132; denies sending copies of works to Queen Victoria, 132–3; resigns as Public Examiner in Mathematics (1864), 139; visits Russia (1867), 140–2; death of father (1868), 143; responsibilities

for welfare of sisters, 143; takes new rooms at Christ Church (1868), 145–7; publishes *Phantasmagoria* (1869), 152; publishes *Through the Looking-Glass* (1871), 154; forswears role of story-teller (1875), 157; ridiculed in *Cakeless* (1874), 171–2, 179–80; pleasure in being known as Lewis Carroll, 174, 231–4; progressive withdrawal from social life, 175, 229; effect of popular fame on life at Christ Church, 175–7; firm action in college affairs, 175; pamphlets on Oxford controversies (1872–4), 177–9, 180; publishes *The Hunting of the Snark* (1876), 183; *Euclid and his Modern Rivals* (1879), 195; *Sylvie and Bruno* (1889), 194; accepts £100 cut in salary at Christ Church at own suggestion (1880), 198; resigns mathematical lectureship at Christ Church (1881), 198; service as Curator of Senior Common Room (1882–92), 198–202; difficulties with Wine Committee, 198–9, 202; retires as Curator (1892, 202–4; later college life; continual complaints and grumbles, 204–6; publishes *A Tangled Tale* (1885), 222; facsimile edition of *Alice's Adventures Under Ground* (1885), 223; *The Game of Logic* (1887), 224–5; intermittent ill-health, 227–8; publishes *Sylvie and Bruno* (1889) and *Sylvie and Bruno Concluded* (1893), 230; distaste for lionisation, 231–4; help for members of family, 234, 239, 245; more contented in the 'nineties, 235–6, 238; addresses readers by advertisements and leaflets, 237–8; publishes last book, *Symbolic Logic* (1896), 238; illness and death (1898), 19, 245; obituaries quoted, 19–20; tributes to, 19–20, 22–4; will, 20–1, 28; directions regarding funeral, 21; funeral, 21; monument over grave, 21; child's suggestion for memorial cot, 22; appeal and presentation to Great Ormond Street Hospital, 22–4; sale of personal effects, 25–6; interest in him slackens, 26; revival in interest after 1914–18 war, 26; increase in

Dodgson, Rev. Charles Lutwidge—cont.

prices paid for manuscripts and first editions, 27; centenary of birth (1932), 27, 28; Lewis Carroll ward at St Mary's Hospital, 28

Amateur theatricals, 157

Animals, love of, 180–1

Anthology, his poems in an, 174

Apartments described, 145–7

Appearance, 78, 131, 239, 241, 249, 254

Artistic tastes and friendships, 84, 135, 137

Autograph-hunters, rebuffs to, 232, 233

Ballet, attitude to, 82

Biographies of, 25, 27–8

Buffaloes, interest in, 46

Character, 25, 31, 35, 36, 67, 83, 159

Child-friends, love of the companionship of children, particularly of little girls, 59, 67, 88–90, 115–16, 167, 207–21, 223, 235; selection of letters published, 27, 103; general aversion to boys, 80, 102, 139, 208–9; gift of winning child's confidence, 115; venture of photographing in the nude, 218–19; girl friends' reminiscences, 249–55

Classics, lack of appeal, 50

Deafness, 55

Death, attitude to, 245

Diaries, 27, 74, 161; 'white stone' entries, 89; missing volumes, 74, 105, 161; extracts, passim

Dinner-parties, 145

Dramatic sense, 47, 231

Drawing ability, 47, 84, 92, 194

Eccentricity, 25

Editions of Works, 27

Family affection, 21, 35

Fire, fear of, 227

Fireplaces, interest in, 147

Games, not good at, 53, 64, 81

Generosity, 196–8

Handwriting, 38, 45, 51–2, 65–6, 76, 106, 173, 235–6, 245

Happiness, on, 58, 244, 252

Humour, personal, 176–7

Interests, wide, 74

Inventions, 236–7

Lectures, contrasting views on his, 79–80

Letters, to his child-friends, 27, 103

letters reproduced, 38, 65,

204; early letters quoted, 37, 50–1, 53–5; Register of Correspondence, 107

Library, 81–2

Literary tastes, 75, 81–2, 187, 227

Longevity of brothers and sisters, 38

Love-affairs, possibility of, discussed, 105, 159–73

Marriage, attitude to, 160, 167, 169, 173, 209

Mathematics, early interest in, 50; estimate of contributions to, 132

Medicine, interest in, 67, 82, 84, 92, 227

Music, taste in, 83

Nom de plume, 'B. B.', 70, 80; suggestions for, 80; Lewis Carroll chosen, 81; author's attitude to, 233–4, 248

Opera, fondness for, 82, 105

Parodies, 188–90

Photograph (1857), 78

Photography, interest in: see Photography

Phrenologist's report, 67, 84

Play-writing attempt, 137, 139

Poet, as a, 183, 184–93

Portrait by Herkomer, 235

Preacher, later reputation as, 238–41

Puppets, interest in, 46–7

Relics discovered under floorboards at Croft Rectory (1950), 44–6, 184, 246

Religious doubts and difficulties, 58, 64, 103–6; substitutes tiger-lily for passion-flower in Through the Looking-Glass, 128, 148, 157

Shyness, 79, 134, 175

Snobbish, 134, 157

Stammer, 48, 64, 79, 87, 99, 101, 105, 106, 126, 235–9, 254

Supernatural, interest in the, 186, 231

Teacher, as a, 79–80, 224

Theatre, passion for the, 47, 82, 105, 137, 139, 140, 162, 165, 166, 212, 255

Thimbles, fascination for, 44–5

Tobacco, horror of, 101, 198

Tricycle 'Velociman', 227

Twin identities, 83, 222, 245

Undergraduates, attitude to, 175, 244, 253

Walking, fondness for, 227

Women, attitude to, 87, 159, 167, 173

Dodgson, Rev. Christopher, 34

Dodgson, Edwin Heron (brother), 20, 38, 231

Dodgson, Elizabeth Lucy (sister), 38, 46, 53, 64, 65, 68, 114, 126

Dodgson, Frances Jane (mother), 34, 44; Collingwood's estimate of, 36–7; list of children, 38; letters quoted, 50, 53, 55; death, 59; D.'s love for, 60, 66

Dodgson, Frances Jane (sister), 38, 114, 126, 161

Dodgson, Frank (cousin), 69, 89

Dodgson, Hassard (uncle), 34, 69

Dodgson, Henrietta Harington (sister), 38

Dodgson, Isabel (sister-in-law), 233

Dodgson, Louisa Fletcher (sister), 38, 48

Dodgson, Margaret Anna Ashley (sister), 38

Dodgson, Mary Charlotte (sister): see Collingwood, Mrs Mary Charlotte

Dodgson, Menella, 16, 161, 202

Dodgson, Skeffington Hume (brother), 38, 51, 233, 239

Dodgson, Wilfred Longley (brother), 20, 38, 48, 105, 161, 167

Dog-fight, D.'s account of, 61

Doublets (game), 194, 237

Douglas, Felicity, 156

Doyle, Sir Arthur Conan, 29, 230

Doyle, Richard, 148

Draper, Rev. W. H., 228

Drew, Mrs Mary, 24

Drinkwater, Jack, 253

Drury, Ella, 134

Drury, Emmie, 134

Drury, Minnie: see Fuller, Mrs Herbert

Drury Lane Theatre, 137

Duckworth, Canon Robinson, 22, 112–15, 117, 126, 225

du Maurier, George, 152

Dyer, Mr and Mrs, 209–10

Dymes, T. J., 196–7

Dynamics of a Particle, 132

Eastbourne, 232, 238, 241; D.'s visits to (1877), 209–10; (1887), 229; child-friends' visits to, 220–1, 250; D.'s letters from, 219; D. preaches at, 239

'Easter Greeting to Every Child who Loves "Alice"', 22, 37, 183

Educators and Holy Orders, 104

Egerton, Lord Francis, 40

'Elections to the Hebdomadal

Council', 191

Elementary Treatise on Determinants, An, 132

Elizabeth, Queen, 28

Elliston family, 174

Elton, Oliver, 26

Enunciations of Euclid, 132

Essays and Reviews, 107

Euclid I and II, 132, 240

Euclid and his Modern Rivals, 47, 132, 146, 195, 222, 234

Evans, Dr Luther, 27

'Faces in the Fire', 38, 147, 160, 167, 169

Fairies, 48, 49, 231

'Fairy, My', 48–9

'Fame's Penny-Trumpet', 181, 190

Family magazines: see Magazines

Farringford, 86, 96, 97

Faussett, Robert, 200

'Feeding the Mind', 228

Figaro, 195

Fortnightly Review, 181

Fosters, Mrs: see Prickett, Miss

Fowler, Dr Thomas, 70–3, 92

Fraser-Simson, H., 29

Frederick of Denmark, Prince, 133

Freiligrath-Kroeker, Kate, 29, 174

Frost, A. B., 195–6

Fuller, Audrey, 22

Fuller, Margaret, 244, 252

Fuller, Mrs Minnie (Minnie Drury), 22, 134, 255

Furniss, Harry, 218, 227, 229, 230

Gabb, Dr, 245, 247

Gaisford, Thomas, Dean of Christ Church, 63, 78

Game of Logic, The, 224–5, 238

Games, 107, 115, 132, 237

Gamlen, Ruth (Mrs Waterhouse), 209, 221, 241, 249–51

'Garden of Live Flowers', 148

Gathorne-Hardy, G., 132

Gatty, Mrs, 139

Germany, D.'s visit (1867), 140, 141–2

Gernsheim, Helmut, 27, 86, 137, 165

Gilbert, W. S., 148, 187

Girl friends, D.'s: see Dodgson, Rev. Charles Lutwidge: Child-friends

Gladstone, W. E., 24, 64, 132, 142, 156

Goathland, 69–70

Godstow, 114, 115, 126

Godwin, E. W., 165

Gogarth Abbey, Llandudno, 109

Goldsmith, Oliver, parody of, 190

Grahame, Kenneth, 103

Grant, Canon, 21

Great Exhibition (1851), 65, 84–5

Great Ormond Street Hospital, 22–4, 70, 123

Green, Roger Lancelyn, edits D.'s diaries, 16, 27, 72, 74, 103, 109; diaries cited, *passim*

Guida di Bragia, La (play for marionettes), 47

Guide to the Mathematical Student, 132

Guildford (*see also* 'Chestnuts, The'), D.'s sisters move to, 157, 182, 239, 241, 245; D.'s sermons at, 239; D.'s death at, 246; burial, 21

Guildford Gazette Extraordinary, The, 157, 256

Hamilton, Edward, 67

Hamilton, Bishop Walter Kerr, 141, 191

Handbook of the Literature of the Rev. C. L. Dodgson, 27, 107, 183, 258

Harben, Guy, 28

Harcourt, Aubrey, 171

Harcourt, A. G. Vernon, 115

Hargreaves, Mrs Alice Pleasance (earlier Alice Liddell), first meeting with D. (1856), 88–9; D.'s friendship for, 89–90, 109–10, 115–16, 134; taught drawing by Ruskin, 92; visits Llandudno, 109–10; life at Christ Church, 111; D. tells her the story of *Alice's Adventures Under Ground* during boat trip from Oxford to Godstow (1862), 22, 71, 113–15; asks D. to commit the story to paper, 115; receives manuscript book of 'Alice' (1864), 117–18; special vellum-bound copy of published version (1865), 121; copy exchanged for new one, 123, 131; the original Alice, 124; meets Princess of Wales at bazaar, 133; D.'s adult relationship with, 159, 167–9, 172; marriage (1880), 161, 169, 172, 235; receives morocco-bound copy of *Through the Looking-Glass*, 170; mentioned in *Cakeless*, 170–2; D. asks permission to print facsimile edition of original version of 'Alice', 223; manuscript returned to and later sold, 223; gift copy of *The Nursery Alice*, 225;

wreath from at D.'s funeral, 21; supports memorial to D., 22, 28

Hargreaves, Caryl, 89, 169

Hargreaves, Reginald, 169, 219

Harland, Ethel, 244

Harper's Magazine, 216

Harrowby, Lord, 64

Hartshorne, F. M., 123

Harvard College Library, 16, 43, 50, 65

Hastings, 110

Hatch, Evelyn, 207, 209, 210

Hatfield House, 157, 194

Haydock Park, 34

Haymarket Theatre, 139, 231

Heaphy, Thomas, 137

Herbert, A. P., 28

Herkomer, Sir Hubert von, 24, 235

Hewitt Graily, 28, 144

'Hiawatha's Photographing', 152, 189

Hicks, Edward Lee, 177

Hicks-Beach, Sir Michael, 23, 64

High Churchmen, 58, 68, 78, 191

Hoghton, Sir Charles, 34

Holiday, Henry, 92, 182, 183, 250

Holland, Canon Henry Scott, 79, 171

Holloway College, 20

Hollyer, Frederick, 24

Holywell Music Room, Oxford, 25

Homoeopathy, 26, 67, 228

Hone, Canon H. E., 241

Hood, Thomas, 148, 187

Hood, Tom, 238

Hope-Hawkins, Anthony, 23

Hospitals, copies of D.'s books for, 123, 196; profits of books for, 223

Howitt, Mary, parody of, 125

Hughes, Arthur, 84, 135, 137

Hughes, Mrs Vivian, 156

Hull, Agnes, 210–12

Hume, Caroline, 34

Hume, Lucy, 34

Hunt, Holman, 24, 84, 91, 135, 137

Hunt, Dr James, 101

Hunt, Leigh, 187

Hunting of the Snark, The, reference to thimbles in, 44–5; Newman and the dedicatory poem, 64; 'last line' occurs to D. by itself, 126, 182; not influenced by de Morgan's tiles, 147; D. at work on, 181–3; published (1876), 182; mixed reception, 183; concluding verses quoted, 185; probable

influence of *Bab Ballads*, 187; included in 1883 collection of verse, 195; gift copies, 252, 255

French translation, 185

Illustrations, 92, 182, 183, 250

Musical version, 29

Huntington Library, San Marino, 16, 53, 152, 254

Hurcomb, Lord, 253

Hutchinson, C. E., 185

Illustrated Times, 123

Irving, Sir Henry, 24

'Jabberwocky', 76–7, 148, 153–4, 182, 188

James I and the loin of beef, 34

James, Rev. Thomas, 118

Jelf, Canon, 64

Jenkins, Rev. John Howe, *Cakeless*, 170–2, 179–80

Jerome, J. K., 23

Johnson, Eldridge R., 27

Johnson, R. Brimley, 81

Jowett, Benjamin, 107, 132

Joyce, James, 231

Joyce, Sidney, 69

Jupp, E. K., 131

Kean, Charles, 82, 162

Keble, John, 64, 66

Kelly, Charles, 165

Kendal, Madge, 24

Kenealy, Edward Vaughan (anagram), 177

Kilvert, Rev. Francis, 212, 217

Kingsley, Charles, 84; *Alton Locke*, 75; *Hypatia*, 82; *Water Babies*, 120, 128, 131

Kingsley, Henry, 117, 154

Kipling, Rudyard, 191

Lady, The, 237

'Lady of the Ladle, The', 70

Lamb, Charles, 159

Landseer, Sir Edwin, 84, 85

Langford, G. W., parody of, 125

Lanrick (game), 237

Laski, Marghanita, 224–5

Latin verses and inscription by D., 52

Laurencin, Marie, 29

Lawn Tennis Tournaments, 195

'Lays of Sorrow', 57

Lear, Edward, 51, 58, 84, 128, 184, 190, 192

Leathes, Stanley, 198

Lennon, Mrs F. B., 53, 169

Leonide, Bishop, 141

Leopold, Prince, 171

Leslie, G. D., 198

Letter-writing, D.'s pamphlet on, 236–7

Lewin, Dr, 99

Lewis, Arthur, 162

Lewis, Kate Terry: *see* Terry, Kate

Lewis Carroll Picture Book, 26, 258

Liddell, Mrs (wife of Dr H. G. Liddell), unfriendly attitude to D., 89–90, 109, 112, 115–16, 168–9; ridiculed in *Cakeless*, 170–2, 179

Liddell, Alice Pleasance: *see* Hargreaves, Mrs Alice Pleasance

Liddell, Edith, 88, 112–16, 126, 171, 219

Liddell, Frederika, 87, 88

Liddell, Gertrude, 88

Liddell, Harry, 88, 89, 95

Liddell, Dr H. G., Dean of Christ Church, reforms at Christ Church, 63; appointed to Christ Church (1855), 78, 87, 88; D.'s uneasy relations with, 89, 109, 177–9, 235; winters in Madeira, 89–90; on D. and Holy Orders, 106; house at Llandudno, 109–10; D.'s correspondence with regarding Junior Studentships, 139; ancestry, 169; D.'s 'New Belfry' and 'Three T's' aimed at, 177–9; ridiculed in *Cakeless*, 170–2, 179; D. ridicules reforms, 175; portrait, 235; retirement (1891), 235

Liddell, Lorina (Ina), 88, 89, 112–16, 126, 170

Liddell, Rhoda, 171

Liddell, Violet, 171

Liddell children, D.'s friendship for, 88–9, 109–16, 126, 168; painting by Richmond, 116; D.'s friendship ridiculed in *Cakeless*, 170–2

Liddon, Dr H. P., 104, 140–2, 153, 176

'Lion and the Unicorn, The', 148

Literature, 81

Little Holland House, 162, 166

Llandudno, 109–10

Locker, Frederick, 131, 187

Longfellow, H. W., parody of, 189

Longley, Sir Henry, 64

Lothian, Lord, 64

Lucas, E. V., 28

Lutwidge, Charles, of Holmrook, 34

Lutwidge, Frances Jane: *see* Dodgson, Frances Jane (mother)

Lutwidge, Lucy (aunt), 53, 55, 78, 123, 219

Lutwidge, Skeffington (uncle),

21, 65, 75, 85, 152
Lutwidge, Thomas, 34

Macaulay, Lord, 43, 53
MacDonald, George, 23, 91,
    101, 102, 117
MacDonald, Mrs George, 117
MacDonald, Greville, 102
MacDonald, Mary, 102–3
MacDonald, Ramsay, 28
Macmillan, Alexander, 152,
    153, 154–5, 187, 195, 234
Macmillan, Frederick, 28
Macmillan's, Messrs, D.'s
    exacting correspondence
    with, 21, 194, 232; corres-
    pondence with D. on Alice's
    Adventures in Wonderland,
    120–3, 129–30, 131; D. reports on
    his plan for table at dinner-
    party, 145; correspondence
    on Through the Looking-Glass,
    148, 155, 170, 194, 237; atti-
    tude to anthologies, 174;
    correspondence on The
    Hunting of the Snark, 182–3;
    on Sylvie and Bruno, 194, 227,
    231; on Rhyme? and Reason?,
    195; on A Tangled Tale, 222;
    on The Game of Logic, 224;
    on The Nursery Alice, 225;
    D. asks for better terms, 234
Macmillan's Magazine, 258
Mad Hatter, identification, 63,
    126
Madan, Falconer, quoted, 26,
    126, 181, 195, 206; 'Hand-
    book' to D.'s works, 27, 107,
    183, 258
Madeira, 89
Maeterlinck, Maurice, The Blue
    Bird, 231
Magazines, family manuscript
    (see also under their titles), 47–
    50, 56–8
Malcolm of Poltalloch, 64
Mallett, Sir Charles, 63, 68
Mannheim, Dr M. J., analysis
    of D.'s handwriting, 16, 36,
    65–6, 76, 173, 235–6
Manning, Henry Edward, 64
Markham, Violet, 156
Marmalade, D. and, 202
Marriott, C. H. R., 169
Marshall, Julia, 95
Marx Brothers, 128
Mayhew, Rev. A. L., 218
Mayhew, Margaret, 209, 218–
    19, 241, 244, 253–5
Mayhew, Ruth, 218
Mechanics' Institutes, copies of
    D.'s books for, 196, 238
Meredith, George, 23
Meynell, Alice, 23
Millais, Effie, 137
Millais, Sir John, 84, 135, 137

Miller, May, 221
Milne, A. A., 28
Milner, Florence, 50
Mischmasch, 27, 50, 72, 76, 194
Molesworth, Mrs, 195
Montgomery, Dr Lall G., 16
Monthly Packet, 222
Moore, Thomas, parody of, 80
Morning Clouds, 137, 139, 165
Moxon, Mr, 96, 98
Mulock, Dinah Maria, 75
Munro, Alexander, 102, 135

New Belfry of Christ College, The,
    177–8
New Method of Evaluation, The,
    108
New Museum, 142
Newcastle, Duke of, 64
Newman, Cardinal, 64, 141
Newry, Lord, 115
Nonsense poetry, 76–7, 156,
    181–2, 192–3
Notes by an Oxford Chiel, 177
Nuneham, 114, 126
Nursery Alice, The, 225–7, 238
Nyctograph, 26

Observer, 78, 114
Oman, Sir Charles, 27
O'Neill, Norman, 29, 231
Orloff, Prince, 141
Ossoli, Marchioness: see Fuller,
    Margaret
Oswald, Mr, 64
Ottewill, T., 86
Owen, Alice, 208
Owen, James, 208
Owen, S. G., 208
Oxford in 1851, 63
Oxford English Dictionary,
    words from 'Jabberwocky'
    recognised in, 156
Oxford–Godstow trip (July
    1862), 22, 113–15, 126
Oxford Infirmary, 123
Oxford University (see also
    Christ Church), in 1851, 63;
    First Commission (1850), 64,
    68; D.'s account of Encaenia
    ceremony, 65; contest for
    Parliamentary seat (1865),
    132; D. resigns as Public
    Examiner in Mathematics,
    139; installation of Lord
    Salisbury as Chancellor, 157;
    D.'s pamphlet on new
    examination schools, 177
Oxonian Advertiser, The, 70, 80

Paget, Francis, Dean of Christ
    Church, 20, 21, 71, 117, 235
Paget, Sir James, 208
Palgrave, Francis Turner, 95
Pall Mall Gazette, 123, 178, 181
Papy, Jacques, 156

'Parallelepiped', 54
Parisot, Henri, 27, 156
Parrish, Morris L., 27
Patmore, Coventry, 82, 187, 208
Patmore, Francis Epiphanius, 208
Paton, Sir Noel, 148
Pear's Soap, 237
Peel, Sir Robert, 40–1
'Penmorfa', Llandudno, 109
Peters, Mrs and Miss, 112
Phantasmagoria, 54, 152, 160,
    185, 195
Philaret, Archbishop, 141
'Photographer's Day Out, A',
    108
Photographic Society, 85, 95
Photography, D.'s interest and
    achievements in, 26, 84–6,
    88–9, 92–6, 133, 137, 142,
    162; D. buy his first camera,
    85–6; D. sells photographs,
    92; D. embarks on nude
    studies, 218–19, 254; photo-
    graphy abandoned by D.,
    194, 218
'Photography Extraordinary',
    85
Pillow Problems, 173, 237, 249
'Poeta Fit, non Nascitur', 108,
    152, 187
'Poet's Farewell, The', 58
Polytechnic, 174, 180
Poole, Catherine Lucy, 123
'Postage-Stamp Case, Wonder-
    land', 236–7
Potter, Beatrix, 103
Powell, Prof. York, 26, 27, 175
Praed, Winthrop M., 48, 87,
    187, 209
Pre-Raphaelites, 135
Price, Prof. Bartholomew, 69–
    70, 126, 139
Prickett, Miss, 89, 112, 116,
    126, 172
Prince Consort, 133
Prince of Wales' Theatre, 224
Princess's Theatre, 82, 162
Problems: see Conundrums and
    problems
Profits of Authorship, The, 195
Punch, 20, 80, 118, 137, 156,
    177, 191
Pusey, Dr E. B., 68, 104
Pusey, Philip, 63
Puzzles, 194, 207, 237

Rackham, Authur, 29
Radley College, 52
Raikes, Alice (cousin), 152
Railway game, 43, 55, 246
Read, Sir Herbert, 128
Reader, The, 123
Rectory Magazine, The 50
Rectory Umbrella, The, 27, 43,
    50, 56–8, 67
Reed, Langford, 27, 124, 166

Reform Bill (1832), 34
Reynolds, Sir Joshua, 146
Rhyme? and Reason?, 195–6
Richmond, W. B., 116
Richmond Grammar School,
    50–2, 65
Ripon, 36, 40, 74
Ritchie, Lady: see Thackeray,
    Anne Isabella
Rivington, Dolly, 165
Robertson, Graham, 166
Rosebud, The, 50
Roselle, Percy, 137, 139
Rosenbach, Dr A. S. W., 27
Rossetti, Christina, 124, 135,
    225
Rossetti, D. G., 124, 135, 187
Rossetti, W. M., 23
Routledge, Messrs, 174
Rowell, Mrs, 241, 244, 252–3
Rowell, Ethel, 20, 172, 216, 241
Rowell, Hettie, 209, 241, 244,
    251–3
Royal Academy, 121, 162
Royal Court Theatre, 255
'Rules and Regulations', 48
Runcorn, 38
Ruskin, John, 91–2, 103
Russell, Lord John, 123
Russia, D.'s visit to (1867),
    140–2
Ryman's, 84, 92

Sadler, Mrs, 206
Sadler, M. E., 198, 201, 204–6
St Aldates School, Oxford, 79
St Bartholomew's Hospital, 84
St Jame's Gazette, 22, 23, 71, 225
St Mary's Church, Guildford,
    21, 239, 241
St Mary's Hospital, Paddington,
    28
St Petersburg, 140–1
Saki, The Westminster Alice, 26
Salisbury, Lord and Lady, 157–
    8, 174, 194
Sampson, Rev. E. F., 171, 211
Sanday, Prof. William, 20
Sandown, 182, 209, 220
Saunders, Max, 29
Sayles, J. M., 115
Scott, Clement, 162
Scott, Dr Robert, 78, 258
Scottish Guardian, The, 63
'Sea Dirge, A', 108, 109
'Sequel to "The Shepherd of
    Salisbury Plain"', 191–2
Shakespeare, D. and, 128; skit
    on, 187; proposed edition
    for girls, 227, 230
Sharp, Farquharson, 234
Shawyer, Mrs Enid: see Stevens,
    Enid
Sheridan, R. B., parody of, 178,
    190
Sherriff, R. C., Journey's End, 26

'She's all my fancy painted him', 72, 80
Shute, Alice, 256
Silver, A., 232
Sim, Fred, 79
Simon, Lord, 241, 248–9
Skene, W. B., 170
Skene, Mrs W. B.: *see* Liddell, Lorina
Slaughter, Walter, 29
Smedley, Frank, 34, 80
Smedley, Mary, 59
Smedley, Menella (cousin), 80
Smith, Sydney, 192
Snow, C. P., *The Masters*, 178
'Solitude', 66–7, 80, 168
'Song of Love', 186
Soulsby, Miss, 254
Southey, Reginald, 86, 87, 88
Southey, Robert, parody of, 125, 188
Squire, J. C., 28
Stage, The, 225
Stanley, Lady A., 134
Star, The, 50
Steer, P. Wilson, 28
Stephenson, George, 114
Stevens, Mrs, 249, 250
Stevens, Enid, 147, 209, 221, 249–50, 254
Stewart, J. A., 199
'Stolen Waters', 160
Strong, Bishop T. B., 25, 126, 132, 157, 197, 202, 235
Sullivan, Sir Arthur, 97
Sunderland, 72, 76
Swinburne, Algernon C., 187
Syllabus of Plane Algebraical Geometry, A, 107
Sylvie and Bruno, baby-talk in, 38; reference to buffaloes, 46; 'Bruno's Revenge' as nucleus of, 139–40 D. recites embryo chapters of, 157, 194; D.'s slow progress with, 194, 198, 204, 227–8; published (1889), 230; discussed, 230–1, 235; abridged edition, 231; gift copy, 255
  Illustrations, 195–6, 218, 229, 230
Sylvie and Bruno Concluded, 65, 147, 230, 231, 234
Symbolic Logic, 133, 224, 238, 245, 251
Synge, W. W. Follett, 157, 223, 256
Syzygies (game), 237

Tait, Dr A. C., 55
Talbot, Mr, 64
'Tale of a Tail, A', 49
Tangled Tale, A, 222
Tate, Mr (schoolmaster), 50, 52
Taylor, Alexander L., 71, 157
Taylor, Deems, 29

Taylor, Jane, parody of, 125
Taylor, Tom, 118, 137, 139, 162
Tenniel, Sir John, recommended as illustrator, 117, 137; agrees to collaborate with D., 118; model for Alice, 119; illustrations for *Alice's Adventures in Wonderland*, 120, 130, 133, 225, 254; complains of printing of illustrations, 121–3; D.'s own illustrations compared with Tenniel's, 124–5; illustrations for *Through the Looking-Glass*, 148–9, 152–5, 156; gives up book illustrating, 154; D.'s search for successor to, 194, 195–6; pictures as design on wall-paper, 232; and proposed memorial to D., 22–3
Tennyson, Mrs, 95, 98
Tennyson, Alfred Lord, 128, 187; 'Maud', 82, 91; D.'s photograph of home, 86; D.'s relationship with, 95–101; D.'s index to 'In Memoriam', 96; D.'s parody of 'The Two Voices', 148
Tennyson, Sir Charles, 96
Tennyson, Hallam, 95, 96
Tennyson, Lionel, 95, 96, 99
Tent Lodge, Coniston, 95
Terry, Ellen, D.'s admiration for, 82; D.'s friendship with, 116, 137, 162–7, 172; marriage to Watts, 162
Terry, Kate, 24, 162, 165
Thackeray, Anne Isabella (later Lady Ritchie), 23, 227, 228–9
Thackeray, Francis St John, 92
Thackeray, W. M., 91, 92, 230
Theatre, The, 114
Theatres, D.'s love of: *see under* Dodgson, Rev. Charles Lutwidge
Thompson, H. L., 63, 109, 208, 240
Thompson, John Barclay, 194, 198–9
Thomson, Gertrude, 160, 217, 225
'Three Sunsets', 160–1, 217
Three Voices, The, 196
Three Years in a Curatorship, 202
Through the Looking-Glass, D. at work on, 148–52; title chosen, 153; production difficulties, 153–4; published (1871), 154; comparison with 'Alice', 155–6; no direct hidden meanings in, 156–7; dedication, 169; Alice Liddell's copy, 170; popularity, 174; D.'s efforts to prevent exploitation, 174; error in forty-second thou-

sand, 194; offer of exchange for faulty sixtieth thousand, 155, 196, 237; original manuscript not discovered, 223; sales, 239; gift copy, 255
  Dramatic versions, 28, 156, 174
  Illustrations, by Tenniel, 119, 148–9, 152–5; suggestions of political caricature, 156
  Introduction, 34
  'Jabberwocky': *see that title*
  Musical settings, 29, 174
  Tiger-lily substituted for passion-flower on religious grounds, 128, 148, 157
  Translations, 156
  White Knight: *see that title*
Tiles, William de Morgan's 146–7
Times, The, 19, 20, 28, 238
Times Literary Supplement, The, 72
Toynbee, Mr (aurist), 55
Tractarian Movement, 64
Tragedy of King John, The (play for marionettes), 47
Train, The, 80, 81
Tricycle 'Velociman', 227
Trollope, A., 157
Tuckwell, W., 175
Tupper, Martin, 64, 84, 118, 134, 178, 187, 230
'Turtle Soup', 115
Tutor's Assistant, The, inscription in, 52
'Tweedledum' and 'Tweedledee', 148
Twelve Months in a Curatorship, 202
Twiss, Quintin, 92
Tynemouth, 87

United States, Lewis Carroll collections in, 27, 29; sympathisers present 'Alice' manuscript to British Museum, 27, 223; enthusiasm for 'Alice' in, 27, 29; editions of Lewis Carroll's works, 121, 129, 140, 183; rights and editions questions, 153
'Upon the Lonely Moor', 45, 81, 96, 148
Ural Mountains, The (game), 115
Useful and Instructive Poetry, 47–50, 51, 54, 101, 147, 187, 246

Vanity Fair, 197, 216
'Victor and Arnion', 239
Victoria, Queen, 132–4, 238; D.'s fake letter from, 134

Vision of the Three T's, The, 172, 177, 178, 180
Vivisection, 181, 190

Wales, Prince and Princess of, 133
'Walking-Stick of Density, The', 56
'Walrus and the Carpenter, The', 71–2, 148, 188, 224
Walton, Izaak, parody of, 178
Ward, E. M., 216–17
Ward, Leslie, 216
Warner, Canon William, 240
Warrington, 37
Warwick Castle, 171
'Waterford', The, 192
Waterhouse, Mrs A. T.: *see* Gamlen, Ruth
Watts, G. F., 162
Watts, Isaac, parody of, 125
Weaver, Warren, 16, 29, 107, 236
Weld, Agnes Grace, 95
Weld, Mrs Charles, 95
Westminster School, 69
Whitburn, Sunderland, 72, 76, 87
Whitby, reading-party at (1854), 69–72, 92
Whitby Gazette, 70, 80
White, Kirke, 190
White Knight's Song, 45, 81, 148, 167
White Rabbit, origins, 45, 84
Who's Who, 234
Wilberforce, Bishop Samuel, 102, 104, 105, 106, 128, 141
Wilcox, Misses (cousins), 72, 76
Wilcox, William (cousin), 104
Wilde, Oscar, 174
'Wilhelm von Schmitz', 70
Will-o'-the-Wisp, The, 50
Williams, Rev. Dr Rowland, 191
Williams, S. H., 'Handbook' to D.'s works, 27, 108, 122, 258
Williams, Lord Justice Vaughan, 64
Wilson, Edmund, 192
Wiseman, Cardinal, 128
Woodhouse, Rev. G., 63, 64
'Wool and Water', 148
Word-links, 194
Wordsworth, William, 187; parody, of, 81, 148, 188
World, The, 195
Wright, Rear-Adm. Noel, 72

Yates, Edmund, 80, 81
Yonge, Charlotte M., 139, 222
Young, G. M., 50, 75

Zanetti, Prof. J. E., 169
'Zoological Papers', 56